Lecture Notes in Computer Science   14277

Founding Editors

Gerhard Goos
Juris Hartmanis

Editorial Board Members

The series Lecture Notes in Computer Science (LNCS), including its subseries Lecture Notes in Artificial Intelligence (LNAI) and Lecture Notes in Bioinformatics (LNBI), has established itself as a medium for the publication of new developments in computer science and information technology research, teaching, and education.

LNCS enjoys close cooperation with the computer science R & D community, the series counts many renowned academics among its volume editors and paper authors, and collaborates with prestigious societies. Its mission is to serve this international community by providing an invaluable service, mainly focused on the publication of conference and workshop proceedings and postproceedings. LNCS commenced publication in 1973.

Islem Rekik · Ehsan Adeli · Sang Hyun Park ·
Celia Cintas · Ghada Zamzmi
Editors

Predictive Intelligence in Medicine

6th International Workshop, PRIME 2023
Held in Conjunction with MICCAI 2023
Vancouver, BC, Canada, October 8, 2023
Proceedings

 Springer

Editors
Islem Rekik 🆔
Imperial College London
London, UK

Ehsan Adeli 🆔
Stanford University
Stanford, CA, USA

Sang Hyun Park 🆔
Daegu Gyeongbuk Institute of Science
and Technology
Daegu, Korea (Republic of)

Celia Cintas 🆔
IBM Research - Africa
Nairobi, Kenya

Ghada Zamzmi 🆔
United States Food and Drug Administration
Silver Spring, MD, USA

ISSN 0302-9743   ISSN 1611-3349 (electronic)
Lecture Notes in Computer Science
ISBN 978-3-031-46004-3   ISBN 978-3-031-46005-0 (eBook)
https://doi.org/10.1007/978-3-031-46005-0

This Springer imprint is published by the registered company Springer Nature Switzerland AG
The registered company address is: Gewerbestrasse 11, 6330 Cham, Switzerland

Paper in this product is recyclable.

Preface

It would constitute stunning progress in medicine if, in a few years, we were to engineer a *predictive intelligence* able to predict missing clinical data with high precision. Given the explosion of big and complex medical data with multiple modalities (e.g., structural magnetic resonance imaging (MRI) and resting function MRI (rsfMRI)) and multiple acquisition time points (e.g., longitudinal data), more intelligent predictive models are needed to improve diagnosis of a wide spectrum of diseases and disorders *while leveraging minimal medical data*. Basically, the workshop Predictive Intelligence in Medicine (PRIME-MICCAI 2023) aimed to diagnose in the earliest stage using minimal clinically non-invasive data. For instance, PRIME would constitute a breakthrough in early neurological disorder diagnosis as it would allow accurate early diagnosis using multimodal MRI data (e.g., diffusion and functional MRIs) and follow-up observations *all predicted* from only T1-weighted MRI acquired at a baseline timepoint.

Existing computer-aided diagnosis methods can be divided into two main categories: (1) analytical methods, and (2) predictive methods. While analytical methods aim to efficiently analyse, represent and interpret data (static or longitudinal), predictive methods leverage the data currently available to predict observations at later time points (i.e., forecasting the future) or to predict observations at earlier time points (i.e., predicting the past for missing data completion). For instance, a method which only focuses on classifying patients with mild cognitive impairment (MCI) and patients with Alzheimer's disease (AD) is an analytical method, while a method that predicts whether a subject diagnosed with MCI will remain stable or convert to AD over time is a predictive method. Similar examples can be established for various neurodegenerative or neuropsychiatric disorders, degenerative arthritis or in cancer studies, in which the disease/disorder develops over time.

Following the success of the past editions of PRIME-MICCAI in 2018, 2019, 2020, 2021 and 2022, the sixth edition, PRIME[1], aimed to drive the field of 'high-precision predictive medicine', where late medical observations are predicted with high precision, while providing explanation via machine and deep learning, and statistically, mathematically or physically based models of healthy or disordered development and aging. Despite the terrific progress that analytical methods have made in the last twenty years in medical image segmentation, registration, or other related applications, efficient predictive intelligent models and methods are somewhat lagging behind. As such predictive intelligence develops and improves – and it is likely to do so exponentially in the coming years – this will have far-reaching consequences for the development of new treatment procedures and novel technologies. These predictive models will begin to shed light on one of the most complex healthcare and medical challenges we have ever encountered, expanding our basic understanding of who we are.

---

[1] http://basira-lab.com/prime-miccai-2023/.

What are the Key Challenges We Aim to Address?

The main aim of PRIME-MICCAI is to propel the advent of predictive models in a broad sense, with application to medical data. Particularly, the workshop accepted 8 to 12-page papers describing new cutting-edge predictive models and methods that solve challenging problems in the medical field. We envision that the PRIME workshop will become a nest for high-precision predictive medicine, one that is set to transform multiple fields of healthcare technologies in unprecedented ways. Topics of interest for the workshop included but were not limited to predictive methods dedicated to the following topics:

- Modeling and predicting disease development or evolution from a limited number of observations;
- Computer-aided prognostic methods (e.g., for brain diseases, prostate cancer, cervical cancer, dementia, acute disease, neurodevelopmental disorders);
- Forecasting disease or cancer progression over time;
- Predicting low-dimensional data (e.g., behavioral scores, clinical outcome, age, gender);
- Predicting the evolution or development of high-dimensional data (e.g., shapes, graphs, images, patches, abstract features, learned features);
- Predicting high-resolution data from low-resolution data;
- Prediction methods using 2D, 2D+t, 3D, 3D+t, ND and ND+t data;
- Predicting data of one image modality from a different modality (e.g., data synthesis);
- Predicting lesion evolution;
- Predicting missing data (e.g., data imputation or data completion problems);
- Predicting clinical outcome from medical data (genomic, imaging data, etc).

Key Highlights

This workshop intersects ideas from both machine learning and mathematical/statistical/physical modeling research directions in the hope to provide a deeper understanding of the foundations of predictive intelligence developed for medicine, as well as of where we currently stand and what we aspire to achieve through this field. PRIME-MICCAI 2023 featured a single-track workshop with keynote speakers with deep expertise in high-precision predictive medicine using machine learning and other modeling approaches – which are believed to point in opposing directions. PRIME 2023 ran in a hybrid format (with both in-person and virtual modalities), and keynote talks were streamed live this year. Eventually, this will increase the outreach of PRIME publications to a broader audience while steering a wide spectrum of MICCAI publications from being 'only analytical' to being 'jointly analytical and predictive.'

We received a total of 18 submissions and accepted 17 papers. All papers underwent a rigorous double-blinded review process by at least 2 program committee members composed of 23 well-known research experts in the field. The papers were selected based on technical merit, significance of results, and relevance and clarity of presentation. Based on the reviewing scores and critiques, all but one PRIME submission scored highly with the reviewers, i.e., all had an average score of at least above the acceptance threshold.

This year we merged the proceedings with two other workshops, Ambient Intelligence for Healthcare (AmI4HC)[2] and Computational and Affective Intelligence for Computer Assisted Interventions (AICAI)[3]. Dr. Ghada Zamzmi joined us as a co-editor of this LNCS edition. The joined AmI4HC and AICAI workshops received 9 total submissions and the papers were double-blind peer-reviewed by at least 3 expert reviewers. 7 papers were accepted for publication, all of which received high scores from the reviewers.

Diversity and **inclusion** have been one of main focuses of the PRIME-MICCAI workshop. This year we strongly supported gender balance and geographic diversity in the program committee. The authors of the accepted PRIME papers were affiliated with institutions on four continents: Africa, Europe, South America, and Asia. This year, we have also provided one BASIRA Scholarship[4] to register the papers of talented minority students in low-middle income countries (one from the African continent). The eligibility criteria for the BASIRA Scholarship were included in the CMT submission system. We will strive to continue this initiative in the upcoming years and see a similar trend in other conferences and workshops.

August 2023

Islem Rekik
Ehsan Adeli
Sang Hyun Park
Celia Cintas
Ghada Zamzmi

---

[2] http://ami4hc.stanford.edu/.
[3] https://aicai2023.site/.
[4] https://basira-lab.com/.

Organization

Chairs

Islem Rekik	Imperial College London, UK
Ehsan Adeli	Stanford University, USA
Sang Hyun Park	DGIST, South Korea
Celia Cintas	IBM Research Africa, Kenya
Ghada Zamzmi	Food and Drug Administration, USA

Program Committee

Ahmed Nebli	Forschungszentrum Jülich, Germany
Andrea Lara	Galileo University, Guatemala
Gang Li	University of North Carolina at Chapel Hill, USA
Hao Chen	Hong Kong University of Science and Technology, China
Ilwoo Lyu	Ulsan National Institute of Science and Technology, South Korea
Jaeil Kim	Kyungpook National University, South Korea
Jiahong Ouyang	Stanford University, USA
Lequan Yu	University of Hong Kong, China
Li Wang	University of North Carolina at Chapel Hill, USA
Lichi Zhang	Shanghai Jiao Tong University, China
Manhua Liu	Shanghai Jiao Tong University, China
Maria A. Zuluaga	EURECOM, France
Moti Freiman	Technion - Israel Institute of Technology, Israel
Pew-Thian Yap	University of North Carolina at Chapel Hill, USA
Philip Chikontwe	Daegu Gyeongbuk Institute of Science and Technology, Korea
Qian Tao	Delft University of Technology, The Netherlands
Qingyu Zhao	Stanford University, USA
Reza Azad	RWTH University, Germany
Seungyeon Shin	National Institutes of Health, USA
Soochahn Lee	Kookmin University, South Korea
Su Ruan	LITIS, France
Tolga Tasdizen	University of Utah, USA
Won-Ki Jeong	Korea University, South Korea

Yalin Wang   Arizona State University, USA
Yonggang Shi   University of Southern California, USA
Ziga Spiclin   University of Ljubljana, Slovenia
Ashwag Alasmari   University of Maryland, USA
Gaetano Manzo   National Institutes of Health, USA

Contents

Longitudinal Self-supervised Learning Using Neural Ordinary Differential
Equation   1
    Rachid Zeghlache, Pierre-Henri Conze, Mostafa El Habib Daho,
    Yihao Li, Hugo Le Boité, Ramin Tadayoni, Pascal Massin,
    Béatrice Cochener, Ikram Brahim, Gwenolé Quellec,
    and Mathieu Lamard

Template-Based Federated Multiview Domain Alignment for Predicting
Heterogeneous Brain Graph Evolution Trajectories from Baseline   14
    Emircan Gündoğdu and Islem Rekik

Feature-Based Transformer with Incomplete Multimodal Brain Images
for Diagnosis of Neurodegenerative Diseases   25
    Xingyu Gao, Feng Shi, Dinggang Shen, and Manhua Liu

RepNet for Quantifying the Reproducibility of Graph Neural Networks
in Multiview Brain Connectivity Biomarker Discovery   35
    Hizir Can Bayram, Mehmet Serdar Çelebi, and Islem Rekik

SynthA1c: Towards Clinically Interpretable Patient Representations
for Diabetes Risk Stratification   46
    Michael S. Yao, Allison Chae, Matthew T. MacLean, Anurag Verma,
    Jeffrey Duda, James C. Gee, Drew A. Torigian, Daniel Rader,
    Charles E. Kahn Jr., Walter R. Witschey, and Hersh Sagreiya

Confounding Factors Mitigation in Brain Age Prediction Using MRI
with Deformation Fields   58
    K. H. Aqil, Tanvi Kulkarni, Jaikishan Jayakumar, Keerthi Ram,
    and Mohanasankar Sivaprakasam

Self-supervised Landmark Learning with Deformation Reconstruction
and Cross-Subject Consistency Objectives   70
    Chun-Hung Chao and Marc Niethammer

DAE-Former: Dual Attention-Guided Efficient Transformer for Medical
Image Segmentation   83
    Reza Azad, René Arimond, Ehsan Khodapanah Aghdam,
    Amirhossein Kazerouni, and Dorit Merhof

Diffusion-Based Graph Super-Resolution with Application
to Connectomics   96
    Nishant Rajadhyaksha and Islem Rekik

Deep Survival Analysis in Multiple Sclerosis   108
    Xin Zhang, Deval Mehta, Chao Zhu, Daniel Merlo, Yanan Hu,
    Melissa Gresle, David Darby, Anneke van der Walt,
    Helmut Butzkueven, and Zongyuan Ge

Federated Multi-trajectory GNNs Under Data Limitations for Baby Brain
Connectivity Forecasting   120
    Michalis Pistos, Gang Li, Weili Lin, Dinggang Shen, and Islem Rekik

Learning Task-Specific Morphological Representation for Pyramidal Cells
via Mutual Information Minimization   134
    Chunli Sun, Qinghai Guo, Gang Yang, and Feng Zhao

DermoSegDiff: A Boundary-Aware Segmentation Diffusion Model
for Skin Lesion Delineation   146
    Afshin Bozorgpour, Yousef Sadegheih, Amirhossein Kazerouni,
    Reza Azad, and Dorit Merhof

Self-supervised Few-Shot Learning for Semantic Segmentation:
An Annotation-Free Approach   159
    Sanaz Karimijafarbigloo, Reza Azad, and Dorit Merhof

Imputing Brain Measurements Across Data Sets via Graph Neural
Networks   172
    Yixin Wang, Wei Peng, Susan F. Tapert, Qingyu Zhao, and Kilian M. Pohl

Multi-input Vision Transformer with Similarity Matching   184
    Seungeun Lee, Sung Ho Hwang, Saelin Oh, Beom Jin Park,
    and Yongwon Cho

Federated Multi-domain GNN Network for Brain Multigraph Generation   194
    Chun Xu and Islem Rekik

An Ambient Intelligence-Based Approach for Longitudinal Monitoring
of Verbal and Vocal Depression Symptoms   206
    Alice Othmani and Muhammad Muzammel

Dynamic Depth-Supervised NeRF for Multi-view RGB-D Operating
Room Videos   218
    Beerend G. A. Gerats, Jelmer M. Wolterink, and Ivo A. M. J. Broeders

Revisiting N-CNN for Clinical Practice 231
  Leonardo Antunes Ferreira, Lucas Pereira Carlini,
  Gabriel de Almeida Sá Coutrin, Tatiany Marcondes Heideirich,
  Marina Carvalho de Moraes Barros, Ruth Guinsburg,
  and Carlos Eduardo Thomaz

Video-Based Hand Pose Estimation for Remote Assessment
of Bradykinesia in Parkinson's Disease 241
  Gabriela T. Acevedo Trebbau, Andrea Bandini, and Diego L. Guarin

More Than Meets the Eye: Analyzing Anesthesiologists' Visual Attention
in the Operating Room Using Deep Learning Models 253
  Sapir Gershov, Fadi Mahameed, Aeyal Raz, and Shlomi Laufer

Pose2Gait: Extracting Gait Features from Monocular Video of Individuals
with Dementia 265
  Caroline Malin-Mayor, Vida Adeli, Andrea Sabo, Sergey Noritsyn,
  Carolina Gorodetsky, Alfonso Fasano, Andrea Iaboni, and Babak Taati

Self-Supervised Learning of Gait-Based Biomarkers 277
  R. James Cotton, J. D. Peiffer, Kunal Shah, Allison DeLillo,
  Anthony Cimorelli, Shawana Anarwala, Kayan Abdou,
  and Tasos Karakostas

Author Index 293

Longitudinal Self-supervised Learning Using Neural Ordinary Differential Equation

Rachid Zeghlache[1,2(✉)], Pierre-Henri Conze[1,3], Mostafa El Habib Daho[1,2], Yihao Li[1,2], Hugo Le Boité[5], Ramin Tadayoni[5], Pascal Massin[5], Béatrice Cochener[1,2,4], Ikram Brahim[1,2,6], Gwenolé Quellec[1], and Mathieu Lamard[1,2]

[1] LaTIM UMR 1101, Inserm, Brest, France
[2] University of Western Brittany, Brest, France
rachid.zeghlache@univ-brest.fr
[3] IMT Atlantique, Brest, France
[4] Ophtalmology Department, CHRU Brest, Brest, France
[5] Lariboisière Hospital, AP-HP, Paris, France
[6] LBAI UMR 1227, Inserm, Brest, France

Abstract. Longitudinal analysis in medical imaging is crucial to investigate the progressive changes in anatomical structures or disease progression over time. In recent years, a novel class of algorithms has emerged with the goal of learning disease progression in a self-supervised manner, using either pairs of consecutive images or time series of images. By capturing temporal patterns without external labels or supervision, longitudinal self-supervised learning (LSSL) has become a promising avenue. To better understand this core method, we explore in this paper the LSSL algorithm under different scenarios. The original LSSL is embedded in an auto-encoder (AE) structure. However, conventional self-supervised strategies are usually implemented in a Siamese-like manner. Therefore, (as a first novelty) in this study, we explore the use of Siamese-like LSSL. Another new core framework named neural ordinary differential equation (NODE). NODE is a neural network architecture that learns the dynamics of ordinary differential equations (ODE) through the use of neural networks. Many temporal systems can be described by ODE, including modeling disease progression. We believe that there is an interesting connection to make between LSSL and NODE. This paper aims at providing a better understanding of those core algorithms for learning the disease progression with the mentioned change. In our different experiments, we employ a longitudinal dataset, named OPHDIAT, targeting diabetic retinopathy (DR) follow-up. Our results demonstrate the application of LSSL without including a reconstruction term, as well as the potential of incorporating NODE in conjunction with LSSL.

Keywords: Longitudinal analysis · longitudinal self supervised learning · neural ODE · disease progression · diabetic retinopathy

I. Rekik et al. (Eds.): PRIME 2023, LNCS 14277, pp. 1–13, 2023.
https://doi.org/10.1007/978-3-031-46005-0_1

1 Introduction

In recent years, the deep learning community has enthusiastically embraced the self-supervised learning paradigm, by taking advantage of pretext tasks to learn better representations to be used on a downstream task. Most of the existing works are based on contrastive learning [4] or hand-crafted pretext task [20]. When using hand-crafted pretext tasks, the model learns automatically by obtaining supervisory signals extracted directly from the nature of the data itself, without manual annotation performed by an expert. An adequate objective function teaches robust feature representations to the model, which are needed to solve downstream tasks (e.g., classification, regression). However, to design an effective pretext task, domain-specific knowledge is required.

Recently, several approaches that involve pretext tasks in a longitudinal context have appeared with the purpose of encoding disease progression. These approaches aim to learn longitudinal changes or infer disease progression trajectories at the population or patient levels [5,15,18,21].

Longitudinal self-supervised learning (LSSL) was initially introduced in the context of disease progression as a pretext task by [16], which involved the introduction of a longitudinal pretext task utilizing a Siamese-like model. The model took as input a consecutive pair of images and predicted the difference in time between the two examinations. Since then, more sophisticated algorithms have been proposed, including the advanced version of LSSL proposed in [21]. The framework attempted to theorize the notion of longitudinal pretext task with the purpose of learning the disease progression. LSSL was embedded in an auto-encoder (AE), taking two consecutive longitudinal scans as inputs. The authors added to the classic reconstruction term a cosines alignment term that forces the topology of the latent space to change in the direction of longitudinal changes.

Moreover, as conducted in [8,16] employed a Siamese-like architecture to compare longitudinal imaging data with deep learning. The strength of this approach was to avoid any registration requirements, leverage population-level data to capture time-irreversible changes that are shared across individuals and offer the ability to visualize individual-level changes. Neural Ordinary Differential Equations (NODEs) is a new core algorithm that has a close connection to modeling time-dependant dynamics. NODE, introduced in [3], deals with deep learning operations defined by the solution of an ODE. Whatever the involved architecture and given an input, a NODE defines its output as the numerical solution of the underlying ordinary differential equation (ODE). One advantage is that it can easily work with irregular time series [17], which is an inherent aspect of the disease progression context. This is possible because the NODEs are able to deal with continuous time. Additionally, NODEs leverage the inductive bias that time-series originates from an underlying dynamical process, where the rate of change of the current state depends on the state itself. NODEs have been used to model hidden dynamics in disease progression using neural networks. Authors in [14] have developed a Neural ODE-based model in order to learn disease progression dynamics for patients under medication for COVID-19. Thus, Lachinov et al. proposed in [10] a U-Net-based model coupled with a neural ODE to predict the progression of 3D volumic data in the context of geographic atrophy using retinal OCT volumes and predicting the brain ventricle change with MRI for the quantification of progression of Alzheimer's disease. Thus, the main objectives of our work are to examine if:

1. By including Neural ODEs, it becomes possible to generate a latent representation of the subsequent scan without the explicit need for feeding an image pair to the model. Due to the inherent characteristics of NODE, there is potential to encode the latent dynamic of disease progression and longitudinal change. We believe this established a natural connection between NODE and LSSL algorithms, warranting further investigation to gain a deeper understanding of these newly introduced frameworks.
2. Most of the current self-supervised learning frameworks are embedded in a Siamese-like paradigm, using only an encoder and optimizing different loss functions based on various similarity criteria. While the reconstruction term offers a way to encode anatomical change, successful longitudinal pretext tasks [7, 8, 16] have only used an encoder in terms of design, which justify the potential of extending it to LSSL. In order to examine this hypothesis, we are constructing a Siamese-like variant of the LSSL framework to evaluate the significance of the reconstruction term within LSSL.

2 Method

In this section, we briefly introduce the concepts related to LSSL [21] and NODE [3], and we investigate the longitudinal self-supervised learning framework under different scenarios: standard LSSL (Fig. 1b), Siamese-like LSSL (Fig. 1a) as well as their NODE-based versions (Fig. 1c-d). Let $\mathcal{X}$ be the set of subject-specific image pairs extracted from the full collection of color fundus photographs (CFP). $\mathcal{X}$ contains all $(x^{t_i}, x^{t_{i+1}})$ image pairs that are from the same subject with image x^{t_i} scanned before image $x^{t_{i+1}}$. These image pairs are then provided as inputs of an auto-encoder (AE) network (Fig. 1). The latent representations generated by the encoder are denoted by $z^{t_i} = f(x^{t_i})$ and $z^{t_{i+1}} = f(x^{t_{i+1}})$ where f is the encoder. From this encoder, we can define the trajectory vector $\Delta z = (z^{t_{i+1}} - z^{t_i})$. The decoder g uses the latent representation to reconstruct the input images such that $\tilde{x}^{t_i} = g(z^{t_i})$ and $\tilde{x}^{t_{i+1}} = g(z^{t_{i+1}})$.

2.1 Longitudinal Self-supervised Learning (LSSL)

Longitudinal self-supervised learning (LSSL) exploits a standard AE (Fig. 1b). The AE is trained with a loss that forces the trajectory vector Δz to be aligned with a direction that could rely in the latent space of the AE called τ. This direction is learned through a subnetwork composed of single dense layers which map dummy data (vector full of ones) into a vector τ that has the dimension of the latent space of the AE. Enforcing the AE to respect this constraint is equivalent to encouraging $\cos(\Delta z, \tau)$ to be close to 1, i.e., a zero-angle between

τ and the direction of progression in the representation space. With $\mathbf{E}$ being the mathematical expectation, the objective function is defined as follows:

$$\mathbf{E}_{(x^{t_i}, x^{t_{i+1}}) \sim \mathcal{X}} \left(\lambda_{recon} \cdot (\| x^{t_i} - \tilde{x}^{t_i} \|_2^2 + \| x^{t_{i+1}} - \tilde{x}^{t_{i+1}} \|_2^2) - \lambda_{dir} \cdot \cos(\Delta z, \tau) \right)$$
(1)

When $\lambda_{dir} = 0$ and $\lambda_{recon} > 0$, the architecture is reduced to a simple AE. Conversely, using $\lambda_{dir} > 0$ and $\lambda_{recon} = 0$ amounts to a Siamese-like structure with a cosine term as a loss function (Fig. 1c).

2.2   Neural Ordinary Differential Equations (NODE)

NODEs approximate unknown ordinary differential equations by a neural network [2] that parameterizes the continuous dynamics of hidden units $\mathbf{z} \in \mathbb{R}^n$ over time with $\mathbf{t} \in \mathbb{R}$. NODEs are able to model the instantaneous rate of change of $\mathbf{z}$ with respect to $\mathbf{t}$ using a neural network u with parameters θ.

$$\lim_{h \to 0} \frac{\mathbf{z}_{t+h} - \mathbf{z}_t}{h} = \frac{d\mathbf{z}}{dh} = u(t, \mathbf{z}, \boldsymbol{\theta})$$
(2)

The analytical solution of Eq. 2 is given by:

$$\mathbf{z}_{t_1} = \mathbf{z}_{t_0} + \int_{t_0}^{t_1} u(t, \mathbf{z}, \boldsymbol{\theta}) dt = \text{ODESolve}(\mathbf{z}(t_0), u, t_0, t_1, \theta)$$
(3)

where $[t_0, t_1]$ represents the time horizon for solving the ODE, u being a neural network, and θ is the trainable parameters of u.

2.3   LSSL-NODE

By using a black box ODE solver introduced in [2], we are able to approximately solve the initial value problem (IVP) and calculate the hidden state at any desired time using Eq. 3. We can differentiate the solutions of the ODE solver with respect to the parameters θ, the initial state $\mathbf{z}_{t_0}$ at initial time t_0, and the solution at time t. This can be achieved by using the adjoint sensitivity method [3]. This allows to backpropagate through the ODE solver and train any learnable parameters with any optimizer. Typically, NODE is modelized by a feedforward layer, where we solve the ODE from t_0 to a terminal time t_1, or it can be used to output a series, by calculating the hidden state at specific times $\{t_1, ..., t_i, t_{i+1}\}$. For a given patient, instead of giving a pair of consecutive images to the model, we only provide the first image of the consecutive pair. In our case, through the latent representation of this image, we define an IVP problem that aims to solve: $\dot{z}(t) = u(z(t), t, \theta)$, with the initial value $z(t_i) = z^{t_i}$. This results in the following update of the equations from the previous notation. The latent representations generated by the encoder are denoted by $z^{t_i} = f(x^{t_i})$ and $z_{node}^{t_{i+1}} = \text{ODESolve}(z^{t_i}, u, t_i, t_{i+1}, \theta)$ where f is the encoder and u is the defined neural network for our NODE. From this encoder and the NODE, we can define the trajectory vector $(\Delta_z^{node}) = (z_{node}^{t_{i+1}} - z^{t_i})$. The same decoder g uses the latent representation to reconstruct the input images such that $\tilde{x}^{t_i} = g(z^{t_i})$ and $\tilde{x}^{t_{i+1}} = g(z_{node}^{t_{i+1}})$. The objective function is defined as:

$$\mathbb{E}_{(x^{t_i},x^{t_{i+1}})\sim\mathcal{X}} \left(\lambda_{recon} \cdot (\| x^{t_i} - \tilde{x}^{t_i} \|_2^2 + \| x^{t_{i+1}} - \tilde{x}^{t_{i+1}} \|_2^2) - \lambda_{dir} \cdot \cos(\Delta_z^{node}, \tau)) \right) \tag{4}$$

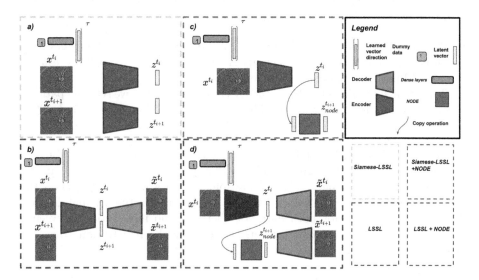

Fig. 1. Illustration of original LSSL and the proposed extension of the LSSL, in figure a) the Siamese-like LSSL(S-LSSL), b) original LSSL and in figure c) and d) their NODE-based version respectively.

3   Experiments and Results

3.1   Dataset

The proposed models were trained and evaluated on OPHDIAT [12], a large CFP database collected from the Ophthalmology Diabetes Telemedicine network consisting of examinations acquired from 101,383 patients between 2004 and 2017. Within 763,848 interpreted CFP images, 673,017 are assigned with a DR severity grade, the others being nongradable. The image sizes range from 1440 × 960 to 3504 × 2336 pixels. Each examination has at least two images for each eye. Each subject had 2 to 16 scans, with an average of 2.99 scans spanning an average time interval of 2.23 years. The age range of patients is from 9 to 91. The dataset is labeled according to the international clinical DR severity scale (ICDR) where the classes include: no apparent DR, mild non-proliferative diabetic retinopathy (NPDR), moderate NPDR, severe NPDR, and proliferative diabetic retinopathy (PDR), respectively labeled as grades 0, 1, 2, 3, and 4. NPDR (grades 1, 2, 3) corresponds to the early-to-middle stage of DR and deals with a progressive microvascular disease characterized by small vessel damages.

Image Selection. The majority of patients from the OPHDIAT database have multiple images with different fields of view for both eyes. To facilitate the selection, we chose to randomly take a single image per eye for each examination. In addition, we defined two sub-datasets from patients that have a longitudinal follow-up to fit our experiment setup.

1. *Pair-wise dataset*: From the OPHDIAT database, we selected pairs from patients with at least one DR severity change in their follow-up. This resulted in 10412 patients and 49579 numbers of pairs.
2. *Sequence-wise dataset*: From the OPHDIAT database, we selected patients that have at least four visits. This resulted in 7244 patients and 13997 sequences.

For both datasets, the split was conducted with the following distribution: training (60%), validation (20%), and test (20%) based on subjects, i.e., images of a single subject belonged to the same split and in a way that preserves the same proportions of examples in each class as observed in the original dataset. We also ensured that for both datasets, there was no intersection between a patient in training/validation/test sets. Except for the registration stage, we followed the same image processing performed in [19].

3.2   Implementation Details

As conducted in [13,19,21], a basic AE was implemented in order to focus on the methodology presented. We used the same encoder and decoder as used in [19]. This encoder provides a latent representation of size $64 \times 4 \times 4$. The different networks were trained for 400 epochs by the AdamW optimizer, with a learning rate of 5×10^{-4}, OneCycleLR as scheduler, and a weight decay of 10^{-5}, using an A6000 GPU with the PyTorch framework and trained on the pair-wise dataset. The regularization weights were set to $\lambda_{dir} = 1.0$ and $\lambda_{recon} = 1.0$. Concerning NODE, we used the torchdiffeq framework, which provides integration of NODE in Pytorch with the possibility to use a numeric solver with the adjoint method, which allows constant memory usage. Our neural ODE function consists of the succession of dense layers followed by a tanh activation function. We employed the fifth-order "dopri5" solver with an adaptive step size for the generative model, setting the relative tolerance to 1e-3 and the absolute tolerance to 1e-4. When using the dopri solver with the adjoint method, the torchdiffeq package does not provide support for a batched time solution, so during training for the forward batch in the NODE we used the workaround introduced in [11] to enable a batched time solution.

3.3 Evaluating the Learned Feature Extractor

To evaluate the quality of the encoder from the different experiments, we will use two tasks with a longitudinal nature. We only perform fine-tuning scenarios, as performed in [7] to assess the quality of the learned weights. We initialize the weights of the encoder that will be used for the two tasks, with the weights of the longitudinal pre-training method presented in Fig. 1. An additional AE and AE-NODE were added for comparison purposes. Each task was trained for 150 epochs with a learning rate of 10^{-3} and a weight decay of 10^{-4} and OneCycleLR as a scheduler. The first one is the prediction of the patient's age in years, using a CFP (this task is called *age regression* for the rest of the manuscript), and the second task is the prediction of the development of the DR for the next visit using the past three examinations (task called *predict next visit*). For the age regression, the model developed is a combination of the implemented encoder and a multi-layer perceptron. The model is trained with the Mean Squared Error (MSE) on the image selected for the sequence-wise dataset. For predict next visit, we used a CNN+RNN [6], a standard approach for tackling sequential or longitudinal tasks. The RNN we used is a long short-term memory (LSTM). The model is trained using cross-entropy, on the sequence-wise dataset. We used the Area Under the receiver operating characteristic Curve (AUC) with three binary tasks which are the following: predicting at least NPDR in the next visit (**AUC Mild+**), at least moderate NPDR in the next visit denoted (**AUC Moderate+**) and finally at least severe NPDR in the next visit (**AUC severe+**) for evaluating the models.

Table 1. Results for the age regression task reporting the Mean Squared Error (MSE) in squared years. Best results for the LSSL and S-LSSL are in underline, best results for their NODE version are in bold.

Weights	λ_{dir}	λ_{recon}	NODE	MSE
From scratch	–	–	-	0.0070
AE	0	1	No	0.0069
AE	0	1	Yes	0.0069
LSSL	1	1	No	0.0050
LSSL	1	1	Yes	**0.0048**
Siamese LSSL	1	0	No	0.0049
Siamese LSSL	1	0	Yes	**0.0046**

According to the results of both Table 1 and 2, we observe that longitudinal pre-training is an efficient pre-training strategy to tackle a problem with a longitudinal nature compared to training from scratch of classic autoencoder, which is aligned with the following studies [7,13,19,21]. For the age regression task, according to the results presented in Table 1, the best longitudinal pre-training strategy is the Siamese LSSL version with NODE. However, the difference in

Table 2. Results for the predict next visit label for the different longitudinal pretext task for the three binary tasks using the AUC. Best results for the LSSL and S-LSSL are in underline, best results for their NODE version are in bold.

Weights	λ_{dir}	λ_{recon}	NODE	AUC Mild+	AUC Moderate +	AUC severe+
From scratch	–	–	–	0.574	0.602	0.646
AE	0	1	No	0.563	0.543	0.636
AE	0	1	Yes	0.569	0.565	0.649
LSSL	1	1	No	0.578	0.618	0.736
LSSL	1	1	Yes	**0.604**	**0.630**	**0.760**
Siamese LSSL	1	0	No	0.578	0.596	0.708
Siamese LSSL	1	0	Yes	**0.569**	**0.549**	**0.756**

performance is marginal, indicating that the Siamese LSSL could also be used as pretext task. The cosine alignment term in the loss function, which is the one responsible for forcing the model to encode longitudinal information, seems to be beneficial in solving longitudinal downstream tasks.

For the predict next visit task (Table 2), the LSSL-NODE version performs better than the rest. An observation that could explain the difference is that during the training of the LSSL-NODE, the reconstruction term and the direction alignment (second term of Eq. 4) in the loss function reach 0 at the end of the training. While for the LSSL, only the reconstruction term converges to 0. The direction alignment term faces a plateau of around 0.3. One way to explain this convergence issue is the fact that the longitudinal pair were selected randomly. Even if it is the same patient, the image may have a very different field of view which could increase the difficulty for the model to both minimize the reconstruction loss and cosine alignment term. The LSSL-NODE does not have this issue since only one image is given to the CNN, which we suspect ease the problem solved by the LSSL+NODE. Another way to explain this phenomena is the fact that the LSSL was trained with λ_{recon} and λ_{dir} set to 1, a more advanced weight balanced between the two terms in the loss could reduce this issue. This observation could be the explanation for the difference in performance when using the LSSL-NODE vs classic LSSL. Another simple explanation could be the fact that we did not use any registration method for the longitudinal pairs. Surprisingly, according to both Table 1 and 2, the model with the NODE extension performed well compared to their original version. We believe that the NODE forces the CNN backbone to learn a representation that is more suitable for modeling the dynamics of the disease progression.

3.4   Analysis of the Norm of Δ_z

Using the same protocol introduced in [13,21], we computed the norm of the trajectory vector. The intuition behind this computation is the following: Δ_z can be seen as some kind of vector that indicates the speed of disease progression because it can be regarded as an instantaneous rate of change of $\mathbf{z}$ normalized by 1. For the different extensions of LSSL, we evaluate pregnancy factor [9] and type of diabetes [1], which are known factors that characterize the speed of the disease progression in the context of DR. This is done to analyze the capacity of Δ_z to capture the speed of disease progression.

1. **Pregnancy**: Pregnant vs not pregnant (only female). For the pregnant group, we selected longitudinal pairs from patients that were in early pregnancy and in close monitoring. For the rest, we selected longitudinal pair from female patients without antecedent of pregnancy.
2. **Diabetes type**: Patients with known diabetes type. We only selected a longitudinal pair of patients for known diabetes type 1 or 2.

First, patients present in the training set for the longitudinal pretext task were not allowed to be selected as part of any group. For the first group, we randomly selected 300 patients for each category. For the second group, we randomly selected 2000 patients for the two categories. We applied a statistical test (student t-test) to explore if the mean value of the norm of the trajectory vector with respect to both defined factors has a larger mean value for patients with pregnancy than for patients without pregnancy. And if the patient with type 1 diabetes had a higher mean than type 2. We observe that the norm of the trajectory vector (Δz) is capable of dissociating the two types of diabetes (t-test p-value < 0.01) and pregnancy type (t-test p-value < 0.00001) for all models that have a cosine alignment term (except the AE and the AE+NODE extension). Regarding the type of diabetes, a specific study in the OPHDIAT dataset [1] indicated that the progression of DR was faster in patients with type 1 diabetes than for patients with type 2 diabetes. Furthermore, pregnancy is a known factor [9] in the progression speed of DR. Those observations are aligned with the expected behavior of the two factors. In addition, as observed in [13,19,21], standard AE is not capable of encoding disease progression.

3.5 Evaluation of the NODE Weights

For models trained with a NODE, we design a protocol to assess the capacity of NODE to learn a meaningful representation related to disease progression. The protocol to evaluate the weights of the NODE is as follows. We implemented a NODE classifier (NODE-CLS) illustrated in Fig. 2. The NODE classifier is constructed as the concatenation of a backbone, a NODE, and a multilayer perceptron (MLP). The architecture of the backbone and the NODE is the same that was used with the LSSL method. The MLP consists of two fully connected layers of dimensions 1024 and 64 with LeakyReLU activation followed by a last single perceptron, which project the last layer representation into the number of class, and the network is trained using the pairwise dataset. The NODE-CLS only requires a single CFP denoted x^{t_i} and $\Delta_t = t_{i+1} - t_i$, which is the time lapse between examinations x^{t_i} and $x^{t_{i+1}}$. The image is first given to the backbone, which produces the latent representation z^{t_i}, then this vector is fed to the black box NODE, using the same IPV defined for the LSSL-NODE we can define the latent representation of the next visit. Using the predicted latent representation by the NODE, we predicted the severity grade of the next visit with the MLP. The same loss and metrics were used for the predict next visit task.

Table 3. Comparaison of AUC for the NODE classifier using different initialize weights, best results in bold.

Weights	λ_{dir}	λ_{recon}	NODE	AUC Mild+	AUC moderate+	AUC severe+
From scratch	–	–	–	0.552	0.600	0.583
AE	0	1	Yes	0.561	0.609	0.590
LSSL	1	1	Yes	**0.547**	**0.609**	**0.641**
Siamese LSSL	1	0	Yes	**0.558**	**0.617**	**0.670**

For the NODE-CLS, Table 3 shows a clear performance gain compared to the method trained from scratch. The best weights are obtained with the Siamese-LSSL. The classical LSSL also provides descent result, for the different subtask. We suspect that the LSSL model is more affected by the design of our experiments. Since we randomly selected images per examination, we did not perform any registration step. These results suggest that the classical LSSL is more likely to underperform than the Siamese-like method when the pair are not registered, aligned with the finding of [8].

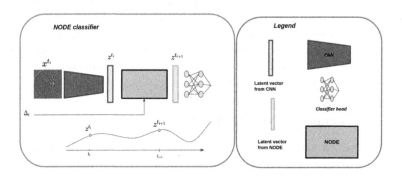

Fig. 2. Illustration of proposed NODE classifier for evaluating the weights of the method with a backbone + NODE

4   Discussion and Conclusion

In this paper, we investigated the use of the LSSL under different scenarios in order to get a better understanding of the LSSL framework. Our result demonstrated that the use of Siamese-like LSSL is possible. The S-LSSL might be more suitable when not registered pairs are given to the model. Moreover, for the various tasks that were used to evaluate the quality of the weights, a performance gain was observed when the LSSL and S-LSSL coupled with the NODE compared to their standard versions, while the reasons for such performance remain unclear. We hypothesize that adding the NODE in training forces the linked backbone to provide an enriched representation embedded with longitudinal information. Thus, since the formulation of the original LSSL [21] is based on a differential equation, which resulted in the introduction of the cosine alignment term in the objective function. Including the NODE is aligned with the formulation of the LSSL problem, which is reflected in our results. In this direction, we are interested in looking at the representation of the learned neural ODE, in order to understand if the neural ODE is able to interpolate the spatial feature and thus give the opportunity not even to need the registration. If so, the use of NODE with longitudinal self-supervised learning could also overcome the need of heavy registration step. LSSL techniques are quite promising and we believe that they will continue to grow at a fast pace. We would like to extend this study by including more frameworks [5,7,8,13] as well as more longitudinal datasets.

Some limitations should be pointed out, since we selected a random view of CFP for each examination, we did not apply any registration step. Using a better pairing strategy with the right registration step could enhance the results presented for LSSL. Moreover, we did not perform any elaborate hyperparameter search to find the correct loss weights in order to reach a complete loss convergence for the LSSL.

This work also opens up interesting research questions related to the use of neural ODE. The formulation and hypotheses of the LSSL framework are based on a differential equation that could be directly learned via a Neural ODE which could explain the better performance of the LSSL+NODE version. In the future, we will work on a theoretical explanation as to why this blending works.

In addition, for the models trained with a NODE, our experiments demonstrated the possibility of using pretext tasks on Neural ODE in order to provide an enhanced representation. In the classic SSL pretext task paradigm, the goal is to learn a strong backbone that yields good representation to solve specific downstream task. The results from the NODE-CLS experiments indicated that pre-training techniques where a NODE is involved can be reused on longitudinal downstream tasks and have the ability to enhance the results when a NODE is part of the model. In the future, we would like to explore time-aware pretraining in general, with a pretext task that has longitudinal context to be reused on longitudinal tasks.

Acknowledgement. The work takes place in the framework of Evired, an ANR RHU project. This work benefits from State aid managed by the French National Research Agency under the "Investissement d'Avenir" program bearing the reference ANR-18-RHUS-0008.

References

1. Chamard, C., et al.: Ten-year incidence and assessment of safe screening intervals for diabetic retinopathy: the OPHDIAT study. British J. Ophthal. **105**(3), 432–439 (2020)
2. Chen, R.T.Q., Rubanova, Y., Bettencourt, J., Duvenaud, D.: Neural ordinary differential equations (2018). https://doi.org/10.48550/ARXIV.1806.07366, https://arxiv.org/abs/1806.07366
3. Chen, R.T.Q.: torchdiffeq (2018). https://github.com/rtqichen/torchdiffeq
4. Chen, T., Kornblith, S., Norouzi, M., Hinton, G.: A simple framework for contrastive learning of visual representations (2020). https://doi.org/10.48550/ARXIV.2002.05709, https://arxiv.org/abs/2002.05709
5. Couronné, R., Vernhet, P., Durrleman, S.: Longitudinal self-supervision to disentangle inter-patient variability from disease progression, September 2021. https://doi.org/10.1007/978-3-030-87196-3_22
6. Cui, R., Liu, M.: Rnn-based longitudinal analysis for diagnosis of alzheimer's disease. Comput. Med. Imaging Graph. **73**, 1–10 (2019)
7. Emre, T., Chakravarty, A., Rivail, A., Riedl, S., Schmidt-Erfurth, U., Bogunović, H.: pp. 625–634. Springer Nature Switzerland (2022).https://doi.org/10.1007/978-3-031-16434-7_60
8. Kim, H., Sabuncu, M.R.: Learning to compare longitudinal images (2023)
9. Klein, B.E.K., Moss, S.E., Klein, R.: Effect of pregnancy on progression of diabetic retinopathy. Diabetes Care 13(1), 34–40 (1990). https://doi.org/10.2337/diacare.13.1.34
10. Lachinov, D., Chakravarty, A., Grechenig, C., Schmidt-Erfurth, U., Bogunovic, H.: Learning spatio-temporal model of disease progression with neuralodes from longitudinal volumetric data (2022)
11. Lechner, M., Hasani, R.: Learning long-term dependencies in irregularly-sampled time series. arXiv preprint arXiv:2006.04418 (2020)
12. Massin, P., Chabouis, A., et al.: Ophdiat: a telemedical network screening system for diabetic retinopathy in the ile-de-france. Diab. Metabol. **34**, 227–34 (2008). https://doi.org/10.1016/j.diabet.2007.12.006
13. Ouyang, J., et al.: Self-supervised longitudinal neighbourhood embedding
14. Qian, Z., Zame, W.R., Fleuren, L.M., Elbers, P., van der Schaar, M.: Integrating expert odes into neural odes: pharmacology and disease progression (2021)
15. Ren, M., Dey, N., Styner, M.A., Botteron, K., Gerig, G.: Local spatiotemporal representation learning for longitudinally-consistent neuroimage analysis (2022)
16. Rivail, A., et al.: Modeling disease progression in retinal OCTs with longitudinal self-supervised learning. In: Rekik, I., Adeli, E., Park, S.H. (eds.) PRIME 2019. LNCS, vol. 11843, pp. 44–52. Springer, Cham (2019). https://doi.org/10.1007/978-3-030-32281-6_5
17. Rubanova, Y., Chen, R.T.Q., Duvenaud, D.: Latent odes for irregularly-sampled time series (2019). https://doi.org/10.48550/ARXIV.1907.03907, https://arxiv.org/abs/1907.03907
18. Vernhet, P., Durrleman, S.: Longitudinal self-supervision to disentangle inter-patient variability, pp. 231–241 (2021). https://doi.org/10.1007/978-3-030-87196-3
19. Zeghlache, R., et al.: Detection of diabetic retinopathy using longitudinal self-supervised learning. In: Antony, B., Fu, H., Lee, C.S., MacGillivray, T., Xu, Y., Zheng, Y. (eds.) Ophthalmic Medical Image Analysis, pp. 43–52. Springer International Publishing, Cham (2022)

20. Zhang, R., Isola, P., Efros, A.A.: Colorful image colorization. In: Leibe, B., Matas, J., Sebe, N., Welling, M. (eds.) ECCV 2016. LNCS, vol. 9907, pp. 649–666. Springer, Cham (2016). https://doi.org/10.1007/978-3-319-46487-9_40
21. Zhao, Q., Liu, Z., Adeli, E., Pohl, K.M.: Longitudinal self-supervised learning. Med. Image Anal. **71** (2021). https://doi.org/10.1016/j.media.2021.102051

Template-Based Federated Multiview Domain Alignment for Predicting Heterogeneous Brain Graph Evolution Trajectories from Baseline

Emircan Gündoğdu[1,2] and Islem Rekik[1(✉)] (iD)

[1] BASIRA Lab, Imperial-X and Department of Computing, Imperial College London,
London, UK
i.rekik@imperial.ac.uk
[2] Faculty of Computer and Informatics Engineering, Istanbul Technical University,
Istanbul, Turkey
https://basira-lab.com/

Abstract. Predicting the brain graph (or connectome) evolution trajectory can aid in the *early* diagnosis of neurological disorders or even prior to onset. However, when dealing with heterogeneous datasets collected from various hospitals, each representing a unique domain (e.g., functional connectivity), the task of prediction becomes even more challenging within a federated learning (FL) context. To the best of our knowledge, no FL method was designed to predict brain graph evolution trajectory with hospitals trained on separate data domains, which presents one of the complex non-IID and data heterogeneity cases that existing FL methods struggle to solve in general. To address this issue, we introduce the concept of *template-based domain alignment*, where we leverage a *prior universal* connectional brain template (CBT), encoding shared connectivity patterns across the available domains. Specifically, we propose a *template-based federated multiview domain alignment* (TAF-GNN). Our TAF-GNN architecture consists of two parts: (1) *template-based alignment* where we align each distinct domain (i.e., hospital) to the *prior* universal CBT trajectory domain by using our proposed graph-based domain aligner network, and (2) *GNN-based trajectory federation* where we train a 4D graph neural network (GNN) for each hospital on its *CBT-aligned* brain trajectories. Our results on both real and simulated longitudinal connectivity datasets demonstrate that our TAF-GNN significantly outperforms other architectures with different alignment methods in both centralized and federated learning paradigms. Our TAF-GNN code is available on GitHub at https://github.com/basiralab/TAF-GNN.

Keywords: Brain graph evolution trajectory prediction · Federated learning · Connectional brain template · Template-based domain alignment

1 Introduction

Over the past decades, network neuroscience [1] coupled with sophisticated medical image processing techniques [2,3], aimed to debunk the brain construct through non-invasive magnetic resonance imaging (MRI) by extracting the brain connectivity matrix (also called graph or connectome), which models the connectivity between pairs of

I. Rekik et al. (Eds.): PRIME 2023, LNCS 14277, pp. 14–24, 2023.
https://doi.org/10.1007/978-3-031-46005-0_2

anatomical regions of interest (ROIs). In particular, learning how to predict the brain connectivity evolution over time across different *domains* or *views* (e.g., functional and morphological) and at various timepoints can aid in the early diagnosis of neurodegenerative disorders such as Alzheimer's Disease (AD) and mild cognitive impairment (MCI) [4,5]. However, the availability of brain connectomes in multiple domains and at various timepoints remains very limited, hospital-specific and confidential, which restricts the generalizability of geometric deep learning models, in particular graph neural networks (GNNs) to such diagnostic tasks [6]. Notwithstanding, the synergy between federated learning (FL) [7] and graph neural networks (GNNs) can present a promising lead for predicting brain graph evolution trajectory from a single observation while jointly (i) overcoming data scarcity and confidentiality issues, (ii) depicting longitudinal brain connectivity alterations and (iii) boosting the prediction performance.

On one hand, a few GNN models including an adversarial GNN [8] and a recurrent GNN [9], were proposed for predicting the temporal evolution of brain connectomes as reviewed in [6]. On the other hand, a variety of federated learning methods were designed to tackle the issue of non-IID data heterogeneity by leveraging meta-learning [10] or variants of the original aggregation technique FedAvg [7] such as FedProx [11] and FedBN [12]. Recently, a prime paper [13] aimed to design such a synergetic predictive framework where 4D (or longitudinal) GNN models are federated to predict the evolution of a brain graph trajectory from a single timepoint, while addressing the challenge of highly temporally-varying training data with independently missing timepoints across local hospitals. Although [13] presented compelling prediction results even in the most severe learning case where a hospital has only a baseline timepoint to train on, such framework cannot easily federate *heterogeneous multiview 4D brain graph trajectories, drawn from disparate domains* -same applies to existing FL and GNN methods. To the best of our knowledge, this paper presents the first attempt to learn how to boost the prediction of a 4D graph trajectory while federating from disparate domains.

To address this challenge, we introduce the concept of *template-based domain alignment in FL*, where we leverage a *prior universal* connectional brain template (CBT) [14], capturing the shared connectivity patterns across the available domains. Recently, CBTs have shown compelling results across a variety of brain connectivity learning tasks including classification, regression and fingerprinting [14]. Specifically, we root our FL prediction framework in the following assumption: *Using a universal graph template that is learned from a blend of all FL domains, by aligning each domain separately to such universal template domain, one can eliminate distribution fractures between disparate domains and boost predictions across all FL domains.* To this aim, we propose a template-based federated multiview domain alignment (TAF-GNN) network to predict heterogeneous brain graph trajectories from decentralized hospitals trained on separate data domains. *First*, we design a graph-based domain aligner to align distinct domains to a common template domain. We define our prior universal CBT trajectory using an *independent* multiview brain connectivity dataset (e.g., public dataset). *Second*, we align each brain graph trajectory to the corresponding time-specific universal CBT using our aligner network. *Third*, given the *CBT-aligned* brain graph trajectories, we leverage a GNN-based federation framework to predict brain graph evo-

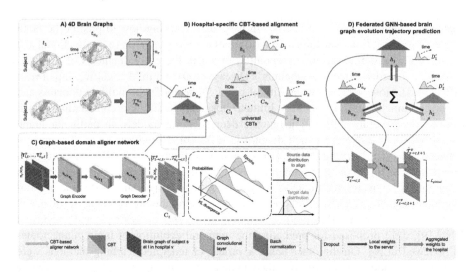

Fig. 1. *Illustration of the proposed template-based federated multiview domain alignment (TAF-GNN) for predicting brain graph evolution trajectory from baseline.* (**A**) **4D brain graph trajectories.** Each hospital has 4D brain graphs and temporal trajectories for each subject. (**B**) **Hospital-specific CBT-based alignment.** We have a prior universal CBT trajectory that is learned via Deep Graph Normalizer (DGN) from an independent multi-domain dataset at each timepoint. We use the prior universal CBT trajectory as a target domain in our graph-based aligner network to align the distribution of brain graphs of each hospital at each acquisition timepoint. (**C**) **Graph-based domain aligner network.** We design a generic domain aligner network, which maps the distribution of each source training graph to the distribution of the target CBT graph at each timepoint by minimizing a KL-divergence loss. (**D**) **Federated GNN-based brain graph evolution trajectory prediction.** We plug-in the 4D CBT-aligned trajectories to train a longitudinal brain graph prediction GNN in federated manner.

lution from baseline across various domains and timepoints. The contributions of our work are three-fold:

1. *On a methodological level.* TAF-GNN presents the first *template-based* federated learning to align all domain-specific hospital trajectories to a prior universal one (here of the CBT). We design a CBT-aligner network and plug with a downstream GNN model to predict brain graph evolution trajectories across disparate domains.
2. *On a clinical level.* Predicting multi-domain brain graph trajectories from a single timepoint can be leveraged for early disease diagnosis in a translational setting.
3. *On a generic level.* Our template-based federation paradigm can be coupled with other downstream tasks such as classification and regression –turning the weakness of data heterogeneity into a strength to predict better across different domains.

2 Methods

In this section, we detail our template-based federated multiview domain aligner network (TAF-GNN) as shown in Fig. 1. Specifically, we set out to federate a set of hospitals, each collecting 4D brain graphs drawn from a unique connectivity domain, e.g., morphological or functional. We view the 4D brain graph as a time-dependent graph trajectory, each representing an individual subject. We also assume the public availability of a prior universal CBT trajectory learned from an independent multi-domain dataset –using for instance the state-of-the-art method Deep Graph Normalizer (DGN) [14]. Given the severe case of federating from disparate domains with different distributions, we propose to align existing domains to a common base (or template). Hence, we design a *generic* graph-based domain aligner network to map the distributions of source trajectories to a universal CBT trajectory as a fixed target by minimizing the Kullback-Leibler (KL) divergence between both distributions. Last, for each hospital, we plug in the CBT-aligned 4D trajectories to train their local predictive GNN models in a federated manner.

Problem Statement. Let $\mathcal{T}_s^v$ denote the brain graph evolution trajectory for subject s and domain (or view) v. We define each trajectory $\mathcal{T}_s^v = \{\mathbf{T}_{s,1}^v, ..., \mathbf{T}_{s,n_t}^v\}$ as a three-dimensional tensor $\mathcal{T}_s^v \in \mathbb{R}^{n_r \times n_r \times n_t}$, where n_r and n_t denote the number of ROIs and timepoints, respectively. $\mathbf{T}_{s,t}^v$ denotes the brain graph connectivity matrix storing the edge weights $\mathbf{e}_{s,t,i}^v$ for each node $i \in \{1, ..., n_r\}$. Given n_v hospital, each with a dataset driven from a distinct domain D_v, where $v \in \{1, ..., n_v\}$, let D_v denote its local longitudinal 4D dataset including brain graph trajectories as $D_v = \{\mathcal{T}_1^v, ..., \mathcal{T}_{n_s}^v\}$ (Fig. 1-A), where n_s denotes the number of subjects with n_t timepoints. Here we set out to learn how to boost both the accuracy and the generalizability of a local hospital-specific GNNs when federating using brain graph trajectories collected in distinct domains.

Definition 1. Let $\mathbf{C}_t \in \mathbb{R}^{n_r \times n_r}$ denote a time-dependent CBT, which is a well-centered representation of a multiview brain graph population at timepoint $t \in \{1, ..., n_t\}$. $\mathbf{C}_t$ is a point on the prior universal CBT trajectory.

Hospital-specific CBT-Based Alignment. Since our main goal is to predict the dynamics of a brain graph over time within a federated system, the presence of different domains across hospitals can significantly impair the performance of the system. Therefore, prior to the federated training stage, aligning domains from each hospital to a common 'template domain' that is accessible to all hospitals minimizes domain fractures between them. To this aim, we first learn a prior template and then use it to align domains. This alignment step also acts as a global regularizer of the multi-domain local models. The second block of TAF-GNN (Fig. 1-**B**) shows hospital-specific CBT-based alignment based on a domain aligner network to align the distribution of each domain to that of the universal CBT.

i. CBT Trajectory Learning From an Independent Multi-domain Dataset. The universal template must be generated from a dataset that is both *independent* to ensure that the resulting template is not affected by the datasets in the hospitals, and *multi-domain* to capture the shared brain connectivity patterns across all domains. To this aim, we use a state-of-art CBT generator, namely DGN [14, 15], a graph neural network architecture that learns how to create a representative average of a heterogeneous population of multiview brain graphs. Specifically, we learn a universal CBT $\mathbf{C}_t$ at each timepoint t, thereby generating a universal CBT trajectory $\mathbf{C} = \{\mathbf{C}_1, ..., \mathbf{C}_{n_t}\}$, which will be used as a fixed target prior in the following alignment step.

ii. Domain Alignment to a Prior Universal CBT Distribution. Given the prior universal CBT trajectory, we aim to align the brain graphs from each hospital to the prior CBT at each timepoint t. Therefore, we design a generic graph-based domain aligner network Fig. 1-**C**). Specifically, given a timepoint t and a hospital in domain v, we train an aligner network locally where the learned CBT $\mathbf{C}_t$ is used as a target domain and the local training brain graphs $\{\mathbf{T}_{s,t}^v\}_{s=1}^{n_s}$ are used as the source domain. Eventually, the domain aligner network trained by each hospital, learns how to map a given domain distribution to the target prior CBT distribution. Next, we utilize the trained aligner to align all 4D brain graph trajectories of each hospital to the prior universal CBT trajectory, independently.

Graph-Based Domain Aligner Network. Here we detail the aligner architecture in our TAF-GNN (Fig. 1-**C**). The network is composed of three layers, each with a graph convolutional neural network, batch normalization, and dropout, respectively. The network uses a dynamic edge-conditioned filter proposed by [16] in graph convolutional layers and is also motivated by encoder-decoder pairs in the U-Net architecture [17]. Specifically, we use batch normalization to improve the efficiency of the network training by ensuring faster convergence of the loss function, while dropout helps prevent overfitting and simplify the network training. To train our aligner network for domain v, we use a set of training source brain graphs $\{\mathbf{T}_{s,t}^v\}_{s=1}^{n_s}$ and the target prior graph $\mathbf{C}_t$. For each source brain graph of subject s and at each timepoint t, our domain aligner network outputs a tensor encoding the CBT-aligned graphs, $\mathcal{T}_{s\rightarrow c,t}^v$, with a distribution that is similar to that of the target prior brain graph template. To do so, we use KL divergence as a loss function where we minimize the difference between the output and the target distributions. KL divergence encourages the aligner network to learn a mapping that closely matches the target distribution. Particularly, we compute the KL divergence loss between the fixed target prior universal CBT distribution Q_t, where $\mathbf{C}_t$ follows the probability distribution Q_t ($\mathbf{C}_t \sim Q_t$), and the output distribution $P_{s,t}^v$ of the aligned networks, where $\mathcal{T}_{s\rightarrow c,t}^v \sim P_{s,t}^v$, as follows: $\mathcal{L}_{\mathrm{KL}} = \sum_{s=1}^{n_s} \mathrm{KL}(Q_t \| P_{s,t}^v)$, where the KL divergence between $\mathbf{C}_t$ and $\mathcal{T}_{s\rightarrow c,t}^v$ is defined as: $\mathrm{KL}(Q_t \| P_{s,t}^v) = \int_{-\infty}^{+\infty} Q_t \log \frac{Q_t}{P_{s,t}^v} dx$.

GNN-Based Federation to Predict Brain Evolution Trajectory. The last block of our TAF-GNN (Fig. 1-**D**) presents the GNN-based federation process to predict brain graph evolution trajectory, where each hospital uses the CBT-aligned 4D trajectories resulting from our domain aligner network. Specifically, hospital v has $\{\mathcal{T}_{1\rightarrow c,t}^v, ..., \mathcal{T}_{n_s\rightarrow c,t}^v\}$. In FL, each hospital also has a GNN-based model to predict brain graph at the next timepoint $\mathcal{T}_{s\rightarrow c,t+1}^v$ from a current observation $\mathcal{T}_{s\rightarrow c,t}^v$. Without any loss of generality, we use the Recurrent Brain Graph Mapper (RBGM) [9] as a brain graph prediction model.

4D-FED-GNN. As presented in [13], 4D-FED-GNN federates RBGM architecture to predict the evolution of a brain graph trajectory in a data-preserving manner.

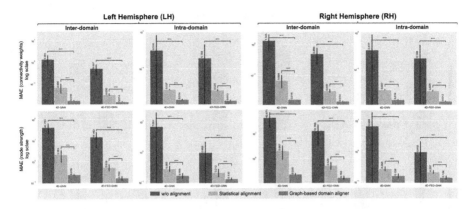

Fig. 2. *Prediction results using mean absolute error (MAE) between predicted and ground-truth graphs at t_2 in both centralized (4D-GNN) and federated (4D-FED-GNN) learning paradigms.* The top row shows the MAE in connectivity weights and the bottom row displays the MAE in node strengths. Bar charts and error bars represent the mean and standard deviation of MAE of each hospital, respectively. ****: p−value < 0.001 using two-tailed paired t-test.

Specifically, RBGM consists of a graph convolutional layer which is followed by ReLU. The graph convolutional layer is inspired by the dynamic edge-conditioned filters introduced in [16]. However, it is redesigned by adding edge-based recurrent GNN [9]. Moreover, each hospital outputs $\{\hat{T}^v_{2 \to c,t}, ..., \hat{T}^v_{n_s \to c,t}\}$ with the same dimensions as the CBT-aligned 4D trajectories. FL in 4D-FED-GNN is based on a layer-wise weight aggregation where each hospital sends the weights of its local GNN model to a central server after a predetermined number of epochs, defining a federation round. The server aggregates the received weights by simple averaging then broadcasts the averaged weights back to all hospitals as in FedAvg [7]. To train RBGM architecture, we use a global loss function comprising a topological subloss to preserve the brain graph topology and an $l1$ subloss to minimize the distance between the predicted and ground-truth graphs. We use node strength centrality as a topological measure. Therefore, our topological loss is expressed as follows: $\mathcal{L}_{tp}(\mathbf{N}^v_{s \to c,t,i}, \hat{\mathbf{N}}^v_{s \to c,t,i}) = \frac{1}{n_r} \sum_{i=1}^{n_r} (\mathbf{N}^v_{s \to c,t,i} - \hat{\mathbf{N}}^v_{s \to c,t,i})^2$, where $\mathbf{N}^v_{s \to c,t,i}$ denotes the node strength of node i of the CBT-aligned brain graph for subject s and view v at timepoint t, and $\hat{\mathbf{N}}^v_{s \to c,t,i}$ denotes the node strength of model prediction. The global loss function is expressed as follows:

$$\mathcal{L}_{\text{global}} = \mathcal{L}_{L1}(\mathcal{T}^v_{s \to c,t+1}, \hat{\mathcal{T}}^v_{s \to c,t+1}) + \lambda_{tp}\mathcal{L}_{tp}(\mathbf{N}^v_{s \to c,t,i}, \hat{\mathbf{N}}^v_{s \to c,t,i})$$

3   Results and Discussion

Longitudinal Brain Graph Dataset. We evaluated our TAF-GNN architecture on 67 subjects from the longitudinal ADNI dataset [18], including 32 subjects diagnosed with Alzheimer's Disease (AD) and 35 with Late Mild Cognitive Impairment (LMCI). Each

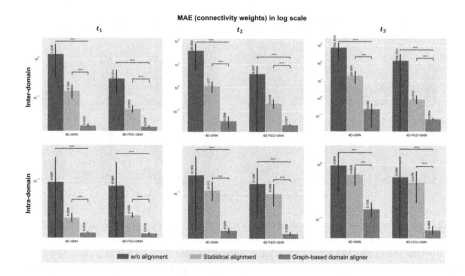

Fig. 3. *Prediction results using mean absolute error (MAE) in connectivity weights between predicted and CBT-aligned graph at t_1, t_2 and t_3 using the simulated brain graph trejectory dataset.* Bar charts and error bars represent the mean and standard deviation of MAE across each hospital, respectively. ****: $p-$value < 0.001 using two-tailed paired t-test.

subject is characterized by four cortical brain networks constructed from T1-weighted MRI for the left and right hemisphere (LH and RH, respectively) at two timepoints, a baseline and 6-month follow up. We use the Desikan-Killiany cortical atlas to parcellate each cortical hemisphere into 35 ROIs where we derive 4 cortical morphological networks using the protocol described in [19] and the following measures: maximum principal curvature, the mean cortical thickness, the mean sulcal depth, and the average curvature, where each represents a distinct domain. Additionally, we generated a simulated 4D multiview brain graph dataset including 200 subjects and 4 timepoints. To simulate the 4D brain graph trajectories that closely resemble the LMCI-AD dataset, we use mean connectivity weights and correlation matrices of the dataset, as they effectively capture its statistical properties. Moreover, we use PyTorch and PyTorch Geometric [20] libraries to implement our TAF-GNN.

Hyperparameters. We have two different networks in our TAF-GNN architecture, which are the proposed graph-based domain aligner and the RBGM in FL. We use AdamW [21] as our optimizer with a learning rate of 0.025 for the aligner network. As for RBGM, we use Adam [22] with a learning rate of 0.001 and we empirically set the hyperparameter λ_{tp} to 10 in our global loss function.

Evaluation and Comparison Methods. To evaluate the generalizability of our TAF-GNN architecture on intra- and inter-domain brain graph prediction, we design two different training strategies using 5-fold cross-validation: **(1) intra-domain** where each hospital is trained on local four folds and tests on the remaining local fold; **(2) inter-domain** where we create a global multi-domain test set by taking one fold from each domain and let each hospital train on their local remaining four folds while testing on the global multi-domain test set. Since our TAF-GNN is the first method aiming to predict the brain graph evolution trajectory using FL where hospitals have disparate domains, we benchmark our architecture against its variants and ablated versions in which we replace both the domain aligner within two learning paradigms. In total, these include: **(1) w/o alignment** where there is no alignment step; **(2) statistical alignment** where we align brain graphs to the mean and standard deviation of the universal CBT trajectory without learning a model; **(3) graph-based domain aligner network** which is the learnable model that we propose in TAF-GNN. Furthermore, we evaluate two learning paradigms: **(1) 4D-GNN** where each hospital is trained without federation (i.e., centralized learning); **(2) 4D-FED-GNN** where we adopt FedAvg [7] to train a personalized (at the hospital level) and a global (at the server level) model.

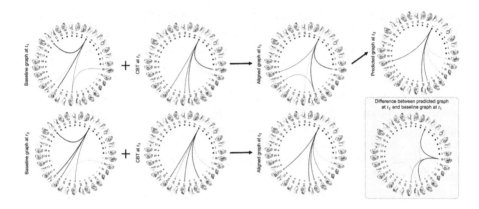

Fig. 4. *Comparison between the predicted, aligned, and ground-truth baseline graphs.* We display the top 5 strongest morphological cortical connectivities for left hemisphere (LH) of a random ADNI subject in domain 1 (i.e., maximum principal curvature) at t_1 and t_2. Thicker edges indicate stronger connectivity.

ADNI Dataset. Figure 2 displays the MAE in connectivity weight as well as node strength between the predicted and ground-truth brain graphs using the longitudinal ADNI dataset for the left and right cortical hemispheres. **Fig.** 4 displays the top 5 connectivities of ground-truth baseline, aligned, and predicted brain graph cortical regions for LH of a random subject from hospital 1 at the follow-up timepoint t_2. Our federated strategy performs effectively in predicting the top 2 strongest morphological connections between the predicted brain graph and the ground-truth brain graph at t_2, which are: (1) fusiform gyrus (ROI 7) with superior frontal gyrus (ROI 28) and (2) fusiform gyrus (ROI 7) with superior parietal cortex (ROI 29). Moreover, the difference between the predicted graph at t_2 and the baseline graph at t_1 shows that the insula cortex (ROI 35) is the most altered cortical region, sharing the same findings of previous studies [23,24] on AD and LMCI. As Fig. 2 shows, our TAF-GNN, which utilizes a federated learning paradigm with prior CBT-based alignment, outperforms benchmarks in all 8 experiments. Also Fig. 2 shows that CBT-based alignment with our domain aligner surpasses the performance of other alignment methods by consistently demonstrating *significantly* improved performance across all experiments in both centralized and federated learning paradigms. These findings highlight the advantages of using a prior CBT-based domain alignment when working with multiple disparate domains, strengthening local model robustness to data heterogeneity.

Simulated 4D Dataset[1]. Further, we conduct the same experiments on the simulated brain graph trajectory dataset including more timepoints and subjects, which allows us to better investigate the generalizability of TAF-GNN. Fig. 3 shows that our TAF-GNN *significantly* outperforms its variants and ablated versions across all 6 experiments. Our findings emphasize the importance of addressing domain shifts across hospitals in federated learning through alignment to a universal domain for effective prediction of brain graph evolution trajectory from a single timepoint.

Limitations and Future Directions. Although our TAF-GNN boosted the performance of predicting brain graph evolution across different domains from heterogeneous datasets by aligning each trajectory to a prior universal CBT, it has several limitations. First, our solution inherently assumes that all trajectories are matched in time, hence may not handle trajectories with missing timepoints. Thus in our future work, we intend to design a multi-domain GNN federated model that can handle incomplete brain trajectories. Second, our FL aggregation step simply averages the layer weights across hospitals. Although the CBT-aligned brain graph is robust to data heterogeneity and multi-domain data federation, layer-wise weight averaging may not present the optimal solution. Hence, we will design a novel aggregation strategy that is tailored to multi-domain FL [11, 12].

4 Conclusion

In this paper, we proposed the first template-based federated brain graph evolution trajectory prediction, namely TAF-GNN, where local hospitals have brain graph trajectories drawn from distinct domains (e.g., functional, morphological, etc.). Our method unprecedentedly addresses data heterogeneity by aligning the local domains to a universal domain, captured by a prior universal CBT. Our TAF-GNN achieved the best prediction results on both real and simulated 4D brain connectivity datasets. This is a first step towards building a federated predictive intelligence that is strengthened by heterogeneous non-IID datasets. In our future work, we will generalize our TAF-GNN towards learning from incomplete training trajectories (i.e., with varying missing timepoints across hospitals). Our framework can be used for predicting other types of brain graphs such as structural and functional and easily plugged in with alternative GNN architectures [6] for brain connectivity prediction over time. It could be also use to design *federated CBT-guided* brain graph superresolution [25], registration [26] and diagnosis [27].

---

[1] The TAF-GNN code is available at https://github.com/basiralab/TAF-GNN.

References

1. Bassett, D.S., Sporns, O.: Network neuroscience. Nat. Neurosci. **20**, 353–364 (2017)
2. Duncan, J.S., Ayache, N.: Medical image analysis: progress over two decades and the challenges ahead. IEEE Trans. Pattern Anal. Mach. Intell. **22**, 85–106 (2000)
3. Shen, D., Wu, G., Suk, H.I.: Deep learning in medical image analysis. Annu. Rev. Biomed. Eng. **19**, 221–248 (2017)
4. Fornito, A., Zalesky, A., Breakspear, M.: The connectomics of brain disorders. Nat. Rev. Neurosci. **16**, 159–172 (2015)
5. van den Heuvel, M.P., Sporns, O.: A cross-disorder connectome landscape of brain dysconnectivity. Nat. Rev. Neurosci. **20**, 435–446 (2019)
6. Bessadok, A., Mahjoub, M.A., Rekik, I.: Graph neural networks in network neuroscience. IEEE Trans. Pattern Anal. Mach. Intell. (2022)
7. McMahan, B., Moore, E., Ramage, D., Hampson, S., y Arcas, B.A.: Communication-efficient learning of deep networks from decentralized data. Artifi. Intell. Stat., 1273–1282 (2017)
8. Nebli, A., Kaplan, U.A., Rekik, I.: Deep EvoGraphNet architecture for time-dependent brain graph data synthesis from a single timepoint. In: Rekik, I., Adeli, E., Park, S.H., Valdés Hernández, M.C. (eds.) PRIME 2020. LNCS, vol. 12329, pp. 144–155. Springer, Cham (2020). https://doi.org/10.1007/978-3-030-59354-4_14
9. Tekin, A., Nebli, A., Rekik, I.: Recurrent brain graph mapper for predicting time-dependent brain graph evaluation trajectory. In: Albarqouni, S., et al. (eds.) DART/FAIR -2021. LNCS, vol. 12968, pp. 180–190. Springer, Cham (2021). https://doi.org/10.1007/978-3-030-87722-4_17
10. Shen, Z., Cervino, J., Hassani, H., Ribeiro, A.: An agnostic approach to federated learning with class imbalance. In: International Conference on Learning Representations (2022)
11. Li, T., Sahu, A.K., Zaheer, M., Sanjabi, M., Talwalkar, A., Smith, V.: Federated optimization in heterogeneous networks. Proc. Mach. Learn. Syst. **2**, 429–450 (2020)
12. Li, X., Jiang, M., Zhang, X., Kamp, M., Dou, Q.: Fedbn: federated learning on non-iid features via local batch normalization. arXiv preprint arXiv:2102.07623 (2021)
13. Gürler, Z., Rekik, I.: Federated brain graph evolution prediction using decentralized connectivity datasets with temporally-varying acquisitions. IEEE Trans. Med. Imaging (2022)
14. Chaari, N., Akdağ, H.C., Rekik, I.: Comparative survey of multigraph integration methods for holistic brain connectivity mapping. Med. Image Anal. 102741 (2023)
15. Gurbuz, M.B., Rekik, I.: Deep graph normalizer: a geometric deep learning approach for estimating connectional brain templates. In: Martel, A.L., et al. (eds.) MICCAI 2020. LNCS, vol. 12267, pp. 155–165. Springer, Cham (2020). https://doi.org/10.1007/978-3-030-59728-3_16
16. Simonovsky, M., Komodakis, N.: Dynamic edge-conditioned filters in convolutional neural networks on graphs. In: Proceedings of the IEEE Conference on Computer Vision and pattern Recognition, pp. 3693–3702 (2017)
17. Ronneberger, O., Fischer, P., Brox, T.: U-Net: convolutional networks for biomedical image segmentation. In: Navab, N., Hornegger, J., Wells, W.M., Frangi, A.F. (eds.) MICCAI 2015. LNCS, vol. 9351, pp. 234–241. Springer, Cham (2015). https://doi.org/10.1007/978-3-319-24574-4_28
18. Mueller, S.G., et al.: The alzheimer's disease neuroimaging initiative. Neuroimaging Clin. **15**, 869–877 (2005)
19. Nebli, A., Rekik, I.: Gender differences in cortical morphological networks. Brain Imaging Behav. **14**, 1831–1839 (2020)

20. Fey, M., Lenssen, J.E.: Fast graph representation learning with pytorch geometric. arXiv preprint arXiv:1903.02428 (2019)
21. Loshchilov, I., Hutter, F.: Decoupled weight decay regularization. arXiv preprint arXiv:1711.05101 (2017)
22. Kingma, D.P., Ba, J.: Adam: a method for stochastic optimization. arXiv preprint arXiv:1412.6980 (2014)
23. Yang, H., et al.: Study of brain morphology change in alzheimer's disease and amnestic mild cognitive impairment compared with normal controls. General Psych. **32** (2019)
24. Xie, C., et al.: Abnormal insula functional network is associated with episodic memory decline in amnestic mild cognitive impairment. Neuroimage **63**, 320–327 (2012)
25. Pala, F., Mhiri, I., Rekik, I.: Template-based inter-modality super-resolution of brain connectivity. In: Rekik, I., Adeli, E., Park, S.H., Schnabel, J. (eds.) PRIME 2021. LNCS, vol. 12928, pp. 70–82. Springer, Cham (2021). https://doi.org/10.1007/978-3-030-87602-9_7
26. Gürler, Z., Gharsallaoui, M.A., Rekik, I., Initiative, A.D.N., et al.: Template-based graph registration network for boosting the diagnosis of brain connectivity disorders. Comput. Med. Imaging Graph. **103**, 102140 (2023)
27. Chaari, N., Gharsallaoui, M.A., Akdağ, H.C., Rekik, I.: Multigraph classification using learnable integration network with application to gender fingerprinting. Neural Netw. **151**, 250–263 (2022)

Feature-Based Transformer with Incomplete Multimodal Brain Images for Diagnosis of Neurodegenerative Diseases

Xingyu Gao[1,2], Feng Shi[3(✉)], Dinggang Shen[3,4(✉)], and Manhua Liu[1,2(✉)]

[1] School of EIEE, Shanghai Jiao Tong University, Shanghai 200240, China
[2] MoE Laboratory of Artificial Intelligence, AI Institute,
Shanghai Jiao Tong University, Shanghai 200240, China
mhliu@sjtu.edu.cn
[3] Department of Research and Development, Shanghai United Imaging Intelligence
Co., Ltd., Shanghai 200232, China
feng.shi@uii-ai.com
[4] School of Biomedical Engineering, ShanghaiTech University, Shanghai 201210,
China
dinggang.shen@gmail.com

Abstract. Benefiting from complementary information, multimodal brain imaging analysis has distinct advantages over single-modal methods for the diagnosis of neurodegenerative diseases such as Alzheimer's disease. However, multi-modal brain images are often incomplete with missing data in clinical practice due to various issues such as motion, medical costs, and scanner availability. Most existing methods attempted to build machine learning models to directly estimate the missing images. However, since brain images are of high dimension, accurate and efficient estimation of missing data is quite challenging, and not all voxels in the brain images are associated with the disease. In this paper, we propose a multimodal feature-based transformer to impute multimodal brain features with missing data for the diagnosis of neurodegenerative disease. The proposed method consists of a feature regression subnetwork and a multimodal fusion subnetwork based on transformer, for completion of the features of missing data and also multimodal diagnosis of disease. Different from previous methods for the generation of missing images, our method imputes high-level and disease-related features for multimodal classification. Experiments on the ADNI database with 1,364 subjects show better performance of our method over the state-of-the-art methods in disease diagnosis with missing multimodal data.

Keywords: Multimodal brain imaging · Neurodegenerative disease · Feature regression · Multi-modal transformer

© The Author(s), under exclusive license to Springer Nature Switzerland AG 2023
I. Rekik et al. (Eds.): PRIME 2023, LNCS 14277, pp. 25–34, 2023.
https://doi.org/10.1007/978-3-031-46005-0_3

1   Introduction

Multimodal brain images such as magnetic resonance imaging (MRI) and positron emission tomography (PET) could provide complementary information to enhance the diagnosis performance of neurodegenerative diseases e.g., Alzheimer's disease (AD) and its prodromal phase as mild cognitive impairment (MCI) [1,2]. However, when the multimodal brain images are incomplete, traditional multimodal fusion methods directly discard the samples with missing data [3,4]. This kind of method reduces the available data. To address this problem, another category of methods tries to divide the incomplete data into several groups according to availability, followed by building different models for different groups [5,6]. These methods can include incomplete data, which increases the complexity of the process of building different models.

Reconstructing the missing modality data becomes a hotspot in the research field of medical image computing and computer-assisted intervention. For the MRI-to-CT generation, Nie et al. [7] proposed an end-to-end nonlinear mapping with the fully convolutional network, from which the neighborhood information of generated CT could be better preserved compared with the convolutional neural network. And Huynh et al. [8] proposed a random forest-based auto-context network. In this method, a patch-wise structured random forest is first adopted to initialize the CT patches and then an auto-context model is used to refine the prediction iteratively. At last, the predicted CT patches are clustered to output the final prediction. Recently, generative adversarial network (GAN) achieves great success in estimating the missing data. Considering the disease-related information that could be conveyed between the different multi-modalities, Pan et al. [9] presented a disease-specific Cycle-GAN for AD and MCI prognosis. From that, a disease-specific neural network is first built for the classification, then the classification task is embedded to aid the image generation. Instead of estimating the missing data, an auto-encoder-based data completion network was proposed to learn common representations for AD diagnosis [10]. From this, the complete data are first mapped to a latent space through the auto-encoder network, then the latent representations are used to complement the kernel matrix for the incomplete view. Meanwhile, the Hilbert-Schmidt Independence Criterion constraints and graph regularization are adapted to maintain the correlations between different modalities. Finally, an SVM classifier is used to predict the disease status.

With the complete multimodal brain images, taking effective interaction between different modalities for disease diagnosis is also a meaningful process. Song et al. [11] proposed a 3D multi-scale CNN method on the group of gray matter (GM) tissue areas of MRI and PET regions for disease classification. Zhang et al. [12] proposed a hierarchical attention-based multimodal fusion method for AD diagnosis, which has three data streams. Specifically, the data streams of MRI and PET are independent during the process of feature extraction, and the attention mechanism is adopted to fuse the information of two modalities at each stage as the third stream. To make full use of complementary information between different modalities, a consistent metric constraint method is proposed for AD analysis [13]. In this method, each MRI and PET modality is first used to calculate the similarity individually by random forest. Then, a group of sample similarity constraint regularization terms and sparsity regularization terms are used to conduct the objective function for feature extraction from multiple modalities. Finally, these features are fused by a multi-kernel SVM for disease classification. Although many efforts have been made for multimodal analysis, it is still challenging to make use of incomplete multimodal brain images and improve diagnostic performance and efficiency.

Motivated by the success of the transformer for modeling data correlations, we propose a multimodal feature-based transformer for the diagnosis of AD with incomplete multimodal brain images. First, a feature regression transformer subnetwork is proposed to estimate the disease-related high-level features of missing modality from the available scans. Then, a multimodal transformer is proposed to combine the complete multimodal features for disease diagnosis. The proposed method can not only make full use of the available multimodal data but also model the correlations between different modalities. Experiments on 1,364 subjects from the ADNI dataset show the effectiveness of the tasks of data estimation and disease diagnosis.

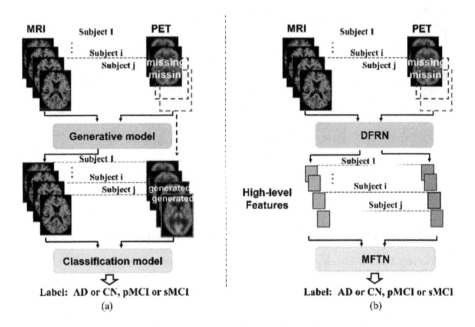

Fig. 1. Strategies of disease diagnosis with incomplete multi-modalities: (a) existing typical method; (b) our proposed framework with disease-related feature regression subnetwork (DFRN) and multimodal feature-based transformer subnetwork (MFTN).

2   Method

2.1   Overview

To deal with the problem of incomplete multimodal data, most of the existing methods aim to estimate the missing original image with generative models, then the complete multimodal images are used as the inputs for the classification models in disease diagnosis, as shown in Fig. 1(a). Different from that, we propose a deep learning multimodal classification framework based on a transformer for disease diagnosis with incomplete multimodal brain images including MRI and PET. The proposed framework consists of a disease-related feature regression subnetwork (DFRN) and a multimodal transformer subnetwork (MFTN), for imputing the high-level disease-related features of missing modality and predicting the disease status of subjects, respectively. The flowchart of our method is shown in Fig. 1(b), and the details of each subnetwork will be described in the following subsections.

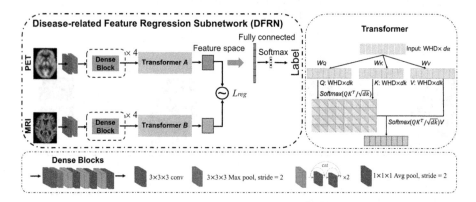

Fig. 2. The architecture of our proposed disease-related feature regression subnetwork (DFRN) which is used to impute the missing PET features.

2.2   Feature Regression for Imputation of Missing Data

Considering that neurodegenerative disease is not associated with all voxels of brain images, which contain redundant information for disease diagnosis. Instead of imputing whole brain images, we propose a regression subnetwork to predict the disease-related high-level features of missing modality, as shown in Fig. 2. The DFRN consists of two stages: 1) features extraction, and 2) features regression. Dense blocks with convolution layers are used to learn the disease-related high-level features from original brain images, and transformers are used to model the long-range spatial correlations of extracted high-level features. Specifically, a $3 \times 3 \times 3$ convolution layer with a $3 \times 3 \times 3$ max-pooling operation is first used to reduce the spatial size of the original brain images. Then, 4 dense blocks followed by a transformer module are assembled to impute the high-level features. The transformer is added to model the spatial correlations of high-level features. Finally, to learn the disease-related features, fully connected layers with Softmax activation are included for disease classification.

Suppose that $Z_i^{(1)}$ and $Z_i^{(2)}$ are the high-level features extracted from MRI and PET images for ith subject, respectively. The complete multimodal feature set can be denoted as $C = \left\{ Z_i^{(1)}, Z_i^{(2)} \right\}_{i=1}^{M}$, and the incomplete feature set is denoted as $I = \left\{ Z_i^{(1)} \right\}_{i=M}^{N}$ with the number of missing data is $N - M$. The network with PET inputs is first pre-trained for feature extraction, then we train the feature regression branch with MRI inputs to predict the PET features. The DFRN can be considered as a non-linear mapping from one modality to another. Let f denote the non-linear mapping function of DFRN, the objective loss is defined as:

$$L_{reg} = \sum_{i=1}^{M} \| f(x_i; \Theta) - Z_i^{(2)} \|_F^2) \tag{1}$$

where x_i is the original image of available MRI; Θ is the parameters of weights and bias; $Z_i^{(2)}$ is the ground truth of PET features. After training DFRN with complete data set C, the features of missing modality can be predicted as $\hat{Z}_i^{(2)} = f(x_i; \Theta)$. If the missing data are MRI scans, DFRN could be adjusted to a bi-direction regression.

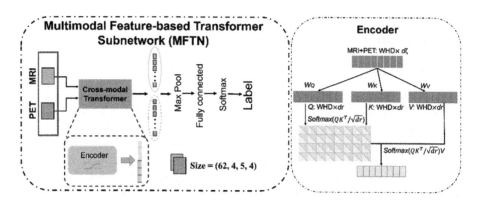

Fig. 3. The architecture of our multimodal feature-based transformer subnetwork (MFTN).

2.3 Multimodal Transformer for Disease Diagnosis

After the feature regression, data set I is completed as $I = \left\{ \left\{ Z_i^{(1)}, Z_i^{(2)} \right\}_{i=1}^{M} \right.$, $\left. \left\{ Z_i^{(1)}, \hat{Z}_i^{(2)} \right\}_{i=M}^{N} \right\}$. With the complete high-level features of MRI and PET, we propose a multimodal feature-based transformer network (MFTN) for disease diagnosis as shown in Fig. 3.

The transformer is used to model the interactions and correlations of high-level features from different modalities for a more accurate disease prediction. In this work, the size of the feature vector is $(62, 4, 5, 4)$, so the training process is efficient. The cross-modal transformer is essentially an encoder, which is used to take information interactions between different modalities by self-attention. In detail, the vectors of Query, Key, and Value are obtained from the aggregation of MRI and PET features and defined as $Q = W_Q Z_i$, $K = W_K Z_i$, $V = W_V Z_i$ respectively, where W_Q, W_K, W_V are the projection matrix and Z_i denotes an aggregation of $\left\{Z_i^{(1)}, Z_i^{(2)}\right\}$ or $\left\{Z_i^{(1)}, \hat{Z}_i^{(2)}\right\}$. Through the cross-modal transformer, the output can be computed as:

$$J = Softmax(QK^T/\sqrt{d_r})V \tag{2}$$

where d_r indicates the dimension of the Q, K and V. To the output J, a $3\times3\times3$ max-pooling layer followed by a fully connected layer with Softmax activation is used to predict the probabilities of disease. With the complete multimodal feature space $\{C, I\}$, our MFTN can be defined as $g(Z_i; \Theta) = \hat{y}_i$, where $\hat{y}_i$ is the predicted label. The cross-entropy loss is used in our MFTN and can be denoted as:

$$L_{cls} = -\sum_{i=1}^{N}[y_i * \log(g(Z_i; \Theta)) + (1 - y_i) * \log(g(Z_i; \Theta))] \tag{3}$$

3   Experiments and Results

3.1   Materials

In this work, MRI and PET data from ADNI-1 and ADNI-2 baseline datasets are used to test our method. In ADNI 1 dataset, there are 395 subjects (including 92 AD, 100 CN, 76 pMCI, and 127 sMCI) with complete MRI and PET images while 425 subjects (including 104 AD, 127 CN, 92 pMCI, 102 sMCI) with only MRI scans. In ADNI-2, there are 487 (including 144 AD, 185 CN, 65 pMCI, and 93 sMCI) data-complete subjects and 57 (including 12 AD, 15 CN, 1 pMCI, and 19 sMCI) data-incomplete subjects. Overall, there is a total of 1,364 subjects with 482 subjects having incomplete data. The pre-processing procedures contain skull-stripping and linear registration. Finally, the original images are downsampled to $76 \times 94 \times 76$ as the inputs of our method for efficiency.

3.2   Implementation

Our proposed models are implemented on the Pytorch framework with the Ubuntu operating system. The DFRN is trained with epoch = 60, learning rate = 0.001, and batch size = 4. Adam optimizer is applied with the weight decay = 0.0001 to avoid overfitting. Due to the input size of MFTN being very small, the classification model can converge quickly. Hence the epoch, learning rate, and batch size are set to 40, 0.001, and 8, respectively. The training of DFRN and MFTN are both accelerated by 1 GPU of Nvidia RTX 2080 Ti.

The DFRN and MFTN are both trained on ADNI-1 and tested on ADNI-2. Specifically, at the stage of DFRN, only the complete pair of MRI and PET are used for training and testing. After the missing modalities are estimated, the subjects with missing data in ADNI-1 are included for data augmentation in the training process of MFTN. Meanwhile, the subjects with missing data in ADNI-2 are involved in testing.

3.3 Results of Features Regression

To evaluate the effectiveness of our feature regression model, we visually show two typical results from the testing set in Fig. 4. The feature size in our model is $(62, 4, 5, 4)$, which is reshaped to $(62, 4 \times 5 \times 4)$ for better display. From the results in Fig. 4, we can see that the generated high-level features are close to their ground truths (as the value range is [-1, 1]). Subject 1 is healthy and subject 2 is with cognitive impairment.

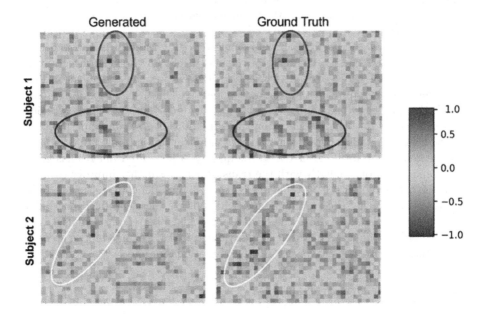

Fig. 4. Illustration of the generated high-level PET features and the ground truths for two typical subjects on ADNI-2, where the models are trained on ADNI-1.

Second, we use the classification model (as mentioned in Sect. 2.3) to evaluate the quality of generated high-level features rather than measure the distance between the generated features and their ground truths. Our DFRN is compared

Table 1. Performance of generated PET modalities through four different methods on ADNI-2, where the models are trained on ADNI-1.

Method	AD vs CN (%)				pMCI vs sMCI (%)			
	AUC	ACC	SEN	SPE	AUC	ACC	SEN	SPE
Cycle-GAN [14]	68.0	62.6	61.1	63.8	64.0	62.0	60.0	62.4
TPA-GAN [15]	88.3	83.6	**81.9**	84.9	72.4	69.6	70.8	68.8
CNN(w/o Transformer)	89.6	82.4	77.1	86.5	79.4	70.9	**72.3**	69.9
Our DFRN	**93.0**	**86.9**	79.2	**93.0**	**80.9**	**75.3**	67.6	**80.6**

with two generative models and one CNN-based regression model: (1) Cycle-consistent GAN (Cycle-GAN) [14]; (2) Task-induced Pyramid and Attention GAN (TPA-GAN) [15]; and (3) DFRN framework without transformer blocks, which is named as CNN(w/o Transformer). These four models are both trained on modality-complete subjects in ADNI-1 and tested on modality-complete subjects in ADNI-2. Four measures are used to evaluate the quality of generated modalities (whether in the form of images or features), including (1) accuracy (ACC); (2) sensitivity (SEN); (3) specificity (SPE), and (4) area under the receiver operating characteristic (AUC).

Table 1 reports the performances of generated PET modalities through four different methods. There are three observations: First, for the generative adversarial models of Cycle-GAN and TPA-GAN, embedding the classification task into generation is important. Since the Cycle-GAN is a bi-directional mapping model, the quality of the generated image is very poor because the generation process does not fuse the classification task. In addition to embedding the classification task, pyramid convolution layers, and attention module are combined into the generation for TPA-GAN, so the quality of generated images has great improvement. Second, DFRN with the transformer can further improve the performance compared with CNN. The CNN regression model converges fast and is easy to overfit during the training stage, which limits the generalization ability of the regression model. Third, the DFRN can achieve better performance than existing state-of-the-art generative adversarial networks, which demonstrates the effectiveness of our method for the completion of missing modalities.

3.4   Results of Disease Diagnosis

In the task of disease classification, we compare our MFTN with other state-of-the-art multimodal methods, including (1) group-constrained sparse learning model (GSLM) [16]; (2) landmark-based deep learning model (LDLM) [17]; (3) pathwise transfer model (PTM) [15]; and (4) MLP framework without cross-modal transformer. These models are both trained on ADNI-1 and tested on ADNI-2. The subjects with missing data are involved after the operation of modality completion with DFRN. Table 2 compares the classification results of five different methods.

From Table 2, we can see that the methods of LDLM and PTM perform better than GSLM. MFTN without the cross-modal transformer can achieve better performance than PTM. Nevertheless, our MFTN with transformer achieves the best performance in the diagnosis of AD vs CN and pMCI vs sMCI. The results indicate the effectiveness of our method.

Table 2. Classification results achieved by five different multimodal methods on ADNI-2, where the models are trained on ADNI-1. All subjects are used in experiments.

Method	AD vs CN (%)				pMCI vs sMCI (%)			
	AUC	ACC	SEN	SPE	AUC	ACC	SEN	SPE
GSLM [16]	92.0	87.4	84.2	90.0	75.0	71.0	74.4	70.6
LDLM [17]	96.1	90.9	87.9	93.3	80.9	73.5	74.4	73.4
PTM [15]	95.6	92.0	**89.1**	94.0	78.6	75.3	77.3	74.1
MLP(w/o Transformer)	96.2	90.2	87.8	92.0	86.4	77.8	**78.5**	77.4
Our MFTN	**96.7**	**92.4**	88.5	**95.5**	**87.2**	**77.8**	75.4	**79.6**

4   Conclusion

In this paper, we propose a disease-related feature regression network (DFRN) and a multimodal feature-based transformer network (MFTN). The DFRN is employed to regress the missing modality in high-level feature space. Specifically, the transformer module can capture the disease-related mapping between the MRI and PET. After the missing modalities are estimated, we further design a MFTN to fuse the features from different modalities for the final disease prediction. Experiments on the ADNI dataset demonstrate the effectiveness of our proposed method.

Acknowledgements. This study was supported in part by the National Natural Science Foundation of China (No.62171283), Natural Science Foundation of Shanghai (20ZR1426300), in part by the National Key R&D Program of China (National key research and development program of China) under Grant (2022YFC2503302/2022YFC2503305), by Shanghai Jiao Tong University Scientific and Technological Innovation Funds (No.2019QYB02), CAAI-Huawei MindSpore Open Fund, Shanghai Municipal Science and Technology Major Project (2021SHZDZX0102), the Fundamental Research Funds for the Central Universities, Supported by Shanghai Municipal Science and Technology Major Project (No.2018SHZDZX01), Key Laboratory of Computational Neuroscience and Brain-Inspired Intelligence (LCNBI) and ZJLab.

References

1. Zhang, D., Wang, Y., Zhou, L., Yuan, H., Shen, D.: Multimodal classification of Alzheimer's disease and mild cognitive impairment. Neuroimage **55**(3), 856–867 (2011)

2. Liu, M., Cheng, D., Wang, K., Wang, Y.: Multi-modality cascaded convolutional neural networks for Alzheimer's disease diagnosis. Neuroinformatics **16**(3–4), 295–308 (2018)
3. Cheng, B., Liu, M., Zhang, D., Shen, D.: Robust multi-label transfer feature learning for early diagnosis of Alzheimer's disease. Brain Imaging Behav. **13**(1), 138–153 (2019)
4. Zhou, T., Thung, K., Zhu, X., Shen, D.: Effective feature learning and fusion of multimodality data using stage-wise deep neural network for dementia diagnosis. Hum. Brain Mapp. **40**(3), 1001–1016 (2019)
5. Xiang, S., Yuan, L., Fan, W., Wang, Y., Thompson, P.M., Ye, J.: Bi-level multi-source learning for heterogeneous block-wise missing data. Neuroimage **102**, 192–206 (2014)
6. Liu, M., Gao, Y., Yap, P.-T., Shen, D.: Multi-hypergraph learning for incomplete multimodality data. IEEE J. Biomed. Health Inform. **22**(4), 1197–1208 (2018)
7. Nie, D., Cao, X., Gao, Y., Wang, L., Shen, D.: Estimating CT image from MRI Data Using 3D Fully convolutional networks. In: Carneiro, G., et al. (eds.) LABELS/DLMIA -2016. LNCS, vol. 10008, pp. 170–178. Springer, Cham (2016). https://doi.org/10.1007/978-3-319-46976-8_18
8. Huynh, T., et al.: Estimating CT image From MRI data using structured random forest and auto-context model. IEEE Trans. Med. Imaging **35**(1), 174–183 (2016)
9. Pan, Y., Liu, M., Lian, C., Xia, Y., Shen, D.: Disease-image specific generative adversarial network for brain disease diagnosis with incomplete multi-modal neuroimages. In: Shen, D., et al. (eds.) MICCAI 2019. LNCS, vol. 11766, pp. 137–145. Springer, Cham (2019). https://doi.org/10.1007/978-3-030-32248-9_16
10. Liu, Y., et al.: Incomplete multi-modal representation learning for Alzheimer's disease diagnosis. Med. Image Anal. **69**, 101953 (2021)
11. Song, J., Zheng, J., Li, P., Lu, X., Zhu, G., Shen, P.: An effective multimodal image fusion method Using MRI and PET for Alzheimer's disease diagnosis. Front. Digit. Health **3**, 637386 (2021)
12. Zhang, T., Shi, M.: Multi-modal neuroimaging feature fusion for diagnosis of Alzheimer's disease. J. Neurosci. Methods **341**, 108795 (2020)
13. Hao, X., et al.: Multi-modal neuroimaging feature selection with consistent metric constraint for diagnosis of Alzheimer's disease. Med. Image Anal. **60**, 101625 (2020)
14. Pan, Y., Liu, M., Lian, C., Zhou, T., Xia, Y., Shen, D.: Synthesizing missing PET from MRI with cycle-consistent generative adversarial networks for alzheimer's disease Diagnosis. In: Frangi, A.F., Schnabel, J.A., Davatzikos, C., Alberola-López, C., Fichtinger, G. (eds.) MICCAI 2018. LNCS, vol. 11072, pp. 455–463. Springer, Cham (2018). https://doi.org/10.1007/978-3-030-00931-1_52
15. Gao, X., Shi, F., Shen, D., Liu, M.: Task-induced pyramid and attention GAN for multimodal brain image imputation and classification in Alzheimer's disease. IEEE J. Biomed. Health Inform. **26**(1), 36–43 (2022)
16. Wee, C.-Y., Yap, P.-T., Zhang, D., Wang, L., Shen, D.: Group-constrained sparse fMRI connectivity modeling for mild cognitive impairment identification. Brain Struct. Funct. **219**(2), 641–656 (2014)
17. Liu, M., Zhang, J., Nie, D., Yap, P.-T., Shen, D.: Anatomical landmark based deep feature representation for MR images in brain disease diagnosis. IEEE J. Biomed. Health Inform. **22**(5), 1476–1485 (2018)

RepNet for Quantifying the Reproducibility of Graph Neural Networks in Multiview Brain Connectivity Biomarker Discovery

Hizir Can Bayram[1,2], Mehmet Serdar Çelebi[2], and Islem Rekik[1]($\boxtimes$) (iD)

[1] BASIRA Lab, Imperial-X and Department of Computing, Imperial College London, London, UK
i.rekik@imperial.ac.uk
[2] Faculty of Computer and Informatics Engineering, Istanbul Technical University, Istanbul, Turkey
https://basira-lab.com/

Abstract. The brain is a highly complex multigraph that presents different types of connectivities (i.e., edge types) linking pairs of anatomical regions. Each edge type captures a connectional view of the neural roadmaps such as function and morphology. Recently, several graph neural networks (GNNs) have been used to learn the representation of the brain multigraph for disease classification, stratification and outcome prediction. However, such works primarily focus on boosting the accuracy performance without investigating the reproducibility of a trained GNN model in biomarker discovery across data views and perturbations in distribution. Here, we propose RepNet, a framework that ranks various GNN architectures by quantifying their biomarker reproducibility. Specifically, we lay the mathematical foundation for inter-view and inter-model reproducibility and validates it through extensive intra-and and inter-consistency experiments. Our results showed that RepNet can identify the most reproducible GNN model, able to identify trustworthy and consistent biomarkers with a superior performance to state-of-the-art methods. Our RepNet code is available at https://github.com/basiralab/RepNet.

Keywords: model reproducibility · graph neural networks · connectomic biomarkers

1 Introduction

The study of brain connectivity and the analysis of brain networks have become popular in the field of network neuroscience [11]. However, the intricate network structure of the brain presents a hurdle for researchers attempting to pinpoint the underlying mechanisms of neurological and psychiatric disorders such as Alzheimer's and Autism [3,26]. Graph neural networks (GNNs), on the other hand, have gained momentum thanks to their ability to learn graph representations of brain connectivity while preserving its inherent topology [25,29]. GNNs

© The Author(s), under exclusive license to Springer Nature Switzerland AG 2023
I. Rekik et al. (Eds.): PRIME 2023, LNCS 14277, pp. 35–45, 2023.
https://doi.org/10.1007/978-3-031-46005-0_4

have shown remarkable success in brain connectomes including applications such as biomarker discovery and neurological disorder diagnosis [1,2,6,16,19,27]. Despite the success of GNNs in such applications, researchers have expressed concerns regarding the lack of *model reproducibility* in these works [4]. *Reproducibility refers to the capability of obtaining the same top biomarkers across various trainings with different connectivity measures, distribution shifts, and various hyperparameters.* Recently, a few landmark works have aimed to quantify the reproducibility of GNNs.

[13] proposed a primer method to identify the most reproducible connectomic features given various feature selection (FS) methods. This method hypothesizes that the top biomarkers discovered by other FS methods should be replicated by the most reliable FS method. Although promising, it relies on simple FS methods and is not suited for quantifying the reproducibility of graph neural networks. Further, [15] offered the first graph-topology based framework to select the most reproducible GNN model across different views of a multigraph connectomic dataset. The method involves quantifying the reproducibility of each GNN model by examining the degree of overlap in the top features of the last layer of these architectures. This is accomplished by constructing a GNN-to-GNN matrix for each view (i.e., brain connectivity type) and different numbers of top biomarkers (i.e., connectivities) and computing the overlap scores between pairs of GNN models. While this approach quantifies the reproducibility of GNN models, it does not take into account the *inter-view* reproducibility score of GNNs. To solve this issue [23] suggested a framework called RG-Select, a method that generates a distinct view-to-view matrix based on the degree of overlap between the top biomarkers of a GNN across different views. RG-Select constructs a reproducibility matrix by summing GNN-to-GNN and view-to-view matrices for each view and while varying number of top biomarkers. It then simply averages the reproducibility matrices to obtain a final matrix, and calculates a reproducibility score for each GNN model as the strength of the GNN node in the GNN-to-GNN reproducibility graph.

Despite the promising results achieved by the aforementioned approaches, there are several challenges that are overlooked. First, a significant amount of information is often lost due to the use of the averaging operation on matrices. Second, existing methods have not been validated using biomarker intra-and inter-consistency check experiments. Lastly, They measure inter-view and inter-model reproducibilities using a single method, which causes both not to be quantified properly. To overcome these limitations, we propose RepNet, a method that quantifies the reproducibility of each GNN model by designing novel inter-view and inter-model reproducibility scores. Our major contributions are summarized as follows:

1. *On a methodological level.* RepNet presents the first work that lays the mathematical foundation for inter-view and inter-model reproducibility and validates it through extensive intra-and and inter-consistency experiments.

2. *On a clinical level.* Our work detects the most significant biomarkers that are linked to disordered brain alterations across different brain connectivity measures.
3. *On a generic level.* RepNet can be used to robustly quantify the reproducibility of a GNN architecture within and across different brain connectivity types (e.g., functional and morphological) and against different noises and perturbations.

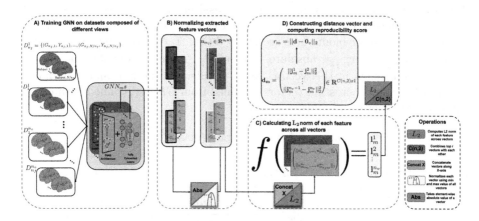

Fig. 1. Proposed RepNet framework for quantifying the reproducibility of graph neural networks. **(A)** The dataset D is partitioned into n_v separate datasets across views. Each of these datasets D^v is then divided using n_f-fold cross-validation strategy to perturb training and testing data distributions. Subsequently, the GNN_m model is trained using each of these datasets. **(B)** The features in the last layer of each resulting GNN models are extracted and normalized across all features. **(C)** View-based matrices are obtained by concatenating all features in each view along the x-axis and view-based vectors are obtained by taking their row-wise L_2 norm. **(D)** The distance vector $\mathbf{d}_m$ is acquired by calculating the squared L_2 norm of each combination of view-based vectors. The inter-view reproducibility score of the relevant GNN model is then calculated by measuring the Euclidean distance of this vector to $\mathbf{0}_v$.

2   Method

In this section, we provide a detailed overview of RepNet for quantifying the reproducibility of a given GNN (Fig. 1).

Problem Statement. We denote $D = (G, Y)$ as the dataset containing brain connectivity multigraphs with a set of classes respective to different brain neurological states to classify. Let $G = \{G_1, G_2, ..., G_{n_n}\}$ and $Y = \{y_1, y_2, ..., y_{n_n}\}$ denote the set of the brain connectivity multigraphs and their labels, respectively. Each connectivity multigraph G_n is represented by an adjacency tensor

$\mathcal{X}_n \in \mathbb{R}^{n_r \times n_r \times n_v}$ and a label $y_n \in \{0,1\}$ where n_r and n_v denote the number of ROIs and the number of views (i.e., edge types) of the brain multigraph, respectively. Let $D_f^v = (G_f^v, Y_f)$ be the dataset constructed from the folds excluding the fth fold in the vth view (i.e., connectivity type), where $v \in 1, ..., n_v$ and $f \in 1, ..., n_f$. Given a set of n_m GNN models $\{GNN_1, GNN_2, ..., GNN_{n_m}\}$, we are interested in quantifying and ranking GNN models when they are trained on separate single-view datasets $\{D^v\}_{v=1}^{n_v}$ in order to differentiate between two brain states.

Training GNN Models and Preprocessing Their Last Layers. Let $\mathbf{r}_{m_{fv}}, \in \mathbb{R}^{n_r}$ denote the biomarker vector of GNN_m, after training with view v in fold f and its top r biomarkers are selected (Fig. 1–A). We define $\mathbf{w}_{m_{fv}} \in \mathbb{R}^{n_r}$ such that $\mathbf{w}_{m_{fv}}^i = |\mathbf{r}_{m_{fv}}^i|$, absolute value of $\mathbf{r}_{m_{fv}}^i$, where i denotes the ith top biomarker (element) in this vector. Next, we identify the min and max values among all elements across all vectors obtained from GNN_m, trained with different subsets of views and folds.

$$min = \min_{f,v,i} w_{m_{fv}}^i, max = \max_{f,v,i} w_{m_{fv}}^i$$

Next, we define $\mathbf{n}_{m_{fv}} \in \mathbb{R}^{n_r}$ such that

$$n_{m_{fv}}^i = \frac{w_{m_{fv}}^i - min}{max - min}$$

Taking the absolute value and normalizing a biomarker vector enables us to determine the degree of influence that each biomarker has on the classification outcome, and allows us to quantify the impact of different biomarkers (Fig. 1–B).

View-Specific Biomarker Vectors. To investigate the importance of each biomarker, we group biomarker vectors by view, regardless of which cross-validation and fold they are trained on. To do so we form a matrix $\mathbf{M}_m^v \in \mathbb{R}^{n_r \times n_f}$, where its column vectors $n_{m_{fv}}$ belong to the same view v:

$$\mathbf{M}_m^v = \begin{pmatrix} n_{m_{1v}}^1 & \cdots & n_{m_{n_fv}}^1 \\ \vdots & \ddots & \vdots \\ n_{m_{1v}}^{n_r} & \cdots & n_{m_{n_fv}}^{n_r} \end{pmatrix}$$

In order to measure how important each biomarker is, we define a function $f : \mathbb{R}^{n_r \times n_f} \to \mathbb{R}^{n_r}$ such that

$$f(\mathbf{M}_m^v) = \mathbf{l}_m^v = \begin{pmatrix} ||n_{m_{1v}}^1, ..., n_{m_{n_fv}}^1||_2 \\ \vdots \\ ||n_{m_{1v}}^{n_r}, ..., n_{m_{n_fv}}^{n_r}||_2 \end{pmatrix}$$

The reason we chose the L_2 norm is to allow for highly discriminative biomarkers' scores to stand out. We also define $\mathbf{j}_m^v$ and $\mathbf{t}_m^v \in \mathbb{R}^r$ as the first top r biomarkers of $\mathbf{l}_m^v$ and the indices of its top biomarkers based on their magnitude values, respectively (Fig. 1–C).

Inter-View Reproducibility Score. To measure the consistency of each biomarker across views, we define a distance vector $\mathbf{d}_m \in \mathbb{R}^{C(n_v,2)}$, whose elements are the squared L_2 norm of pairwise $\mathbf{j}_m^v$ vectors. $C(n_v,2)$ represents the number of possible binary combinations of the vectors $\mathbf{l}_m^v$.

$$\mathbf{d}_m = \begin{pmatrix} ||\mathbf{j}_m^1 - \mathbf{j}_m^2||_2^2 \\ \vdots \\ ||\mathbf{j}_m^{n_v-1} - \mathbf{j}_m^{n_v}||_2^2 \end{pmatrix}$$

In this way, we obtain a distance vector showing how successfully the scores of biomarkers obtained from different datasets are *consistently* reproduced. Since in the best case we get a $\mathbf{0}_v$ as a distance vector, the length of this distance vector from the $\mathbf{0}_v$ will give us the reproducibility score of the model.

$$r_m = ||\mathbf{d}_m - \mathbf{0}_v||_2 = ||\mathbf{d}_m||_2$$

There is a positive correlation between the reproducibility ability of a model and a score close to 0 because we defined reproducibility score as a distance (Fig. 1–D).

Inter-Model Reproducibility Score. For each GNN_m, its index vectors $\{\mathbf{t}_m^1, ..., \mathbf{t}_m^{n_v}\}$ are averaged in an element-wise manner and $\mathbf{t}_m$ is defined similarly. We build a GNN-to-GNN matrix $\mathbf{G}_m^v \in \mathbb{R}^{n_m \times n_m}$ such that G_{ij} is the number of normalized top r biomarkers shared between GNN_i and GNN_j divided by r for normalization. Finally, by summing this matrix along any axis, we obtain a list of inter-model reproducibility scores that contains each GNN's score.

3   Experiments

Evaluation Dataset and Pool of GNNs. We evaluated our method and benchmarked it against RG-Select on a dataset sampled from the Autism Brain Imaging Data Exchange ABIDE I including 150 Autism Spectrum Disorder (ASD) patients and 150 normal controls (NC) patients [10]. We used FreeSurfer [5] to create cortical morphological networks for each participant from structural T1-w MRI scans [9,21]. We then divided the left and right cerebral hemispheres (LH and RH) into 35 cortical areas of interest (ROIs) using the Desikan-Killiany cortical atlas [8,20]. Six cortical measures were used to create multigraphs for both the RH and LH brain including maximum principal curvature, cortical thickness, sulcal depth and average curvature, cortical surface area, and minimum principle area. We considered RH and LH as two separate datasets for

GNN training. In our experiments, we used 5 different GNN architectures: Diff-Pool [28], GAT [24], GCN [17], SAGPool [18], Graph-U-Net [12], tuning them as in RG-Select [15] for a fair comparison.

Inter-view reproducibility scores of GNNs trained with LH dataset

Settings/GNNs	g-U-net	DiffPool	GAT	GCN	SAG
RepNet (t = 15)	11.13	2.51	3.86	**0.59**	15.15
RG-Sel (t = 15)	0.19	**0.60**	0.38	0.58	-0.20
RepNet (t = 10)	8.51	1.36	2.88	**0.39**	11.19
RG-Sel (t = 10)	0.17	0.26	0.15	**0.45**	0.18
RepNet (t = 5)	5.42	0.58	1.24	**0.23**	6.97
RG-Sel (t = 15)	-0.17	0.070	-0.12	**0.087**	0.082

Inter-view reproducibility scores of GNNs trained with RH dataset

Settings/GNNs	g-U-net	DiffPool	GAT	GCN	SAG
RepNet (t = 15)	5.47	2.04	12.06	**1.18**	28.27
RG-Sel (t = 15)	0.39	0.24	-0.15	**0.49**	-0.05
RepNet (t = 10)	4.04	1.10	8.88	**0.85**	18.28
RG-Sel (t = 10)	0.34	0.37	0.09	0.31	**0.46**
RepNet (t = 5)	2.14	**0.47**	6.55	0.48	8.48
RG-Sel (t = 15)	0.46	0.12	-0.05	**0.48**	-0.14

Fig. 2. Inter-view reproducibility scores of GNNs trained with LH and RH ASD/NC datasets. Graph-U-Net and SAGPool are abbreviated as g-U-net and SAG.

Comparing Inter-View Reproducibility Scores. We conducted a comparison between RepNet and RG-Select to assess their inter-view reproducibility scores. A higher score for RG-Select is an indication of better reproducibility whereas a score close to 0 for RepNet indicates a better reproducibility of the relevant GNN model. Reproducibility scores can be found in Fig. 2. Since these methods measure reproducibility scores differently, we compare them based on how they ranked GNNs in terms of their reproducibility capacity. We expect the internally consistent method to provide the same ranking, regardless of the dataset used for training and the number of top biomarkers selected. We show GNNs ranked by these two methods in Fig. 3.

Comparing Inter-Model Reproducibility Scores. We compare RepNet and RG-Select in terms of their inter-model reproducibility scores. However, since RG-Select used the same method for inter-view and inter-model reproducibility scores, we used its scores for both. The reproducibility scores for both methods can be seen in Fig. 4.

Quantifying Inter-View Reproducibility Scores. RepNet and RG-Select measure reproducibility scores differently. Thus, it would be appropriate to refer to a third evaluation strategy for a more rigorous comparison. We grouped biomarker ranks from trainings with different datasets and calculated their interquartile ranges. In this way, we can experimentally see the variation of the rank of each biomarker against different training data distributions. We define $\mathbf{u}_{m_{fv}} \in \mathbb{R}^{n_r}$ such that $\mathbf{u}_{m_{fv}} = rank(rank\mathbf{w}_{m_{fv}})$, ranking the vector in ascending order. Let $\mathbf{k}_m^i$ be a set $\{\mathbf{t}_{m_{fv}}^i\}_{f,v=1}^{n_f,n_v}$. We define $q_m^i = IQR(\mathbf{k}_m^i)$, where IQR is an inter-quartile range. Grouping them into a list, we obtain the set $\mathbf{I}_m = \{q_m^1, q_m^2, ..., q_m^{n_r}\}$, which consists of each biomarker's deviation across different trainings. We display each $\mathbf{I}_m$ in a scatter chart, representing each GNN_m, with a unique colour. We also fit a line to the IQR scores of the biomarkers for

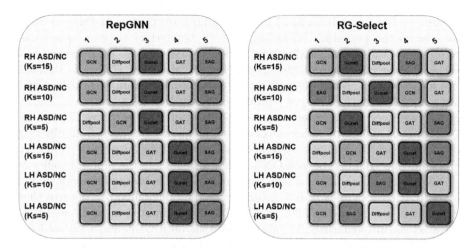

Fig. 3. Ranking GNN models according to their reproducibility scores in ASD/NC classification. Notwithstanding the dataset used in training and the number of top biomarkers selected to quantify reproducibility, RepNet achieved a more robust and consistent GNN rankings than RG-Select.

each model in order to compare them easily. The ranking of models shows the line of the most reproducible model at the bottom, while the least reproducible model is at the top. The results are displayed in Fig. 6.

Inter-model reproducibility scores of GNNs trained with LH dataset

Settings/GNNs	g-U-net	DiffPool	GAT	GCN	SAG
RepNet (t = 15)	0.43	0.41	**0.48**	0.41	0.45
RG-Sel (t = 15)	0.19	**0.60**	0.38	0.58	-0.20
RepNet (t = 10)	**0.37**	0.25	0.35	0.3	0.32
RG-Sel (t = 10)	0.17	0.26	0.15	**0.45**	0.18
RepNet (t = 5)	**0.15**	0.05	0.15	0.1	0.15
RG-Sel (t = 15)	-0.17	0.070	-0.12	**0.087**	0.082

Inter-model reproducibility scores of GNNs trained with RH dataset

Settings/GNNs	g-U-net	DiffPool	GAT	GCN	SAG
RepNet (t = 15)	0.48	0.46	0.46	**0.5**	0.38
RG-Sel (t = 15)	0.39	0.24	-0.15	**0.49**	-0.05
RepNet (t = 10)	0.275	0.275	0.225	**0.275**	0.25
RG-Sel (t = 10)	0.34	0.37	0.09	0.31	**0.46**
RepNet (t = 5)	0.1	0.05	0.1	**0.15**	0.1
RG-Sel (t = 15)	0.46	0.12	-0.05	**0.48**	-0.14

Fig. 4. Inter-model reproducibility scores of GNNs trained with LH and RH datasets. Graph-U- Net and SAGPool are abbreviated as g-U-net and SAG.

4   Discussion

Investigating Inter-View Reproducibility Scores. First, we internally analyze the RepNet and discuss the comparison with state-of-the-art method RG-Select [15]. We see in Fig. 3 that RepNet ranks GNNs more consistently than RG-Select, regardless of the training dataset and number of top biomarkers selected. This is because, RepNet takes L_2 norm by grouping each of the selected biomarkers after normalizing the features of all trained models. In this way Rep-Net enables the potential differences between biomarkers to grow quadratic, revealing the true reproducibility capabilities of these models. We see that GCN is chosen as the most reproducible model (Fig. 2). Moreover, GCN and DiffPool were found to be significantly better than other models evaluated, while being closer to each other in terms of reproducibility capabilities as shown in Fig. 2. Second, we carry out an inter-consistency validation. In Fig. 6, we display the IQR scores calculated by index ranks of each biomarker obtained from different trainings of each GNN model. IQR scores shows the deviation of each biomarker across different trainings of each GNN. A few insights into the reproducibility of a GNN model can be inferred by examining the IQR scores, where biomarkers having IQR scores closer to 0 indicate better reproducibility. We observe that GCN has higher reproducibility than DiffPool, as reflected by the lower IQR scores across all biomarkers. We also notice that both GCN and DiffPool have lower IQR scores than the other three models, indicating greater reproducibility. Another significant finding is that there is a noticeable quantitative difference between the reproducibility of GCN and DiffPool compared to the other models. Our findings are more consistent with RepNet quantification method, providing further evidence of RepNet superiority over RG-Select [15].

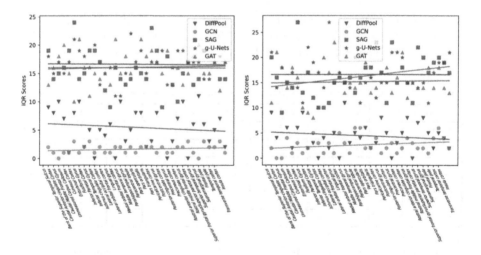

Fig. 5. IQR scores of each GNN biomarkers across different trainings.

Investigating Inter-Model Reproducibility Scores. Here, we can see that GCN is the most reproducible model, however with lower scores than the inter-view ones **Fig.** 4. This could be due to the assumption made while calculating the inter-model reproducibility score, which states that the model with the highest inter-model reproducibility shares the same biomarkers as all other models. The fact that GCN is the most reproducible model in terms of both inter-view and inter-model reproducibility shows that we can trust it to differentiate two brain states.

Most Reproducible Biomarkers. The precuneus cortex, bank of the superior temporal sulcus and lateral orbital frontal cortex are the most discriminative biomarkers produced by GCN across views for ASD/NC dataset (Fig. 6). Supporting our findings, [7] discovered that patients with autism have weaker functional connections between the precuneus cortex and several brain regions that play a crucial role in social cognition and self-referential processing. In addition, [14] demonstrated that autistic brains have reduced activation in the superior temporal sulcus when processing vocal sounds, especially emotional speech sounds. [22] reported that individuals with autism exhibit lower gray matter volume in the orbital cortex, as well as other brain regions involved in social cognition, corroborating our results. Demonstrating both inter- and inner-reproducibility, RepNet can identify biomarkers in clinical trials for neural disconnectivity diagnosis and treatment.

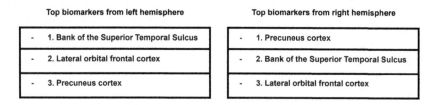

Fig. 6. Top 3 biomarkers by the reproducible GCN architecture trained on ASD/NC LH and RH datasets, respectively.

5   Conclusion

This study presents RepNet, a novel approach for quantifying the reproducibility of a GNN model for consistent biomarker discovery. RepNet distinguishes between inter-view and inter-model reproducibility and ranks different GNN models based on their biomarker reproducibility across views and against perturbations in training/testing data distributions. Our study demonstrates that Rep-Net outperforms state-of-the-art methods by producing results that are simultaneously intra-and inter-consistent. In our future work, we will replicate the findings of RepNet using large-scale connectomic datasets. We will also explore how RepNet can optimize GNN models in terms of reproducibility and its impact on the GNN accuracy measures.

References

1. Aktı, Ş, et al.: A comparative study of machine learning methods for predicting the evolution of brain connectivity from a baseline timepoint. J. Neurosci. Methods **368**, 109475 (2022)

2. Banka, A., Rekik, I.: Adversarial connectome embedding for mild cognitive impairment identification using cortical morphological networks. In: Schirmer, M.D., Venkataraman, A., Rekik, I., Kim, M., Chung, A.W. (eds.) CNI 2019. LNCS, vol. 11848, pp. 74–82. Springer, Cham (2019). https://doi.org/10.1007/978-3-030-32391-2_8

3. Bassett, D.S., Sporns, O.: Network neuroscience. Nat. Neurosci. **20**(3), 353–364 (2017)

4. Bessadok, A., Mahjoub, M.A., Rekik, I.: Graph neural networks in network neuroscience. IEEE Trans. Pattern Anal. Mach. Intell. (2022)

5. Bruce, F.: Freesurfer. Neuroimage **62**(2), 774–781 (2012)

6. Chaari, N., Akdağ, H.C., Rekik, I.: Comparative survey of multigraph integration methods for holistic brain connectivity mapping. Med. Image Anal., 102741 (2023)

7. Cherkassky, V.L., Kana, R.K., Keller, T.A., Just, M.A.: Functional connectivity in a baseline resting-state network in autism. NeuroReport **17**(16), 1687–1690 (2006)

8. Desikan, R.S., et al.: An automated labeling system for subdividing the human cerebral cortex on mri scans into gyral based regions of interest. Neuroimage **31**(3), 968–980 (2006)

9. Dhifallah, S., Rekik, I., Initiative, A.D.N., et al.: Estimation of connectional brain templates using selective multi-view network normalization. Med. Image Anal. **59**, 101567 (2020)

10. Di Martino, A., et al.: The autism brain imaging data exchange: towards a large-scale evaluation of the intrinsic brain architecture in autism. Mol. Psychiatry **19**(6), 659–667 (2014)

11. Douw, L., et al.: The road ahead in clinical network neuroscience. Netw. Neurosci. **3**(4), 969–993 (2019)

12. Gao, H., Ji, S.: Graph u-nets. In: International Conference on Machine Learning, pp. 2083–2092. PMLR (2019)

13. Georges, N., Mhiri, I., Rekik, I., Initiative, A.D.N., et al.: Identifying the best data-driven feature selection method for boosting reproducibility in classification tasks. Pattern Recogn. **101**, 107183 (2020)

14. Gervais, H., et al.: Abnormal cortical voice processing in autism. Nat. Neurosci. **7**(8), 801–802 (2004)

15. Gharsallaoui, M.A., Tornaci, F., Rekik, I.: Investigating and quantifying the reproducibility of graph neural networks in predictive medicine. In: Rekik, I., Adeli, E., Park, S.H., Schnabel, J. (eds.) PRIME 2021. LNCS, vol. 12928, pp. 104–116. Springer, Cham (2021). https://doi.org/10.1007/978-3-030-87602-9_10

16. Jie, B., Shen, D., Zhang, D.: Brain connectivity hyper-network for MCI classification. In: Golland, P., Hata, N., Barillot, C., Hornegger, J., Howe, R. (eds.) MICCAI 2014. LNCS, vol. 8674, pp. 724–732. Springer, Cham (2014). https://doi.org/10.1007/978-3-319-10470-6_90

17. Kipf, T.N., Welling, M.: Semi-supervised classification with graph convolutional networks. arXiv preprint arXiv:1609.02907 (2016)

18. Lee, J., Lee, I., Kang, J.: Self-attention graph pooling. In: International Conference on Machine Learning, pp. 3734–3743. PMLR (2019)

19. Li, X., Dvornek, N.C., Zhou, Y., Zhuang, J., Ventola, P., Duncan, J.S.: Graph neural network for interpreting task-fMRI biomarkers. In: Shen, D., et al. (eds.) MICCAI 2019. LNCS, vol. 11768, pp. 485–493. Springer, Cham (2019). https://doi.org/10.1007/978-3-030-32254-0_54
20. Lisowska, A., Rekik, I.: Pairing-based ensemble classifier learning using convolutional brain multiplexes and multi-view brain networks for early dementia diagnosis. In: Wu, G., Laurienti, P., Bonilha, L., Munsell, B.C. (eds.) CNI 2017. LNCS, vol. 10511, pp. 42–50. Springer, Cham (2017). https://doi.org/10.1007/978-3-319-67159-8_6
21. Mahjoub, I., Mahjoub, M.A., Rekik, I.: Brain multiplexes reveal morphological connectional biomarkers fingerprinting late brain dementia states. Sci. Rep. 8(1), 1–14 (2018)
22. McAlonan, G.M., et al.: Mapping the brain in autism, a voxel-based MRI study of volumetric differences and intercorrelations in autism. Brain 128(2), 268–276 (2005)
23. Nebli, A., Gharsallaoui, M.A., Gürler, Z., Rekik, I., Initiative, A.D.N., et al.: Quantifying the reproducibility of graph neural networks using multigraph data representation. Neural Netw. 148, 254–265 (2022)
24. Veličković, P., Cucurull, G., Casanova, A., Romero, A., Lio, P., Bengio, Y.: Graph attention networks. arXiv preprint arXiv:1710.10903 (2017)
25. Wang, M.Y.: Deep graph library: towards efficient and scalable deep learning on graphs. In: ICLR Workshop on Representation Learning on Graphs and Manifolds (2019)
26. Wang, P.Y., Sapra, S., George, V.K., Silva, G.A.: Generalizable machine learning in neuroscience using graph neural networks. Front. Artifi. Intell. 4, 618372 (2021)
27. Xing, X., et al.: Dynamic spectral graph convolution networks with assistant task training for early MCI diagnosis. In: Shen, D., et al. (eds.) MICCAI 2019. LNCS, vol. 11767, pp. 639–646. Springer, Cham (2019). https://doi.org/10.1007/978-3-030-32251-9_70
28. Ying, Z., You, J., Morris, C., Ren, X., Hamilton, W., Leskovec, J.: Hierarchical graph representation learning with differentiable pooling. In: Advances in Neural Information Processing Systems 31 (2018)
29. Zhang, Z., Cui, P., Zhu, W.: Deep learning on graphs: a survey. IEEE Trans. Knowl. Data Eng. 34(1), 249–270 (2020)

SynthA1c: Towards Clinically Interpretable Patient Representations for Diabetes Risk Stratification

Michael S. Yao[1,2], Allison Chae[2], Matthew T. MacLean[3],
Anurag Verma[4], Jeffrey Duda[3], James C. Gee[3], Drew A. Torigian[3],
Daniel Rader[4], Charles E. Kahn Jr.[2,3], Walter R. Witschey[2,3],
and Hersh Sagreiya[2,3(✉)]

[1] Department of Bioengineering, University of Pennsylvania, Philadelphia 19104,
USA
[2] Perelman School of Medicine, University of Pennsylvania, Philadelphia 19104, USA
[3] Department of Radiology, University of Pennsylvania, Philadelphia, PA 19104, USA
hersh.sagreiya@pennmedicine.upenn.edu
[4] Department of Medicine, University of Pennsylvania, Philadelphia, PA 19104, USA

Abstract. Early diagnosis of Type 2 Diabetes Mellitus (T2DM) is crucial to enable timely therapeutic interventions and lifestyle modifications. As the time available for clinical office visits shortens and medical imaging data become more widely available, patient image data could be used to opportunistically identify patients for additional T2DM diagnostic workup by physicians. We investigated whether image-derived phenotypic data could be leveraged in tabular learning classifier models to predict T2DM risk in an automated fashion to flag high-risk patients *without* the need for additional blood laboratory measurements. In contrast to traditional binary classifiers, we leverage neural networks and decision tree models to represent patient data as 'SynthA1c' latent variables, which mimic blood hemoglobin A1c empirical lab measurements, that achieve sensitivities as high as 87.6%. To evaluate how SynthA1c models may generalize to other patient populations, we introduce a novel generalizable metric that uses vanilla data augmentation techniques to predict model performance on input out-of-domain covariates. We show that image-derived phenotypes and physical examination data together can accurately predict diabetes risk as a means of opportunistic risk stratification enabled by artificial intelligence and medical imaging. Our code is available at https://github.com/allisonjchae/DMT2RiskAssessment.

Keywords: Disease Prediction · Representation Learning · Radiomics

1 Introduction

Type 2 Diabetes Mellitus (T2DM) affects over 30 million patients in the United States, and is most commonly characterized by elevated serum hemoglobin A1c

M. S. Yao and A. Chae—Equal contribution as co-first authors.
W. R. Witschey and H. Sagreiya—Equal contribution as co-senior authors.

I. Rekik et al. (Eds.): PRIME 2023, LNCS 14277, pp. 46–57, 2023.
https://doi.org/10.1007/978-3-031-46005-0_5

(HbA1c) levels measured through a blood sample [1,2]. Formally, a patient is considered diabetic if their HbA1c is greater than 6.5% A1c. While patients diagnosed with T2DM are at an increased risk of many comorbidities, early diagnosis and lifestyle interventions can improve patient outcomes [3].

However, delayed diagnosis of T2DM is frequent due to a low rate of screening. Up to a third of patients are not screened for T2DM as recommended by current national guidelines [4,5], and Porter et al. [6] estimate that it would take over 24 h per day for primary care physicians to follow national screening recommendations for every adult visit. Furthermore, T2DM screening using patient bloodwork is not routinely performed in acute urgent care settings or emergency department (ED) visits. Given these obstacles, machine learning (ML) is a promising tool to predict patient risk of T2DM and other diseases [7].

Simultaneously, the usage of radiologic imaging in clinical medicine continues to increase every year [8,9]. Over 70 million computed tomography (CT) scans are performed annually and their utilization has become increasingly common in both primary care and ED visits [10]. Consequently, the wealth of CT radiographic data can potentially be used to estimate patient risk of T2DM as an incidental finding in these clinical settings. For example, T2DM risk factors include central adiposity and the buildup of excess fat in the liver that can be readily estimated from clinical CT scans. Liver fat excess can be estimated by calculating the spleen-hepatic attenuation difference (SHAD), which is the difference between liver and spleen CT attenuation [11]. These metrics are examples of **image-derived phenotypes** (IDPs) derived from patient CT scans and other imaging modalities. Other IDPs, such as volume estimation of subcutaneous fat and visceral fat, can also be used to quantify central adiposity. Using these metrics, a prediction model could report estimated T2DM risk as an incidental finding during an unrelated outpatient imaging study or ED visit workup as a means of opportunistic risk stratification from analysis of CT scans and patient information, with automated referral of high-risk patients for downstream screening without the need for intermediate physician intervention.

Existing machine learning methods for disease prediction have largely focused on developing classification models that output probability values for different physiologic states [12–14]. However, these metrics are difficult for clinicians to interpret at face value and cannot be intelligently integrated into existing clinician workflows, such as diagnostic pathways based on clinical lab findings [15].

In this study, we hypothesized that radiomic metrics derived from CT scans could be used in conjunction with physical examination data to predict patient T2DM risk using SynthA1c, a novel synthetic *in silico* measurement approximating patient blood hemoglobin A1c (HbA1c) (Fig. 1). To predict model generalizability, we also propose a generalizable data augmentation-based model smoothness metric that predicts SynthA1c accuracy on previously unseen out-of-domain patient datasets.

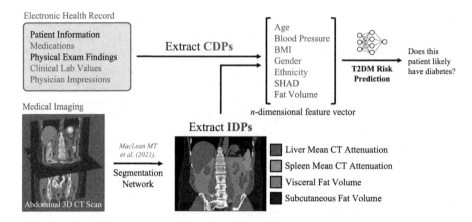

Fig. 1. Overview of our proposed work. Using the IDP extraction pipeline from MacLean et al. [11], we can estimate quantitative IDPs from abdominal CT scans associated with an increased risk for T2DM. IDPs and CDPs from corresponding patient electronic health records can then be used to train T2DM risk prediction models. *IDP*: image-derived phenotype; *CT*: computed tomography; *T2DM*: Type 2 Diabetes Mellitus; *CDP*: clinically derived phenotype.

2   Materials and Methods

2.1   Patient Cohort and Data Declaration

The data used for our retrospective study were made available by the Penn Medicine BioBank (PMBB), an academic biobank established by the University of Pennsylvania. All patients provided informed consent to utilization of de-identified patient data, which was approved by the Institutional Review Board of the University of Pennsylvania (IRB protocol 813913).

From the PMBB outpatient dataset, we obtained patient ages, genders, ethnicities, heights, weights, blood pressures, abdominal CT scans, and blood HbA1c measurements. Notably, the only clinical laboratory value extracted was HbA1c to be used as a ground truth- no blood biomarkers were used as model inputs. Patients with any missing features were excluded.

Using the pre-trained abdominal CT segmentation network trained and reported by MacLean et al. [11], we estimated four IDPs from any given CT of the abdomen and pelvis study (either with or without contrast) to be used as model inputs. Our four IDPs of interest were mean liver CT attenuation, mean spleen CT attenuation, and estimated volume of subcutaneous fat and visceral fat. Briefly, their segmentation network achieved mean Sørenson-Dice coefficients of at least 98% for all IDP extraction tasks assessed (including our four IDPs of interest) and is detailed further in their work.

Any patient i has a set of measured values of any particular feature within the dataset. To construct a feature vector $\mathbf{x}$ associated with an HbA1c measurement y_i, we selected the patient's measurements that minimized the time between the date the feature was measured and the date y_i was measured.

2.2   Machine Learning Models: GBDT, NODE, and FT-Transformer

Current supervised methods for disease detection work with feature vectors derived from patient physical examinations and clinical laboratory values [7,12,13]. Our work builds on these prior advances by incorporating IDPs as additional input vector dimensions. Previously, Chen and Guestrin [16] introduced gradient-boosted decision trees (**GBDTs**) that incorporate scalable gradient boosting with forest classifiers for state-of-the-art prediction accuracy across tasks. A separate class of machine learning models is deep neural networks (DNNs). Recently, neural oblivious decision ensemble (**NODE**) DNNs achieved classification performance on par with decision tree models on certain tasks [17] and the Feature Tokenizer + Transformer (**FT-Transformer**) [18] effectively adopts transformer architectures to tabular data. Here, we assessed NODE, FT-Transformer, and GBDT architectures as backbones for our SynthA1c encoders.

We sought to compare our proposed SynthA1c models against a number of baselines. We looked at Ordinary Least Squares (OLS) encoders and traditional diabetes *binary classifier* models with the same three architectures as proposed above, in addition to a zero-rule classifier and a multi-rule questionnaire-based classifier currently recommended for clinical practice by the American Diabetes Association and Centers for Disease Control and Prevention [19].

2.3   Model Training and Evaluation Strategy

Our model inputs can be divided into two disjoint sets: clinically derived phenotypes (CDPs), which are derived from physical examination, and image-derived phenotypes (IDPs) that are estimated from abdominal CT scans herein. The specific CDPs and IDPs used depended on the model class- broadly, we explored two categories of models, which we refer to as r-type and p-type. r-type models were trained on 'raw' data types (CDPs: height, weight, race, gender, age, systolic blood pressure [SBP], diastolic blood pressure [DBP]; IDPs: liver CT attenuation, spleen CT attenuation, subcutaneous fat [SubQ Fat], visceral fat [Visc Fat]), while p-type models were trained on 'processed' data types (CDPs: BMI, race, gender, age, SBP, DBP; IDPs: SHAD, SubQ Fat, Visc Fat). Comparing the performance of r- and p- type models could help us better understand if using derivative processed metrics that are better clinically correlated with T2DM risk yields better model performance.

SynthA1c encoders were trained to minimize the L_2 distance from the ground truth HbA1c laboratory measurement, and evaluated using the root mean square error (RMSE) and Pearson correlation coefficient (PCC). We then compared the predicted SynthA1c values with the traditional HbA1c $\geq 6.5\%$ A1c diabetes cutoff to assess the utility of SynthA1c outputs in diagnosing T2DM. A p value of $p < 0.05$ was used to indicate statistical significance.

2.4   Implementation Details

NODE models were trained with a batch size of 16 and a learning rate of $\eta = 0.03$, which decayed by half every 40 epochs for a total of 100 epochs. FT-

Transformer models were trained with a batch size of 128 and a learning rate of $\eta = 0.001$, which decayed by half every 50 epochs for a total of 100 epochs. GBDT models were trained using 32 boosted trees with a maximum tree depth of 8 with a learning rate of $\eta = 0.1$.

2.5   Assessing Out-of-Domain Performance

An important consideration in high-stakes clinical applications of machine learning is the generalizability of T2DM classifiers to members of previously unseen patient groups. Generalizability is traditionally difficult to quantify and can be affected by training data heterogeneity and the geographic, environmental, and socioeconomic variables unique to the PMBB dataset.

Prior work has shown that model smoothness can be used to predict out-of-domain generalization of neural networks [20, 21]. However, these works largely limit their analysis to classifier networks. To evaluate SynthA1c encoder robustness, we develop an estimation of model manifold smoothness $\mathbb{M}$ for our encoder models. Under the mild assumption that our SynthA1c encoder function $y : \mathbb{R}^{|\mathbf{x}|} \to \mathbb{R}$ is Lipschitz continuous, we can define a local manifold smoothness metric μ at $\mathbf{x} = \tilde{\mathbf{x}}$ given by

$$
\begin{aligned}
\mu(\tilde{\mathbf{x}}) &= \mathbb{E}_{\mathcal{N}(\tilde{\mathbf{x}})} \left[\frac{\sigma_y^{-1} \|y(\mathbf{x}) - y(\tilde{\mathbf{x}})\|_1}{\|\delta\mathbf{x} \oslash \sigma_{\mathbf{x}}\|_2} \right] \\
&= \mathcal{V}[\mathcal{N}(\tilde{\mathbf{x}})]^{-1} \cdot \oint_{\mathcal{N}(\tilde{\mathbf{x}}) \in \mathcal{D}} d\mathbf{x} \; \frac{\sigma_y^{-1}|y(\mathbf{x}) - y(\tilde{\mathbf{x}})|}{\sqrt{(\delta\mathbf{x} \oslash \sigma_{\mathbf{x}})^T (\delta\mathbf{x} \oslash \sigma_{\mathbf{x}})}}
\end{aligned}
\tag{1}
$$

where we have a feature vector $\mathbf{x}$ in domain $\mathcal{D}$ and a neighborhood $\mathcal{N}(\tilde{\mathbf{x}}) \in \mathcal{D}$ around $\mathbf{x}$ with an associated volume of $\mathcal{V}[\mathcal{N}(\tilde{\mathbf{x}})]$. We also define $\delta\mathbf{x} = \mathbf{x} - \tilde{\mathbf{x}}$, $\oslash$ as the Hadamard division operator, and $\sigma_{\mathbf{x}}$ as the vector of the estimated standard deviations of each feature over $\mathcal{D}$. The exact expectation value over a given neighborhood $\mathcal{N}(\tilde{\mathbf{x}})$ is computationally intractable, but we can approximate it with a Monte Carlo integration through an empirical sampling of $Q \gg 1$ random feature points $\mathbf{x}_k$ from $\mathcal{N}(\tilde{\mathbf{x}})$:

$$
\mu(\tilde{\mathbf{x}}) = \frac{1}{Q} \sum_{k=1}^{Q} \frac{\sigma_y^{-1}|y(\mathbf{x}_k) - y(\tilde{\mathbf{x}})|}{\sqrt{(\delta\mathbf{x}_k \oslash \sigma_{\mathbf{x}})^T (\delta\mathbf{x}_k \oslash \sigma_{\mathbf{x}})}}
\tag{2}
$$

We can now define a metric $\mathbb{M}$ for the global encoder manifold smoothness over a domain $\mathcal{D}$ as the expectation value of $\mu(\tilde{\mathbf{x}})$ over $\mathcal{D}$, which can similarly be approximated by an empirical sampling of N feature vectors $\mathbf{x}_1, \mathbf{x}_2, \ldots, \mathbf{x}_N \in \mathcal{D}$. We hypothesized that this global smoothness metric $\mathbb{M}$ inversely correlates with model performance on out-of-domain datasets. To evaluate this experimentally, we assessed model performance on two previously unseen T2DM datasets: (1) the Iraqi Medical City Hospital dataset [22]; and (2) the PMBB inpatient dataset. The Iraqi dataset contains 1,000 sets of patient age, gender, BMI, and HbA1c measurements. Because of this limited feature set, we trained additional Syn-thA1c encoders (referred to as p'-type models) on the PMBB outpatient dataset using only these features. The PMBB inpatient dataset consists of 2,066 measurements of the same datatypes as the outpatient dataset (Sect. 3.1).

3 Results

3.1 Summary Statistics

Our model-building dataset from the PMBB consisted of 2,077 unique HbA1c measurements (1,159 diabetic, 619 prediabetic, 299 nondiabetic) derived from 389 patients (Table 1). 208 (10%) samples were set aside as a holdout test set partition disjoint by patient identity. Each HbA1c measurement was used to construct an associated feature vector from that patient's data collected closest in time to each HbA1c measurement. To quantify the temporal association between a given patient's measurements, we defined the daterange of an observation vector $\mathbf{x}$ as the maximum length of time between any two features/imaging studies. The median daterange in our dataset was 18 days.

3.2 SynthA1c Encoder Experimental Results

Our results suggest that the GBDT encoder predicted SynthA1c values closest to ground truth HbA1c values, followed by both the NODE and FT-Transformer DNN models (Table 2). All the learning-based architectures assessed outperformed the baseline OLS encoder. When comparing SynthA1c outputs against the clinical HbA1c cutoff of 6.5% A1c for the diagnosis of diabetes, the r-GBDT SynthA1c model demonstrated the highest sensitivity of the assessed models at 87.6% on par with the best-performing binary classifier model assessed. In terms of an opportunistic screening modality for T2DM, a high sensitivity ensures that a large proportion of patients with diabetes can be identified for additional lab-based diagnostic work-up with their primary care physicians. Although the accuracy of SynthA1c encoders was lower than the corresponding binary classifier models assessed, this may be partially explained by the fact that the latter's threshold value for classification was empirically tuned to maximize the model's accuracy. In contrast, our SynthA1c encoders used the fixed clinical HbA1c cutoff of 6.5% A1c for diabetes classification. When comparing r- and p- type SynthA1c models, we did not observe a consistently superior data representation strategy.

To further interrogate our SynthA1c encoders, we investigated whether model performance varied as a function of demographic features. Defining the difference between the model prediction and ground truth HbA1c values as a proxy for model performance, all SynthA1c encoders showed no statistically significant difference in performance when stratified by gender or BMI (Fig. 2).

3.3 Ablation Studies: Relative Importance of CDPs and IDPs

Until now, prior T2DM classifiers have used only blood lab measurements and physical examination data to predict T2DM. In contrast, our models presented herein are the first to incorporate IDPs as input model features for the task of diabetes risk stratification. To better

Table 1. PMBB outpatient dataset characteristics. To reduce the effects of selection bias, all patients presenting to the University of Pennsylvania Health System were given the opportunity to enroll in the PMBB so as to best capture the population of patients that seek medical care and avoid overrepresentation of healthy patients as in traditional office visit patient recruitment strategies. However, the PMBB is still affected by hesitancies of patient sub-populations in study enrollment and the unique socioeconomic factors affecting different groups of patients. *HTN*: Hypertension.

Self-Reported Ethnicity	**Count (%)**
White	720 (34.7)
Hispanic	40 (1.9)
Black	1248 (60.1)
Asian	36 (1.7)
Pacific Islander	6 (0.3)
Native American	5 (0.2)
Other/Unknown	22 (1.1)
Self-Reported Gender	**Count (%)**
Male	880 (42.4)
Female	1197 (57.6)
Age Decade	**Count (%)**
20-29	31 (1.5)
30-39	89 (4.3)
40-49	362 (17.4)
50-59	593 (28.6)
60-69	680 (32.7)
70-79	299 (14.4)
80-89	23 (1.1)
Blood Pressure	**Count (%)**
Normal (SBP $<$ 120 mmHg and DBP $<$ 80 mmHg)	421 (20.2)
Elevated (120 $\leq$ SBP $<$ 130 mmHg and DBP $<$ 80 mmHg)	398 (19.2)
Stage 1 HTN (130 $\leq$ SBP $<$ 140 mmHg or 80 $\leq$ DBP $<$ 90 mmHg)	652 (31.4)
Stage 2 HTN (SBP $\geq$ 140 mmHg or DBP $\geq$ 90 mmHg)	606 (29.2)
BMI	**Count (%)**
Underweight or Healthy Weight (BMI $<$ 25.0)	275 (13.2)
Overweight (25.0 $\leq$ BMI $<$ 30.0)	443 (21.3)
Class 1 Obesity (30.0 $\leq$ BMI $<$ 35.0)	556 (26.8)
Class 2 Obesity (35.0 $\leq$ BMI $<$ 40.0)	389 (18.7)
Class 3 Obesity (BMI $\geq$ 40.0)	414 (20.0)
HbA1c	**Count (%)**
Not Diabetic (HbA1c $<$ 6.5% A1c)	918 (44.2)
Diabetic (HbA1c $\geq$ 6.5% A1c)	1159 (55.8)
CT Abdomen and Pelvis Enhancement	**Count (%)**
With Contrast	1570 (75.6)
Without Contrast	507 (24.4)
Image Derived Phenotypes (IDPs) Statistics	**Mean $\pm$ SD**
Spleen CT Attenuation (HU)	36.2 $\pm$ 16.7
Liver CT Attenuation (HU)	42.8 $\pm$ 20.2
Subcutaneous Fat Area (cm^2)	321.3 $\pm$ 170.1
Visceral Fat Area (cm^2)	172.4 $\pm$ 104.9
Total Count	**2077**

Table 2. SynthA1c prediction results using different encoder models. r- (p-) prefixed models are fed raw (processed) inputs as outlined in Sect. 2.3. RMSE in units of % A1c. For the SynthA1c encoder models, recall, precision, specificity, and accuracy metrics are reported based on the traditional T2DM cutoff of 6.5% A1c. The Multi-Rule binary classifier is the current deterministic risk stratification tool recommended by American Diabetes Association [19].

SynthA1c Encoder	RMSE	PCC	Recall	Precision	Specificity	Accuracy
r-OLS	1.67	0.206	85.3	56.0	26.3	57.2
p-OLS	1.73	0.159	80.7	57.5	34.3	58.6
r-FT-Transformer	1.44	0.517	87.6	63.4	55.9	70.7
p-FT-Transformer	1.51	0.441	83.5	61.4	54.1	67.8
r-NODE	1.60	0.378	85.6	55.0	38.7	60.6
p-NODE	1.57	0.649	77.3	59.5	54.1	64.9
r-GBDT	1.36	0.567	87.2	66.4	51.5	70.2
p-GBDT	1.36	0.591	77.1	72.4	67.7	72.6
Binary Classifier	**AUROC (%)**	**Recall**	**Precision**	**Specificity**	**Accuracy**	
Zero-Rule	–	100	52.4	0.0	52.4	
Multi-Rule	56.3	67.0	54.9	39.4	53.8	
r-FT-Transformer	82.1	85.3	73.8	66.7	76.4	
r-NODE	83.5	82.6	76.9	72.7	77.9	
r-GBDT	83.1	87.2	76.6	70.7	79.3	

understand the benefit and value-add of using IDPs in conjunction with CDPs, we evaluated classifier performance on models trained using either only CDPs or only IDPs and compared them to corresponding models trained using both input types.

Our results suggest that while classifier models trained only on CDPs generally outperform those trained only on IDPs, the best performance is achieved when combining CDPs and IDPs together (Table 3). This further validates the clinical utility of incorporating IDPs into patient diagnosis and disease risk stratification first proposed by MacLean et al. [11] and related work.

3.4   Characterizing Out-of-Domain Model Performance

As our proposed global smoothness metric $\mathbb{M}$ decrease across the three evaluated models, the RMSE in SynthA1c prediction decreases and the PCC increases, corresponding to better predictive performance on the out-of-domain Iraqi Medical Center Dataset (Table 4). This supports our initial hypothesis that smoother models may generalize better to unseen datasets. We also noted larger RMSE values using the Iraqi Medical Center Dataset when compared to the PMBB outpatient test dataset results (Table 2).

Interestingly, we found that this relationship did not ostensibly hold when considering the PMBB inpatient dataset; in fact, model predictive performance was *inversely* correlated with global smoothness. This suggested that the PMBB inpatient and outpatient dataset distributions were more similar than initially predicted. To validate this hypothesis, we computed the Kullback-Leibler (KL) divergence between each of the test dataset distributions and the training dataset distribution with respect to the features available in all datasets: ethnicity, gender, age, BMI, and HbA1c. We assumed the PMBB-derived outpatient training dataset was sampled from a distribution $\mathcal{Q}$ and each of the PMBB outpatient test, PMBB inpatient, and Iraqi

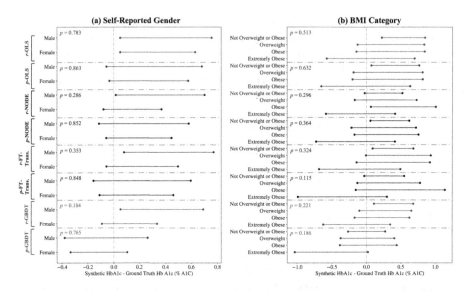

Fig. 2. Assessing for algorithmic bias in SynthA1c encoders. We plotted the 95% confidence interval of the mean difference between the SynthA1c model output and ground truth HbA1c as a function of self-reported (a) gender and (b) BMI category. p values comparing the differences in SynthA1c model performance when stratified by gender (two-sample T-test) and BMI category (one-way ANOVA) are shown.

Table 3. Ablation study assessing model performance as a function of clinically derived phenotypes (CDPs) and/or image-derived phenotypes (IDPs).

r-**NODE**	Recall	Precision	Specificity	Accuracy
CDPs Only	77.1	73.7	69.7	73.5
IDPs Only	73.4	76.9	75.8	74.5
CDPs + IDPs	82.6	76.9	72.7	77.9
r-**FT-Transformer**	Recall	Precision	Specificity	Accuracy
CDPs Only	78.0	76.6	73.7	75.9
IDPs Only	71.6	60.5	48.5	60.6
CDPs + IDPs	85.3	73.8	66.7	76.4
r-**GBDT**	Recall	Precision	Specificity	Accuracy
CDPs Only	80.7	68.6	59.6	70.7
IDPs Only	73.4	75.5	73.7	73.6
CDPs + IDPs	87.2	76.6	70.7	79.3

medical center datasets were sampled from $\mathcal{P}_{\text{Outpatient}}$, $\mathcal{P}_{\text{Inpatient}}$, and $\mathcal{P}_{\text{Iraqi}}$, respectively. The greatest KL divergence was between the Iraqi medical center and training dataset distributions, as expected ($D_{KL}[\mathcal{P}_{\text{Iraqi}} \| \mathcal{Q}] = 31.2$). Despite the fact that our training set included outpatient data alone, we found the KL divergence between the inpatient test and training

Table 4. SynthA1c model sensitivity and out-of-domain generalization results. Global smoothness metric values $\mathbb{M}$ were evaluated on the PMBB outpatient dataset. r-type models could not be evaluated on the Iraqi dataset because IDPs and medical imaging data were not available. RMSE in units of % A1c.

SynthA1c Encoder	$\mathbb{M}$	Iraqi Dataset		PMBB Inpatient	
		RMSE	PCC	RMSE	PCC
p'-/r- NODE	1.43	3.62/-	0.154/ -	1.76/1.23	0.512/0.795
p'-/r- FT-Transformer	1.07	3.04/ -	0.246/-	1.90 / 1.58	0.331/0.617
p'-/r- GBDT	3.28	6.25/-	0.021/ -	1.54/1.12	0.674/0.823

datasets ($D_{KL}[\mathcal{P}_{\text{Inpatient}}||\mathcal{Q}] = 0.227$) was lower than that between the outpatient test and training dataset ($D_{KL}[\mathcal{P}_{\text{Outpatient}}||\mathcal{Q}] = 1.84$).

To further characterize the feature distributions within our datasets, we analyzed the pairwise relationships between BMI, age, and HbA1c. Individual feature distributions were statistically significant between either of the PMBB datasets and the Iraqi Medical Center dataset (two-sample Kolmogorov-Smirnov (KS) test; $p < 0.0001$ between [PMBB inpatient dataset, Iraqi Medical Center dataset] and [PMBB outpatient dataset, Iraqi Medical Center dataset] pairs for individual age, HbA1c, and BMI quantitative features), but not between the PMBB inpatient and outpatient datasets (two-sample KS test; age: $p = 0.315$, HbA1c: $p = 0.463$, BMI: $p = 0.345$). These results suggest that inpatients are a compact subset of outpatients within the PMBB with respect to T2DM risk assessment. This helps explain our initial findings regarding the relationship between $\mathbb{M}$ and model generalization. Further work is warranted to validate the proposed metric $\mathbb{M}$ across other tasks.

4 Conclusion

Our work highlights the value of using CT-derived IDPs and CDPs for opportunistic screening of T2DM. We show that tabular learning architectures can act as novel SynthA1c encoders to predict HbA1c measurements noninvasively. Furthermore, we demonstrate that model manifold smoothness may be correlated with prediction performance on previously unseen data sampled from out-of-domain patient populations, although additional validation studies on separate tasks are needed. Ultimately, we hope that our proposed work may be used in every outpatient and ED imaging study, regardless of chief complaint, for opportunistic screening of type 2 diabetes. Our proposed SynthA1c methodology will by no means replace existing diagnostic laboratory workups, but rather identify those at-risk patients who should consider consulting their physician for downstream clinical evaluation in an efficient and automated manner.

Acknowledgment. MSY is supported by NIH T32 EB009384. AC is supported by the AΩA Carolyn L. Kuckein Student Research Fellowship and the University of Pennsylvania Diagnostic Radiology Research Fellowship. WRW is supported by NIH R01 HL137984. MTM received funding from the Sarnoff Cardiovascular Research Foundation. HS received funding from the RSNA Scholar Grant.

References

1. Khan, M.A.B., Hashim, M.J., King, J.K., Govender, R.D., Mustafa, H., Al Kaabi, J.: Epidemiology of type 2 diabetes - Global burden of disease and forecasted

trends. J. Epi. Glob. Health **10**(1), 107–111 (2020). https://doi.org/10.2991/jegh.k.191028.001

2. Xu, G., et al.: Prevalence of diagnosed type 1 and type 2 diabetes among US adults in 2016 and 2017: Population based study. BMJ **362** (2018). https://doi.org/10.1136/bmj.k1497

3. Albarakat, M., Guzu, A.: Prevalence of type 2 diabetes and their complications among home health care patients at Al-Kharj military industries corporation hospital. J. Family Med. Prim. Care **8**(10), 3303–3312 (2019). https://doi.org/10.4103/jfmpc.jfmpc_634_19

4. Polubriaginof, F.C.G., Shang, N., Hripcsak, G., Tatonetti, N.P., Vawdrey, D.K.: Low screening rates for diabetes mellitus among family members of affected relatives. In: AMIA Annual Symposium Proceedings, pp. 1471–1417 (2019)

5. Kaul, P., Chu, L.M., Dover, D.C., Yeung, R.O., Eurich, D.T., Butalia, S.: Disparities in adherence to diabetes screening guidelines among males and females in a universal care setting: a population-based study of 1,380,697 adults. Lancet Regional Health (2022). https://doi.org/10.1016/j.lana.2022.100320

6. Porter, J., Boyd, C., Skandari, M.R., Laiteerapong, N.: Revisiting the time needed to provide adult primary care. J. Gen. Intern. Med. (2022). https://doi.org/10.1007/s11606-022-07707-x

7. Farran, B., Channanath, A.M., Behbehani, K., Thanaraj, T.A.: Predictive models to assess risk of type 2 diabetes, hypertension and comorbidity: machine-learning algorithms and validation using national health data from Kuwait—A cohort study. BMJ Open **3**(5) (2013). https://doi.org/10.1136/bmjopen-2012-002457

8. Dowhanik, S.P.D., Schieda, N., Patlas, M.N., Salehi, F., van der Pol, C.B.: Doing more with less: CT and MRI utilization in Canada 2003–2019. Canadian Assoc. Radiol. J. **73**(3), 592–594 (2022). https://doi.org/10.1177/08465371211052012

9. Hong, A.S., Levin, D., Parker, L., Rao, V.M., Ross-Degnan, D., Wharam, J.F.: Trends in diagnostic imaging utilization among Medicare and commercially insured adults from 2003 through 2016. Radiology **294**(2), 342–350 (2020). https://doi.org/10.1148/radiol.2019191116

10. Smith, J.W., Everhart, J.E., Dickson, W.C., Knowler, W.C., Johannes, R.S.: Using the ADAP learning algorithm to forecast the onset of diabetes mellitus. In: Proceedings of Symposium on Computer Application in Medical Care, 261–265 (1988)

11. MacLean, M.T., et al.: Quantification of abdominal fat from computed tomography using deep learning and its association with electronic health records in an academic biobank. J. Am. Med. Inform. Assoc. **28**(6), 1178–1187 (2021). https://doi.org/10.1093/jamia/ocaa342

12. Uddin, S., Khan, A., Hossain, M.E., Moni, M.A.: Comparing different supervised machine learning algorithms for disease prediction. BMC Med. Inform. Decis. Mak. **19**(281) (2019). https://doi.org/10.1093/jamia/ocaa342

13. Kopitar, L., Kocbek, P., Cilar, L., Sheikh, A., Stiglic, G.: Early detection of type 2 diabetes mellitus using machine learning-based prediction models. Nat. Sci. Rep. (2020). https://doi.org/10.1038/s41598-020-68771-z

14. Deberneh, H.M., Kim, I.: Prediction of type 2 diabetes based on machine learning algorithm. Int. J. Environ. Res. Public Health **18**(6), 3317 (2021). https://doi.org/10.3390/ijerph18063317

15. Sivaraman, V., Bukowski, L.A., Levin, J., Kahn, J.M., Perer, A.: Ignore, trust, or negotiate: Understanding clinician acceptance of AI-based treatment recommendations in health care. arXiv (2023). https://doi.org/10.48550/arxiv.2302.00096

16. Chen, T., Guestrin, C.: XGBoost: a scalable tree boosting system. In: Proceedings of ACM SIGKDD International Conference on Knowledge Discovery and Data Mining, pp. 785–794 (2016). https://doi.org/10.1145/2939672.2939785
17. Popov, S., Morozov, S., Babenko, A.: Neural oblivious decision ensembles for deep learning on tabular data. arXiv (2019). https://doi.org/10.48550/arxiv.1909.06312
18. Gorishniy, Y., Rubachev, I., Khrulkov, V., Babenko, A.: Revisiting deep learning models for tabular data. arXiv (2021). https://doi.org/10.48550/arxiv.2106.11959
19. Bang, H., et al.: Development and validation of a patient self-assessment score for diabetes risk. Ann. Intern. Med. **151**(11), 775–783 (2009). https://doi.org/10.7326/0003-4819-151-11-200912010-00005
20. Ng, N., Hulkund, N., Cho, K., Ghassemi, M.: Predicting out-of-domain generalization with local manifold smoothness. arXiv (2022). https://doi.org/10.48550/arxiv.2207.02093
21. Jiang, Z., Zhou, J., Huang, H.: Relationship between manifold smoothness and adversarial vulnerability in deep learning with local errors. Chin. Phys. B **30**(4) (2021). https://doi.org/10.1088/1674-1056/abd68e
22. Rashid, A.: Iraqi Diabetes Dataset (2020). www.data.mendeley.com/datasets/wj9rwkp9c2/1, https://doi.org/10.17632/wj9rwkp9c2.1

Confounding Factors Mitigation in Brain Age Prediction Using MRI with Deformation Fields

K. H. Aqil[1]([⊠])[iD], Tanvi Kulkarni[1], Jaikishan Jayakumar[2], Keerthi Ram[3], and Mohanasankar Sivaprakasam[1,2,3]

[1] Indian Institute of Technology Madras, Chennai, India
aqil.mec@gmail.com
[2] Centre for Computational Brain Research, IIT Madras, Chennai, India
[3] Healthcare Technology Innovation Centre, IIT Madras, Chennai, India

Abstract. The aging brain is characterized by a decline in physical and mental capacities and susceptibility to neurological disorders. Magnetic resonance imaging (MRI) has proven to be a critical tool in detecting age-related structural and morphological changes. One of the effective biomarkers for healthy aging is the difference between predicted brain age and chronological brain age (Predicted Age Difference: PAD). While deep learning networks give accurate brain age predictions, they are highly affected by confounding factors like variable noise levels from different MRI scanners/sites, gender, etc. This study focuses on the development of an algorithm leveraging deformation fields with debiasing in T1-W MRI images obtained from the OpenBHB dataset to learn representation vectors that capture the biological variability (age). To achieve this, we explore the use of learnable deformation fields combined with a contrast invariant training method (SynthMorph). We evaluate the accuracy of our method on the large publicly available dataset, OpenBHB, which consists of MRI scans from multiple sites and scanners and compare it with a standard available method, ResNet.

1 Introduction

Brain aging is a multifaceted process characterized by intricate biological transformations, such as cortical thinning, reduction in overall volume, and reduction in the gray matter and white matter [21]. "Brain Age" is one of the fundamental elements that determine both normal brain aging and the aging brain's susceptibility to neurodegenerative disorders such as Alzheimer's, Parkinson's, and dementia. One important technique to determine this parameter is Structural Magnetic resonance imaging (MRI) [19]. The disparity between predicted age and chronological age, often referred to as PAD (Predicted Age Delta), serves as an effective biomarker for distinguishing healthy individuals from various patient groups, including those with Alzheimer's disease and mild cognitive impairment [23]. In recent years, the field of brain age prediction has witnessed significant advancements through the utilization of machine learning algorithms applied to neuroimaging data. These methods have demonstrated remarkable accuracy and hold great potential for clinical applications. However, challenges such as limited generalizability and vulnerability to variations in imaging protocols and scanner characteristics persist. Numerous studies have explored the estimation of brain age using

© The Author(s), under exclusive license to Springer Nature Switzerland AG 2023
I. Rekik et al. (Eds.): PRIME 2023, LNCS 14277, pp. 58–69, 2023.
https://doi.org/10.1007/978-3-031-46005-0_6

machine learning techniques on magnetic resonance imaging (MRI) data, including SVM, RVR, and CNN models [1,11,20,24].

These investigations have made substantial contributions to our understanding of brain aging processes and have shed light on the complex interplay between neuroimaging features and chronological age. Addressing the issues of generalizability and robustness in brain age prediction remains a crucial endeavor, necessitating the development of approaches that effectively handle inter-scanner variability, acquisition protocol differences, and confounding factors. By overcoming these challenges, the reliability and applicability of brain age prediction models can be enhanced, enabling more accurate assessments of brain aging-related pathologies and facilitating personalized medicine approaches. Continued research efforts in this field have the potential to unlock valuable insights into brain development, aging, and neurodegenerative disorders, leading to early detection and intervention strategies for improved patient outcomes. Neuroimaging techniques have proven to be invaluable tools for investigating the brain, enabling the non-invasive visualization of its structure and function. In particular, recent advances in magnetic resonance imaging (MRI) technology has allowed for high-resolution, multi-modal imaging that can capture detailed information about the brain's anatomy, connectivity, and activity, in particular for PAD estimation. The importance of multimodal MRI in characterizing brain tissue and its potential application for individual age prediction has been highlighted in Cherubini et al. 2016 [5]. Cole et al. conducted an extensive study utilizing Gaussian Process regression to explore the association between brain age and mortality. Their findings revealed that brain age can serve as a predictive factor for mortality, with a mean absolute prediction error of 5.02 years and a root mean square error of 6.31 years [7]. Building upon this work, Jonsonn et al. applied ResNet to predict brain age and successfully identified sequence variants associated with this prediction, achieving an MAE of 4.006 and R-squared of 0.829 [15]. Furthermore, Cole et al. used CNN to predict brain age from raw imaging data, achieving a correlation coefficient ($\mathbf{r}$) of 0.94 and a mean absolute error (MAE) of 4.65 years [6]. In a related study, Kauffman explored the correlation between common brain disorders and heritable patterns of apparent brain aging [18].

Several recent works have significantly contributed to the field of brain age prediction, utilizing different approaches and techniques. One of the promising techniques to more accurately predict brain age uses deformation fields [9]. Other techniques use a generative approach for aging brain images while utilizing diffeomorphic registration and fast three-dimensional image generation to capture healthy brain aging patterns [12]. These studies demonstrate the diverse strategies and advancements made in leveraging neuroimaging data for accurate brain age prediction. The application of the predicted brain age difference (PAD) biomarker has garnered significant attention in recent years. Several machine learning (ML) papers have explored its potential and presented various approaches for brain age prediction not only for older brains but also for the adolescent brain [17]. Behesthi et al. conducted a comprehensive evaluation of different ML algorithms to assess their effectiveness in brain age prediction [2]. In another study, Beheshti introduced an improved version of the least squares twin support vector regression (SVR) method for accurate brain age prediction [13]. Cheng proposed cascade networks with ranking loss to estimate brain age from MRI data [4]. Lastly,

Xiong compared various machine learning models using six different imaging modalities to predict brain age in middle-aged and older adults [25]. Additionally, Dufumier et al. introduced a new public benchmarking resource, utilizing the large-scale multi-site brain MRI dataset OpenBHB [8]. While these models have shown promising results, the variation in MRI scan properties arising from differences in scanner types and acquisition parameters can introduce biases when machine learning models are trained and tested on imbalanced samples collected with different protocols [16,20]. Previous debiasing methods have predominantly relied on regression-based approaches, including Random-effects regression models [26] and the scale-and-shift random effects regression of ComBat [10]. Direct image-to-image transfer has been investigated in supervised (paired) tasks, where explicitly paired data is required, ensuring that the same brains are scanned at all sites [3,22].

In this paper, we propose a novel methodology for brain age prediction utilizing deep learning-based registration networks, making significant contributions to the field. Our approach introduces a unique perspective by leveraging the deformation information derived from the registration process between a subject and a standard atlas to estimate brain age. By incorporating spatial relationships captured during registration, our method takes into account anatomical variations, thereby enhancing predictive accuracy. To validate the efficacy of our network, we conduct a preliminary experiment using MNIST digits as a surrogate dataset, wherein we predict the scale of the subject image relative to the standard atlas. This experiment serves as a proof-of-concept, showcasing the age-predictive capability of our model and highlighting its potential for brain age estimation. To address the challenges associated with variable noise levels originating from different MRI scanners, we employ a contrast-invariant training strategy. This technique normalizes image contrast across different scanners, mitigating the impact of scanner-induced variations and bolstering the robustness of our model. In addition, we perform clustering analysis on both the input and latent space representations, enabling us to investigate the "debiasing" effect of site-specific confounding factors inherent in MRI scanner data.

1.1 Dataset Description

We conducted our experiments on the OpenBHB dataset. The dataset consists of 3984 T1-Weighted (T1W) brain scans taken from different subjects using over 60 different scanners. All T1 images were uniformly pre-processed using CAT12 (SPM), FreeSurfer (FSL), and Quasi-Raw (in-house minimal pre-processing) methods, passed a visual quality check, and were subsequently affine registered to a common MNI152 template. The dataset has 3227 training scans and 757 test volume scans while maintaining similar age distribution in both sets. Each scan had dimensions of $160 \times 160 \times 192$ and was resampled with a voxel spacing of 1.2 mm. Figure 2 showcases examples from diverse sites within the dataset.

2 Methods

Our proposed model shown in Fig. 1 is a unified architecture that integrates a debiasing and diffeomorphic registration network and a fully connected prediction network to effectively capture brain aging. Drawing inspiration from the SynthMorph architecture [14], our registration network comprises an encoder and a decoder. The encoder extracts informative features from input images, while the decoder generates a deformation field that aligns the input image with a target image.

We utilized unsupervised learning-based registration frameworks to perform non-linear registration between a fixed 3D image (f) and a moving 3D image (m), which serves as our template image. The registration was performed using a CNN (h_θ) with parameters (θ), which outputs the deformation $(\varphi_\theta = h_\theta(m, f))$ for the image pair m, f. At each training iteration, the network h_θ was given a pair of images m, f, and parameters were updated by optimizing a loss function $L(\theta; m, f, \varphi_\theta)$ using stochastic gradient descent. The loss function included an image dissimilarity term $L_{dis}(m \circ \varphi_\theta, f)$, which penalized differences in appearance between the warped image $(m \circ \varphi_\theta)$ and the fixed image (f), and a regularization term $L_{reg}(\varphi)$, which encouraged smooth deformations. The loss function is given by:

$$L(\theta; m, f, \varphi_\theta) = L_{dis}(m \circ \varphi_\theta, f) + \lambda L_{reg}(\varphi_\theta)$$

where λ controlled the weighting of the terms.

The encoder consists of several three-dimensional convolutional blocks with a kernel size of $3 \times 3 \times 3$, followed by a Leaky ReLU activation function. Each convolutional block is followed by a max-pooling operation with a stride of 2, which reduces the resolution of the feature maps. The number of filters in the convolutional blocks gradually increases from 32 to 256 in the deepest layers.

The decoder consists of several upsampling blocks, each of which consists of a transposed convolutional layer with a kernel size of $4 \times 4 \times 4$ and a stride of 2, followed by a concatenation operation with the corresponding encoder block. The concatenated features are then passed through a three-dimensional convolutional block with a kernel size of $3 \times 3 \times 3$ and a Leaky ReLU activation function, which generates a deformation field. To achieve contrast invariance and robustness to anatomical variability, we employed a method inspired by SynthMorph, which allows us to overcome the limitations of relying solely on acquired training data. We start with the, we leveraged the SynthMorph model [14] where two paired 3D label maps denoted as sm, sf, are generated using the function $g_s(z) = sm, sf$ with a random seed z. Additionally, the function $g_I(sm, sf, z)$ is employed to synthesize two 3D intensity volumes, represented as m, f, based on the generated label maps sm, sf and the seed z. By training a registration network $h_\theta(m, f)$ using the generated images, we expose it to arbitrary contrasts and shapes at each iteration, thus removing the dependency on a specific MRI contrast. By synthesizing label maps first, we can use a similarity loss that measures label overlap independent of image contrast, thus eliminating the need for a cost function that depends on the contrasts being registered at that iteration. We use a stationary velocity field (SVF) $\mathbf{v}$ to parameterize the deformation field ϕ, which is integrated within the network to obtain a diffeomorphism that is invertible by design. We regularize ϕ using $L_{reg}(\phi) = 1/2 \|\nabla u\|^2$, where u is the displacement of the deformation field $\phi = I_d + u$. Figure 3 provides a visual representation of the non-linear registration process.

The age prediction network is a fully connected, single-layered network. The latent space from the registration network is flattened and input to the age prediction network.

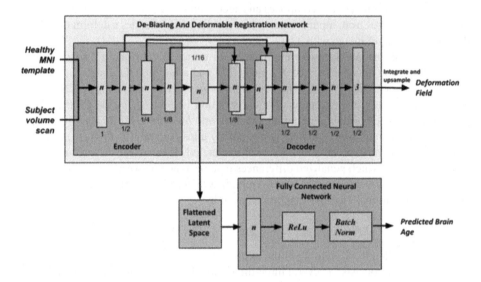

Fig. 1. Our architecture with $\phi_\theta = h_\theta(m, f)$ for deformable mapping and FCN for brain age prediction. The encoder features blocks with 3D convolutions ($n = 256$ filters) and LeakyReLU layers (0.2). Stride-2 convolutions reduce input resolution. In the decoder, each convolution is followed by an upsampling layer and a skip connection (long arrows). SVF v_θ is obtained at half resolution, yielding warp ϕ_θ after integration and upsampling. Kernel size: $3 \times 3 \times 3$. Final layer: $n = 3$ filters.

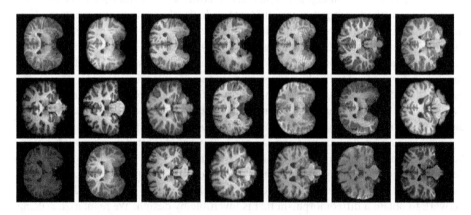

Fig. 2. MRI Images from diverse sites in the dataset, demonstrating the multi-site and heterogeneous nature of the MRI data used in this study

The dense FCN block is preceded by a dropout layer (0.2) with a ReLU activation function, followed by a batch normalization layer to predict the final brain age.

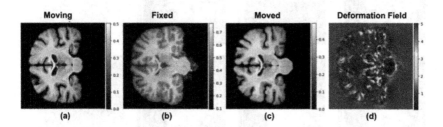

Fig. 3. Visualization of the non-linear registration process: (a) Template image, (b) Fixed image, (c) Moved image, and (d) Deformation field representing the spatial transformations applied to align the moving image with the fixed image.

3   Experiments and Results

3.1   Quantifying Debiasing

To evaluate the effectiveness of our debiasing method, we employed UMAP (Uniform Manifold Approximation and Projection) clustering on both the original MRI images and our feature space. Figure 5 showcases the 2D projections of the UMAP clustering applied to both the original image space and our derived feature space. These projections provide visual representations of the complex multidimensional relationships within the data, condensed into a 2D format for easier analysis and interpretation. We observed that in the original image space, distinct clusters could be observed, highlighting the presence of shared characteristics and patterns among images. Notably, certain clusters correspond to images acquired from specific sites, indicating the influence of site-related bias in the dataset. However, in the feature space, we observed a significant reduction in clustering based on the imaging site, indicating the successful removal of the site bias. Additionally, we conducted a quantitative evaluation of the clustering performance using three distinct metrics: Silhouette Score, Calinski-Harabasz Score, and Davies-Bouldin Score. The results in Table 1 show that the original image space exhibits well-defined and distinct clusters, as indicated by a positive Silhouette Score (0.178), high Calinski-Harabasz Score (20.162), and low Davies-Bouldin Score (2.518). However, after applying debiasing, the debiased space demonstrates poorer cluster separation, with a negative Silhouette Score (–0.100), lower Calinski-Harabasz Score (9.997), and higher Davies-Bouldin Score (9.983) (Fig. 4).

These findings provide empirical evidence for the effectiveness of our debiasing approach in mitigating the influence of site-related variability in brain MRI data. By mitigating the confounding effects of scanner variations, our model is better able to capture the true underlying patterns of brain development and maturation. This is crucial for improving the accuracy and reliability of predictions and interpretations in the field of brain development research.

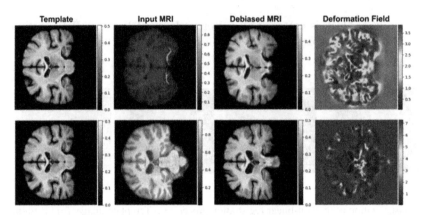

Fig. 4. Illustration of extreme examples showcasing the effectiveness of our de-biasing model in brain MRI. By leveraging our model, the intensity biases are successfully mitigated, resulting in the corresponding debiased outputs shown in the third column

Table 1. Quantitative evaluation of the clustering

	Silhouette	Calinski-Harabasz	Davies-bouldin
Input	0.178	20.162	2.518
Embeddings	–0.100	9.997	9.983

3.2   Assessing Generalizability

In this study, we aimed to address site bias and evaluate the generalizability of our method by conducting experiments with a reduced training set from the OpenBHB dataset. By focusing on site debiasing and assessing performance under data scarcity, we aimed to test the robustness and applicability of our predictive models in real-world scenarios. By including samples from multiple sites in the reduced training dataset, we ensured that the models could learn representative features and patterns without being biased toward a specific imaging site. We assessed the impact of training size on our model and the state-of-the-art ResNet baseline [16], as shown in Fig. 6. Increasing the training size from 100 to 500 consistently improved Mean Absolute Error (MAE), Mean Squared Error (MSE), and coefficient of determination (R2) for both models. Our model consistently outperformed ResNet, demonstrating superior predictive accuracy and reduced errors. Notably, our model achieved lower MAE and MSE values compared to ResNet, with the performance gap widening as the training size increased. Remarkably, as the training set size is expanded to 3000 as shown in Table 2, our model demonstrates substantial enhancements in performance, showcasing the lowest Mean Absolute Error (MAE) and Mean Squared Error (MSE) values. Moreover, our model consistently maintains higher R-squared (R2) values, indicating a superior alignment with the data. This analysis provides valuable insights into the efficacy of our model in mitigating the influence of scanner-related biases and effectively handling the increased heterogeneity in the dataset. In contrast, ResNet [16] exhibited lower performance, indi-

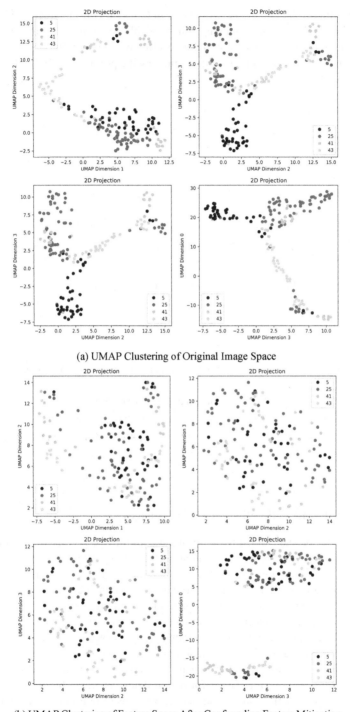

(a) UMAP Clustering of Original Image Space

(b) UMAP Clustering of Feature Space After Confounding Factors Mitigation

Fig. 5. Visualization of Debiasing Effect using UMAP Clustering in Brain MRI Data

cating its inability to handle the heterogeneity in the data. Our method effectively captures age-related information, achieving commendable performance as indicated by the mean absolute error metric. This highlights its effectiveness in extracting relevant age-related features while accounting for biases, making it a promising solution for accurate brain age prediction (Fig. 7).

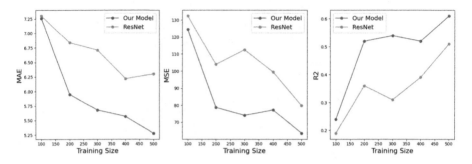

Fig. 6. Comparison of Performance Metrics between "Our Model" and ResNet for Different Training Set Sizes

Table 2. Comparison of Prediction Performance on OpenBHB dataset: Our Model vs.ResNet

	No. of Training Samples	MAE	MSE	R2
ResNet	3000	9.303	145.360	0.107
Our model	3000	**4.554**	**38.919**	**0.806**

3.3 Localized Scale Estimation on MNIST Images

In this study, our primary objective is to investigate the age-predictive capabilities of our neural network architecture by simulating the scaling effect observed in cortical thinning and ventricular enlargement in T1-weighted (T1w) MRI scans. To achieve this, we employ a random scaling procedure on MNIST images, which spans a range of 0.7 to 1.3, serving as a surrogate for anatomical scaling variations. The predicted scale factor derived from our network's output serves as an indicative measure of age prediction. We perform this investigation individually on each of the ten digits (0–9) as the template. To facilitate the age prediction process, we input the scaled image along with the corresponding template into our neural network. The output of our network then estimates the scale factor. The deformation fields generated by our network successfully capture the spatial contractions and expansions responsible for accomplishing the downstream task of scale prediction. The findings depicted in Fig. 8 unequivocally

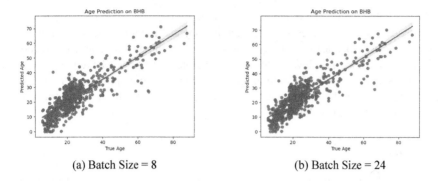

(a) Batch Size = 8   (b) Batch Size = 24

Fig. 7. Comparative Scatter Plots of Predicted Age vs. Actual Age for Different Batch Sizes

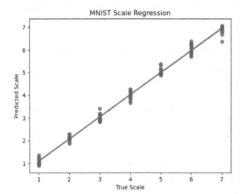

Digits	MAE	MSE	R2
0	0.020	0.001	0.978
1	0.032	0.002	0.944
2	0.021	0.001	0.977
3	0.025	0.001	0.965
4	0.022	0.001	0.975
5	0.017	0.000	0.987
6	0.021	0.001	0.977
7	0.023	0.001	0.972
8	0.019	0.001	0.980
9	0.020	0.001	0.979

Fig. 8. The Scatter plot depicting the scale estimation results on MNIST Images. Each data point represents an image from the MNIST dataset, with the x-axis indicating the true scale and the y-axis representing the estimated scale. The table displays the Mean Absolute Error (MAE), Mean Squared Error (MSE), and R-squared (R2) values.

demonstrate the commendable accuracy exhibited by our network in accurately predicting the scale factor for each digit, thus substantiating its inherent potential as a robust predictor of anatomical aging with remarkable reliability.

This simple and fast proof-of-concept experiment demonstrates the ability of our network to capture subtle changes in anatomical structures and predict age-related changes.

4   Conclusion

Our study proposed a novel deep learning framework for the reliable estimation of brain age, incorporating a debiasing component to mitigate the influence of confounding factors. Debiasing in MRI is crucial for the accurate and unbiased interpretation of the data. It helps reduce the potential confounding effects and enables more meaningful comparisons and analyses across different subjects, populations, or imaging sites. The integration of debiasing techniques has improved the generalizability and robustness of our framework, allowing for more accurate and unbiased predictions across diverse populations. Our findings highlight the potential of our approach for addressing the challenges of site bias and enhancing the clinical utility of brain age estimation in applications such as early detection of neurodegenerative disorders.

References

1. Baecker, L., et al.: Brain age prediction: a comparison between machine learning models using region-and voxel-based morphometric data. Hum. Brain Mapp. **42**(8), 2332–2346 (2021)
2. Beheshti, I., Ganaie, M.A., Paliwal, V., Rastogi, A., Razzak, I., Tanveer, M.: Predicting brain age using machine learning algorithms: a comprehensive evaluation. IEEE J. Biomed. Health Inform. **26**, 1432–1440 (2021)
3. Cetin Karayumak, S., Kubicki, M., Rathi, Y.: Harmonizing diffusion MRI data across magnetic field strengths. In: Frangi, A.F., Schnabel, J.A., Davatzikos, C., Alberola-López, C., Fichtinger, G. (eds.) MICCAI 2018. LNCS, vol. 11072, pp. 116–124. Springer, Cham (2018). https://doi.org/10.1007/978-3-030-00931-1_14
4. Cheng, J., et al.: Brain age estimation from MRI using cascade networks with ranking loss. IEEE Trans. Med. Imaging **40**, 3400–3412 (2021)
5. Cherubini, A., Caligiuri, M.E., Péran, P., Sabatini, U., Cosentino, C., Amato, F.: Importance of multimodal MRI in characterizing brain tissue and its potential application for individual age prediction. IEEE J. Biomed. Health Inform. **20**, 1232–1239 (2016)
6. Cole, J.H., et al.: Predicting brain age with deep learning from raw imaging data results in a reliable and heritable biomarker. Neuroimage **163**, 115–124 (2016)
7. Cole, J.H., et al.: Brain age predicts mortality. Mol. Psych. **23**, 1385–1392 (2017)
8. Dufumier, B., Grigis, A., Victor, J., Ambroise, C., Frouin, V., Duchesnay, E.: Openbhb: a large-scale multi-site brain mri data-set for age prediction and debiasing. NeuroImage **263** (2022)
9. de Fátima Machado Dias, M., de Carvalho, P., Duarte, J.V., Castelo-Branco, M.: Deformation fields: a new source of information to predict brain age. J. Neural Eng. **19** (2022)
10. Fortin, J.P., et al.: Harmonization of multi-site diffusion tensor imaging data. Neuroimage **161**, 149–170 (2017)
11. Franke, K., Ziegler, G., Klöppel, S., Gaser, C., Initiative, A.D.N., et al.: Estimating the age of healthy subjects from t1-weighted MRI scans using kernel methods: exploring the influence of various parameters. Neuroimage **50**(3), 883–892 (2010)
12. Fu, J., Tzortzakakis, A., Barroso, J., Westman, E., Ferreira, D., Moreno, R.: Generative aging of brain images with diffeomorphic registration. ArXiv abs/ arXiv: 2205.15607 (2022)
13. Ganaie, M.A., Tanveer, M., Beheshti, I.: Brain age prediction with improved least squares twin svr. IEEE J. Biomed. Health Inform. **27**, 1661–1669 (2022)
14. Hoffmann, M., Billot, B., Greve, D.N., Iglesias, J.E., Fischl, B., Dalca, A.V.: Synthmorph: learning contrast-invariant registration without acquired images. IEEE Trans. Med. Imaging **41**(3), 543–558 (2021)
15. Jonsson, B.A., et al.: Brain age prediction using deep learning uncovers associated sequence variants. Nat. Commun. **10** (2019)
16. Jónsson, B.A., et al.: Brain age prediction using deep learning uncovers associated sequence variants. Nat. Commun. **10**(1), 1–10 (2019)

17. Kassani, P.H., Gossmann, A., Ping Wang, Y.: Multimodal sparse classifier for adolescent brain age prediction. IEEE J. Biomed. Health Inform. **24**, 336–344 (2019)
18. Kaufmann, T., et al.: Common brain disorders are associated with heritable patterns of apparent aging of the brain. Nat. Neurosci. **22**(10), 1617–1623 (2019)
19. Koutsouleris, N., et al.: Accelerated brain aging in schizophrenia and beyond: a neuroanatomical marker of psychiatric disorders. Schizophr. Bull. **40**(5), 1140–1153 (2014)
20. Liem, F., et al.: Predicting brain-age from multimodal imaging data captures cognitive impairment. Neuroimage **148**, 179–188 (2017)
21. Mishra, S., Beheshti, I., Khanna, P.: A review of neuroimaging-driven brain age estimation for identification of brain disorders and health conditions. IEEE Rev. Biomed. Eng. **16**, 371–385 (2021)
22. Ning, L., et al.: Muti-shell diffusion MRI harmonisation and enhancement challenge (MUSHAC): progress and results. In: Bonet-Carne, E., Grussu, F., Ning, L., Sepehrband, F., Tax, C.M.W. (eds.) MICCAI 2019. MV, pp. 217–224. Springer, Cham (2019). https://doi.org/10.1007/978-3-030-05831-9_18
23. Salih, A., et al.: A new scheme for the assessment of the robustness of explainable methods applied to brain age estimation. In: 2021 IEEE 34th International Symposium on Computer-Based Medical Systems (CBMS), pp. 492–497. IEEE (2021)
24. Valizadeh, S., Hänggi, J., Mérillat, S., Jäncke, L.: Age prediction on the basis of brain anatomical measures. Hum. Brain Mapp. **38**(2), 997–1008 (2017)
25. Xiong, M., Lin, L., Jin, Y., Kang, W., Wu, S., Sun, S.: Comparison of machine learning models for brain age prediction using six imaging modalities on middle-aged and older adults. Sensors (Basel, Switzerland) **23** (2023)
26. Zavaliangos-Petropulu, A., et al.: Diffusion MRI indices and their relation to cognitive impairment in brain aging: the updated multi-protocol approach in adni3. Front. Neuroinform. **13**, 2 (2019)

Self-supervised Landmark Learning with Deformation Reconstruction and Cross-Subject Consistency Objectives

Chun-Hung Chao[✉] and Marc Niethammer

University of North Carolina at Chapel Hill, Chapel Hill, USA
chchao@cs.unc.edu

Abstract. A Point Distribution Model (PDM) is the basis of a Statistical Shape Model (SSM) that relies on a set of landmark points to represent a shape and characterize the shape variation. In this work, we present a self-supervised approach to extract landmark points from a given registration model for the PDMs. Based on the assumption that the landmarks are the points that have the most influence on registration, existing works learn a point-based registration model with a small number of points to estimate the landmark points that influence the deformation the most. However, such approaches assume that the deformation can be captured by point-based registration and quality landmarks can be learned solely with the deformation capturing objective. We argue that data with complicated deformations can not easily be modeled with point-based registration when only a limited number of points is used to extract influential landmark points. Further, landmark consistency is not assured in existing approaches In contrast, we propose to extract landmarks based on a given registration model, which is tailored for the target data, so we can obtain more accurate correspondences. Secondly, to establish the anatomical consistency of the predicted landmarks, we introduce a landmark discovery loss to explicitly encourage the model to predict the landmarks that are anatomically consistent across subjects. We conduct experiments on an osteoarthritis progression prediction task and show our method outperforms existing image-based and point-based approaches.

Keywords: Landmark proposal · Image registration · Self-supervised learning

1 Introduction

A Point Distribution Model (PDM) is an important approach to describe shape variations for biomedical applications [8,9,11]. PDMs rely on a set of landmark points (hereafter "landmarks") that usually correspond to certain anatomical structures to represent the geometry of each shape instance. As designing landmarks for unseen data or tasks and annotating them is labor intensive, many

I. Rekik et al. (Eds.): PRIME 2023, LNCS 14277, pp. 70–82, 2023.
https://doi.org/10.1007/978-3-031-46005-0_7

works have been proposed to automatically identify or place the landmarks [2,3,12].

To extract the landmarks for PDMs, conventional approaches require prior knowledge of the shape-of-interest or point-of-interest and rely on segmentation, meshing, or other pre-processing in addition to the image itself to provide guidance for landmark localization. Cates et al. [5] proposed a way to extract landmarks by optimizing a set of surface points with the objective of simultaneously maximizing geometric accuracy and statistical simplicity. Similarly, for left atrium modeling in ShapeWorks [4], the binary segmentation of the shape-of-interest is also needed to find landmarks. Agrawal et al. [1] proposed a deep-learning approach based on a supervised Siamese training paradigm which is the basis of existing landmarks localization approaches [4,5]. To minimize pre-processing steps, such as region-of-interest delineation, DeepSSM [2] directly trains a network to predict landmarks under a supervised learning setting with the labels coming from conventional PDM landmark localization methods. As the above approaches require additional labels for supervised learning, the recent work by Bhalodia et al. [3] presented a self-supervised learning approach to regress landmarks by learning a point-based image registration model. This method assumes that its point-based parametric registration using only a limited number of points can lead to accurate registration. Therefore it can not capture complex deformations. Using a toy example with this approach [3] (Fig. 1) to find 30 corresponding control point pairs to register a 2D image pair that is deformed by a synthesized stationary velocity field, we observe that a correspondence error exists among the found optimal point pairs for registration. Hence, without making assumptions of which registration model is the best fit for the data, we instead treat the landmark estimation in a knowledge distillation manner and extract the points that are most crucial to the deformation and their correspondences based on a *given* registration model.

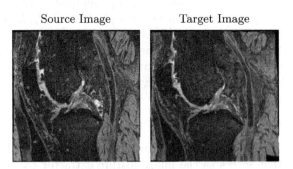

Source Image   Target Image

Fig. 1. Toy example using the approach by Bhalodia et al. [3] to find landmarks on a synthesized image pair. Red crosses on the target image indicate the found landmarks; red crosses on the source image indicate the found corresponding landmarks on the source image; and the cyan crosses denote the gold-standard correspondences for the found landmarks on the target image. (Color figure online)

Moreover, the discovered landmarks should not only be important to the deformation, but should also consistently appear on anatomically corresponding locations across the image population, i.e., they should exhibit anatomical consistency. Thus, we design a landmark discovery loss that minimizes the distance between the same landmarks from a triplet of images after mapping them to a common coordinate to enforce the consistency of our landmark predictions. Additionally, since there are a lot of different deforming parts in the data with complex deformations, the model needs to generate a sufficient number of landmarks to be able to select the best points to describe the deformation. As traditional point proposal architectures, e.g., based on a multilayer perceptron (MLP) [2,3] or a heatmap [14,15], require a significant amount of memory when adopted for applications in 3D medical images, we propose to use a grid-based architecture to reduce computational resource consumption.

Contributions: (1) We design a framework that extracts landmarks in a registration-model-agnostic manner, so it can be applied to data that requires state-of-the-art registrations rather than using simple point-based registration models with a limited number of control points. (2) We introduce a landmark discovery loss that enforces anatomical consistency between the landmarks. (3) We demonstrate the effectiveness of our framework in proposing landmarks to predict osteoarthritis disease progression based on the challenging Osteoarthritis Initiative (OAI) data set.

2   Methodology

2.1   Overview

Given three images $\{I_a, I_b, I_c\}$ sampled from a set of training images, we feed them separately into our point proposal network to obtain three sets of landmark predictions, $\{P_a, P_b, P_c\}$. Along with the landmark predictions, we also perform image registration on the image pairs (I_c, I_a) and (I_c, I_b) with the given registration model and obtain transformation fields Φ_{ca}^{-1} and Φ_{cb}^{-1}. Based on the landmark predictions and the transformation fields, we compute the deformation reconstruction loss $\mathcal{L}_{recon}$ and landmark discovery loss $\mathcal{L}_d$ to train our point proposal network. Figure 2 gives an overview of our framework.

2.2   Point Proposal Network

Our point proposal network consists of two modules: (1) a convolutional neural network (CNN) that serves as the image feature extractor ψ_f and (2) a point proposal head ψ_p that predicts landmark coordinates from the extracted image features. Given a 3D image I of size $D \times H \times W$, the image feature extractor ψ_f outputs features $f \in \mathbb{R}^{(d \times h \times w) \times c}$ of image I. Let $G_i \in \mathbb{R}^3$ denote the coordinate of the i-th grid point on a regular grid with $N = d \times h \times w$ grid points and uniform spacing δ such that $[D, H, W]^T = \delta[d, h, w]^T$. Our grid-based point

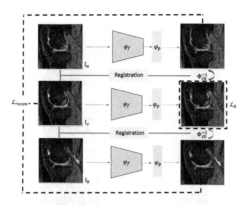

Fig. 2. Overview of our framework. Our framework takes three images I_a, I_b, and I_c as input. Through feature extractor ψ_f and point-proposal head ψ_p, our framework predicts a set of landmarks on each image. Leveraging the transformation field Φ^{-1}, we compute the deformation reconstruction loss $\mathcal{L}_{recon}$ and map all the landmarks to I_c to compute the landmark discovery loss $\mathcal{L}_d$.

proposal head $\psi_p : \mathbb{R}^c \rightarrow \mathbb{R}^3$ predicts a displacement vector for each grid point to produce the coordinate of the i-th landmark, p_i:

$$p_i = \psi_p(f_i) + G_i, \tag{1}$$
$$f = \psi_f(I), \tag{2}$$

where $f = \{f_1, f_2, \cdots, f_n\}$ denotes all predicted features at n different locations, f_i is the i-th feature, and all the landmark predictions of image I are:

$$P = \{p_i | i \in \mathbb{Z}^+, 1 \le i \le N\}. \tag{3}$$

2.3 Landmark Discovery Loss

Based on the assumption that a landmark point is a point that can be consistently identified on most images in a population of images, we propose a triplet loss to encourage the point proposal network to discover such consistent landmark points. In other words, we want the landmarks proposed by our model to be anatomically corresponding across images. Achieving the landmark consistency goal requires accurate correspondences of each landmark point between images. Although, in the most ideal scenario, accurate landmark correspondences can be learned simultaneously in a multi-task learning setting where our model jointly learns to perform image registration and landmark prediction, practically this multi-task learning setting often leads to inexact landmark correspondences due to the limited expressive capabilities of landmark-based registration when only a small number of landmarks are extracted. Hence, we advocate decoupling

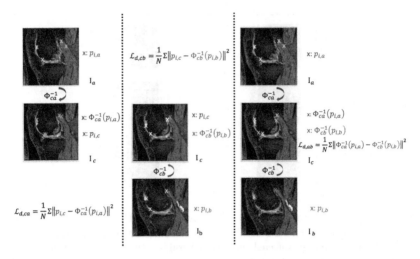

Fig. 3. Graphical Illustration of landmark discovery loss. The red crosses, green crosses, and blue crosses are the detected landmarks on image I_a, I_b, and I_c. With given transformation field Φ^{-1}, we can map the red crosses and the blue crosses to the coordinate system of I_b, where we denote the mapped landmarks with the magenta and cyan crosses and compute landmark discovery loss terms $\mathcal{L}_{d,ab}$, $\mathcal{L}_{d,ca}$, and $\mathcal{L}_{d,cb}$. (Color figure online)

the registration task from the landmark prediction task and leverage provided image registration models to obtain landmark correspondences between images. As there is no constraint on the choice for the registration model as long as it can provide a high quality transformation field for a pair of images, we can choose the model that is best for our data, e.g., optimization-based fluid-based registration models or deep-learning multi-step registration models that normally have better registration performance [18,19].

Let ψ_{reg} denote the given registration model from which we obtain transformation fields $\Phi_{ca}^{-1} = \psi_{reg}(I_c, I_a)$ and $\Phi_{cb}^{-1} = \psi_{reg}(I_c, I_b)$, where Φ_{ca}^{-1} is the map that warps image I_a to image I_c defined in the coordinate system of I_c. For the landmark predictions of I_a, P_a, and the landmark predictions of I_b, P_b, if they are anatomically equivalent, their corresponding points on I_c should be close to each other. From this idea, we can define our loss:

$$\mathcal{L}_{d,ab} = \frac{1}{N} \sum_{i=1}^{N} \|\Phi_{ca}^{-1}(p_{i,a}) - \Phi_{cb}^{-1}(p_{i,b})\|^2, \tag{4}$$

where $p_{i,a}$ is the i-th landmark in P_a and $p_{i,b}$ is the i-th landmark in P_b. To further exploit the input image triplet and the two transformation fields, Φ_{ca}^{-1} and Φ_{cb}^{-1}, we can use P_c to define two extra terms:

$$\mathcal{L}_{d,ca} = \frac{1}{N} \sum_{i=1}^{N} \|p_{i,c} - \Phi_{ca}^{-1}(p_{i,a})\|^2, \tag{5}$$

$$\mathcal{L}_{d,cb} = \frac{1}{N} \sum_{i=1}^{N} \|p_{i,c} - \Phi_{cb}^{-1}(p_{i,b})\|^2, \tag{6}$$

where $p_{i,c}$ is the i-th landmark in P_c. Then we define our complete landmark discovery loss as:

$$\mathcal{L}_d = \mathcal{L}_{d,ab} + \mathcal{L}_{d,ca} + \mathcal{L}_{d,cb}. \tag{7}$$

Figure 3 graphically illustrates each term in the landmark discovery loss.

Although we may also be able to encourage one-directional landmark consistency with one image pair and one transformation field by using the loss

$$\frac{1}{N} \sum_{i=1}^{N} \|p_{i,a} - \Phi_{ab}^{-1}(p_{i,b})\|^2, \tag{8}$$

we hypothesize that using a triplet of images and our formulation of $\mathcal{L}_d$ is more symmetric and provides more regularity with an acceptable trade-off of performing image registration on one extra pair of images.

2.4 Deformation Reconstruction Loss

In addition to landmark consistency, another important attribute for the landmarks is that they are placed on anatomical locations that are able to characterize the deformation as well as possible and can thereby serve as a good structure representation for the PDM. In fact, if we solely rely on the landmark discovery loss $\mathcal{L}_d$ as our training loss, the point proposal network may degenerate to placing all the landmarks on a single location since it can easily minimize $\mathcal{L}_d$ in this manner. To ensure the quality of landmark distribution and motivate the point proposal network to find the points that are crucial towards characterizing the deformation, we introduce a deformation reconstruction loss that penalizes the difference between the original deformation field and the deformation field reconstructed from the landmarks. When reconstructing a dense deformation field from sparse points, a vital design decision to make is the choice of the interpolation method. Common choices in biomedical image registration, like B-splines [16] or thin plate splines [7], do not fit well for our task since the former only work for regular grid points, which are not placed according to anatomical information, and the latter involves solving the inverse of a $(N + 4) \times (N + 4)$ matrix and becomes computationally costly when we have more landmarks, i.e., a larger N. Thus, we propose using Nadaraya-Watson interpolation:

$$\tilde{D}_{ab}^{-1}(\mathbf{x}) = \frac{\sum_i K(\mathbf{x}, \mathbf{p}_{i,b})(\mathbf{p}_{i,a} - \mathbf{p}_{i,b})}{\sum_i K(\mathbf{x}, \mathbf{p}_{i,b})}, \tag{9}$$

where $\tilde{D}_{ab}^{-1}$ is the reconstructed deformation field, $\mathbf{x}$ is the location where we want to evaluate the displacement field in the I_b space, and $K(\cdot, \cdot)$ is the kernel function:

$$K(\mathbf{x}, \mathbf{p}) = e^{-\frac{\|\mathbf{x}-\mathbf{p}\|^2}{2\sigma^2}}. \tag{10}$$

The reconstructed transformation field $\tilde{\Phi}_{ab}^{-1}$ can then be obtained by adding the identity map Id to the reconstructed displacement field:

$$\tilde{\Phi}_{ab}^{-1} = \tilde{D}_{ab}^{-1} + \text{Id}. \tag{11}$$

With the reconstructed transformation field, we should be able to obtain a warped source image that is similar to the target image:

$$I_a \circ \tilde{\Phi}_{ab}^{-1} \approx I_a \circ \Phi_{ab}^{-1} \approx I_b. \tag{12}$$

Thus, we define the deformation reconstruction loss for the image triplet as:

$$\mathcal{L}_{recon} = MSE(I_a \circ \tilde{\Phi}_{ac}^{-1}, I_c) + MSE(I_b \circ \tilde{\Phi}_{bc}^{-1}, I_c) \tag{13}$$

where $MSE(\cdot)$ is the mean squared error. Although we can compute the difference with $MSE(\tilde{\Phi}_{ac}^{-1}, \Phi_{ac}^{-1})$, using the image similarity loss reflects the alignment quality between anatomical structure better and directly minimizing the mean squared error between $\tilde{\Phi}_{ac}^{-1}$ and Φ_{ac}^{-1} does not guarantee the alignment of the foreground.

2.5   Complete Training Loss

We train our model by combining the landmark discovery loss and the deformation reconstruction loss:

$$\mathcal{L} = \lambda_d \mathcal{L}_d + \lambda_{recon} \mathcal{L}_{recon}, \tag{14}$$

where $\lambda_d > 0$ and $\lambda_{recon} > 0$ are the hyper-parameters which denote the weight of each individual loss.

3   Experimental Results

3.1   Experimental Setting

Implementation Details. We modified DenseNet121 [13] as our backbone for the feature extractor in the point proposal network. The feature extractor outputs a feature map corresponding to a regular grid of size $10 \times 24 \times 24$, which gives us $5,760$ landmark predictions for each image. For the external registration model, we use the 4 stages of GradICON [19] to obtain the transformation fields. We fixed our σ in the kernel function of Nadaraya-Watson interpolation at 3 mm. λ_d and λ_{recon} are set to be 0.005 and 0.05 respectively. The network was trained with an ADAM optimizer for 35 epochs, with the learning rate set to 0.001 and a learning rate scheduler that decreases the learning rate by 1% after each epoch. The batch size was set to 4 throughout the training. We implemented the entire network and the Nadaraya-Wastson interpolation module with PyTorch and PyKeops [6]. The training was done on one NVIDIA RTX A6000 GPU.

Dataset. We build our OA progression dataset based on the train-val-test patient split of the OA registration dataset in AVSM [18]. After filtering out the patients without progression labels, we obtain 474 subjects for training, 20 for validation, and 63 for testing. We determine OA progression based on the often-used Kellgren and Lawrence grading system (KLG) which classifies the OA severity in clinical practice by checking if the KLG score increases. Among the 63 subjects in the testing set, 39 subjects are non-progressive and the rest are progressive.

Evaluation Metrics. For the classification tasks in our experiments, we report the accuracy and the average precision (AP) scores. While not every baseline predicts an ordered landmark set, we use two metrics, one for both ordered and non-ordered landmark sets and another one solely for ordered landmark sets, to evaluate the landmark consistency. For both consistency metrics, we first randomly sample a third image from a different subject for each pair of input images and map the detected landmarks on both input images in each pair to the sampled third image using an oracle registration model that provides an oracle transformation map Φ^{-1}. As the two landmark sets are mapped to the third image and form two point clouds in a common coordinate system, we use the mean symmetric Chamfer distance d_{CD} of the two landmark sets:

$$\frac{1}{2N}\left(\sum_{i=1}^{N}\min_{j=1,\ldots,N}\|\Phi_{ca}^{-1}(p_{i,a}) - \Phi_{cb}^{-1}(p_{j,b})\|_2 + \sum_{i=1}^{N}\min_{j=1,\ldots,N}\|\Phi_{cb}^{-1}(p_{i,b}) - \Phi_{ca}^{-1}(p_{j,a})\|_2\right)$$

for the ordered and non-ordered landmark predictions. Specifically for the ordered landmark sets, we can further evaluate the consistency error using

$$\frac{1}{N}\sum_{i=1}^{N}\|\Phi_{ca}^{-1}(p_{i,a}) - \Phi_{cb}^{-1}(p_{i,b})\|_2 .$$

3.2 OA Progression Prediction

Table 1. Quantitative results of OA progression prediction.

		DenseNet	GraphRegNet	Bhalodia et al	Ours w/o $\mathcal{L}_d$	Ours
Acc		65.08%	58.73%	61.90%	60.32%	68.25%
AP		54.10%	37.55%	37.86%	43.28%	61.00%
Chamfer Dist. (mm)		-	7.38 ± 1.77	7.71 ± 2.45	4.71 ± 0.46	2.41 ± 0.47
Ordered	X	-	-	2.46 ± 0.76	3.57 ± 1.56	1.11 ± 0.33
Consist.	Y	-	-	3.21 ± 1.37	3.48 ± 1.27	0.95 ± 0.35
Error	Z	-	-	2.09 ± 0.84	3.42 ± 0.90	1.03 ± 0.33
(mm)	All	-	-	5.33 ± 1.76	7.10 ± 1.99	2.14 ± 0.65

Osteoarthritis (OA) is a joint disease that develops slowly over the years. To study the effectiveness of the proposed landmarks, we choose knee OA progression prediction as our downstream task. Given the first two knee Magnetic Resonance (MR) scans separated by 12 months, our goal is to correctly predict if OA will get worse within the next 72 months. For the OA progression prediction task, our model first detects two sets of estimated landmarks on the two initial scans. Then we combine and process the landmarks across patients, which are ordered, by generalized Procrustes analysis and train a linear distance-weighted discrimination (DWD) classification model with the proposed points from the training set to predict whether OA progression will occur.

In order to compare the results, we use one image-based and two point-based methods as our baselines. For the image-based baseline, we train a 3D DenseNet121 to predict the progression directly with the two given scans using a binary cross entropy loss. The first point-based baseline is GraphRegNet [10], which performs registration using the handcrafted Forstner keypoints. We combine the detected Förstner keypoints on the second input scan and their corresponding points on the first input scan, which are obtained with the transformation field estimated by GraphRegNet, to form the point representation. The second point-based baseline is the work done by Bhalodia et al. [3]. Bhalodia et al. proposed to train a network to predict landmarks on the two input scans by learning a point-based registration model with regularization on the coefficients of the thin-plate spline interpolation. Due to the memory intensive nature of the work by Bhalodia et al., this baseline only predicts 152 landmarks so it can fit in the GPU we used. We process the point representation of the baselines using the same protocol we used to process the landmarks for our approach. Ordered landmarks are processed with generalized Procrustes analysis.

Table 1 shows the quantitative OA progression prediction results. Training a DenseNet classifier directly from images yields 65.08% in accuracy and 54.10% in average precision and serves as a strong baseline for OA progression prediction. Our method produces 68.25% in accuracy and 61.00% in average precision. This shows that our method successfully extracts the disease-related information and is an efficient representation, as each input image is characterized using $5,760$ landmarks. With handcrafted Förstner keypoints, GraphRegNet produces the lowest performance as the keypoints are originally designed for lung CT and might not be suitable for knee MR. Due to memory constraints, the approach by Bhalodia et al. can only predict 152 landmarks and yields an average precision score of only 37.86%, which is possibly due to the fact that the number of landmarks insufficient to characterize images pairs with complex deformations. In fact, for our method with merely 152 landmarks, it could only reach AP of 38.4%. We observe that the Chamfer landmark distance consistency evaluation is correlated with the average precision score. In fact, by comparing the results between our method with and without $\mathcal{L}_d$, we can conclude it is advantageous to enforce landmark consistency when building the point representation.

3.3   Qualitative Results

In this section, we visualize the top influential landmarks and their gradient activation map to provide visual interpretations for the landmark predictions.

Gradient Activation Map. We adopt a strategy similar to GradCAM [17] by computing the gradient activation using the magnitude of $\frac{\partial \|\psi_p(f_i)\|^2}{\partial I(x)}$ to highlight the voxels that have the greatest impact on the landmark predictions. From Fig. 4, we can see that the gradient responses primarily occur on local structures near the landmarks.

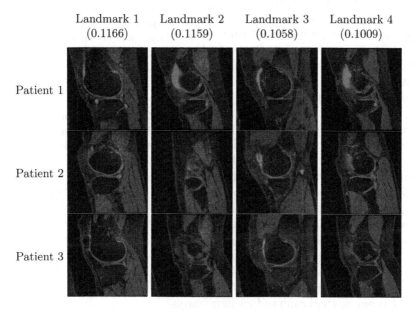

Landmark 1 (0.1166)   Landmark 2 (0.1159)   Landmark 3 (0.1058)   Landmark 4 (0.1009)

Patient 1

Patient 2

Patient 3

Fig. 4. Qualitative results of landmark predictions. The intensity of the purple indicates the magnitude of the gradient activation. The red crosses indicate the landmarks. The numbers in the parentheses are the corresponding DWD coefficient magnitudes. (Color figure online)

Top Influential Landmarks. As we use linear DWD for progression prediction, we can quantify the importance of each landmark by comparing the sum of the weights operating on each landmark value, which indicates the landmark influence for identifying a positive case. Figure 5 shows the weight distribution of our trained DWD model and Fig. 4 shows the landmarks randomly sampled from the top twenty influential landmarks from different patients. We can observe that the predicted landmarks are anatomically consistent across different patients. Critically, since these landmarks are important factors for the linear DWD model, these landmarks have the potential to serve as image markers for OA progression prediction.

In addition, we discuss the relationship between the number of landmarks and the classification performance (shown in Table2). We trained DWD using different numbers of top influential landmarks. Using the top 50 landmarks yields the average precision value of 51.8%, and increasing the number of landmarks generally has a positive effect on the classification performance. It is worth noticing that when using 152 landmarks (same number as Bhalodia et al.), our method outperforms Bhalodia et al. with a large margin (55.6% vs 37.9%). This shows that our method can produce more meaningful landmarks even with a limited number of landmarks.

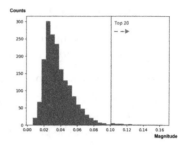

Fig. 5. Histogram of the DWD coefficient weights and occurrence frequencies. The few but important (larger weight) landmarks are ideal image markers for OA progression prediction.

Table 2. Relationship between the number of landmarks and the average precision of classification

N of landmarks	AP (%)
50	51.8
150	56.3
152	57.2
250	55.6
550	57.9
1250	61.0

4   Conclusion

In this work, we presented a learning-based landmark proposal framework. With our deformation reconstruction and consistency objectives, the model learns to predict the points that not only characterize the deformation well but also are anatomically consistent across patients and constitute landmarks points. In our experiments on OA progression prediction, our method achieves the best prediction performance as well as the lowest consistency error. Based on the quantitative and qualitative results, we demonstrated that our proposed landmarks can serve as point representations of images and can potentially be used to discover prognostic image markers for early disease diagnosis.

Acknowledgements. This work was supported by NIH grants 1R01AR072013 and R41MH118845. The work expresses the views of the authors, not of NIH. The knee imaging data were obtained from the controlled access datasets distributed from the Osteoarthritis Initiative (OAI), a data repository housed within the NIMH Data Archive. OAI is a collaborative informatics system created by NIMH and NIAMS to provide a worldwide resource for biomarker identification, scientific investigation and OA drug development. Dataset identifier: NIMH Data Archive Collection ID: 2343.

References

1. Agrawal, P., Whitaker, R.T., Elhabian, S.Y.: Learning deep features for shape correspondence with domain invariance. arXiv preprint arXiv:2102.10493 (2021)
2. Bhalodia, R., Elhabian, S.Y., Kavan, L., Whitaker, R.T.: DeepSSM: a deep learning framework for statistical shape modeling from raw images. In: Reuter, M., Wachinger, C., Lombaert, H., Paniagua, B., Lüthi, M., Egger, B. (eds.) ShapeMI 2018. LNCS, vol. 11167, pp. 244–257. Springer, Cham (2018). https://doi.org/10.1007/978-3-030-04747-4_23
3. Bhalodia, R., Kavan, L., Whitaker, R.T.: Self-supervised discovery of anatomical shape landmarks. In: MICCAI 2020. LNCS, vol. 12264, pp. 627–638. Springer, Cham (2020). https://doi.org/10.1007/978-3-030-59719-1_61
4. Cates, J., Elhabian, S., Whitaker, R.: ShapeWorks: particle-based shape correspondence and visualization software. In: Statistical Shape and Deformation Analysis, pp. 257–298. Elsevier (2017)
5. Cates, J., Fletcher, P.T., Styner, M., Shenton, M., Whitaker, R.: Shape modeling and analysis with entropy-based particle systems. In: Karssemeijer, N., Lelieveldt, B. (eds.) IPMI 2007. LNCS, vol. 4584, pp. 333–345. Springer, Heidelberg (2007). https://doi.org/10.1007/978-3-540-73273-0_28
6. Charlier, B., Feydy, J., Glaunes, J.A., Collin, F.D., Durif, G.: Kernel operations on the GPU, with Autodiff, without memory overflows. J. Mach. Learn. Res. **22**(1), 3457–3462 (2021)
7. Duchon, J.: Splines minimizing rotation-invariant semi-norms in Sobolev spaces. In: Schempp, W., Zeller, K. (eds.) Constructive Theory of Functions of Several Variables. Lecture Notes in Mathematics, vol. 571, pp. 85–100. Springer, Heidelberg (1977). https://doi.org/10.1007/BFb0086566
8. Gardner, G., Morris, A., Higuchi, K., MacLeod, R., Cates, J.: A point-correspondence approach to describing the distribution of image features on anatomical surfaces, with application to atrial fibrillation. In: 2013 IEEE 10th International Symposium on Biomedical Imaging, pp. 226–229. IEEE (2013)
9. Gerig, G., Styner, M., Jones, D., Weinberger, D., Lieberman, J.: Shape analysis of brain ventricles using SPHARM. In: Proceedings IEEE Workshop on Mathematical Methods in Biomedical Image Analysis, MMBIA 2001, pp. 171–178. IEEE (2001)
10. Hansen, L., Heinrich, M.P.: GraphRegNet: deep graph regularisation networks on sparse keypoints for dense registration of 3D lung CTs. IEEE Trans. Med. Imaging **40**(9), 2246–2257 (2021)
11. Harris, M.D., Datar, M., Whitaker, R.T., Jurrus, E.R., Peters, C.L., Anderson, A.E.: Statistical shape modeling of cam femoroacetabular impingement. J. Orthop. Res. **31**(10), 1620–1626 (2013)
12. Hill, A., Taylor, C.J., Brett, A.D.: A framework for automatic landmark identification using a new method of nonrigid correspondence. IEEE Trans. Pattern Anal. Mach. Intell. **22**(3), 241–251 (2000)

13. Huang, G., Liu, Z., Van Der Maaten, L., Weinberger, K.Q.: Densely connected convolutional networks. In: Proceedings of the IEEE Conference on Computer Vision and Pattern Recognition, pp. 4700–4708 (2017)
14. Ma, T., Gupta, A., Sabuncu, M.R.: Volumetric landmark detection with a multi-scale shift equivariant neural network. In: 2020 IEEE 17th International Symposium on Biomedical Imaging (ISBI), pp. 981–985. IEEE (2020)
15. Nibali, A., He, Z., Morgan, S., Prendergast, L.: Numerical coordinate regression with convolutional neural networks. arXiv preprint arXiv:1801.07372 (2018)
16. Rueckert, D., Sonoda, L.I., Hayes, C., Hill, D.L., Leach, M.O., Hawkes, D.J.: Non-rigid registration using free-form deformations: application to breast MR images. IEEE Trans. Med. Imaging **18**(8), 712–721 (1999)
17. Selvaraju, R.R., Cogswell, M., Das, A., Vedantam, R., Parikh, D., Batra, D.: Grad-CAM: visual explanations from deep networks via gradient-based localization. In: Proceedings of the IEEE International Conference on Computer Vision (2017)
18. Shen, Z., Han, X., Xu, Z., Niethammer, M.: Networks for joint affine and non-parametric image registration. In: Proceedings of the IEEE/CVF Conference on Computer Vision and Pattern Recognition, pp. 4224–4233 (2019)
19. Tian, L., Greer, H., Vialard, F.X., Kwitt, R., Estépar, R.S.J., Niethammer, M.: GradICON: approximate diffeomorphisms via gradient inverse consistency. arXiv preprint arXiv:2206.05897 (2022)

DAE-Former: Dual Attention-Guided Efficient Transformer for Medical Image Segmentation

Reza Azad[1]([✉]), René Arimond[1], Ehsan Khodapanah Aghdam[2],
Amirhossein Kazerouni[3], and Dorit Merhof[4,5]

[1] Faculty of Electrical Engineering and Information Technology, RWTH Aachen University, Aachen, Germany
rezazad68@gmail.com
[2] Department of Electrical Engineering, Shahid Beheshti University, Tehran, Iran
[3] School of Electrical Engineering, Iran University of Science and Technology, Tehran, Iran
[4] Faculty of Informatics and Data Science, Institute of Image Analysis and Computer Vision, University of Regensburg, Regensburg, Germany
dorit.merhof@ur.de
[5] Fraunhofer Institute for Digital Medicine MEVIS, Bremen, Germany

Abstract. Transformers have recently gained attention in the computer vision domain due to their ability to model long-range dependencies. However, the self-attention mechanism, which is the core part of the Transformer model, usually suffers from quadratic computational complexity with respect to the number of tokens. Many architectures attempt to reduce model complexity by limiting the self-attention mechanism to local regions or by redesigning the tokenization process. In this paper, we propose DAE-Former, a novel method that seeks to provide an alternative perspective by efficiently designing the self-attention mechanism. More specifically, we reformulate the self-attention mechanism to capture both spatial and channel relations across the whole feature dimension while staying computationally efficient. Furthermore, we redesign the skip connection path by including the cross-attention module to ensure the feature reusability and enhance the localization power. Our method outperforms state-of-the-art methods on multi-organ cardiac and skin lesion segmentation datasets, without pre-training weights. The code is publicly available at GitHub.

Keywords: Transformer · Segmentation · Deep Learning · Medical

1 Introduction

Medical image segmentation has become one of the major challenges in computer vision. For physicians to monitor diseases accurately, visualize injuries, and select the correct treatment, stable and accurate image segmentation algorithms are

I. Rekik et al. (Eds.): PRIME 2023, LNCS 14277, pp. 83–95, 2023.
https://doi.org/10.1007/978-3-031-46005-0_8

necessary [2]. Deep learning networks perform very well in medical imaging, surpassing non-deep state-of-the-art (SOTA) methods. However, an immense volume of data must be trained to achieve a good generalization with a large number of network parameters. Additionally, the great need for large annotated data is another limitation of deep models, specifically in the medical domain. Unfortunately, per-pixel labeling is necessary for medical image segmentation, making annotation tedious and expensive.

The U-Net by Ronneberger et al. [23] is one of the successful fully convolutional neural networks proposed to address the automatic segmentation task. Several extensions to the U-Net have been proposed to enhance the performance of the network [3]. These methods aim to enrich the feature representation either by incorporating the attention mechanisms [17], or redesigning the skip connection path [4], or replacing the backbone module [19]. Although these extensions improve the feature representation, the locality restriction of the convolution layer limits the representational power of these networks to capture the shape and structural information, which is crucial for medical image segmentation. It has been shown that exploiting shape information in CNNs by fine-tuning the input images can boost the representational power of the network. However, including shape representations inside the CNN networks requires modeling long-range dependencies in the latent space, which is still an open challenge in CNN architectures.

To address CNN limitation, the Vision Transformer (ViT) [13] model has been proposed. The ViT architecture is purely based on the multi-head self-attention mechanism. This enables the network to capture long-range dependencies and encode shape representations. ViT, however, requires large amounts of training data to perform similarly to CNNs, and the self-attention mechanism suffers from a quadratic computation complexity with respect to the number of tokens. The naive ViT model also renders poor performance compared to the CNN model for capturing the local representation. To address the weak local representation of the Transformer model, several methods have been proposed to build a hybrid CNN-Transformer network [7,10,15,21,31]. TransUNet [10], as a pioneer work in this direction, offers a hierarchical Transformer that captures global and fine-grained local context by combining convolutions and an attention mechanism. However, the downside of TransUNet is its high number of parameters and computational inefficiency. Additionally, although HiFormer [15] and contextual network [6] effectively bridge a CNN and a Transformer for medical image segmentation, it still relies on a heavy CNN backbone. HyLT [21] uses the Transformer counterparts to complement convolutional operations to capture global dependencies. This pipeline utilizes a two-path encoding design that embodies standalone convolution and Transformer operation in each path. Moreover, RAT-Net [31] investigates SegFormer [29] as a sparse attention mechanism in its region-aware attention mechanism in a U-shaped structure.

To address the computational complexity of the Transformer model, recent designs suggest either imposing a restriction on the self-attention mechanism to perform in a local region [9,12,20], or defining a scaling factor to reduce the spatial dimension [18], or calculating channel attention instead of spatial attention [1]. However, the global context is only partially captured in such methods. Swin-Unet [8] takes a different perspective and offers a U-Net-like pure Transformer architecture that operates at different scales and fuses the features from different layers using skip connections. Swin-Unet uses two consecutive Transformer blocks with different windowing settings (shifted windows to reduce the computational burden) to attempt to recapture context from neighboring windows. Although the multi-scale representation of the Swin-Unet enhances the feature representation, the spatial context is still limited in the process.

To address the aforementioned limitations, we propose a dual attention module that operates on the full spatial dimension of the input feature and also captures the channel context. To this end, we apply efficient attention by Shen et al. [25], which reduces the complexity of self-attention to linear while producing the same output as the regular self-attention mechanism. Moreover, to capture the input feature's channel context, we reformulate the attention mechanism with the cross-covariance method [1]. We integrate our redesigned Transformer block in a hierarchical U-Net-like pure Transformer architecture, namely, the DAE-Former . In order to reliably fuse multi-scale features from different layers, we propose a cross-attention module in each skip connection path. Our contributions are as follows: ❶ a novel efficient dual attention mechanism to capture the full spatial and channel context of the input feature vector, ❷ a skip connection cross attention (SCCA) module to fuse features from encoder and decoder layers adaptively, and ❸ a hierarchical U-Net-like pure Transformer structure for medical image segmentation.

2 Proposed Method

We introduce the DAE-Former (Fig. 1), a convolution-free U-Net-like hierarchical Transformer. Given an input image $x^{H \times W \times C}$ with spatial dimension $H \times W$ and C channels, the DAE-Former utilizes the patch embedding module [8,18] to gain overlapping patch tokens of size 4×4 from the input image. The tokenized input $(x^{n \times d})$ then goes through the encoder module, with 3 stacked encoder blocks, each consisting of two consecutive dual Transformer layers and a patch merging layer. During patch merging, 2×2 patch tokens are merged to reduce the spatial dimension while doubling the channel dimension. This allows the network to gain a multi-scale representation in a hierarchical fashion. In the decoder, the tokens are expanded again by a factor of 2 in each block. The output of each patch expanding layer is then fused with the features forwarded by the skip connection from the parallel encoder layer using SCCA. The resulting features are fed into two consecutive dual Transformer layers. Finally, a linear projection layer produces the output segmentation map. In the next sections, we will first provide a brief overview of the efficient and transpose attentions. Then we will introduce our efficient dual attention and the SCCA modules.

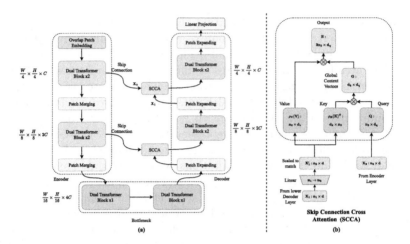

Fig. 1. (a): The structure of our DAE-Former . Both the encoder and decoder of the U-Net-like architecture are each comprised of 3 blocks. Our dual attention block consists of efficient attention followed by transpose attention. (b): The skip connection cross attention (SCCA) module.

2.1 Efficient Attention

The standard self-attention mechanism Eq. (1) suffers from a quadratic computational complexity ($\mathcal{O}(n^2)$), which limits the applicability of this architecture for high-resolution images. $\mathbf{Q}$, $\mathbf{K}$, and $\mathbf{V}$ in Eq. (1) shows the query, key, and value vectors, and d is the embedding dimension,

$$S(\mathbf{Q}, \mathbf{K}, \mathbf{V}) = \text{softmax}\left(\frac{\mathbf{Q}\mathbf{K}^{\mathbf{T}}}{\sqrt{d_{\mathbf{k}}}}\right)\mathbf{V}. \tag{1}$$

Efficient attention by Shen et al. [25] uses the fact that regular self-attention produces a redundant context matrix to propose an efficient way to compute the self-attention procedure Eq. (2):

$$\mathbf{E}(\mathbf{Q}, \mathbf{K}, \mathbf{V}) = \rho_{\mathbf{q}}(\mathbf{Q})(\rho_{\mathbf{k}}(\mathbf{K})^{\mathbf{T}}\mathbf{V}), \tag{2}$$

where ρ_q and ρ_k are normalization functions for the queries and keys. It has been shown in [25] that the module produces an equivalent output of dot-product attention when ρ_q and ρ_k are applied, which are softmax normalization functions. Therefore, efficient attention normalizes the keys and queries first, then multiplies the keys and values, and finally, the resulting global context vectors are multiplied by the queries to produce the new representation. Unlike dot-product attention, efficient attention does not first compute pairwise similarities between points. Instead, the keys are represented as d_k attention maps $\mathbf{k}^{\mathbf{T}}{}_j$, with j referring to position j in the input feature. These global attention maps represent a semantic aspect of the whole input feature instead of similarities to the position of the input. This shifting of orders drastically reduces the computational complexity of the attention mechanism while maintaining high representational power. The memory complexity of efficient attention is $\mathcal{O}(dn + d^2)$ while the computational complexity is $\mathcal{O}(d^2 n)$ when $d_v = d, d_k = \frac{d}{2}$ - which is a typical setting. In our structure, we use efficient attention to capture the spatial importance of the input feature map.

2.2   Transpose Attention

Cross-covariance attention also called transpose attention [1], is a channel attention mechanism. This strategy employs transpose attention only to enable the processing of larger input sizes. However, we reformulate the problem and propose a transpose attention mechanism to efficiently capture the full channel dimension. The transpose attention is shown in Eq. (3):

$$\mathbf{T}(\mathbf{Q}, \mathbf{K}, \mathbf{V}) = \mathbf{V}\mathcal{C}_T(\mathbf{K}, \mathbf{Q}), \quad \mathcal{C}_T(\mathbf{K}, \mathbf{Q}) = Softmax(\mathbf{K}^\mathbf{T}\mathbf{Q}/\tau) \qquad (3)$$

The keys and queries are transposed, and, therefore, the attention weights are based on the cross-covariance matrix. $\mathcal{C}_T$ refers to the context vector of the transpose attention. The temperature parameter τ is introduced to counteract the scaling with the l_2-norm that is applied to the queries and keys before calculating the attention weights. This increases stability during training but removes a degree of freedom, thus reducing the representational power of the module.

Transpose attention has a time complexity of $\mathcal{O}(nd^2/h)$, whereas standard self-attention requires $\mathcal{O}(n^2 d)$. The space complexity is $\mathcal{O}(hn^2 + nd)$ for transpose attention and $\mathcal{O}(d^2/h + nd)$ for self-attention. Self-attention scales quadratically with the number of tokens n, whereas transpose attention scales quadratically with the embedding dimension d, which is usually smaller than n.

2.3   Efficient Dual Attention

A literature review [14] on the attention mechanism shows that combining spatial and channel attention enhances the capacity of the model to capture more contextual features than single attention. Therefore, we construct a dual Transformer block that combines transpose (channel) attention and efficient (spatial) attention. The structure of our efficient dual attention block is shown in Fig. 2. Our efficient dual attention block Eq. (8) consists of efficient attention Eq. (4), followed by an add & norm Eq. (5), and a transpose attention block that performs the channel attention Eq. (6), followed by an add & norm Eq. (7).

$$\mathbf{E}_{\mathbf{block}}(\mathbf{X}, \mathbf{Q_1}, \mathbf{K_1}, \mathbf{V_1}) = \mathbf{E}(\mathbf{Q_1}, \mathbf{K_1}, \mathbf{V_1}) + \mathbf{X}, \qquad (4)$$

$$\mathrm{MLP}_1(\mathbf{E}_{\mathbf{block}}) = \mathrm{MLP}(\mathrm{LN}(\mathbf{E}_{\mathbf{block}})), \qquad (5)$$

$$\mathbf{T}_{\mathbf{block}}(\mathbf{E}_{\mathbf{block}}, \mathbf{Q_2}, \mathbf{K_2}, \mathbf{V_2}) = \mathbf{T}(\mathrm{MLP}_1(\mathbf{E}_{\mathbf{block}}) + \mathbf{E}_{\mathbf{block}}) + \mathrm{MLP}_1(\mathbf{E}_{\mathbf{block}}), \qquad (6)$$

$$\mathrm{MLP}_2(\mathbf{T}_{\mathbf{block}}) = \mathrm{MLP}(\mathrm{LN}(\mathbf{T}_{\mathbf{block}})), \qquad (7)$$

$$\mathrm{DualAttention}(\mathbf{T}_{\mathbf{block}}) = \mathrm{MLP}_2(\mathbf{T}_{\mathbf{block}}) + \mathbf{T}_{\mathbf{block}}. \qquad (8)$$

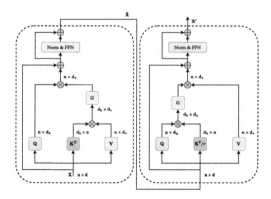

Fig. 2. The efficient dual attention block. It consists of an efficient attention block, followed by a Norm & FFN, and a channel attention block followed by a Norm & FFN to perform spatial and channel attentions.

$\mathbf{E}(\cdot), \mathbf{T}(\cdot)$ refer to efficient and transpose attentions, and $\mathbf{T_{block}}$ and $\mathbf{E_{block}}$ denote the transpose and efficient attention blocks, respectively. $\mathbf{Q_1, K_1, V_1}$ are the keys, queries, and values calculated from the input feature $\mathbf{X}$. $\mathbf{Q_2, K_2, V_2}$ are the queries, keys, and values computed from the input to the transpose attention block. MLP denotes the Mix-FFN feed-forward network [18]: MLP$(\mathbf{X}) =$ FC(GELU(DW-Conv(FC$(\mathbf{X})$)))) with FC being a fully connected layer. GELU refers to GELU activation [16] and DW-Conv is depth-wise convolution. It is worthwhile to mention that our dual attention module is novel in terms of performing both channel and spatial attention in a linear form.

2.4   Skip Connection Cross Attention

The SCCA module is shown in Fig. 1(b). Instead of simply concatenating the features from the encoder and decoder layers, we cross-attend them to preserve the underlying features more efficiently. Our proposed module can effectively provide spatial information to each decoder so that it can recover fine-grained details when producing output masks. In our structure, the skip connection cross attention (SCCA) applies efficient attention, but instead of using the same input feature for keys, queries, and values, the input used for the query is the output of the encoder layer forwarded by a skip connection $\mathbf{X_2}$, hence the name. The input used for keys and values is the output of the lower decoder layer $\mathbf{X_1}$. To fuse the two features, $\mathbf{X_1}$ needs to be scaled to the same embedding dimension as $\mathbf{X_2}$ using a linear layer Eq. (9). The motivation behind using $\mathbf{X_2}$ as an input for the query is to model the multi-level representation within the efficient attention block.

$$\mathbf{X'_1} = FC(\mathbf{X_1}), \quad \mathbf{K, V} = Proj(\mathbf{X'_1}), \quad \mathbf{Q} = Proj(\mathbf{X_2})$$
$$\mathbf{E} = \rho_\mathbf{v}(\mathbf{V})\rho_\mathbf{k}(\mathbf{K^T})\mathbf{Q}. \tag{9}$$

Here, ρ_v, ρ_k are normalization functions, and $Proj$ refers to a projection function. In this case, it is a linear projection.

3   Experimental Setup

Our proposed method is implemented in an end-to-end manner using the PyTorch library and is trained on a single RTX 3090 GPU. The training is done with a batch size of 24 and a stochastic gradient descent with a base learning rate of 0.05, a momentum of 0.9, and a weight decay of 0.0001. The model is trained for 400 epochs using both cross-entropy and Dice losses ($Loss = 0.6 \cdot L_{dice} + 0.4 \cdot L_{ce}$).

Dataset and Evaluation Metrics: We use the publicly available Synapse dataset for the evaluation process, which constitutes a multi-organ segmentation dataset with 30 cases with 3779 axial abdominal clinical CT images [8,18]. We follow the setting presented in [10] for the evaluation. We further use the [6] setting to evaluate our method on the skin lesion segmentation challenge using the ISIC 2018 [11] dataset.

Quantitative and Qualitative Results: Table 1 presents the performance of our proposed DAE-Former on the Synapse dataset. DAE-Former surpasses the previous SOTA methods in terms of DSC score. It also outperforms CNN-based methods by a large margin. We confirm an increase of the Dice score by +0.67 compared to the previous SOTA, MISSFormer [18]. We observe that the segmentation performance increases, especially for the gallbladder, kidney, liver, and spleen. In addition, we present the performance of our method when utilizing only the efficient attention mechanism without the SCCA and transpose attention (EffFormer), as well as the performance of our method without SCCA module. Eliminating each of these components results in a noticeable drop in performance, as observed.

Figure 3 shows the visualization of the segmentation maps. It can be observed that the competitive methods fail to predict the small organs (e.g., pancreas) while our model produces a smooth segmentation map for all organs.

Table 1. Comparison results of the proposed method on the *Synapse* dataset. Blue indicates the best result, and red indicates the second-best. We exclusively report each method's parameter numbers in order of millions (M).

Methods	# Params (M)	DSC ↑	HD ↓	Aorta	Gallbladder	Kidney(L)	Kidney(R)	Liver	Pancreas	Spleen	Stomach
U-Net [23]	14.8	76.85	39.70	89.07	69.72	77.77	68.60	93.43	53.98	86.67	75.58
Att-UNet [24]	34.88	77.77	36.02	89.55	68.88	77.98	71.11	93.57	58.04	87.30	75.75
TransUNet [10]	105.28	77.48	31.69	87.23	63.13	81.87	77.02	94.08	55.86	85.08	75.62
Swin-Unet [8]	27.17	79.13	21.55	85.47	66.53	83.28	79.61	94.29	56.58	90.66	76.60
LeVit-Unet [30]	52.17	78.53	16.84	78.53	62.23	84.61	80.25	93.11	59.07	88.86	72.76
MT-UNet [27]	79.07	78.59	26.59	87.92	64.99	81.47	77.29	93.06	59.46	87.75	76.81
TransDeepLab [5]	21.14	80.16	21.25	86.04	69.16	84.08	79.88	93.53	61.19	89.00	78.40
HiFormer [15]	25.51	80.39	14.70	86.21	65.69	85.23	79.77	94.61	59.52	90.99	81.08
MISSFormer [18]	42.46	81.96	18.20	86.99	68.65	85.21	82.00	94.41	65.67	91.92	80.81
EffFormer (baseline model)	22.31	80.79	17.00	85.81	66.89	84.10	81.81	94.80	62.25	91.05	79.58
DAE-Former (without SCCA)	40.75	81.59	17.31	87.41	69.57	85.22	80.46	94.68	63.71	91.47	78.23
DAE-Former	48.01	82.63	16.39	87.84	71.65	87.66	82.39	95.08	63.93	91.82	80.77

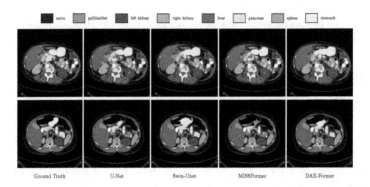

Fig. 3. Comparative segmentation results on the *Synapse* dataset. DAE-Former shows finer and smooth boundaries for the stomach, spleen, and liver organs and a less false positive for the gallbladder compared to Swin-Unet and MISSFormer.

The skin lesion segmentation benchmark results are presented in Table 2a and 2b. It can be seen that, compared to both CNN and Transformer-based methods, our network produces better performance in almost all metrics. Our model performs better than the most competitive and similar approach (TMU-Net). The TMU-Net requires extra information (boundary and foreground distribution information) and suffers from a large number of parameters (165.1M vs. 48.1M parameters for our model). We also observe that the dual attention mechanism performs better than the base structure, indicating our suggested modules' effectiveness for better performance gain.

Table 2. (a) Performance comparison of the proposed method against the SOTA approaches on the *ISIC 2018* skin lesion segmentation task. (b) Visual comparisons on the *Synapse* dataset. Ground truth boundaries are shown in green, and predicted boundaries are shown in blue.

(b) Qualitative results

(a) Quantitative results

Methods	DSC	SE	SP	ACC
U-Net [23]	0.8545	0.8800	0.9697	0.9404
Att U-Net [22]	0.8566	0.8674	**0.9863**	0.9376
TransUNet [10]	0.8499	0.8578	0.9653	0.9452
MedT [26]	0.8389	0.8252	0.9637	0.9358
FAT-Net [28]	0.8903	0.9100	0.9699	0.9578
TMU-Net [6]	0.9059	0.9038	0.9746	0.9603
Swin U-Net [8]	0.8946	0.9056	0.9798	**0.9645**
EffFormer	0.8904	0.8861	0.9698	0.9519
DAE-Former (without SCCA)	0.8962	0.8634	0.9830	0.9578
DAE-Former	**0.9147**	**0.9120**	0.9780	0.9641

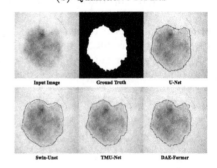

3.1   Ablation Study

In our method, we take into account the computational advantages of the efficient and the transpose attention mechanisms to build our dual attention mechanism. Four different possibilities are explored in this ablation study. These structures are shown in Fig. 4. The first is sequential dual attention, as already used in our method. Next, two variants for additive dual attention were tested; namely, simple additive dual attention (Fig. 4(b)) and complex additive dual attention (Fig. 4(c)). The former was expected to have a more unstable back-propagation as the outputs of each attention block are not normalized. Although the latter has a larger number of parameters, efficient and channel attention outputs were normalized and fed to an FFN before the addition. Lastly, the concatenation dual attention is shown in Fig. 4(d). The outputs of both blocks are normalized, then concatenated. An MLP reduces the dimension from twice the input dimension back to the input dimension, and the resulting tensor is again normalized. A comparison result is shown in Table 3a.

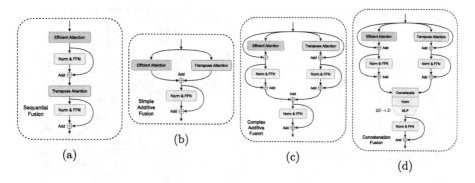

Fig. 4. (a) Sequential dual attention, (b) simple additive dual attention, (c) complex additive dual attention, and (d) concatenation dual attention.

Table 3. Ablation study of our proposed method on the *Synapse* dataset.

(a) Dual Attention Strategy

Strategy	# Params (M)	DSC	HD
Sequential	48.1	82.63	16.39
Simple Additive	48.0	79.51	23.83
Complex Additive	61.1	81.49	19.36
Concatenation	64.0	80.11	27.20

(b) Skip Connection Effect

# Skip Connections	DSC	HD
0	79.71	22.46
1	81.81	21.66
2	82.63	16.39

(c) Size

Image Size	DSC	HD
128 × 128	79.20	15.90
224 × 224	82.63	16.39
288 × 288	82.78	17.85

We also explore the effect of skip connections in our suggested network. In this respect, we reconstructed our model with three settings: no skip connections, one skip connection in the highest layer, and two skip connections, i.e. the base setting. The results are presented in Table 3b. We observe that the model behaves as expected: The more skip connections there are, the better the performance. In particular, fine-grained information from higher layers is critical to the

Dice Score (%)

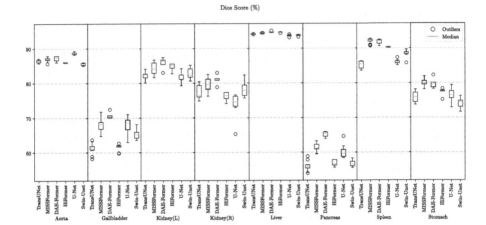

Fig. 5. Statistical analysis between the U-Net [23], TransUNet [10], Swin-Unet [8], HiFormer [15], MISSFormer [18], and our proposed method, DAE-Former.

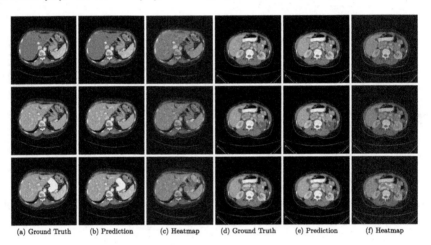

(a) Ground Truth   (b) Prediction   (c) Heatmap   (d) Ground Truth   (e) Prediction   (f) Heatmap

Fig. 6. Visualization of attention maps using Grad-CAM on the *Synapse* dataset demonstrates the effectiveness of DAE-Former in detecting both large (liver, spleen, and stomach) and small (gallbladder, left kidney, and pancreas) organs.

fusion of information. To evaluate the effect of image resolution, we conducted experiments with two different image resolutions besides the original 224×224 resolution we used in our experiments. In this respect, we reduced the input size to 128×128 pixels to observe the low-resolution impact. Furthermore, we slightly increased the image resolution to 288×288 pixels to analyze the effect of higher resolution. The results are shown in Table 3c.

To endorse the validity of the results we conducted a statistical analysis by running 10 times SOTA and our proposed models to report the mean Dice score over each organ. Figure 5 indicates that the DAE-Former performs with low variance and confident performances over Gallbladder, Kidney (L/R), and liver. We also provide attention map visualization (Fig. 6) of the DAE-Former using Grad-CAM to highlight its capacity for capturing local and global dependency.

4   Conclusion

In this paper, we propose DAE-Former , a novel U-Net-like hierarchical pure Transformer that leverages both spatial and channel attention on the full feature dimension. We enrich the representational space by including dual attention while retaining the same number of parameters compared to previous architectures. Furthermore, we perform a fusion of multi-scale features through skip connection cross-attention. Our model achieves the SOTA results on both the Synapse and skin lesion segmentation datasets.

References

1. Ali, A., et al.: XCiT: cross-covariance image transformers. In: Advances in Neural Information Processing Systems, vol. 34 (2021)
2. Antonelli, M., et al.: The medical segmentation decathlon. Nat. Commun. **13**(1), 1–13 (2022)
3. Azad, R., et al.: Medical image segmentation review: the success of U-Net. arXiv preprint arXiv:2211.14830 (2022)
4. Azad, R., Asadi-Aghbolaghi, M., Fathy, M., Escalera, S.: Bi-directional ConvLSTM U-Net with densly connected convolutions. In: Proceedings of the IEEE/CVF International Conference on Computer Vision Workshops (2019)
5. Azad, R., et al.: TransDeepLab: convolution-free transformer-based DeepLab v3+ for medical image segmentation. In: Rekik, I., Adeli, E., Park, S.H., Cintas, C. (eds.) Predictive Intelligence in Medicine, PRIME 2022. LNCS, vol. 13564, pp. 91–102. Springer, Cham (2022). https://doi.org/10.1007/978-3-031-16919-9_9
6. Azad, R., Heidari, M., Wu, Y., Merhof, D.: Contextual attention network: transformer meets U-Net. In: Lian, C., Cao, X., Rekik, I., Xu, X., Cui, Z. (eds.) Machine Learning in Medical Imaging, MLMI 2022. LNCS, vol. 13583, pp. 377–386. Springer, Cham (2022). https://doi.org/10.1007/978-3-031-21014-3_39
7. Azad, R., et al.: Advances in medical image analysis with vision transformers: a comprehensive review. arXiv preprint arXiv:2301.03505 (2023)
8. Cao, H., et al.: Swin-Unet: Unet-Like Pure Transformer for Medical Image Segmentation. In: Karlinsky, L., Michaeli, T., Nishino, K. (eds.) Computer Vision – ECCV 2022 Workshops, ECCV 2022. LNCS, vol. 13803, pp. 205–218. Springer, Cham (2023). https://doi.org/10.1007/978-3-031-25066-8_9
9. Chen, C.F., Panda, R., Fan, Q.: RegionViT: regional-to-local attention for vision transformers. arXiv preprint arXiv:2106.02689 (2021)
10. Chen, J., et al.: TransUNet: transformers make strong encoders for medical image segmentation. arXiv preprint arXiv:2102.04306 (2021)
11. Codella, N., et al.: Skin lesion analysis toward melanoma detection 2018: a challenge hosted by the international skin imaging collaboration (ISIC). arXiv preprint arXiv:1902.03368 (2019)

12. Ding, M., Xiao, B., Codella, N., Luo, P., Wang, J., Yuan, L.: DaViT: dual attention vision transformers. arXiv preprint arXiv:2204.03645 (2022)
13. Dosovitskiy, A., et al.: An image is worth 16×16 words: transformers for image recognition at scale. arXiv preprint arXiv:2010.11929 (2020)
14. Guo, M.H., et al.: Attention mechanisms in computer vision: a survey. Comput. Vis. Media **8**, 331–368 (2022)
15. Heidari, M., et al.: HiFormer: hierarchical multi-scale representations using transformers for medical image segmentation. In: Proceedings of the IEEE/CVF Winter Conference on Applications of Computer Vision, pp. 6202–6212 (2023)
16. Hendrycks, D., Gimpel, K.: Gaussian error linear units (GELUs). arXiv preprint arXiv:1606.08415 (2016)
17. Hu, J., Shen, L., Sun, G.: Squeeze-and-excitation networks. In: Proceedings of the IEEE Conference on Computer Vision and Pattern Recognition, pp. 7132–7141 (2018)
18. Huang, X., Deng, Z., Li, D., Yuan, X., Fu, Y.: MISSFormer: an effective transformer for 2D medical image segmentation. IEEE Trans. Med. Imaging **42**, 1484–1494 (2022). https://doi.org/10.1109/TMI.2022.3230943
19. Karaali, A., Dahyot, R., Sexton, D.J.: DR-VNet: retinal vessel segmentation via dense residual UNet. In: El Yacoubi, M., Granger, E., Yuen, P.C., Pal, U., Vincent, N. (eds.) Pattern Recognition and Artificial Intelligence, ICPRAI 2022. LNCS, vol. 13363, pp. 198–210. Springer, Cham (2022). https://doi.org/10.1007/978-3-031-09037-0_17
20. Liu, Z., et al.: Swin transformer: hierarchical vision transformer using shifted windows. In: Proceedings of the IEEE/CVF International Conference on Computer Vision, pp. 10012–10022 (2021)
21. Luo, H., Changdong, Y., Selvan, R.: Hybrid ladder transformers with efficient parallel-cross attention for medical image segmentation. In: International Conference on Medical Imaging with Deep Learning, pp. 808–819. PMLR (2022)
22. Oktay, O., et al.: Attention U-Net: learning where to look for the pancreas. arXiv preprint arXiv:1804.03999 (2018)
23. Ronneberger, O.: Invited Talk: U-Net convolutional networks for biomedical image segmentation. In: Bildverarbeitung für die Medizin 2017. I, pp. 3–3. Springer, Heidelberg (2017). https://doi.org/10.1007/978-3-662-54345-0_3
24. Schlemper, J., et al.: Attention gated networks: learning to leverage salient regions in medical images. Med. Image Anal. **53**, 197–207 (2019)
25. Shen, Z., Zhang, M., Zhao, H., Yi, S., Li, H.: Efficient attention: attention with linear complexities. In: Proceedings of the IEEE/CVF Winter Conference on Applications of Computer Vision, pp. 3531–3539 (2021)
26. Valanarasu, J.M.J., Oza, P., Hacihaliloglu, I., Patel, V.M.: Medical transformer: gated axial-attention for medical image segmentation. In: de Bruijne, M., et al. (eds.) MICCAI 2021. LNCS, vol. 12901, pp. 36–46. Springer, Cham (2021). https://doi.org/10.1007/978-3-030-87193-2_4
27. Wang, H., et al.: Mixed transformer U-Net for medical image segmentation. In: 2022 IEEE International Conference on Acoustics, Speech and Signal Processing (ICASSP), ICASSP 2022, pp. 2390–2394. IEEE (2022)
28. Wu, H., Chen, S., Chen, G., Wang, W., Lei, B., Wen, Z.: FAT-Net: feature adaptive transformers for automated skin lesion segmentation. Med. Image Anal. **76**, 102327 (2022)

29. Xie, E., Wang, W., Yu, Z., Anandkumar, A., Alvarez, J.M., Luo, P.: SegFormer: simple and efficient design for semantic segmentation with transformers. In: Advances in Neural Information Processing Systems, vol. 34, pp. 12077–12090 (2021)

30. Xu, G., Wu, X., Zhang, X., He, X.: LeViT-UNet: make faster encoders with transformer for medical image segmentation. arXiv preprint arXiv:2107.08623 (2021)

31. Zhu, X., et al.: Region aware transformer for automatic breast ultrasound tumor segmentation. In: International Conference on Medical Imaging with Deep Learning, pp. 1523–1537. PMLR (2022)

Diffusion-Based Graph Super-Resolution with Application to Connectomics

Nishant Rajadhyaksha[1,2] and Islem Rekik[1(✉)] 🆔

[1] BASIRA Lab, Imperial-X and Department of Computing, Imperial College London, London, UK
i.rekik@imperial.ac.uk
[2] K.J. Somaiya College of Engineering, Mumbai, India
https://basira-lab.com/

Abstract. The super-resolution of low-resolution brain graphs, also known as brain connectomes, is a crucial aspect of neuroimaging research, especially in brain graph super-resolution. Brain graph super-resolution revolutionized neuroimaging research by eliminating the need for costly acquisition and data processing. However, the development of generative models for super-resolving brain graphs remains largely unexplored. The state-of-the-art (SOTA) model in this domain leverages the inherent topology of brain connectomes by employing a Graph Generative Adversarial Network (GAN) coupled with topological feature-based regularization to achieve super-resolution. However, training graph-based GANs is notoriously challenging due to issues regarding scalability and implicit probability modeling. To overcome these limitations and fully capitalize on the capabilities of generative models, we propose Dif-GSR (**Dif**fusion based **G**raph **S**uper-**R**esolution) for predicting high-resolution brain graphs from low-resolution ones. Diffusion models have gained significant popularity in recent years as flexible and powerful frameworks for explicitly modelling complex data distributions. Dif-GSR consists of a noising process for adding noise to brain connectomes, a conditional denoiser model which learns to conditionally remove noise with respect to an input low-resolution source connectome and a sampling module which is responsible for the generation of high-resolution brain connectomes. We evaluate Dif-GSR using three-fold cross-validation using a variety of standard metrics for brain connectome super-resolution. We present the first diffusion-based framework for brain graph super-resolution, which is trained on non-isomorphic inter-modality brain graphs, effectively handling variations in graph size, distribution, and structure. This advancement holds promising prospects for multimodal and holistic brain mapping, as well as the development of a multimodal neurological disorder diagnostic frameworks. Our Dif-GSR code is available at https://github.com/basiralab/Dif-GSR.

1 Introduction

Neuroimaging techniques, such as magnetic resonance imaging (MRI) and diffusion tensor imaging (DTI) [1], have greatly advanced the understanding of brain disorders and anatomy. However, the limited availability and high cost of ultra-high field scanners restrict the acquisition of submillimeter resolution MRI data. To address this challenge,

ⓒ The Author(s), under exclusive license to Springer Nature Switzerland AG 2023
I. Rekik et al. (Eds.): PRIME 2023, LNCS 14277, pp. 96–107, 2023.
https://doi.org/10.1007/978-3-031-46005-0_9

researchers have explored super-resolution techniques to enhance low-resolution brain-intensity images to high-intensity images [2–5]. Deep learning methods, including convolutional neural networks (CNNs) and generative adversarial nets (GANs), have been employed for image super-resolution, but the application of recent generative frameworks, such as diffusion, remains unexplored. Previous studies have utilized CNNs [2] to generate high-resolution 7T-like MRI images from 3T MRI data, and regression random forest techniques have been employed to enhance high-resolution MRI images [6]. Despite these advancements in MRI super-resolution, the super-resolution of brain connectomes, which represent the connectivity between different brain regions, remains largely unexplored. The construction of brain connectomes involves multiple complex steps, including skull stripping, cortical thickness estimation, tissue segmentation, and registration to a brain atlas [7]. While MRI super-resolution has received considerable attention, there is a need to investigate super-resolution techniques specifically tailored for brain connectomes.

Brain connectomes present a highly complex non-linear structure that poses challenges for linear models to accurately capture [8]. The conventional approach for generating connectomes at different resolutions involves using a brain atlas or template to divide the brain into predefined anatomical regions of interest (ROIs) based on the desired resolution. The resulting connectome consists of nodes representing each ROI and edge weights indicating the strength of connectivity between ROI pairs [9]. Connectivity strength can be measured based on correlation between neural activity or similarity in brain morphology –among others. However, this connectome generation process has two significant limitations: (1) substantial computational time is required per subject, and (2) preprocessing steps, such as registration and label propagation, are prone to variability and bias, as suggested by previous studies [10, 11].

Another approach to bypass the complexity of neuroimaging pipelines is to establish a mapping between low-resolution brain graphs and higher-resolution counterparts, as low-resolution connectomes are relatively easier to obtain from magnetic resonance imaging (MRI). However, this process of upsampling, or super-resolution, is inherently challenging due to the multiple possible high-resolution solutions for a given low-resolution connectome [12]. Recent studies have turned to deep learning techniques for brain graph super-resolution tasks. One common approach is to employ geometric deep neural networks to handle geometric data. For instance, a pioneering work called GSR-Net utilized a graph U-Net to generate a higher-resolution brain graph with enhanced regions of interest (ROIs) [13]. Currently, the state-of-the-art model for brain graph resolution is IMANGraphNet [14], which combines a graph-GAN-based model with a domain aligner to produce a higher-resolution graph. More recent graph super-resolution models have been proposed which primarily rely on adversarial generative learning [15, 16]. However, graph-based architectures encounter scalability issues due to oversmoothing effects [17]. Utilizing scalable neural networks can yield better results, but this often involves disregarding topological features. Moreover, traditional generative deep neural network models like GANs and Autoencoders, particularly in their generative mode, tend to focus on capturing high-level features and global patterns, potentially overlooking finer and intricate structures. GANs, in particular, face challenges in training due to their implicit modeling of probability distributions [18].

To overcome these limitations, we propose a diffusion-based framework for predicting high-resolution connectomes from low-resolution ones. Diffusion models belong to a more recent class of generative models that have shown promise in various applications, including text-to-image generation, image inpainting, and audio/video generation [19–24]. These models gradually introduce noise into data and align it with a predetermined prior distribution, allowing for the generation of realistic samples by reversing this process. By leveraging diffusion models, we can develop generative models that effectively capture the underlying structures of complex datasets, resulting in high-quality and realistic samples. There are three sub-types within the diffusion model category: denoising diffusion probabilistic models (DDPMs), score-based generative models (SGMs), and stochastic differential equations (SDEs) [25–28]. While each sub-type implements forward and backward diffusion passes differently, they all explicitly model probability distributions. In our work, we focus on the conditional generation capabilities of DDPMs [29]. Diffusion models allow for the incorporation of external conditioning information, which guides the generation process and enables precise control over the generated samples. This conditioning information facilitates the integration of specific desired attributes or characteristics, providing flexibility in aligning the generated samples with specific criteria and enhancing customization and targeted generation capabilities.

Our main contributions can be summarised as follows. (i) We present the first conditioned diffusion framework for brain connectome super-resolution. (ii) We empirically demonstrate that our diffusion-based framework outperforms existing methods for the task of brain graph super-resolution. We present a U-Net [30] based architecture to conditionally denoise noisy target brain connectomes given source connectomes at particular timesteps. By leveraging the power of successful iterative conditional denoising, we can effectively generate higher-resolution brain connectomes from their respective lower-resolution counterparts, achieving superior and more detailed generations.

2   Methodology

Problem Definition. Let $G_i(V_i, E_i)$ denote a brain graph comprising nodes (ROIs) in V_i and edges (connectivity strength) in E_i. Our goal is to learn a mapping from $G_{source}(V_{source}, E_{source})$ to $G_{target}(V_{target}, E_{target})$, representing the source and target brain graphs, respectively. The source graph has n_r nodes, while the target graph has $n_{r'}$ nodes, with $n_{r'} > n_r$. Importantly, these graphs are non-isomorphic, indicating that they exhibit topological differences and lack node and edge correspondence between them. The edges of the graphs can be represented using a symmetric adjacency matrix A, where $A_{(i,j)}$ represents the weight of the edge connecting nodes i and j. Specifically, A^{source} of dimensions $n_r \times n_r$ represents the source adjacency matrix, while A^{target} of dimensions $n_{r'} \times n_{r'}$ represents the target adjacency matrix. A_t denotes the adjacency matrix at timestep t during the diffusion process.

In the context of brain graph super-resolution, the task can be formulated as follows. Given a brain graph G_{source}, our objective is to learn a mapping f : $(V_{source}, E_{source}) \rightarrow (V_{target}, E_{target})$, which maps G_{source} onto G_{target} where $V_{target} > V_{source}$. This implies that we aim to generate a high-resolution brain graph

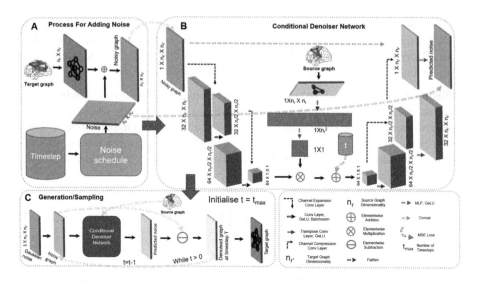

Fig. 1. Illustration of our diffusion-based graph super-resolution framework (Dif-GSR). The framework comprises three key modules: (i) Process for Adding Noise, where the target brain connectomes are perturbed; (ii) Conditional Denoiser Network, which predicts noise by leveraging conditional information from the source brain connectome; and (iii) Sampling, iteratively and conditionally denoising random Gaussian noise to generate the final high-resolution target brain connectome.

G_{taregt} with a larger number of nodes and potentially more complex connectivity patterns from a low-resolution brain graph G_{source}.

Overall Framework. In Figure 1, we detail the proposed diffusion-based framework[1], which consists of the following steps:

(i) Adding Noise. We introduce noise to a brain connectome based on a predefined schedule. This schedule determines the level of noise to be added at each timestep during the diffusion process. The noise is added to the source graph, which serves as the starting point for the super-resolution task.

(ii) Conditional Denoiser Network. We use a conditional denoiser network that takes the noisy graph as input and predicts the noise to be removed at each timestep. The denoiser network is trained to learn the mapping between the noisy graph and the corresponding noise to be removed, conditioned on the specific source graph.

(iii) Noise Removal and Mapping. Using the predicted noise from the denoiser network, we iteratively remove the noise from a graph sampled from a random Gaussian distribution. The noise removal process is conditioned on the source graph, ensuring that the resulting graph aligns with the desired super-resolution mapping. As the diffusion process unfolds, the graph gradually transforms, aiming to resemble the target graph.

---

[1] https://github.com/basiralab/Dif-GSR.

By following this diffusion-based approach, we leverage the denoiser network to guide the noise removal process and generate a high-resolution connectome. The framework effectively captures the underlying structures of the complex brain connectome data, leading to the generation of high-quality and realistic samples.

Diffusion. Diffusion models belong to the class of generative models and can be defined as latent variable models denoted by $p_\theta(x_0) = \int p_\theta(x_{0:T}) dx_{1:T}$, where $x_1, \ldots, x_T$ represent latents of the same dimensionality as the data x_0, sampled from a distribution $q(x_0)$. The joint distribution $p_\theta(x_{0:T})$ is referred to as the reverse process, which is defined as a Markov chain with learned Gaussian transitions starting at $p(x_T) = \mathcal{N}(x_T; 0, I)$:

$$p_\theta(x_{0:T}) = p(x_T) \prod_{t=1}^{T} p_\theta(x_{t-1}|x_t) \tag{1}$$

$$p_\theta(x_{t-1}|x_t) = \mathcal{N}(x_{t-1}; \mu_\theta(x_t, t), \Sigma_\theta(x_t, t)) \tag{2}$$

where μ_θ and Σ_θ are learned parameters. Specifically, $\mu_\theta(x_t, t)$ is the mean value of the conditional probability distribution $p_\theta(x_{t-1}|x_t)$. It indicates the expected value of x_{t-1} given the value of x_t at time t. On the other hand, $\Sigma_\theta(x_t, t)$ represents the covariance matrix of the conditional probability distribution $p_\theta(x_{t-1}|x_t)$. Diffusion models are distinguished from other latent variable models by fixing the approximate posterior $q(x_{1:T}|x_0)$, also known as the forward process or diffusion process, to a Markov chain that gradually adds Gaussian noise to the data according to a variance schedule $\beta_1, \ldots, \beta_T$:

$$q(x_{1:T}|x_0) = \prod_{t=1}^{T} q(x_t|x_{t-1}), \quad q(x_t|x_{t-1}) = \mathcal{N}(x_t; \sqrt{1 - \beta_{t-1}}x_{t-1}, \beta_t I) \tag{3}$$

where I denotes an Identity matrix. The variances β_t in the forward process can be learned through reparameterization or held constant as hyperparameters. The choice of Gaussian conditionals in $p_\theta(x_{t-1}|x_t)$ ensures the expressiveness of the reverse process, as both processes have the same functional form when β_t is small. Notably, the forward process allows for closed-form sampling of x_t at any timestep t. By denoting $\alpha_t = 1 - \beta_t$ and $\overline{\alpha}_t = \prod_{s=1}^{t} \alpha_s$, the closed-form expression for $q(x_t|x_0)$ is [25]:

$$q(x_t|x_0) = \mathcal{N}\left(x_t; \sqrt{\overline{\alpha}_t}x_0, (1 - \overline{\alpha}_t)I\right) \tag{4}$$

Training the diffusion models involves optimizing the variational bound:

$$\mathcal{L} = \mathbb{E}[-\log p_\theta(x_0)] \leq \mathbb{E}_q\left[-\log p_\theta(x_{0:T}) - \sum_{t \geq 1} \log \frac{p_\theta(x_{t-1}|x_t)}{q(x_t|x_{t-1})}\right] \tag{5}$$

While there exists a tractable variational lower-bound on $\log p(x_0)$, better results can be obtained by optimizing a surrogate objective that re-weights the terms in the variational lower bound [25]. To compute this surrogate objective, samples x_t are generated by applying Gaussian noise ϵ meant to perturb x_{t-1} to x_t using Eq 4, and then a model ϵ_θ is trained to predict the added noise using a standard mean-squared error loss:

$$L = \mathbb{E}_{t \sim [1,T], x_0 \sim q(x_0), \epsilon \sim \mathcal{N}(0,I)} \| \epsilon - \epsilon_\theta(x_t, t) \|^2 \qquad (6)$$

Here, ϵ_θ is a function approximator which attempts to predict the noise ϵ. By optimizing this surrogate objective, diffusion models can effectively learn the generative process, allowing for the generation of high-quality samples and providing useful latent representations of the data.

Process for Adding Noise. We diffuse brain connectomes according to a specific noise schedule as denoted in the nosing module in Fig. 1-A. The noise schedule is a design choice for diffusion models. We have chosen the linear noise schedule [31] to add perturbations to our graphs. For a linear schedule, β_t is incremented in a linear manner. A total number of diffusion timesteps are decided where the graph at the last timestep $t_{\max}$ corresponds to a pure Gaussian distribution. To prepare noise-perturbed graphs for training, we first sample a batch of target brain connectomes G_{target} and sample a batch of timesteps, one for each graph, respectively. For a sampled graph with an adjacency matrix A^{target} and a timestep $t \in [1, t_{\max}]$, we diffuse the adjacency matrix to timestep t using Eq. 7 in concordance with Eq. 4:

$$A_t^{target} = \sqrt{\overline{\alpha}_t} A_0^{target} + (1 - \overline{\alpha}_t)\epsilon \qquad (7)$$

Here, A_0^{target} represents the initial sampled adjacency matrix, A_t^{target} represents the diffused adjacency matrix at timestep t, and ϵ denotes the noise perturbation applied to the adjacency matrices.

Conditional Denoiser Network. A neural network can serve as the function approximator $\epsilon_\theta(A_t^{target}, c)$, where c represents conditioning information in the form of the source brain connectome and timestep information. This neural network is designed to predict the noise ϵ that diffused A_{t-1}^{target} to A_t^{target}. In this section, we present our conditional denoiser network, which functions as the mapping approximator. The conditional denoiser network architecture is inspired by U-Net [30], enabling the utilization of Convolutional Neural Networks (CNNs) for graph processing, which offers better scalability compared to Graph Neural Networks (GNNs). Although this approach sacrifices some topological information, it compensates for it by leveraging the stacking of CNN layers, resulting in improved performance over GNNs.

Specifically, we consider a target adjacency matrix $A_0^{target} \in \mathbb{R}^{n_{r'} \times n_{r'}}$ to be a grayscale image of size $X^0 \in \mathbb{R}^{1 \times n_{r'} \times n_{r'}}$. Given this input, the grayscale image is initially passed through a channel expansion layer. This layer consists of convolutional filters of size 3×3, followed by batch normalization [32], GeLU activation function [33], and maximum pooling layers [34] with a kernel size of 2×2. The channel expansion layer transforms X^0 to $X^1 \in \mathbb{R}^{32 \times n_{r'} \times n_{r'}}$. Subsequently, a downsampling block, comprising 3×3 convolutional filters, GeLU activation function, batch normalization, and 2×2 maximum pooling filters, is applied to further reduce the size to X^1 to $X^2 \in \mathbb{R}^{32 \times \frac{n_{r'}}{2} \times \frac{n_{r'}}{2}}$. This process is repeated with another channel expansion layer and downsampling block, resulting in an output of size $X^{enc} \in \mathbb{R}^{64 \times 1 \times 1}$ which represents the output of the U-Net encoder block.

To incorporate conditioning information c, we combine it with the output of the encoder block of the U-Net architecture as denoted in Fig. 1-B. Conditioning information refers to any external data provided to the diffusion framework to guide the generation of a specific output. In our case, the source brain connectome G_{source} and the current timestep serve as the conditioning information, guiding the conditional denoiser network to predict the noise that perturbed the corresponding target brain connectome G_{target}. This effectively establishes a mapping function from the source brain connectome to the target brain connectome by utilizing conditioning information in conjunction with the encoded U-Net output.

To incorporate the source brain connectome, we flatten its adjacency matrix $A^{source} \in \mathbb{R}^{n_r \times n_r}$ to $C^1 \in \mathbb{R}^{1 \times n_r^2}$. We employ a two-layered Multi-Layer Perception (MLP) with GeLU activation function to embed this flattened vector into a scalar value $C^2 \in \mathbb{R}$. Similarly, the current timestep t is mapped to a scalar $t^{embed} \in \mathbb{R}$ using a similar MLP. We then perform $X^{cond} = X^{enc} \times C^2 + t^{embed}$. We apply element-wise multiplication between the encoded output and source brain connectome followed by element-wise addition with the embedded timpestep, to incorporate the conditioning information.

To upsample the conditioned information tensor, we employ an upsampling block, consisting of transposed convolutional filters of size 2×2 and GeLU activation function. This upsampling process teansforms X^{cond} to $X'^1 \in \mathbb{R}^{64 \times \frac{n_{r'}}{2} \times \frac{n_{r'}}{2}}$. Subsequently, a channel compression layer, comprising convolutional layers with GeLU activation function, transforms X'^1 to $X'^2 \in \mathbb{R}^{32 \times \frac{n_{r'}}{2} \times \frac{n_{r'}}{2}}$. Another round of upsampling block and channel compression layer is applied to obtain an output of shape $X^{out} \in \mathbb{R}^{1 \times n_{r'} \times n_{r'}}$.

To generate the predicted noise tensor $\hat{\epsilon}$, we concatenate X^0 with X^{out}, resulting in $X^{concat} \in \mathbb{R}^{1 \times n_{r'} \times 2n_{r'}}$. Finally, an MLP is applied to X^{concat} to produce $\hat{\epsilon} \in \mathbb{R}^{1 \times n_{r'} \times n_{r'}}$. We utilize the Mean Squared Error (MSE) loss function to optimize the discrepancy between ϵ and the output of our conditional denoiser network $\hat{\epsilon}$, as defined in Eq. 6.

Conditional Sampling. The conditional sampling module is responsible for generating a target brain connectome based on a given source brain connectome as illustrated in Fig. 1-C. We initialize the process by introducing random Gaussian noise $A^{target}_{t_{max}} \in \mathbb{R}^{1 \times n_r \times n_r}$ at timestep $t_{\max}$. We guide our conditional denoising network ϵ_θ to progressively denoise this Gaussian noise, producing a specific target brain connectome that corresponds to the provided source brain connectome. To achieve this, we employ conditional generation with classifier-free guidance [35], as described in Eq. 8.

$$\epsilon' = (1 + \gamma) \cdot \epsilon_\theta(A^{target}_t, c) - \gamma \cdot \epsilon_\theta(A^{target}_t, \phi) \tag{8}$$

Here, γ represents a hyperparameter that controls the strength of conditional guidance. $\epsilon_\theta(A^{target}_t, \phi)$ denotes $\hat{\epsilon}$ at timestep t when provided with no conditional information. Equation 8 requires two separately trained models: one with conditional training and another with unconditional training. However, we simplify the process by training a single model capable of generating predicted noise both conditionally and unconditionally. To create training examples containing both conditioned and unconditioned samples, we apply random masking to the conditional source connectome information with a probability p for all examples in a batch. This enables the refinement of the Gaussian noise by subtracting ϵ' at each timestep t, starting from t_{max} and iterating until $t > 0$ to yield $\hat{A}_0^{target}$. Finally, we convert the resulting final output $\hat{A}_0^{target} \in \mathbb{R}^{1 \times n_{r'} \times n_{r'}}$ back into a graph format by suppressing the extra dimension, yielding an output $\hat{A} \in \mathbb{R}^{n_{r'} \times n_{r'}}$. $\hat{A}_0^{target}$ represents the corresponding high resolution brain connectome for the low-resolution source connectome used for conditioning.

3   Results and Discussion

Connectomic Dataset and Parameter Setting. We use three-fold cross-validation to evaluate the proposed Dif-GSR framework on 279 subjects from the Southwest University Longitudinal Imaging Multimodal (SLIM) public dataset, where each subject possesses T1-weighted (T1-w), T2-weighted (T2-w) MRI, and resting-state functional MRI (rsfMRI) scans [36].

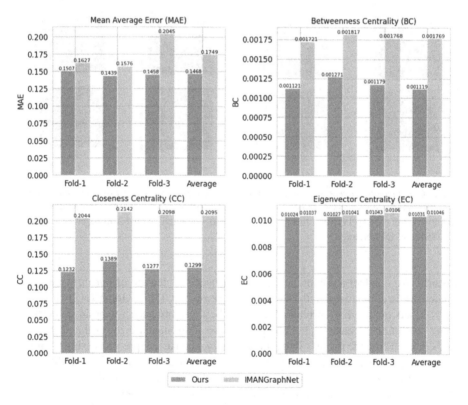

Fig. 2. Bar plots for comparison between different metrics for graph super-resolution task. We present comparison for i) Mean Absolute Error (MAE), ii) Betweeness Centrality (BC), iii) Closeness Centrality (CC) and iv) Eigenvector Centrality (EC) against state-of-the-art IMAN-GraphNet [14].

We utilize FreeSurfer [37] to reconstruct the cortical morphological network (source graphs) based on structural T1-weighted MRI scans. Specifically, we parcellate each cortical hemisphere into 35 cortical regions using the Desikan-Killiany cortical atlas. Finally, by computing the pairwise absolute difference in cortical thickness between pairs of regions of interest, we generate a 35×35 morphological connectivity matrix for each subject. As target graphs, we use 160×160 connectivity matrices [38], where each edge denotes the Pearson correlation coefficient between the average fMRI signals of each pair of ROIs. We utilize the Adam optimizer [39] with a learning rate of 10^{-4} to optimize our conditional denoiser network. The guidance parameter γ is empirically set to 0.5, the dropout probability p to 0.2, and the total number of diffusion timesteps $t_{\max}$ to 400.

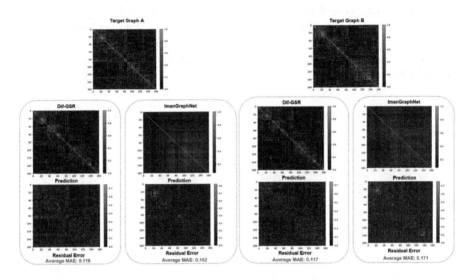

Fig. 3. *Comparison between the ground truth target and predicted target brain connectomes of two representative subjects A and B.* We display the residual error matrix computed using mean absolute error (MAE) between the ground truth and predicted super-resolved brain graphs by Dif-GSR and IMANGraphNet.

Results. We conduct a comprehensive performance evaluation of our diffusion-based framework in comparison to the state-of-the-art method, IMANGraphNet [14], a graph GAN-based model that currently holds the best performance for brain connectome super-resolution. To ensure a fair comparison, we adopt standardized evaluation metrics for benchmarking the results. To begin, we apply a consistent pre-processing technique by cleaning the dataset. This involves replacing any negative values in both the source and target brain connectomes with zeros, denoted as $A_{(i,j)} = 0$ for all $A_{(i,j)} < 0$. This step is carried out for both our framework and the baseline model.

Our results are evaluated using several key metrics: i) Mean Absolute Error (MAE), ii) Eigenvector Centrality (EC), iii) Betweenness Centrality (BC), and iv) Closeness

Centrality (CC). Across all these metrics, our proposed framework achieves state-of-the-art (SOTA) performance, surpassing the baseline model in each category as shown in Fig. 2. Specifically, our framework achieves an average MAE score of 0.1468, while the baseline model achieves a higher MAE score of 0.1749. This substantial reduction in MAE shows the superior accuracy and precision of our framework. Regarding the centrality metrics, our framework achieves the best results in preserving the topological properties of the super-resolved graphs with the lowest MAE in eigenvector centrality, betweenness centrality, and closeness centrality. Overall, our framework consistently outperforms the baseline model across all evaluation metrics, highlighting the effectiveness of diffusion as a powerful mapping function for brain connectome resolution. The achieved superior results demonstrate the capability of our approach to accurately and reliably reconstruct high-resolution brain connectomes. However, Dif-GSR suffers from a slow generation speed, which is a drawback for time-sensitive applications. In addition, the conditional denoiser model exhibits a narrow margin of error, as even modest deviations between the predicted noise and the true noise can result in suboptimal generations. This error propagates across all diffusion timesteps, further compromising the quality of the generated outputs. In the future, we intend to address both issues in designing a more cost-effective and faster Dif-GSR architecture (Fig. 3).

4   Conclusion

This paper introduces a novel diffusion-based framework Dif-GSR for specifically super-resolving brain connectomes. We demonstrate the superior performance of Dif-GSR when compared to the state-of-the-art baseline model for graph super-resolution. However, it is important to acknowledge certain limitations that warrant further investigation and improvement. One notable drawback is the relatively longer time required for graph generation within the diffusion framework compared to its GAN-based counterpart. The iterative nature of the diffusion process, spanning multiple timesteps, results in increased memory usage and computational demands, thus elongating the overall sampling time. To address this limitation, future research should focus on refining the diffusion-based framework to enable faster sampling, potentially through the exploration of consistency models [40] or related techniques. Furthermore, it is worth exploring graph-based diffusion frameworks for the brain connectome super-resolution problem. However, the inherent poor scalability of such approaches may pose challenges when super-resolving graphs with a larger number of nodes. Therefore, careful consideration and innovative solutions are needed to overcome scalability issues and extend the applicability of graph-based diffusion frameworks to effectively handle larger brain connectomes. In conclusion, while our diffusion-based framework currently demonstrates remarkable performance in brain connectome super-resolution, ongoing research efforts should aim to optimize sampling efficiency and explore alternative approaches to address scalability concerns inherent to graph-based frameworks.

References

1. Tournier, J.D., Mori, S., Leemans, A.: Diffusion tensor imaging and beyond. Magn. Reson. Med. **65**, 1532–1556 (2011)

2. Bahrami, K., Shi, F., Rekik, I., Gao, Y., Shen, D.: 7T-guided super-resolution of 3T MRI. Med. Phys. **44**, 1661–1677 (2017)
3. Kaur, P., Sao, A.K., Ahuja, C.K.: Super resolution of magnetic resonance images. J. Imaging **7**, 101 (2021)
4. Sui, Y., Afacan, O., Gholipour, A., Warfield, S.K.: MRI super-resolution through generative degradation learning. Med. Image Comput. Comput. Assist. Interv. **12906**, 430–440 (2021)
5. Zhang, K., et al.: SOUP-GAN: Super-resolution MRI using generative adversarial networks. Tomography **8**, 905–919 (2022)
6. Bahrami, K., Shi, F., Rekik, I., Gao, Y., Shen, D.: 7t-guided super-resolution of 3T MRI. Med. Phys. **44**, 1661–1677 (2017)
7. Bassett, D.S., Sporns, O.: Network neuroscience. Nat. Neurosci. **20**, 353 (2017)
8. van den Heuvel, M.P., Sporns, O.: A cross-disorder connectome landscape of brain dysconnectivity. Nat. Rev. Neurosci. **20**, 435–446 (2019)
9. Fornito, A., Zalesky, A., Breakspear, M.: The connectomics of brain disorders. Nat. Rev. Neurosci. **16**, 159–172 (2015)
10. Qi, S., Meesters, S., Nicolay, K., ter Haar Romeny, B.M., Ossenblok, P.: The influence of construction methodology on structural brain network measures: a review. J. Neurosci. Methods **253**, 170–182 (2015)
11. Bressler, S.L., Menon, V.: Large-scale brain networks in cognition: emerging methods and principles. Trends Cogn. Sci. **14**, 277–290 (2010)
12. Li, Y., Sixou, B., Peyrin, F.: A review of the deep learning methods for medical images super resolution problems. IRBM **42**, 120–133 (2021)
13. Isallari, M., Rekik, I.: GSR-Net: graph super-resolution network for predicting high-resolution from low-resolution functional brain connectomes. In: Liu, M., Yan, P., Lian, C., Cao, X. (eds.) MLMI 2020. LNCS, vol. 12436, pp. 139–149. Springer, Cham (2020). https://doi.org/10.1007/978-3-030-59861-7_15
14. Mhiri, I., Nebli, A., Mahjoub, M.A., Rekik, I.: Non-isomorphic inter-modality graph alignment and synthesis for holistic brain mapping. In: Feragen, A., Sommer, S., Schnabel, J., Nielsen, M. (eds.) IPMI 2021. LNCS, vol. 12729, pp. 203–215. Springer, Cham (2021). https://doi.org/10.1007/978-3-030-78191-0_16
15. Pala, F., Mhiri, I., Rekik, I.: Template-based inter-modality super-resolution of brain connectivity. In: Rekik, I., Adeli, E., Park, S.H., Schnabel, J. (eds.) PRIME 2021. LNCS, vol. 12928, pp. 70–82. Springer, Cham (2021). https://doi.org/10.1007/978-3-030-87602-9_7
16. Mhiri, I., Mahjoub, M.A., Rekik, I.: StairwayGraphNet for inter- and intra-modality multiresolution brain graph alignment and synthesis. In: Lian, C., Cao, X., Rekik, I., Xu, X., Yan, P. (eds.) MLMI 2021. LNCS, vol. 12966, pp. 140–150. Springer, Cham (2021). https://doi.org/10.1007/978-3-030-87589-3_15
17. Chen, D., Lin, Y., Li, W., Li, P., Zhou, J., Sun, X.: Measuring and relieving the over-smoothing problem for graph neural networks from the topological view. Proc. AAAI Conf. Artif. Intell. **34**, 3438–3445 (2020)
18. Ansari, A.F., Scarlett, J., Soh, H.: A characteristic function approach to deep implicit generative modeling. In: Proceedings of the IEEE/CVF Conference on Computer Vision and Pattern Recognition, pp. 7478–7487 (2020)
19. Rombach, R., Blattmann, A., Lorenz, D., Esser, P., Ommer, B.: High-resolution image synthesis with latent diffusion models (2022)
20. Yu, W., Heber, S., Pock, T.: Learning reaction-diffusion models for image inpainting. In: Gall, J., Gehler, P., Leibe, B. (eds.) GCPR 2015. LNCS, vol. 9358, pp. 356–367. Springer, Cham (2015). https://doi.org/10.1007/978-3-319-24947-6_29
21. Leng, Y., et al.: Binauralgrad: a two-stage conditional diffusion probabilistic model for binaural audio synthesis. Adv. Neural. Inf. Process. Syst. **35**, 23689–23700 (2022)

22. Pascual, S., Bhattacharya, G., Yeh, C., Pons, J., Serrà, J.: Full-band general audio synthesis with score-based diffusion. In: ICASSP 2023–2023 IEEE International Conference on Acoustics, Speech and Signal Processing (ICASSP), pp. 1–5. IEEE (2023)

23. Ho, J., Salimans, T., Gritsenko, A., Chan, W., Norouzi, M., Fleet, D.J.: Video diffusion models (2022)

24. Molad, E., et al.: Dreamix: video diffusion models are general video editors (2023)

25. Ho, J., Jain, A., Abbeel, P.: Denoising diffusion probabilistic models (2020)

26. Lee, J.S., Kim, J., Kim, P.M.: Score-based generative modeling for de novo protein design. Nat. Comput. Sci. (2023)

27. Vahdat, A., Kreis, K., Kautz, J.: Score-based generative modeling in latent space. Adv. Neural. Inf. Process. Syst. **34**, 11287–11302 (2021)

28. Jo, J., Lee, S., Hwang, S.J.: Score-based generative modeling of graphs via the system of stochastic differential equations. In: International Conference on Machine Learning, pp. 10362–10383. PMLR (2022)

29. Nichol, A., et al.: Glide: towards photorealistic image generation and editing with text-guided diffusion models. arXiv preprint arXiv:2112.10741 (2021)

30. Ronneberger, O., Fischer, P., Brox, T.: U-Net: convolutional networks for biomedical image segmentation. In: Navab, N., Hornegger, J., Wells, W.M., Frangi, A.F. (eds.) MICCAI 2015. LNCS, vol. 9351, pp. 234–241. Springer, Cham (2015). https://doi.org/10.1007/978-3-319-24574-4_28

31. Chen, T.: On the importance of noise scheduling for diffusion models (2023)

32. Ioffe, S., Szegedy, C.: Batch normalization: Accelerating deep network training by reducing internal covariate shift (2015)

33. Hendrycks, D., Gimpel, K.: Gaussian error linear units (GELUS) (2020)

34. Nagi, J., et al.:. Max-pooling convolutional neural networks for vision-based hand gesture recognition, pp. 342–347 (2011)

35. Ho, J., Salimans, T.: Classifier-free diffusion guidance (2022)

36. Liu, W., et al.: Longitudinal test-retest neuroimaging data from healthy young adults in southwest china. Sci. Data **4** (2017)

37. Fischl, B.: FreeSurfer. Neuroimage **62**, 774–781 (2012)

38. Dosenbach, N.U., et al.: Prediction of individual brain maturity using FMRI. Science **329**, 1358–1361 (2010)

39. Kingma, D.P., Ba, J.: Adam: a method for stochastic optimization (2017)

40. Song, Y., Dhariwal, P., Chen, M., Sutskever, I.: Consistency models (2023)

Deep Survival Analysis in Multiple Sclerosis

Xin Zhang[1,2(✉)], Deval Mehta[1,2,3], Chao Zhu[4], Daniel Merlo[4,5], Yanan Hu[6],
Melissa Gresle[4,5], David Darby[4,5], Anneke van der Walt[4,5],
Helmut Butzkueven[4,5], and Zongyuan Ge[1,2,3]

[1] Faculty of Engineering, Monash University, Melbourne, Australia
`xin.zhang4@monash.edu`
[2] Monash Medical AI, Monash University, Melbourne, Australia
[3] AIM for Health Lab, Faculty of IT, Monash University, Melbourne, Australia
[4] Department of Neuroscience, Central Clinical School, Monash University,
Melbourne, Australia
[5] Department of Neurology, Alfred Hospital, Melbourne, Australia
[6] Monash Centre for Health Research and Implementation, School of Public Health
and Preventive Medicine, Monash University, Melbourne, Australia

Abstract. Multiple Sclerosis (MS) is the most frequent non-traumatic debilitating neurological disease. It is usually diagnosed based on clinical observations and supporting data from auxiliary procedures. However, its course is extremely unpredictable, and traditional statistical survival models fail to perform reliably on longitudinal data. An efficient and precise prognosis model of patient-specific MS time-to-event distributions is needed to aid in joint decision-making in subsequent treatment and care. In this work, we aim to estimate the survival function to predict MS disability progression based on discrete longitudinal reaction time trajectories and related clinical variables. To this end, we initially preprocess two sets of measurements obtained from the same cohort of patients. One set comprises the patients' reaction trajectories recorded during computerized tests, while the other set involves assessing their disability progression and extracting practical clinical information. Then we propose our deep survival model for discovering the connections between temporal data and the potential risk. The model is optimised over the sum of three losses, including longitudinal loss, survival loss and consistent loss. We evaluate our model against other machine learning methods on the same dataset. The experimental results demonstrate the advantage of our proposed deep learning model and prove that such computerized measurements can genuinely reflect the disease stage of MS patients and provide a second opinion for prognosticating their disability progression.

Keywords: Survival analysis · Multiple sclerosis · Disability progression · temporal

I. Rekik et al. (Eds.): PRIME 2023, LNCS 14277, pp. 108–119, 2023.
https://doi.org/10.1007/978-3-031-46005-0_10

1   Introduction

Multiple Sclerosis (MS) is a central nervous system immune-mediated inflammatory and neurodegenerative disease. It affects twice as many females as it does males, and people of Northern European ancestry tend to be at the highest risk [4]. Many treatments for MS aim at reducing the frequency of relapses, which is the main endpoint of clinical trials. Another endpoint is the accumulation of disability. Approximately 85% of patients will have a slowly progressing course after their first symptoms [21]. Clinicians use the Expanded Disability Status Scale (EDSS) score [13] for quantifying disability based on a neurological examination, and also for monitoring changes in the level of disability over time. Other conventional methodologies for prognosticating this progression include evaluating the activity of novel magnetic resonance imaging (MRI) and analyzing cerebrospinal fluid (CSF). [3,4,19], however, these can be costly, invasive and time consuming. This becomes the main obstacle for research and tracking patients. Therefore, it is important to find a simpler way to monitor cognitive changes in individual MS patients to predict disability progression. Fortunately, by using latent class modelling, Merlo et al. [15] have reported a relationship between increased risk of MS disability progression and worsening reaction times. They also reported clinic use of computerized tests is a feasible method to detect cognitive change trajectories in MS patients. Moreover, in order to accurately depict and forecast disability changes through this tests, survival analysis has emerged as the most promising approach, gaining traction in the medical field in recent times [12].

Survival analysis, known as time-to-event analysis, is a statistical and machine learning discipline that aims to estimates a survival function, indicating the probability of a specific event happening after a designated time in the future. Because of data censoring and competing risks in practice, survival analysis varies from conventional regression models. Dealing statistically with interrelated temporal data is essential for some important applications, such as various hemodynamic vital signs [10]. For being consistent with traditional survival regression procedures, common adaptations to survival models for observations include encoding input variables with aggregate statistics acquired over time. Under such circumstances, time series becomes one of the most important data modalities that are not always adequately addressed by inputting a large set of static samples of input covariate vectors. Katzman et al. [11] presented DeepSurv, a proportional hazard model in which relative risks are evaluated using one neural network. DeepSurv is able to simulate non-linear proportional risks, although there are still limited to strong Cox assumptions. Lee et al. [14] proposed Dynamic DeepHit (DDH), which completely eliminates the requirement for explicit model specifications. It can perform dynamic survival analysis with competing hazards on the basis of temporal data, but does not scale well to datasets with large horizons. Recurrent Deep Survival Model (RDSM) proposed by Nagpal et al. [16] is based on his Deep Survival Machines (DSM) [17], which can also handle temporal data with time-varying coefficients. However, it does not perform well with a larger amount of censoring. Meanwhile, Ren et al. [20] also proposed an recurrent neural network (RNN) based model, but this only

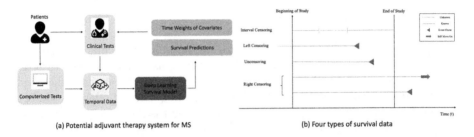

(a) Potential adjuvant therapy system for MS   (b) Four types of survival data

Fig. 1. Illustrations of (a) an adjuvant therapy system for MS based on deep survival framework and (b) four survival data types

considers time-invariant features. Recent machine learning approaches to modelling time-varying covariates remain comparatively unexplored in the survival analysis literature.

In this paper, we propose a unique deep survival model for our in-house MS datasets. Our aim is to accurately predict the survival distribution for MS patients based on longitudinal input variables without competing risks. This model, based on convenient computerized tests, may help doctors make more accurate decisions for patients' health cares and medications in the future. Figure 1(a) illustrates a potential adjuvant therapy system for MS. Specifically, our model adopts RNN for capturing embedding features from longitudinal covariate matrix, computes the time importance of the previous measurements by using last measurement, and considers all unconfirmed cases as right-censoring (All cases of survival data are illustrated in Fig. 1(b)). Three loss functions have been specifically designed and applied for this work: *longitudinal loss* for more accurate longitudinal predictions; *survival loss* and *consistent loss* for a better and rational survival probability distribution. We evaluate the model on the MS dataset and compare with the other existing survival methods. Experimental results show such longitudinal computerized tests can give strong support for tracking and predicting disability progression of MS patients, and that our model can achieve better performance.

2   Method

2.1   Problem Definition

For survival analysis, the data structure is presented in a Time-to-Event data manner. we discretize the survival horizon by δt, resulting in the discretized time intervals $T = \{0, 1, ..., T_k, ..., T_{max}\}$, where δt and T_{max} are pre-defined time resolution and maximum time horizon based on dataset. Based on this time interval, the dataset provides three parts of knowledge: longitudinal observed covariates $S^j = \{s_0^j, s_1^j, ..., s_{Kj}^j\}$, a personalized time interval $\Psi^j = \{\Psi_0^j, \Psi_1^j, ..., \Psi_{Kj}^j\}$, and a sequence of event indicators $e^j = \{e_0^j, e_1^j, ..., e_{Kj}^j\}$ (e.g., 0 for live and 1 for death only in event time horizon), where j indicates the individual patient. An example dataset can be found in Appendix A.

2.2   Deep Survival Model

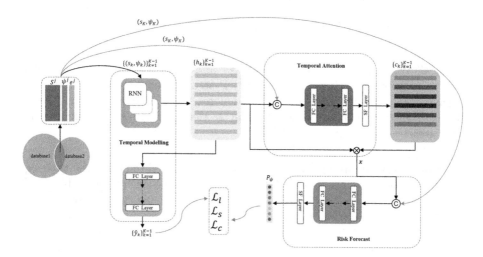

Fig. 2. Pipeline of our proposed model. Longitudinal loss $\mathcal{L}_l$ is generated from temporal modelling module; Survival loss $\mathcal{L}_s$ and consistent loss $\mathcal{L}_c$ are generated from risk forecast module.

Overview. The overall framework of our model is shown in Fig. 2. It is inspired by DDH [14]. The model consists of a temporal modelling (TM) module, temporal attention (TA) module and a risk forecast (RF) module. The TM module takes longitudinal pairs of time-varying covariates and survival time (except the last measurement), extracts the hidden features and predicts the estimation of new covariates at the specified survival time. The TA module takes the hidden features from the TM as well as the last measurement pair to generate the time significance matrix of earlier pairs. This is multiplied by the earlier pairs of measurements to generate a weighted vector. Lastly, the RF module takes this vector and the last pair for the final survival probability prediction. For ease notation, we exclude the explicit dependence on j in the context of these module subsections.

Temporal modelling module is a combination of RNN structure and a fully connected (FC) layer, which is primarily designed to capture features from longitudinal covariates $s^j(t)$ of each individual j. In the training process, a tuple of $(\boldsymbol{s}_k, \boldsymbol{\Psi}_k)$ will be an input for the RNN in the time stamp k, and it will output hidden features $\boldsymbol{h}_k$, which can be expressed as follows if we presume on Long Short-Term Memory (LSTM) [6]

$$\begin{aligned}
\boldsymbol{f}_k &= \sigma_g(W_f[\boldsymbol{s}_k, \boldsymbol{\Psi}_k] + U_f \boldsymbol{h}_{k-1} + b_f) \\
\boldsymbol{i}_k &= \sigma_g(W_i[\boldsymbol{s}_k, \boldsymbol{\Psi}_k] + U_i \boldsymbol{h}_{k-1} + b_i) \\
\boldsymbol{o}_k &= \sigma_g(W_o[\boldsymbol{s}_k, \boldsymbol{\Psi}_k] + U_o \boldsymbol{h}_{k-1} + b_o) \\
\boldsymbol{c}_k &= \boldsymbol{f}_k \odot \boldsymbol{c}_{k-1} + \boldsymbol{i}_k \odot \sigma_c(W_c[\boldsymbol{s}_k, \boldsymbol{\Psi}_k] + U_c \boldsymbol{h}_{k-1} + b_c) \\
\boldsymbol{h}_k &= \boldsymbol{o}_k \odot \sigma_h \boldsymbol{c}_k
\end{aligned} \tag{1}$$

where all W, U and b are weight matrices and bias vector parameters which need to be learned during training, $\sigma_g(\star)$ is sigmoid function, $\sigma_h(\star)$ and $\sigma_c(\star)$ are hyperbolic tangent function and $\odot$ denotes the Hadamard product. Next, FC layers take $\boldsymbol{h}_k$ as input, and output $\hat{\boldsymbol{y}}_k$ as the prediction of the longitudinal covariates.

Temporal Attention Module. This model is designed to clarify the time significance (weights) of the former data in forecasting the survival probability [1]. It predicts the weights of all previous observations by using the last observation. It simply uses $\boldsymbol{h}_k$ from the temporal modelling part as its input, computes and normalizes the attention c_k by another FC layer with a soft-max layer, then outputs a weighted gross vector $\boldsymbol{x}$, which can be expressed as:

$$\boldsymbol{x} = \sum_{k=1}^{K-1} c_k \cdot \boldsymbol{h}_k \tag{2}$$

Risk forecast module contains FC layers in order to acquire relationships between survival risk and the temporal covariates and a soft-max layer for obtaining the appropriate probability. It takes the concatenation of the last observation $[\boldsymbol{s}_K, \boldsymbol{\Psi}_K]$ and the attention c_k as inputs, and outputs the probability mass function (PMF) distribution of the hitting time:

$$p = \{p_1, p_2, ..., p_{T_{max}}\} \tag{3}$$

Training Losses. The overall loss is the weighted sum of all three loss types as:

$$\mathcal{L}_{total} = \mathcal{L}_s + \alpha_l \cdot \mathcal{L}_l + \alpha_c \cdot \mathcal{L}_c \tag{4}$$

where α_l and α_c are hyperparameters. Firstly, longitudinal loss $\mathcal{L}_l$ is operated to penalize the error from the temporal modelling subnetwork. It directly uses mean squared error (MSE) between the longitudinal predictions and the true observations (except the first observation as it cannot be forecasted).

$$\mathcal{L}_l = \sum_{j=1}^{J} \sum_{k=0}^{K-1} (s_{k+1}^j - \hat{y}_k^j)^2 \tag{5}$$

The survival loss $\mathcal{L}_s$ can be calculated as:

$$\mathcal{L}_s = -\sum_{j=1}^{J} \left[e_{K^j}^j \cdot log(p_{k=K^j}^j) + (1 - e_{K^j}^j) \cdot log\left(\sum_{k=K^j+1}^{T_{max}} p_k \right) \right] \tag{6}$$

which aims to treating the survival problem as a T_{max}-class classification problem. It can lead the estimate of PMF concentrates on its event time step for all confirmed cases ($e^j_{Kj} = 1$), and can penalize the PMF before the censoring time for all censored cases ($e^j_{Kj} = 0$). Moreover, the idea of consistent loss $\mathcal{L}_c$ is inspired by concordance [5] and it can penalize the wrong ordering of predicted probability distributions between individuals, while it's the fact that survival probability of one individual who lived until time stamp T_k must larger than another whose event happens at T_k, but not opposite. Therefore, we compare mean lifetimes from different samples to check its consistency. Firstly, the mean lifetime in discrete-time model [7] is calculated as the area under estimated survival curve $\hat{Su}(k)$:

$$\mu^j \approx \sum_{k=0}^{T_{max}} \hat{Su}^j(k) = \sum_{k=0}^{T_{max}} \left(1 - \sum_{n=0}^{k} p^j_n \right) \tag{7}$$

Then, the consistent loss can be calculated as:

$$\mathcal{L}_c = \sum_{j=1}^{J} max\{0, \mathbb{I}(e^j_{Kj}, \Psi^i_{Ki} > \Psi^j_{Kj}) \cdot [(\Psi^i_{Ki} - \Psi^j_{Kj}) - (\mu^i - \mu^j)]\} \tag{8}$$

where, $\mathbb{I}(\star)$ is an indicator function.

3   MS Dataset

To the best of our knowledge, we are unaware of any MS datasets that contain both clinical information and results of task-designed computerized tests used in survival analysis. Here, our work is based on a longitudinal MS dataset by combining useful features from two MS databases. **Database 1** contains time-varying cognitive performance data using reaction time tasks in patients diagnosed with MS. In every test, each patient is required to finish three tasks over 30 times, with the tasks testing psychomotor function, attention and working memory. The patients are instructed to respond as quickly as possible when the stimulus is presented onscreen, and the speed and accuracy of each are recorded.[1] We chose to use aggregated 4 statistics consisting of the mean reaction time and the standard deviation, hit-rate and accuracy of each task, giving us a total of 12 features. **Database 2** contains time-invariant clinical variables such as age, gender, Expanded Disability Status Scale (EDSS), EDSS baseline, Disease Modifying Therapy (DMT) use times, years since the first symptom and relapse times in last two years. We have selected the testing results that matched as closely in time to the tests in Database 1. Among them, EDSS is not considered as a feature but rather serves to validate the occurrence of an event through the six-month disability improvement confirmation rule [8]. This rule mandates that an event is only confirmed to have taken place when there is a significant progression in EDSS compared to its baseline value. It should be noted that there

---

[1] Demo website: https://www.msreactor.com/controls/.

Table 1. Extracted features from two databases and explanations. (Stdev: standard deviation.)

Database 1 Reaction Measurements		Remarks
Task 1/Task 2/Task 3	Mean	Calculated mean of correct response reaction times, in ms
	Stdev	Calculated standard deviation of correct response reaction times, in ms
	Hit-rate	Calculated the proportion of correct responses
	Accuracy	The arcsine transform of the square root of the hit-rate
Database 2 Clinical Information		Remarks
Gender		Female/Male
Age		In years
EDSS baseline		The EDSS score when first measurement happens
DMT used times		Counted DMT used times before each measurement
Year since first symptom		Calculated time gap between the first symptom and each measurement
Relapse times in last 2 years		Counted relapse times for each measurements with 2 years benchmark

is always a time gap between the entry to clinical trials and the date of measurements, so we first align the time of these two events, taking less than three months as the benchmark. More features and dataset pre-processed information can be found in Table 1.

Overall, out of 1,325 patients from Database 1 and 1,029 patients from Database 2, experiments were conducted on 746 individuals with total of 18 features (6 static covariates and 12 time-varying covariates). For each patients, longitudinal measurements were conducted roughly every half-year; the time interval between two adjacent tests range from 0 to 44 months with mean of 4.68 months. The number of yearly follow-ups was from 1 to 6 with mean of 2.20 tests per patients. Among the total of 746 individuals, 148 patients (19.84%) were followed until disease progression and the remaining 598 patients (80.16%) were right-censored. There is no missing clinical features in our processed MS dataset. However, with different pre-defined time resolution, the occurence of missing values happens in longitudinal covariates. We replace these missing values by *last-observation-carried-forward* (LOCF) method and the ones that are still missing after the LOCF method are imputed by mean for these covariates. Eventually, We evaluated the proposed model on this prepared dataset.

4   Experiment and Results

4.1   Implementation Details

All individuals were randomly split into 80%, 20% for training and testing, respectively, and then reserved 20% of the training set as the validation set for early-stopping to avoid over-fitting. For comparison with the baseline models, we applied grid searching for hyperparameters. Considering there are already a large amount of right censored cases, we investigated the model's robustness to

Table 2. The optimal hyperparameters of our model

Dataset	Batch	LR	RNN type	RNN node	RNN dimension	FC structure	α_l	α_c
MS	32	10^{-4}	LSTM	2	50	[100, 100]	0.05	0.1

the censoring without increasing the number of censored data during the training process. The censored and uncensored cases contained the same proportion in training, validation and testing sets. Before training the model, all observed longitudinal covariates were standardized to a normal distribution with zero mean and unit variance. Then we padded the variable-length with null values beforehand due to different numbers of tests for individuals, making sure the equivalent length of time series data was appropriate for RNN requests. The model was trained via ADAM optimizer. T_{max} was set to 100 months based on the largest observed 80 months in the dataset. We further used a grid searching method for other hyperparameter optimization, including batch size from $\{16, 32, 64\}$, learning rate from $\{10^{-3}, 10^{-4}, 5 \cdot 10^{-5}\}$, type of RNN cell from LSTM, GRU and vanilla RNN, number of RNN hidden layers from $\{2, 3\}$, dimensionality of RNN hidden layers from $\{50, 100\}$, the structure of all FC hidden layers, followed by ReLU activations, from $\{[100], [100, 100], [100, 100, 100]\}$, α_l from $\{0.01, 0.05, 0.1, 0.5\}$ and α_c from $\{0.01, 0.05, 0.1, 0.5\}$. Table 2 shows the optimal hyperparameters of our model on MS dataset. All experiments in this paper were conducted in PyTorch [18] on the same environments with fixed random seeds (Hardware: Intel Core i9-9900k CPU, NVIDIA GeForce RTX 2080Ti GPU; Software: Python 3.8.5, PyTorch 1.7.1 and CUDA 11.0).

4.2   Results

We considered Time-Dependent Concordance-Index (TD C-Index) [5], Brier Score and Area Under ROC curve (AUC) for assessing the performance of models, and compared the performance of our model to baseline approaches including DDH [14], RDSM [16], DeepSurv [11], Cox Proportional Hazards (CPH) model [2] and Random Survival Forests (RSF) [9] on MS dataset. We assumed the data was time independent in the last three models. Table 3 shows the comparison of three evaluation metrics with different δt. Compelling evidence suggests that incorporating time-varying factors, such as ours, DDH and RDSM, can enhance the modeling of multivariate longitudinal time series data. Additionally, our proposed model demonstrates superior performance compared to other existing approaches, exhibiting enhanced predictive capabilities specifically within the context of a single risk problem. These findings indicate that employing a PMF-based estimation strategy proves to be more effective when learning from datasets characterized by significant levels of censoring. Furthermore, it is apparent that the overall performance improves gradually as the parameter δt increases. This observation aligns with intuitive expectations, as larger time intervals are introduced along the discrete time axis. Consequently, when evaluating metrics such as the C-Index, the discordant pairs initially identified between two individuals may no longer meet the criteria due to this temporal adjustment. However, due to the substantial proportion of right censoring in comparison to uncensored data, the metrics themselves become unstable, thereby resulting in larger standard deviations than usual.

Table 3. Performances of different approaches on MS dataset. (The unit of δt is in month. Means and standard deviations were obtained via 5 random splits. TD: time dependent)

Methods	TD	TD C-Index ↑			Brier Score ↓			ROC-AUC ↑		
		δt			δt			δt		
		6	3	1	6	3	1	6	3	1
CPH [2]	✗	0.662 (0.043)	0.676 (0.045)	0.618 (0.053)	0.012 (0.003)	0.011 (0.004)	0.016 (0.005)	0.667 (0.043)	0.682 (0.046)	0.617 (0.052)
RSF [9]	✗	0.675 (0.028)	0.667 (0.034)	0.643 (0.031)	0.012 (0.004)	0.014 (0.004)	0.017 (0.003)	0.678 (0.029)	0.665 (0.030)	0.645 (0.032)
DeepSurv [11]	✗	0.678 (0.021)	0.666 (0.026)	0.656 (0.028)	0.009 (0.002)	0.011 (0.003)	0.014 (0.003)	0.679 (0.021)	0.665 (0.020)	0.655 (0.024)
RDSM [16]	✓	0.733 (0.023)	0.725 (0.021)	0.711 (0.025)	0.007 (0.002)	0.008 (0.002)	0.012 (0.004)	0.735 (0.024)	0.726 (0.024)	0.709 (0.027)
DDH [14]	✓	0.738 (0.024)	0.735 (0.023)	0.724 (0.025)	0.006 (0.001)	0.007 (0.002)	0.012 (0.003)	0.741 (0.022)	0.736 (0.021)	0.727 (0.025)
proposed	✓	**0.764 (0.025)**	**0.754 (0.023)**	**0.751 (0.025)**	**0.005 (0.001)**	**0.006 (0.002)**	**0.010 (0.003)**	**0.766 (0.032)**	**0.757 (0.020)**	**0.749 (0.026)**

Ablation Study. Table 4 shows the ablation study of the effects of each loss function. In our observations, we have found that $\mathcal{L}_s$ plays a decisive role during training, as it directly influences the individual's PMF distribution. Furthermore, the inclusion of variable $\mathcal{L}_c$ significantly enhances the C-index, primarily due to its additional consideration of the temporal ordering of survival times between individuals. Additionally, the incorporation of variable $\mathcal{L}_l$ yields a marginal improvement in performance.

Table 4. Ablation study of three loss functions. Experiments run with the optimal hypermeters. (The unit of δt is in month. Means and standard deviations were obtained via 5 random splits.)

Losses			TD C-Index ↑			Brier Score ↓			ROC-AUC ↑		
$\mathcal{L}_s$	$\mathcal{L}_c$	$\mathcal{L}_l$	δt			δt			δt		
			6	3	1	6	3	1	6	3	1
✓			0.715 (0.032)	0.711 (0.033)	0.704 (0.035)	0.008 (0.002)	0.008 (0.002)	0.013 (0.003)	0.717 (0.034)	0.712 (0.033)	0.0705 (0.034)
✓	✓		0.757 (0.029)	0.743 (0.030)	0.737 (0.031)	0.006 (0.001)	0.006 (0.002)	0.011 (0.004)	0.757 (0.028)	0.755 (0.031)	0.752 (0.029)
✓		✓	0.725 (0.027)	0.723 (0.031)	0.712 (0.031)	0.008 (0.002)	0.008 (0.002)	0.012 (0.003)	0.726 (0.027)	0.725 (0.031)	0.713 (0.032)
✓	✓	✓	**0.764 (0.025)**	**0.754 (0.023)**	**0.751 (0.025)**	**0.005 (0.001)**	**0.006 (0.002)**	**0.010 (0.003)**	**0.766 (0.032)**	**0.757 (0.020)**	**0.749 (0.026)**

5   Conclusion and Future Work

In this study, we present a deep survival model for prognostic MS disability progression. Our model is capable of commendably estimating time-to-event in the presence of right censoring, and can be easily applied to any longitudinal survival tabular data. The experiment results on our in-house MS dataset demonstrate our model outperforms other models on predicting survival distributions. Although the utilization of PMF-based loss design obviates the need to consider the monotonicity of the ultimate survival function, this approach is constrained by the length of the temporal axis. Hence, we intend to enhance the loss design in order to alleviate the instability arising from extended time axes. Moreover, we aim to investigate intricate clinical features, such as the number of DMTs, and incorporate a larger volume of uncensored data to enhance the performance of the model. Additionally, an intriguing research avenue involves substituting aggregated measurement data with all fractionated measurement data, which can provide a deeper comprehension of the significance of each test and facilitate effective modifications to testing methodologies.

A   Time-to-Event Data

See Table 5.

Table 5. An example of faked dataset, which is based on a pre-define time resolution $\delta t = 5$. For individual j, e means event indicator, t means actual time stamp, ψ is the discretized time horizon, and s is a matrix for all covariates.

ID j	EDSS	Event e_k^j	Time/months t_k^j	Horizon Ψ_k^j	Covariates s^j
1	1	0	0	−1	$s^1(\Psi = -1)$
1	1	0	6	1	$s^1(\Psi = 1)$
1	1.5	0	12.5	2	$s^1(\Psi = 2)$
2	0	0	0	−1	$s^2(\Psi = -1)$
2	2	0	4	0	$s^2(\Psi = 0)$
2	1	0	10.8	2	$s^2(\Psi = 2)$
3	2	0	0	−1	$s^3(\Psi = -1)$
3	2	0	2.6	0	$s^3(\Psi = 0)$
3	3.5	1	9.2	1	$s^3(\Psi = 1)$
⋮	⋮	⋮	⋮	⋮	⋮
⋮	⋮	⋮	⋮	⋮	⋮

References

1. Bahdanau, D., Cho, K., Bengio, Y.: Neural machine translation by jointly learning to align and translate. arXiv preprint arXiv:1409.0473 (2014)
2. Cox, D.R.: Regression models and life-tables. J. Roy. Stat. Soc.: Ser. B (Methodol.) **34**(2), 187–202 (1972)
3. Fuh-Ngwa, V., et al.: Developing a clinical-environmental-genotypic prognostic index for relapsing-onset multiple sclerosis and clinically isolated syndrome. Brain Commun. **3**(4), fcab288 (2021)
4. Goldenberg, M.M.: Multiple sclerosis review. Pharm. Therap. **37**(3), 175 (2012)
5. Harrell, F.E., Califf, R.M., Pryor, D.B., Lee, K.L., Rosati, R.A.: Evaluating the yield of medical tests. JAMA **247**(18), 2543–2546 (1982)
6. Hochreiter, S., Schmidhuber, J.: Long short-term memory. Neural Comput. **9**(8), 1735–1780 (1997)
7. Hu, S., Fridgeirsson, E., van Wingen, G., Welling, M.: Transformer-based deep survival analysis. In: Survival Prediction-Algorithms, Challenges and Applications, pp. 132–148. PMLR (2021)
8. Hunter, S.F., et al.: Confirmed 6-month disability improvement and worsening correlate with long-term disability outcomes in alemtuzumab-treated patients with multiple sclerosis: post hoc analysis of the care-ms studies. Neurol. Therapy **10**(2), 803–818 (2021)
9. Ishwaran, H., Kogalur, U.B., Blackstone, E.H., Lauer, M.S.: Random survival forests. Annal. Appl. Statist. **2**(3), 841–860 (2008)
10. Kane, G.C., Maradit-Kremers, H., Slusser, J.P., Scott, C.G., Frantz, R.P., McGoon, M.D.: Integration of clinical and hemodynamic parameters in the prediction of long-term survival in patients with pulmonary arterial hypertension. Chest **139**(6), 1285–1293 (2011)
11. Katzman, J.L., Shaham, U., Cloninger, A., Bates, J., Jiang, T., Kluger, Y.: Deepsurv: personalized treatment recommender system using a cox proportional hazards deep neural network. BMC Med. Res. Methodol. **18**(1), 1–12 (2018)
12. Kleinbaum, D.G., Klein, M.: Survival Analysis. SBH, Springer, New York (2012). https://doi.org/10.1007/978-1-4419-6646-9
13. Kurtzke, J.F.: Rating neurologic impairment in multiple sclerosis: an expanded disability status scale (EDSS). Neurology **33**(11), 1444–1444 (1983)
14. Lee, C., Yoon, J., Van Der Schaar, M.: Dynamic-deephit: a deep learning approach for dynamic survival analysis with competing risks based on longitudinal data. IEEE Trans. Biomed. Eng. **67**(1), 122–133 (2019)
15. Merlo, D., et al.: Association between cognitive trajectories and disability progression in patients with relapsing-remitting multiple sclerosis. Neurology **97**(20), e2020–e2031 (2021)
16. Nagpal, C., Jeanselme, V., Dubrawski, A.: Deep parametric time-to-event regression with time-varying covariates. In: Survival Prediction-Algorithms, Challenges and Applications, pp. 184–193. PMLR (2021)
17. Nagpal, C., Li, X., Dubrawski, A.: Deep survival machines: fully parametric survival regression and representation learning for censored data with competing risks. IEEE J. Biomed. Health Inform. **25**(8), 3163–3175 (2021)
18. Paszke, A., et al.: Pytorch: an imperative style, high-performance deep learning library. Adv. Neural Inf. Process. Syst. **32** (2019)

19. Pisani, A.I., Scalfari, A., Crescenzo, F., Romualdi, C., Calabrese, M.: A novel prognostic score to assess the risk of progression in relapsing- remitting multiple sclerosis patients. Eur. J. Neurol. **28**(8), 2503–2512 (2021)
20. Ren, K., et al.: Deep recurrent survival analysis. Proc. AAAI Conf. Artif. Intell. **33**, 4798–4805 (2019)
21. Rudick, R.A., et al.: Disability progression in a clinical trial of relapsing-remitting multiple sclerosis: eight-year follow-up. Arch. Neurol. **67**(11), 1329–1335 (2010)

Federated Multi-trajectory GNNs Under Data Limitations for Baby Brain Connectivity Forecasting

Michalis Pistos[1,2], Gang Li[2], Weili Lin[2], Dinggang Shen[3,4,5], and Islem Rekik[1(✉)]

[1] BASIRA Lab, Imperial-X and Department of Computing, Imperial College London, London, UK
i.rekik@imperial.ac.uk
[2] Department of Radiology and Biomedical Research Imaging Center, University of North Carolina at Chapel Hill, Chapel Hill, NC, USA
[3] School of Biomedical Engineering, ShanghaiTech University, Shanghai 201210, China
[4] Shanghai United Imaging Intelligence Co., Ltd., Shanghai 200230, China
[5] Shanghai Clinical Research and Trial Center, Shanghai 201210, China
https://basira-lab.com/

Abstract. Building accurate predictive models to forecast the trajectory evolution of baby brain networks during the first postnatal year can provide valuable insights into the dynamics of early brain connectivity development. While emerging studies aimed to predict the evolution of brain graphs from a single observation, they suffer from two major limitations: (i) they typically rely on large training datasets to achieve satisfactory performance. However, longitudinal infant brain scans are costly and hard to acquire, and (ii) they adopt a uni-trajectory approach, lacking the ability to generalize to multi-trajectory prediction tasks, where each graph trajectory corresponds to a particular imaging modality (e.g., functional) and at a fixed resolution (graph size). To address these limitations, we propose FedGmTE-Net*, a *federated graph-based multi-trajectory evolution network*. Given a small dataset, we leverage the power of federation through collaborative model sharing among diverse hospitals. This approach not only enhances the performance of the local generative graph neural network (GNN) model of each hospital but also ensures the preservation of data privacy. To the best of our knowledge, our framework is the first federated learning framework designed for brain multi-trajectory evolution prediction. Further, to make the most of the limited data available at each hospital, we incorporate an auxiliary regularizer that modifies the local objective function, for more effective utilization of all the longitudinal brain connectivity in the evolution trajectory. This significantly improves the network performance. Our comprehensive experimental results demonstrate that our proposed FedGmTE-Net* outperforms benchmark methods by a substantial margin. Our source code is available at https://github.com/basiralab/FedGmTE-Net.

Keywords: Multimodal brain graph evolution prediction · Federated learning · Graph neural networks · Longitudinal connectomic datasets

ⓒ The Author(s), under exclusive license to Springer Nature Switzerland AG 2023
I. Rekik et al. (Eds.): PRIME 2023, LNCS 14277, pp. 120–133, 2023.
https://doi.org/10.1007/978-3-031-46005-0_11

1 Introduction

The initial year following birth plays a crucial role in the development of the brain, as it experiences significant structural, morphological, and functional changes [1]. Gaining a deep understanding of the infant brain can provide valuable insights for the early diagnosis of neurodevelopmental diseases. Detecting such conditions early allows for more effective treatment compared to a later-stage prediction [2]. Consequently, the ability to predict a predisposition to disease is highly beneficial as it may prevent its occurrence [3,4].

A brain connectome can be expressed as a graph, where each node represents a distinct region of interest (ROI) [5]. The ROIs correspond to anatomical areas identified in the brain MRI, and their number may vary depending on the MR image parcellation technique employed (e.g., AAL or MNI parcellation templates [6]). The graph edges symbolize the connections between these brain regions, as well as their strength. Recently GNNs [7–9] have been widely adopted in brain network prediction tasks. Notably, within the extensive body of research in this domain, established studies such as [10–12] integrated novel graph neural network architectures, namely GCNs (Graph Convolutional Networks) [13] and gGANs (graph Generative Adversarial Networks) [14] into their predictive models. Additionally, other remarkable papers were introduced in an attempt to forecast the longitudinal developmental trajectory of the brain in the works of [11,15].

While such methods have demonstrated considerable success, they require a substantial amount of training subjects, in order to achieve satisfactory performance and generalization [16]. However, our dataset consists of infant brain scans obtained at various timepoints using multiple imaging modalities, specifically resting-state functional MRI and T1-weighted MRI. This dataset is particularly challenging to obtain due to long acquisition times, high costs, and limited availability of subjects. Another drawback of most of the current approaches is that they are limited to a uni-trajectory prediction. A generalization to multi-trajectory prediction allows the generation of a series of brain graphs from various modalities from a baseline graph. This feature proves highly advantageous since integrating information from diverse modalities provides complementary insights and enables a more comprehensive examination of the brain dynamics and its multi-facet connectivity. Consequently, this leads to improved diagnostic accuracy (i.e., brain tumor classification [17]).

Therefore, there is a pressing need for a multi-trajectory predictive model that addresses *data scarcity*. Only one paper in the existing literature [18] tackled this challenge, where a novel few-shot learning framework was proposed for multi-trajectory evolution, using a TS (Teacher-Student) learning paradigm [19]. Specifically, the teacher network is trained on the original dataset, while the student network is trained on simulated data with the same distribution properties as the original dataset. This enables the integration of simulated data to enhance the training dataset. By utilizing the knowledge of the teacher network, the student network can then mimic its behavior. Despite effectively addressing data scarcity concerns, the TS paradigm introduces some drawbacks, including the following. First, the TS model utilizes two separate networks (one for the student and one for the teacher), which doubles the computational costs in terms of time and storage requirements. Second, since the student heavily relies on the teacher network as its source of ground truth, any noise introduced by the teacher will be further amplified by the student. Third, due to the student dependency on the limited data of the teacher, the student network may become biased and generalize poorly.

In contrast, our paper explores an alternative method called federated learning [20] in an attempt to leverage locally decentralized small datasets. The field of federated learning has recently experienced significant growth thanks to its ability to facilitate the collaboration of multiple independent clients, such as hospitals. This collaboration aims to improve model training by taking advantage of the increase in data that multiple hospitals introduce. This is achieved without compromising the privacy of sensitive information, by sharing and aggregating the different model parameters via a central server (coordinator). By combining local learnings, models can be trained on diverse datasets, enhancing generalization and mitigating biases. Recently, [21,22] primed the first federated brain graph evolution trajectory prediction frameworks. However, the proposed 4D-Fed-GNN framework and its vairants work only on unimodal connectomic datasets.

Beside employing federated learning to address severe data limitations, we incorporate two other strategies. First, in a dataset of trajectories, the issue of data scarcity at different timepoints rises. When confronted with incomplete data for a particular training subject, we have the option to discard it from our training subjects. However, this would further reduce the limited data available. Instead, we utilize a simple yet effective imputation technique called KNN (K-Nearest Neighbors) [23] to fill in the missing values. Second, to optimize the utilization of the longitudinal training multi-trajectory graphs, we introduce an *auxiliary regularizer* in the local objective function. The introduction of this new term enhances our network performance and maximizes data utilization. Third, we add on top of that a topology loss term to effectively capture the topological characteristics of the ground truth graph multi-trajectories in our prediction task. In summary, our main contributions are as follows:

1. We propose Federated Graph Multi-Trajectory Evolution Network (FedGmTE-Net*), which is the first graph multi-trajectory framework that leverages federation for forecasting the infant brain evolution trajectory.
2. We perform two modifications to the standard MAE objective function. Firstly, we include an additional topology loss component to maintain the graph topological patterns. Additionally, we propose a novel auxiliary regularizer to enhance data utilization in a limited data environment.
3. To address the issue of missing data in longitudinal graph datasets, we propose a KNN-based imputation technique. This technique relies on assumptions derived from baseline observations to fill in the missing values.

2   Method

Problem Statement. A brain connectome can be represented as a graph denoted by $\mathcal{G} = \{\mathbf{X}, \mathbf{A}\}$, where $\mathbf{X}$ denotes the different ROIs of the brain. Each ROI acts as a node in the graph, resulting in the construction of the matrix $\mathbf{X} \in \mathbf{R}^{N \times d}$, with N distinct ROIs, each linked to its unique d-dimensional feature vector. The brain graph adjacency matrix, denoted as $\mathbf{A} \in \mathbf{R}^{N \times N}$ is a weighted matrix that represents the connectivity

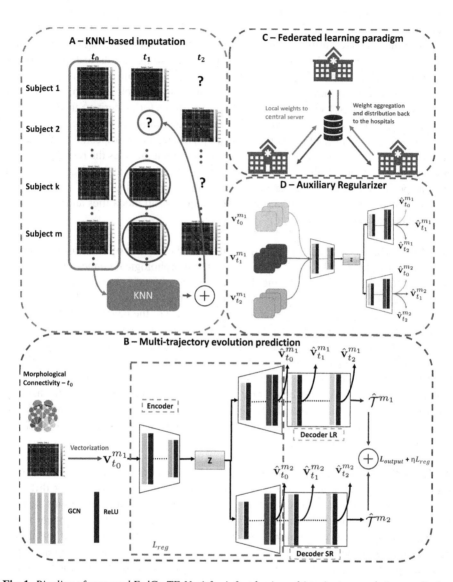

Fig. 1. *Pipeline of proposed FedGmTE-Net* for infant brain multi-trajectory evolution prediction from baseline.* **(A) KNN-based imputation** Imputation technique to complete the missing graphs from our training set by utilizing the similarities of subjects at the baseline timepoint. **(B) Multi-trajectory evolution network** The prediction is made using a single input modality, generating multiple trajectories spanning different modalities. **(C) Federated learning paradigm** A decentralized learning paradigm that allows hospitals to collaborate with each other without sacrificing data privacy. **(D) Auxiliary regularizer** The auxiliary regularizer improves network performance by utilizing the entire training dataset across all timepoints. This enhances the initial prediction at t_0 and consequently leads to improved subsequent predictions.

strength between different brain regions (nodes of the graph). For our framework, we vectorize each brain graph $\mathcal{G}$ into a reduced feature vector, referred to as $\mathbf{v}$, containing a summary of the entire connectivity information within our graph. Given that a brain graph is represented by a symmetric matrix $\mathbf{X}$, we extract its feature vector by vectorizing the off-diagonal upper-triangular part of $\mathbf{X}$. As our problem involves the evolution prediction of multiple trajectories from a single baseline graph, each of our subjects $s \in \{1, ..., n_s\}$ consists of multiple graph trajectories derived from different imaging modalities: $\{\mathcal{T}_s^{m_j}\}_{j=1}^{n_m}$, where n_s denotes the number of training subjects and n_m stands for the number of modalities. The graph trajectory for a specific modality m_j of a subject can be expressed as $\mathcal{T}_s^{m_j} = \{\mathbf{v}_{t_i}^{m_j}\}_{i=1}^{n_t}$, which includes the respective brain graph feature vectors at all n_t timepoints. Our GNN takes in a single graph derived from a specific modality at the baseline timepoint t_0, represented as $\mathbf{v}_{t_0}^{m_1}$. The desired output is the prediction of the trajectory evolution across all modalities and timepoints, given by the multi-trajectories $\{\{\hat{\mathbf{v}}_{t_i}^{m_j}\}_{i=1}^{n_t}\}_{j=1}^{n_m}$.

Population-Based Graphs. In our original dataset, the number of ROIs corresponds to the number of graph nodes, with 35 nodes for the morphological connectome and 116 nodes for the functional connectome. Preserving the original graph structure becomes challenging since we are dealing with different numbers of nodes in a GNN, hence the vectorization step. However, we want to take advantage of the benefits of GNNs. Thus, we construct a population-based graph, which includes the entire population, where each subject corresponds to a node. By doing so, we get a comprehensive representation of the relationships and connections between subjects. Consequently, subjects can learn from others that possess similar structures. There are various methods available to compute the similarity between subjects. In our framework, we measure the dissimilarity between two subjects by calculating the Euclidean distance between their feature vectors, followed by applying the exponential function to generate the adjacency matrix of the graph population.

A - KNN-Based Imputation. Longitudinal medical datasets are often incomplete. Our framework adopts a subject-level availability assumption, which allows for different subjects to have varying acquisition timepoints. Compared to other paradigms such as hospital-level availability, where subjects from the same hospitals have identical availability, this approach is much more realistic by acknowledging the potential variability across subjects. Further, we assume that if a particular modality is missing at a specific timepoint for a subject, then all other modalities are also missing for that same subject since we expect them to be acquired simultaneously. Additionally, the baseline timepoint (t_0) should be available for all subjects. Due to the limited nature of our dataset, we cannot afford to exclude subjects with missing values. Therefore, we employ a KNN-based imputation technique to utilize all available subject graphs. The algorithm works as follows. When a subject has missing graphs at a specific timepoint, we identify its closest neighbors with available graphs at that timepoint. To impute the missing graphs, we calculate the average of the brain graphs from these neighbors. As all subjects have complete data at the baseline timepoint, we determine the nearest neighbors based on their graph similarities at t_0. The underlying idea is that if subjects are similar at baseline, they should exhibit similar patterns over subsequent timepoints.

This imputation procedure is applied independently for each available modality in the dataset. An example of the described imputation technique for morphological graphs can be found in Fig. 1-A.

B - Graph Multi-trajectory Evolution Prediction. The network architecture utilized in this work is inspired by [18]. For each hospital involved in our federated learning framework, we adopt the same autoencoder architecture. This architecture incorporates GCN layers. Initially, an encoder is employed to learn a meaningful latent representation using the input modality at t_0. The encoder module is composed of a two-layer GCN, where each layer is followed by a ReLU activation and a dropout function. Subsequently, a set of decoder networks, denoted as $\{D^{m_j}\}_{j=1}^{n_m}$, is used for each output graph from modality m_j. These decoders take the representation generated by the encoder as input. To account for variations in graph resolution (i.e., node size) between the initial and target modalities and subsequently evolution trajectories, the first decoding step involves a rescaling process to match the dimensions of the corresponding output modality graph. Thus, our decoder is capable of predicting brain graphs even when resolution shifts occur across different graphs. The rescaling module of the decoder follows the same two-layer GCN architecture as the encoder. Finally, following this, an elementary GCN-based module is cascaded $n_t - 1$ times, where each iteration predicts a brain graph matrix at a distinct timepoint.

Our primary prediction loss consists of an L_1 loss and a topological loss term L_{tp}:

$$\mathcal{L}_{output} = \mathcal{L}_{L1}\left(\hat{\mathbf{v}}, \mathbf{v}\right) + \lambda \mathcal{L}_{tp}\left(\hat{\mathbf{N}}, \mathbf{N}\right)$$

$$\mathcal{L}_1\left(\hat{\mathbf{v}}, \mathbf{v}\right) = \frac{1}{n_m n_t} \sum_{j=1}^{n_m} \sum_{i=1}^{n_t} |\hat{\mathbf{v}}_{t_i}^{m_j} - \mathbf{v}_{t_i}^{m_j}|$$

$$\mathcal{L}_{tp}\left(\hat{\mathbf{N}}, \mathbf{N}\right) = \frac{1}{n_m n_t} \sum_{j=1}^{n_m} \sum_{i=1}^{n_t} \left(\hat{\mathbf{N}}_{t_i}^{m_j} - \mathbf{N}_{t_i}^{m_j}\right)^2$$

The L_1 loss measures the difference between the predicted and actual brain graph feature vectors. It quantifies the mean absolute error (MAE) between the predicted and ground truth brain graphs across all modalities. To retain the unique topological properties of brain connectomes and minimize topological dissimilarities between the predicted and ground-truth brain graphs, a topological loss is incorporated, with the node strength [24] as a topological measure. The topological strength of each node is computed by summing all its edge weights. Next, the topological loss is calculated as the mean squared error (MSE) between the true and predicted grpahs. The topological loss is tuned using the hyperparameter λ. Finally, the output loss (L_{output}) described above is combined with an auxiliary regulariser loss (L_{reg}), giving the total loss $\mathcal{L}_{total} = \mathcal{L}_{output} + \eta \mathcal{L}_{reg}$. The auxiliary loss term is also adjusted by a hyperparameter η, and will be introduced below.

C - Federated Learning Paradigm. In our case, the medical datasets of individual hospitals are insufficient to train a generalizable model. Hence, we adopt a federated learning framework, which enables distributed learning. This approach allows hospitals to train their models collaboratively, while preserving the privacy of their subjects and hence improving each hospital individual model, even when trained on a small dataset. In particular, we use FedAvg introduced in [20], which works with K hospitals and a shared global server. At the start of each global federation round, the hospitals receive the current global state of the shared model and undergo local training on their respective datasets. Once the local training is finished, the hospitals send their respective model updates back to the central server/coordinator. The server aggregates these updates using weighted average, resulting in a new global model. This averaging process ensures that the knowledge from all participating hospitals is incorporated into the global model, benefiting everyone. One of the primary challenges in this training paradigm is the high communication cost. To mitigate this, we make a trade-off with computation costs, by performing five local training rounds at each hospital instead of one before sending the updates to the central server. We avoid using a higher number of local training epochs since this can result in divergence issues due to significant differences in clients' parameters.

D - Auxiliary Regularizer. To increase the robustness and accuracy of our training models, we incorporate an auxiliary loss term. The goal of the new term is to better utilize our available longitudinal dataset. The term introduced is defined as L_{reg} and specifically aims at improving the performance of our network encoder and the rescaling process performed by the decoders, which is the module surrounded by a dotted red border in Fig. 1-B. Currently, we only train this using brain graphs from timepoint t_0. However, this module does not seem to rely on the temporal nature of our data, as it simply encodes the input baseline graph into a latent representation and then rescales it to the target modalities. During this process, we do not move forward in time, since the input and target modalities share the same timepoint. Therefore, we can instead utilize all available data, including brain graphs at all timepoints (t_0, t_1, t_2, ..) for our module training. This is precisely what the L_{reg} term addresses, which calculates the loss of the module across all available timepoints (see Fig. 1-D). This loss is computed using the combination of L_1 and L_{tp} loss and is then combined with the standard output loss L_{output} to give the final L_{total}. By improving the performance of this module first, our goal is to enhance the initial prediction of our network at the baseline timepoint (t_0). This raises the question of how subsequent timepoints, such as t_1 and t_2, are affected. Given the nature of time-series prediction scenarios, we anticipate an overall improvement in performance across subsequent timepoints too. The underlying assumption is that a more accurate prediction at a previous timepoint, which is closer to the ground truth, would also lead to improved predictions at the subsequent timepoints. Consequently, our improvement at t_0 is expected to initiate a chain of events that ultimately improves performance across all timepoints.

3   Results and Discussion

Evaluation Dataset. We evaluate our proposed framework using longitudinal multimodal infant brain connectomes. Each subject in the dataset has serial resting-state fMRI, as well as T1-w and T2-w MRI acquired at different timepoints. Using the above data, two types of brain modalities are generated for each subject. Firstly the rsfMRI scans are partitioned into 116 distinct ROIs with the use of an AAL template. Hence, a 116×116 connectivity matrix is created for each subject, where the connectivity strength between the ROIs corresponds to the Pearson correlation between their mean functional signals. In addition to the functional dataset, a morphological dataset is created from the T1-w MR images, where the cortical surfaces are divided into 35 different regions. The connections between these regions contained in the 35×35 morphological graph measure the absolute difference between their cortical thickness. For each subject two morphological graphs are created; one for the left and one for the right hemisphere of the brain. In our experiment, we only focus on one morphological view, hence the final morphological connectivity matrix is created by averaging both hemispheric cortical graphs.

We use three different serial time groupings. The first group, denoted as t_0, includes all brain scans taken between 0–1 months old. The second group, t_1, contains scans taken between 2–4 months old. Finally, the third group, t_2, includes scans taken between 5–7 months old. Not all subjects have complete availability for all time groups and both modalities. In fact, only 9 subjects possess complete data. Hence, to augment the size of our dataset, we include all subjects that have available data for both modalities at t_0, resulting in a total of 25 subjects. For subjects with missing data, we apply the imputation technique proposed during the training process to complete the dataset. However, for the testing dataset, we do not perform any precompletion. Instead, we evaluate only based on the available timepoints and modalities of the real data.

Parameter Setting. The experimental setup is the following. We explore federation between 3 different hospitals and we assess the effectiveness of our framework using a 4-fold cross-validation approach. The dataset is divided into four parts. Unless otherwise specified this is a random and uniform split. One fold is serving as the ground truth test data and the remaining 3 folds are being distributed among the 3 hospitals for local training. To determine the optimal stopping point during training, we employ early stopping with a patience value of 10. This ensures fairness by terminating the training process if there is no significant improvement within the specified limit. The hyperparameter used to monitor the topology loss is set to 0.001. Additionally, for the relevant experiments, the auxiliary regularizer hyperparameter is set to 0.5. Finally, all hospitals are trained for 5 local epochs before the global aggregation.

Evaluation. For our evaluation, we measure two distinct metrics. Firstly, we calculate our primary metric, which is the normal mean average error (MAE) between the predicted graphs and the ground truth ones. This metric allows us to assess the element-wise accuracy of our predictions. As a secondary metric, we compute the MAE among the node strengths (NS) of both graphs. This measure helps us evaluate the topological similarity between the predicted brain graph and the actual graphs. Both of the above metrics are calculated for each timepoint and modality independently.

Experiments. The initial objective of the paper is to investigate whether federated learning improves the quality of the models compared to training hospitals solely on their limited data. To accomplish this, we conducted experiments comparing our FedGmTE-Net framework, which employs the FedAvg algorithm [20] and the no federation approach, named NoFedGmTE-Net. The total graph MAE, as well as the NS MAE for each timepoint, hospital, and method, can be found in Table 1. The federated method demonstrates superior performance in 8/9 scenarios based on the primary metric and in 7/9 scenarios based on the secondary metric. This highlights the significant benefits of federated learning in enhancing model performance.

Table 1. Comparison of FedGmTE-Net and its no federation counterpart (NoFedGmTE-Net). We highlight in bold, blue for MAE (graph), and red for MAE (NS) the best performance at each hospital across timepoints. The performances for the morphological and functional trajectories are averaged.

	Methods	MAE (graph)			MAE (NS)		
		h_1	h_2	h_3	h_1	h_2	h_3
t_0	NoFedGmTE-Net	0.164 ± 0.011	0.167 ± 0.003	0.163 ± 0.008	4.846 ± 0.673	4.899 ± 0.410	4.100 ± 0.460
	FedGmTE-Net	**0.151 ± 0.005**	**0.151 ± 0.006**	**0.150 ± 0.005**	**4.002 ± 0.330**	**3.924 ± 0.309**	**3.935 ± 0.267**
t_1	NoFedGmTE-Net	0.127 ± 0.010	0.129 ± 0.009	0.130 ± 0.007	3.714 ± 0.646	3.446 ± 0.524	3.726 ± 0.819
	FedGmTE-Net	**0.120 ± 0.010**	**0.127 ± 0.010**	**0.119 ± 0.006**	**0.3943 ± 0.0921**	**3.419 ± 0.475**	**3.391 ± 0.695**
t_2	NoFedGmTE-Net	0.168 ± 0.007	**0.160 ± 0.006**	0.159 ± 0.010	**4.019 ± 0.231**	**4.203 ± 0.531**	4.458 ± 0.381
	FedGmTE-Net	**0.154 ± 0.010**	0.162 ± 0.006	**0.152 ± 0.007**	5.156 ± 0.489	4.603 ± 0.422	**3.736 ± 0.573**

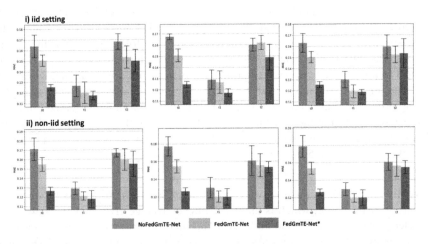

Fig. 2. Total MAE recorded for the three hospitals at all timepoints. The average value across different modalities was taken for the NoFedGmTE-Net, FedGmTE-Net, and FedGmTE-Net* methods. (i) Results in an IID setting where data are uniformly distributed across hospitals. (ii) Results in a non-IID setting where the data are divided into clusters and distinct distributions are assigned to each hospital.

The next experimental design compares our proposed framework after incorporating the auxiliary regularizer (FedGmTE-NET*), against the standard federation framework and the non-federation baseline. The total MAE plots across modalities are provided in Fig. 2-i). These plots demonstrate that our proposed FedGmTE-Net* consistently outperforms the other methods across various timepoints and hospitals, exhibiting a significant improvement, particularly at timepoint t_0. For a more detailed analysis of each modality individually and across both evaluation metrics, refer to Table 2 and Table 3. For both modalities, FedGmTE-Net* outperforms the other approaches in 8/9 scenarios for the primary MAE metric. Regarding the second metric, FedGmTE-Net* also surpasses all other methods in 8/9 scenarios for the morphological connectome trajectory prediction, while the performance for the functional trajectory seems arbitrary.

Table 2. IID data: Morphological brain graph trajectory prediction by NoFedGmTE-Net, FedGmTE-Net, and FedGmTE-Net* (with auxiliary regularizer). We highlight in bold, blue for MAE (graph), and red for MAE (NS) the best performance at each hospital across timepoints.

	Methods	MAE (graph)			MAE (NS)		
		h_1	h_2	h_3	h_1	h_2	h_3
t_0	NoFedGmTE-Net	0.189 ± 0.016	0.194 ± 0.008	0.182 ± 0.014	4.542 ± 0.502	4.536 ± 0.263	3.707 ± 0.477
	FedGmTE-Net	0.162 ± 0.008	0.162 ± 0.009	0.161 ± 0.009	3.728 ± 0.196	3.691 ± 0.367	3.663 ± 0.277
	FedGmTE-Net*	$\mathbf{0.128 \pm 0.006}$	$\mathbf{0.128 \pm 0.007}$	$\mathbf{0.129 \pm 0.008}$	$\mathbf{2.359 \pm 0.128}$	$\mathbf{2.357 \pm 0.103}$	$\mathbf{2.427 \pm 0.169}$
t_1	NoFedGmTE-Net	0.138 ± 0.020	0.135 ± 0.018	0.139 ± 0.007	2.688 ± 0.796	2.490 ± 0.471	2.335 ± 0.546
	FedGmTE-Net	0.124 ± 0.010	0.128 ± 0.016	0.124 ± 0.011	2.126 ± 0.366	2.269 ± 0.741	2.041 ± 0.390
	FedGmTE-Net*	$\mathbf{0.123 \pm 0.005}$	$\mathbf{0.124 \pm 0.006}$	$\mathbf{0.123 \pm 0.005}$	$\mathbf{1.934 \pm 0.119}$	$\mathbf{1.952 \pm 0.122}$	$\mathbf{1.972 \pm 0.230}$
t_2	NoFedGmTE-Net	0.215 ± 0.019	0.205 ± 0.015	0.205 ± 0.017	4.127 ± 0.874	4.229 ± 1.010	3.804 ± 0.659
	FedGmTE-Net	0.194 ± 0.014	0.200 ± 0.019	$\mathbf{0.196 \pm 0.013}$	3.640 ± 0.555	3.865 ± 0.849	$\mathbf{3.510 \pm 0.740}$
	FedGmTE-Net*	$\mathbf{0.193 \pm 0.017}$	$\mathbf{0.193 \pm 0.018}$	0.200 ± 0.023	$\mathbf{3.611 \pm 0.814}$	$\mathbf{3.499 \pm 0.687}$	4.232 ± 1.152

Table 3. IID data: Functional brain graph trajectory prediction by NoFedGmTE-Net, FedGmTE-Net, and FedGmTE-Net* (with auxiliary regularizer). We highlight in bold, blue for MAE (graph), and red for MAE (NS) the best performance at each hospital across timepoints.

	Methods	MAE (graph)			MAE (NS)		
		h_1	h_2	h_3	h_1	h_2	h_3
t_0	NoFedGmTE-Net	0.139 ± 0.008	0.141 ± 0.004	0.144 ± 0.005	5.149 ± 1.004	5.261 ± 1.064	4.494 ± 0.516
	FedGmTE-Net	0.139 ± 0.004	0.140 ± 0.004	0.139 ± 0.004	$\mathbf{4.277 \pm 0.688}$	$\mathbf{4.157 \pm 0.591}$	$\mathbf{4.206 \pm 0.613}$
	FedGmTE-Net*	$\mathbf{0.122 \pm 0.006}$	$\mathbf{0.122 \pm 0.006}$	$\mathbf{0.122 \pm 0.006}$	5.136 ± 1.106	5.300 ± 1.124	4.928 ± 0.990
t_1	NoFedGmTE-Net	0.115 ± 0.006	0.123 ± 0.004	0.120 ± 0.008	$\mathbf{4.740 \pm 0.991}$	$\mathbf{4.402 \pm 0.963}$	5.117 ± 1.631
	FedGmTE-Net	0.116 ± 0.013	0.126 ± 0.006	$\mathbf{0.114 \pm 0.009}$	5.761 ± 1.969	4.569 ± 0.651	4.792 ± 1.387
	FedGmTE-Net*	$\mathbf{0.111 \pm 0.008}$	$\mathbf{0.111 \pm 0.008}$	0.115 ± 0.004	5.139 ± 0.189	5.395 ± 1.401	$\mathbf{4.631 \pm 1.087}$
t_2	NoFedGmTE-Net	0.122 ± 0.007	0.115 ± 0.005	0.114 ± 0.005	$\mathbf{3.911 \pm 0.583}$	$\mathbf{4.176 \pm 0.239}$	5.112 ± 1.397
	FedGmTE-Net	0.113 ± 0.010	0.124 ± 0.013	0.109 ± 0.006	6.672 ± 0.426	5.342 ± 1.029	3.962 ± 1.011
	FedGmTE-Net*	$\mathbf{0.107 \pm 0.006}$	$\mathbf{0.105 \pm 0.006}$	$\mathbf{0.106 \pm 0.004}$	4.770 ± 1.051	5.048 ± 1.274	$\mathbf{3.372 \pm 0.716}$

In the final experiment, instead of randomly distributing the training set across hospitals, we use K-means clustering to group the data and assign one cluster to each hospital. This allows us to investigate the performance of our framework in a scenario where there is both statistical and systems heterogeneity across hospitals (non-IID case). Statistical heterogeneity arises from the differences in data distributions, while systems heterogeneity is created from varying local training dataset sizes in each hospital due to the clusters not being of the same size. The total MAE plots averaged across modalities are provided in Fig. 2-ii), and more specific results for each modality can be found in Table 4 and Table 5. Our results are similar to the IID setting, demonstrating that our proposed framework (FedGmTE-Net*) consistently outperforms the benchmarks even in a heterogeneous setting, highlighting the robustness of our method.

Table 4. Non-IID data: Morphological brain graph trajectory prediction by NoFedGmTE-Net, FedGmTE-Net, and FedGmTE-Net* (with auxiliary regularizer). We highlight in bold, blue for MAE (graph), and red for MAE (NS) the best performance at each hospital across timepoints.

	Methods	MAE (graph)			MAE (NS)		
		h_1	h_2	h_3	h_1	h_2	h_3
t_0	NoFedGmTE-Net	0.198 ± 0.024	0.208 ± 0.019	0.212 ± 0.022	4.652 ± 0.890	4.723 ± 0.768	4.989 ± 1.034
	FedGmTE-Net	0.140 ± 0.012	0.135 ± 0.022	0.141 ± 0.013	3.759 ± 0.189	3.766 ± 0.334	3.625 ± 0.298
	FedGmTE-Net*	**0.130 ± 0.006**	**0.131 ± 0.007**	**0.131 ± 0.006**	**2.361 ± 0.196**	**2.405 ± 0.312**	**2.395 ± 0.218**
t_1	NoFedGmTE-Net	0.140 ± 0.012	0.135 ± 0.022	0.141 ± 0.013	2.510 ± 0.488	2.340 ± 1.002	2.691 ± 0.649
	FedGmTE-Net	0.126 ± 0.009	0.125 ± 0.009	**0.125 ± 0.009**	2.280 ± 0.151	2.141 ± 0.319	**2.094 ± 0.202**
	FedGmTE-Net*	**0.121 ± 0.012**	**0.124 ± 0.014**	0.126 ± 0.017	**1.891 ± 0.214**	**2.111 ± 0.366**	2.259 ± 0.619
t_2	NoFedGmTE-Net	0.217 ± 0.002	0.208 ± 0.026	0.212 ± 0.017	4.166 ± 0.432	**3.600 ± 1.104**	4.116 ± 0.712
	FedGmTE-Net	0.204 ± 0.025	0.199 ± 0.018	0.202 ± 0.024	4.269 ± 1.345	3.897 ± 0.944	**3.971 ± 1.460**
	FedGmTE-Net*	**0.195 ± 0.021**	**0.196 ± 0.009**	**0.200 ± 0.020**	**3.808 ± 1.132**	3.843 ± 0.638	4.084 ± 1.134

Table 5. Non-IID data: Functional brain graph trajectory prediction by NoFedGmTE-Net, FedGmTE-Net, and FedGmTE-Net* (with auxiliary regularizer). We highlight in bold, blue for MAE (graph), and red for MAE (NS) the best performance at each hospital across timepoints.

	Methods	MAE (graph)			MAE (NS)		
		h_1	h_2	h_3	h_1	h_2	h_3
t_0	NoFedGmTE-Net	0.144 ± 0.005	0.147 ± 0.004	0.146 ± 0.006	4.356 ± 0.399	4.749 ± 1.212	4.895 ± 0.779
	FedGmTE-Net	0.142 ± 0.005	0.142 ± 0.006	0.142 ± 0.006	**4.251 ± 0.252**	**4.174 ± 0.278**	**4.241 ± 0.353**
	FedGmTE-Net*	**0.122 ± 0.004**	**0.122 ± 0.005**	**0.122 ± 0.004**	4.842 ± 0.859	4.853 ± 0.501	4.856 ± 0.658
t_1	NoFedGmTE-Net	0.118 ± 0.007	0.125 ± 0.005	0.118 ± 0.004	**4.056 ± 0.787**	**4.524 ± 1.174**	4.939 ± 1.215
	FedGmTE-Net	0.115 ± 0.009	0.116 ± 0.006	0.113 ± 0.005	4.726 ± 0.896	6.337 ± 2.899	4.636 ± 0.843
	FedGmTE-Net*	**0.114 ± 0.106**	**0.115 ± 0.005**	**0.112 ± 0.006**	4.457 ± 0.190	5.214 ± 1.420	**4.635 ± 1.270**
t_2	NoFedGmTE-Net	0.116 ± 0.010	0.113 ± 0.009	0.109 ± 0.006	5.244 ± 1.375	**4.198 ± 0.413**	4.485 ± 0.849
	FedGmTE-Net	0.116 ± 0.011	0.112 ± 0.012	0.110 ± 0.004	**5.237 ± 1.346**	6.515 ± 3.940	4.874 ± 1.367
	FedGmTE-Net*	**0.115 ± 0.020**	**0.111 ± 0.009**	**0.108 ± 0.005**	5.557 ± 2.295	4.426± 1.1074	**4.482 ± 1.313**

To better showcase the effectiveness of our network, we present visual comparisons of the real brain graphs and their corresponding predictions for both morphological and functional graph evolution trajectories in Fig. 3. These visualizations demonstrate the strong performance of our framework, especially considering the challenging scenario and our simplistic encoder-decoder architectures. Despite utilizing only a single modality input (morphological since it is more affordable) at the baseline timepoint along with a very limited dataset, we achieve promising multimodal graph trajectory evolution prediction across time.

In our current model, we make graph predictions at the current timepoint solely based on the information from our network's prediction at the previous timepoint. However, as a future research direction, inspired by [15], one can also consider the history of graph predictions at past timepoints.

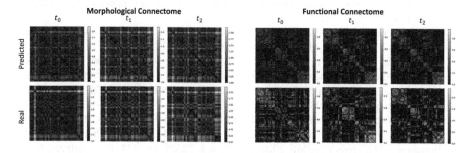

Fig. 3. Predicted against real brain graphs for morphological and functional connectomes at t_0, t_1 and t_2 by FedGmTE-Net*.

4 Conclusion

In this work, we introduced FedGmTE-Net*, the first federated learning framework specifically designed for predicting graph brain multi-trajectory evolution from a single modality graph. By leveraging federated learning, we combine the knowledge gained from diverse hospitals with small local training datasets and hence significantly improve the predictive performance of each hospital's GNN model. Additionally, we introduce an auxiliary regularizer that utilizes all available temporal graphs to substantially improve the initial baseline model prediction. Consequently, this creates a chain reaction that ultimately results in performance improvements across all subsequent timepoints and modalities. Currently, we address missing data in longitudinal brain graph datasets with a KNN-based imputation technique, which helps us expand our training set. As a future direction, we plan to explore dynamic imputation approaches to complete training multi-trajectories in an end-to-end learnable manner.

References

1. Zhang, H., Shen, D., Lin, W.: Resting-state functional MRI studies on infant brains: a decade of gap-filling efforts. Neuroimage **185**, 664–684 (2019)
2. Stoessl, A.J.: Neuroimaging in the early diagnosis of neurodegenerative disease. Transl. Neurodegeneration **1**, 1–6 (2012)

3. Rekik, I., Li, G., Yap, P.T., Chen, G., Lin, W., Shen, D.: Joint prediction of longitudinal development of cortical surfaces and white matter fibers from neonatal MRI. NeuroImage **152**, 411–424 (2017)
4. Rekik, I., Li, G., Lin, W., Shen, D.: Predicting infant cortical surface development using a 4D varifold-based learning framework and local topography-based shape morphing. Med. Image Anal. **28**, 1–12 (2016)
5. Liu, T.: A few thoughts on brain ROIs. Brain Imaging Behav. **5**, 189–202 (2011)
6. Tzourio-Mazoyer, N., et al.: Automated anatomical labeling of activations in SPM using a macroscopic anatomical parcellation of the MNI MRI single-subject brain. Neuroimage **15**, 273–289 (2002)
7. Veličković, P.: Everything is connected: graph neural networks. Curr. Opin. Struct. Biol. **79**, 102538 (2023)
8. Zhou, J., et al.: Graph neural networks: a review of methods and applications. AI Open **1**, 57–81 (2020)
9. Bessadok, A., Mahjoub, M.A., Rekik, I.: Graph neural networks in network neuroscience. IEEE Trans. Pattern Anal. Mach. Intell. **45**, 5833–5848 (2022)
10. Göktaş, A.S., Bessadok, A., Rekik, I.: Residual embedding similarity-based network selection for predicting brain network evolution trajectory from a single observation. In: Rekik, I., Adeli, E., Park, S.H., Valdés Hernández, M.C. (eds.) PRIME 2020. LNCS, vol. 12329, pp. 12–23. Springer, Cham (2020). https://doi.org/10.1007/978-3-030-59354-4_2
11. Nebli, A., Kaplan, U.A., Rekik, I.: Deep EvoGraphNet architecture for time-dependent brain graph data synthesis from a single timepoint. In: Rekik, I., Adeli, E., Park, S.H., Valdés Hernández, M.C. (eds.) PRIME 2020. LNCS, vol. 12329, pp. 144–155. Springer, Cham (2020). https://doi.org/10.1007/978-3-030-59354-4_14
12. Tekin, A., Nebli, A., Rekik, I.: Recurrent brain graph mapper for predicting time-dependent brain graph evaluation trajectory. In: Albarqouni, S., et al. (eds.) DART/FAIR -2021. LNCS, vol. 12968, pp. 180–190. Springer, Cham (2021). https://doi.org/10.1007/978-3-030-87722-4_17
13. Kipf, T.N., Welling, M.: Semi-supervised classification with graph convolutional networks. arXiv preprint arXiv:1609.02907 (2016)
14. Wang, H., et al.: GraphGAN: graph representation learning with generative adversarial nets. In: Proceedings of the AAAI Conference on Artificial Intelligence. Vol. 32 (2018)
15. Ghribi, O., Li, G., Lin, W., Shen, D., Rekik, I.: Multi-regression based supervised sample selection for predicting baby connectome evolution trajectory from neonatal timepoint. Med. Image Anal. **68**, 101853 (2021)
16. Hestness, J., et al.: Deep learning scaling is predictable, empirically. arXiv preprint arXiv:1712.00409 (2017)
17. Usman, K., Rajpoot, K.: Brain tumor classification from multi-modality MRI using wavelets and machine learning. Pattern Anal. Appl. **20**, 871–881 (2017)
18. Bessadok, A., et al.: A few-shot learning graph multi-trajectory evolution network for forecasting multimodal baby connectivity development from a baseline timepoint. In: Rekik, I., Adeli, E., Park, S.H., Schnabel, J. (eds.) PRIME 2021. LNCS, vol. 12928, pp. 11–24. Springer, Cham (2021). https://doi.org/10.1007/978-3-030-87602-9_2
19. Hinton, G., Vinyals, O., Dean, J.: Distilling the knowledge in a neural network. arXiv preprint arXiv:1503.02531 (2015)
20. McMahan, B., Moore, E., Ramage, D., Hampson, S., y Arcas, B.A.: Communication-efficient learning of deep networks from decentralized data. In: Artificial Intelligence and Statistics, PMLR, pp. 1273–1282 (2017)

21. Gürler, Z., Nebli, A., Rekik, I.: Foreseeing brain graph evolution over time using deep adversarial network normalizer. In: Rekik, I., Adeli, E., Park, S.H., Valdés Hernández, M.C. (eds.) PRIME 2020. LNCS, vol. 12329, pp. 111–122. Springer, Cham (2020). https://doi.org/10.1007/978-3-030-59354-4_11

22. Gürler, Z., Rekik, I.: Federated brain graph evolution prediction using decentralized connectivity datasets with temporally-varying acquisitions. IEEE Trans. Med. Imaging **42**(7), 2022–2031 (2022)

23. Peterson, L.E.: K-nearest neighbor. Scholarpedia **4**, 1883 (2009)

24. Newman, M.E.: Analysis of weighted networks. Phys. Rev. E **70**, 056131 (2004)

Learning Task-Specific Morphological Representation for Pyramidal Cells via Mutual Information Minimization

Chunli Sun[1], Qinghai Guo[2], Gang Yang[1], and Feng Zhao[1(✉)]

[1] University of Science and Technology of China, Hefei, China
`fzhao956@ustc.edu.cn`
[2] ACS Lab, Huawei Technologies, Shenzhen, China

Abstract. The morphology of pyramidal cells (PCs) varies significantly among species and brain layers. Therefore, it is particularly challenging to analyze which species or layers they belong to based on morphological features. Existing deep learning-based methods analyze species-related or layer-related morphological characteristics of PCs. However, these methods are realized in a task-agnostic manner without considering task-specific features. This paper proposes a task-specific morphological representation learning framework for morphology analysis of PCs to enforce task-specific feature extraction through dual-task learning, enabling performance gains for each task. Specifically, we first utilize species-wise and layer-wise feature extraction branches to obtain species-related and layer-related features. Applying the principle of mutual information minimization, we then explicitly force each branch to learn task-specific features, which are further enhanced via an adaptive representation enhancement module. In this way, the performance of both tasks can be greatly improved simultaneously. Experimental results demonstrate that the proposed method can effectively extract the species-specific and layer-specific representations when identifying rat and mouse PCs in multiple brain layers. Our method reaches the accuracies of 87.44% and 72.46% on species and layer analysis tasks, significantly outperforming a single task by 2.22% and 3.86%, respectively.

Keywords: Mutual information · Morphology analysis · Type prediction · Task-specific representation

1 Introduction

Pyramidal cells (PCs), a numerically dominant class of neurons found in the cerebral cortex of virtually every mammal, play a crucial role in many important cognitive processes [4,9,23]. Moreover, the function of PCs and their morphologies are intimately linked, and even minor morphological changes might result

---

C. Sun and Q. Guo—Equal contributions.

I. Rekik et al. (Eds.): PRIME 2023, LNCS 14277, pp. 134–145, 2023.
https://doi.org/10.1007/978-3-031-46005-0_12

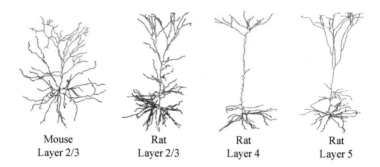

Mouse	Rat	Rat	Rat
Layer 2/3	Layer 2/3	Layer 4	Layer 5

Fig. 1. PCs of mouse and rat in different brain layers. Basal and apical dendrites are drawn with blue and rose red, respectively. (Color figure online)

in functional changes significantly [9,22]. Therefore, studying the morphological differences and categories of PCs is essential to understand brain activity mechanisms better.

As shown in Fig. 1, the morphology of PCs varies markedly between species and brain layers [10,15]. For example, the basal dendrites of mouse PCs are very short and barely branched, while they are long and well-branched in humans [20]. Additionally, the apical dendrites of PCs in layer 2/3 are shorter and more oblique than that of PCs in layer 5 [23]. These morphological differences among species or brain layers make analyzing the type of PCs challenging.

Many methods identify the subtypes of PCs based on morphological features and yield remarkable results [3,14,24,26,27]. For example, Mihaljevic et al. [20] compared the morphology of apical and basal dendritic branches of human and mouse PCs. Besides, Kanari et al. [14] identified 17 types of PCs in the rat somatosensory cortex based on the distance between the persistence images of the apical dendrites. Moreover, Wang et al. [25] identified the subtypes of rat PCs in all layers (i.e., layer 2, layer 3, layer 4, layer5, and layer 6) of the primary somatosensory cortex from a biological perspective. However, these methods only capture related features that contain general features in a task-agnostic way and do not effectively extract task-specific features, which are considered essential for the corresponding tasks. Therefore, a key issue that needs to be solved is effectively capturing discriminative task-specific features from general features to conduct different tasks and improve performance.

To this end, we propose a novel task-specific morphological representation learning framework based on mutual information minimization in a dual-task manner, which effectively extracts task-specific features for species-wise and layer-wise PCs analysis tasks and significantly improves performance (shown in Fig. 2). To be specific, we utilize two feature extraction branches to obtain species-related and layer-related features separately. Then the mutual information between them is estimated and minimized to enforce the model to pay more attention to task-specific rather than common features. Additionally, we introduce an adaptive representation enhancement (ARE) module for each anal-

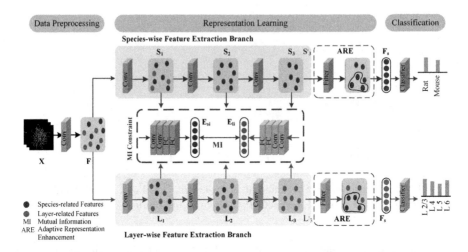

Fig. 2. Overall framework of our method. We first obtain species-related $(S_1, S_2, S_3$ ●) and layer-related features $(L_1, L_2, L_3$ ●) via two feature extraction branches independently. Then, they are transformed into low-dimension features $(E_{S1}, E_{S2}, E_{S2}$ and $E_{l1}, E_{l2}, E_{l2})$. Mutual information (MI) between these low-dimension features is minimized to promote learning task-specific representations of PCs. Finally, an adaptive representation enhancement (ARE) module is introduced to enhance the task-specific features further. (Color figure online)

ysis task to enhance task-specific representations further. In this way, the learned task-specific morphological representations are more proper and reliable for each analysis task, greatly improving the performance of both analysis tasks. Experimental results show that our method can precisely identify species or brain layers that PCs belong to via the learned task-specific features. Furthermore, the performance of our method on species-wise and layer-wise analysis tasks is superior to that of any single analysis task. Ablation experiments also demonstrate the effectiveness of our method.

Our main contributions are summarized as follows:

- We propose a novel task-specific morphological representation learning framework, which significantly enhances the task-specific morphological representation ability of each branch and improves the performance of both analysis tasks simultaneously.
- By minimizing the mutual information of species-related and layer-related features, our model can precisely decompose species-related or layer-related features into task-specific features and obtain more discriminative task-specific features via an ARE module.
- Our method can effectively extract morphological representations to analyze the species and brain layer of PCs. We reach the accuracies of 87.44% and 72.46% on species and layer analysis tasks, significantly outperforming a single task by 2.22% and 3.86%, respectively.

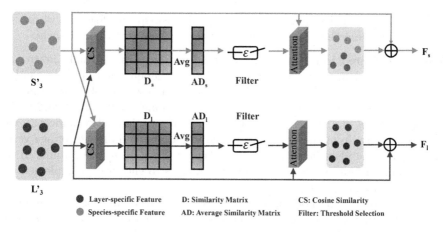

Fig. 3. Adaptive Representation Enhancement (ARE) Module. The distance matrix computed (D) between the feature components of one task and the other task-specific features (S_3' or L_3') is computed by cosine similarity (CS) and then becomes the average distance matrix (AD). When the average distance exceeds the threshold ε, a channel attention module selects and enhances the feature components. The final neuronal morphological descriptor (F_s and F_l) is the addition of enhanced task-specific features and input task-specific features.

2 Methodology

This paper aims to acquire the discriminative task-specific morphological representation from the task-related features that contain both task-specific features and common features and improve the performance of each analysis task simultaneously. To this end, we propose a task-specific morphological representation learning framework (as illustrated in Fig. 2), which mainly consists of feature extraction, mutual information constraint, ARE, and classification modules. Specifically, we first map the high-dimension features into species-related and layer-related features by two feature extraction branches, respectively. Then, we utilize the mutual information to constrain task-related features to be task-specific, containing more exclusive but not common features. Besides, the task-specific features are further enhanced through the ARE module. Finally, the classification results are provided by a simple classifier.

2.1 Model Architecture

Feature Extraction. We first capture high-dimension morphological features F from the PCs data through a convolutional layer (kernel size is 3×3) and a batch normalization layer. Then, we employ two feature extraction branches to extract task-related features[1] from the F from shallow to deep levels respectively, namely species-related features ($S = \{S_1, S_2, S_3\}$) and layer-related features

---

[1] Note that task-related features contain task-specific and common features.

$(L = \{L_1, L_2, L_3\})$. To balance the common and task-specific features, we extract features only from the last three blocks of the feature extraction branches.

Mutual Information Estimator and Minimization. Mutual information estimation is an available tool to determine the dependency between random variables [5–7]. Recently, it is utilized as a regularizer or objective function to constrain independence between variables in many fields [2,12,28,29]. For instance, Hou et al. [12] minimized the mutual information between identity and age components from the same face image to reduce the influence of age variations during the identification process. Likewise, Zhou et al. [29] minimized the mutual information between PAN and MS images to encourage complementary information learning explicitly.

Inspired by the methods above, we introduce mutual information minimization as a regularizer to constrain the task-related features to be task-specific features explicitly. Our basic assumption is that an ideal species-specific or layer-specific morphology feature should carry more exclusive and fewer or no common features. As a result, there should be less dependency between species-related or layer-related features. In order to efficiently measure the dependency between S and L, we first reduce the dimension of S and L through two additional convolution layers with the kernel size of 3×3 and two fully connected layers (see Fig. 2). Consequently, we acquire the low-dimension features, denoted as $E_s = \{E_{s1}, E_{s2}, E_{s3}\}$ and $E_l = \{E_{l1}, E_{l2}, E_{l3}\}$, respectively.

After that, mutual information estimator is adopted to quantify the dependency of E_s and E_l as written as,

$$MI(E_{si}, E_{li}) = MI(E_{li}, E_{si}) = H(E_{si}) + H(E_{li}) - H(E_{si}, E_{li}), \qquad (1)$$

where $H(\cdot)$ indicates the entropy, $i \in \{0, 1, 2\}$, and $H(E_{si}, E_{li})$ presents the joint entropy. We intuitively compute the entropy $H(\cdot)$ through the Kullback-Leibler (KL) divergence,

$$H(E_{si}) = H_{E_{li}}(E_{si}) - KL(E_{si} \parallel E_{li}), \qquad (2)$$

where $H_{E_{li}}(E_{si}) = -\sum E_{si} log(E_{li})$ and $H_{E_{si}}(E_{li}) = -\sum E_{li} log(E_{si})$. $H_{E_{li}}(E_{si})$ and $H_{E_{si}}(E_{li})$ are the cross-entropy. With Eqs. 1 and 2, we can obtain:

$$MI(E_{si}, E_{li}) = -\sum E_{si} log(E_{li}) - \sum E_{li} log(E_{si})$$
$$- KL(E_{si} \parallel E_{li}) - KL(E_{li} \parallel E_{si}) - H(E_{si}, E_{li}). \qquad (3)$$

Note that we utilize the $MI(E_{si}, E_{li})$ estimator at multiple feature levels to effectively strengthen the constraints of mutual information on the feature extraction model (as shown in Fig. 2).

Representation Enhancement. During the task-related feature extraction process, we obtain refined species-specific features S_3' and layer-specific features L_3' via mutual information constraint (as shown in Fig. 2). After that, we introduce an ARE module to obtain more discriminative task-specific features.

As shown in Fig. 3, we first select the feature components with high speci-ficity from the species-specific feature S_3' via a hard filter with a threshold ε. We utilize cosine similarity to measure the distance of task-specific features (i.e., S_3' and L_3'). The averages distance AD_s is obtained from the distance matrix D_s. Only when the averages distance between the feature components of S_3' and L_3' is greater than ε, the feature components will be selected and enhanced through a channel attention module [13]. Furthermore, to efficiently exploit the S_3', we combine the S_3' and the enhanced feature components as the final morphological descriptor F_s for the species-wise analysis task. Similarly, we can obtain mor-phological descriptor F_l for the layer-wise analysis task. These features F_l and F_s serve as the final morphological descriptors to conduct the type prediction.

Classifiers. We obtain the global feature from F_s or F_l for each analysis task via a generalized-mean pooling (GeM pooling) layer [21]. Then they are fed into two classifiers to provide predictions for each task separately. Each classifier is composed of two fully connected layers and one batch normalization layer, where the output dimension of the second fully connected layer is the type number of PCs on species-wise or layer-wise analysis tasks.

2.2 Optimization

Our architecture is trained based on the cross-entropy loss L_{ce} and mutual infor-mation constraint L_{mi}. The L_{ce} is the supervised loss for the species-wise or layer-wise classification. The L_{mi} is conducted to enforce the feature extrac-tion model to learn species-specific and layer-specific features from task-related features. The overall objective function is written as follows:

$$\mathcal{L} = \mathcal{L}_{ce}\left(P_s, Y_s\right) + \mathcal{L}_{ce}\left(P_l, Y_l\right) + \lambda \sum_{i=1}^{3} MI\left(E_{si}, E_{li}\right), \tag{4}$$

where Y_s and Y_l are the ground-truth label for species-wise and layer-wise anal-ysis tasks, respectively, and λ is the hyper-parameter to balance mutual infor-mation constraint.

3   Experiment Results

3.1 Experimental Settings

Dataset. To evaluate our method, we obtain 5951 digital reconstructions of PCs via metadata search from NeuroMorpho.org [1], a publicly available dataset for the neuroscience community. These PCs are in the L2/3, L4, L5, and L6 of the rat somatosensory neocortex and medial prefrontal neocortex as well as the same layers of the mouse somatosensory neocortex and medial prefrontal neocortex. For the species-wise analysis task, there are 2630 and 3321 PCs from the rat and mouse, respectively. For the layer-wise analysis task, there are 2350, 723, 2261, and 617 PCs in L2/3, L4, L5, and L6, respectively. Besides, the training and

Table 1. Performance of our method.

Method	Task 1		Task 2	
	F_1	Acc. (%)	F_1	Acc. (%)
LCCDNN [18]	0.8614	86.57	0.6762	67.06
DRNN [19]	0.7194	74.12	0.6305	63.33
Baseline	0.8524	85.22	0.6785	68.60
Ours	**0.8748**	**87.44**	**0.7228**	**72.46**

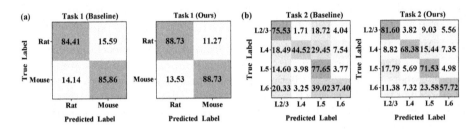

Fig. 4. Confusion matrices of the baseline and our method on the (a) species-wise and (b) layer-wise analysis tasks.

test sets are divided by 8:2 within each class. This guarantees that the test set includes all types of PCs on each task.

Given that the acquired PCs data are 3D data and directly processing 3D PCs data is challenging, we first convert them into three 2D-view images like previous works [16,17]. Then, these three 2D-view images are concatenated along the channel and projected into high-dimension feature space.

Training Details and Metrics. Our model is implemented using the PyTorch framework and trained on a single NVIDIA GeForce RTX 3090 GPU. We utilize ResNet50 [11] as feature extractors for different tasks. The weight of the feature extractor is initialized as the weight of ResNet50 pre-trained on ImageNet [8]. The weights of task classifiers are initialized randomly. Our model is trained using a batch size of 16 across 80 epochs. The Adam optimizer with a learning rate of 0.001 is adopted for optimization. In addition, the parameter λ and ϵ are set as 0.2 and 0.5, respectively.

Evaluation Metrics. We adopt multiple evaluation metrics, including overall accuracy and F_1 score, to verify the effectiveness of our method. Besides, we use the confusion matrix to better demonstrate the effectiveness of our method for the predictions for each category. The feature visualizations more clearly show the task-related features obtained by our method.

Table 2. Performance of our method with different modules evaluated on two tasks. "MI" and "ARE" represent mutual information constraint and the adaptive enhancement module.

MI	ARE	Species-wise Analysis		Layer-wise Analysis	
		F_1	Acc. (%)	F_1	Acc. (%)
×	✓	0.8653	86.47	0.6886	69.32
✓	×	0.8723	87.20	0.6965	69.81
✓	✓	0.8748	87.44	0.7228	72.46

Table 3. Influence of different weights for mutual information constraint.

λ	Species-wise Analysis		Layer-wise Analysis	
	F_1	Acc. (%)	F_1	Acc. (%)
0.05	0.8631	86.35	0.6914	69.38
0.1	0.8684	86.84	0.6954	69.69
0.2	0.8748	87.44	0.7228	72.46
0.3	0.8692	86.96	0.7158	71.74
0.7	0.8658	86.62	0.6766	67.84

3.2 Performance Evaluation

To demonstrate the effectiveness of our method objectively, we employ the method using ResNet50 as the feature extractor as the baseline, which is trained only on the cross-entropy loss as the objective function without the mutual information constraint. We use it to conduct the species-wise and layer-wise analysis tasks for PCs independently. Besides, we compare our method to these task-agnostic methods (e.g., LCCDNN [18] and DRNN [19]) of performing a single analysis task, and the results are shown in Table 1.

Our method performs better on both analysis tasks, with accuracies of 87.44% and 72.46%, respectively. Although single-task-based analysis methods achieve good results, their performance on the layer-wise analysis task needs to be improved, especially DRNN [19]. Compared to the baseline, our method increases the accuracy by 2.22% and 3.86% on the two tasks, respectively. Our approach effectively learns species-specific and layer-specific representations, leading to superior performance.

As illustrated in Fig. 4, our method accurately predicts the species or brain layers that PCs belong to, where the accuracy for each class is considerably increased. Although L4 and L6 PCs are insufficient, our method identifies them precisely and produces impressive results, improving accuracy by 23.86% and 20.32% over the baseline, respectively. This demonstrates that the learned task-specific representations are more discriminative.

Table 4. Evaluation of different thresholds ε.

ε	Species-wise Analysis		Layer-wise Analysis	
	F_1	Acc. (%)	F_1	Acc. (%)
0.1	0.8652	86.47	0.6890	69.08
0.3	0.8750	87.70	0.6957	69.41
0.5	0.8748	87.44	0.7228	72.46
0.7	0.8714	87.20	0.7030	70.53

Table 5. Evaluation of our method with different backbones.

Backbone	Species-wise Analysis		Layer-wise Analysis	
	F_1	Acc. (%)	F_1	Acc. (%)
VGG16	0.8743	87.43	0.7163	71.74
ResNet50	0.8748	87.44	0.7228	72.46
ResNet101	0.8630	86.35	0.6986	70.17

3.3 Ablation Studies

Evaluation of Different Modules. As shown in the first row of Table 2, all evaluation metrics decrease when our model is trained without the MI minimization constraint, especially on the layer-wise analysis task (accuracy only is 69.32%). This demonstrates its beneficial impact on task-specific representation learning. When the ARE module is deleted, our model performs less well on two tasks (see the second row of Table 2). As a result, the ARE module is also essential to improving the effectiveness of our method.

Impact of Different Balance Parameters λ. We verify the effects of different balance parameter values λ on our model, and the results are presented in Table 3. When λ equals 0.2, our method reaches the best performance (accuracies of 87.44% and 72.46, and F_1 scores of 0.8748 and 0.7728 on species-wise and layer-species analysis tasks, respectively). The decomposed task-specific features from test-related ones contain fewer common features. When λ is set as 0.05, our model becomes nearly free from mutual information constraint. When λ equals 0.7, performance degrades on both tasks. This is because the learned task-specific representations are too refined to recognize PCs. Therefore, it is optimal to set λ to 0.2.

Influence of Different Thresholds ε. Here, we investigate the impact of different thresholds ε on performance improvement as shown in Table 4. Our method performs best on the species-wise analysis task when ε equals 0.3 (accuracy of 87.70% and F_1 scores of 0.8750). In contrast, our method reaches the optimal performance on the layer-wise analysis task when ε is set to 0.5 (accuracy of 72.46% and F_1 scores of 0.7228). Identifying PCs on the layer-wise analysis task is more challenging because of more categories and data imbalance. Therefore, we set ε as 0.5 at other experiments based on the performance of the layer-wise analysis task.

(a)   (b)

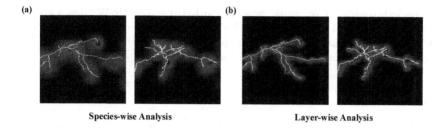

Species-wise Analysis   Layer-wise Analysis

Fig. 5. Feature visualization for both tasks.

Evaluation of Different Backbones. We test the effectiveness of our approach by conducting experiments with different backbones, such as VGG16, ResNet50, and ResNet101. As shown in Table 5, our approach that utilizes VGG16 as the feature extractor produces similar results to that of ResNet50 when it comes to species-wise analysis. However, our method based on ResNet50 performs better in layer-wise analysis than VGG16. As the backbone becomes deeper, the performance of our approach slightly decreases on both tasks. Hence, we utilize ResNet50 as the feature extractor.

3.4 Visualization

As shown in Fig. 5, our approach can efficiently capture the distinguishing morphology features for both analysis tasks. When analyzing the species of PCs, our approach focuses more on relatively large morphological regions (shown in Fig. 5(a)). When analyzing the brain layer of PCs, our method focuses on more detailed morphology features, such as bifurcations and terminal points (presented in Fig. 5(b)). This demonstrates that our approach effectively captures task-specific features for species-wise and layer-wise analysis tasks.

4   Conclusions

In this paper, we develop a task-specific representation learning framework, which effectively extracts species-specific and layer-specific features via mutual information minimization through dual-task learning. We first capture task-related features and then constrain them as task-specific representations by minimizing their mutual information. Moreover, the adaptive representation module increases the discriminability of task-specific representations, significantly boosting the performance. Experimental results show that our method can effectively learn distinctive species-specific and layer-specific features while remarkably improving the performance of species-wise and layer-wise analysis tasks. In future work, we will explore utilizing our model for multiple analysis tasks (more than two). Besides, how to take advantage of intra-task specificity and inter-task commonality to boost performance will be exploited.

Acknowledgments. This work was supported by the JKW Research Funds (20-163-14-LZ-001-004-01) and the Anhui Provincial Natural Science Foundation (2108085UD12). We acknowledge the support of GPU cluster built by MCC Lab of Information Science and Technology Institution, USTC.

References

1. Ascoli, G.A., Donohue, D.E., Halavi, M.: Neuromorpho. org: a central resource for neuronal morphologies. J. Neurosci. **27**(35), 9247–9251 (2007)
2. Bachman, P., Hjelm, R.D., Buchwalter, W.: Learning representations by maximizing mutual information across views. In: Proceedings of the Advances in Neural Information Processing Systems, pp. 15509–15519 (2019)
3. Batabyal, T., Condron, B., Acton, S.T.: Neuropath2path: classification and elastic morphing between neuronal arbors using path-wise similarity. Neuroinformatics **18**(3), 479–508 (2020)
4. Bekkers, J.M.: Pyramidal neurons. Curr. Biol. **21**(24), R975 (2011)
5. Belghazi, M.I., et al.: Mutual information neural estimation. In: Proceedings of the International Conference on Machine Learning, pp. 531–540 (2018)
6. Chen, X., et al.: Infogan: interpretable representation learning by information maximizing generative adversarial nets. In: Proceedings of the Advances in Neural Information Processing Systems, pp. 2180–2188 (2016)
7. Cheng, P., et al.: Club: a contrastive log-ratio upper bound of mutual information. In: Proceedings of the International Conference on Machine Learning, pp. 1779–1788 (2020)
8. Deng, J., et al.: Imagenet: a large-scale hierarchical image database. In: Proceedings of the IEEE Conference on Computer Vision Pattern Recognition, pp. 248–255 (2009)
9. Elston, G.N.: Cortex, cognition and the cell: new insights into the pyramidal neuron and prefrontal function. Cereb. Cortex **13**(11), 1124–1138 (2003)
10. Gao, W.J., Zheng, Z.H.: Target-specific differences in somatodendritic morphology of layer v pyramidal neurons in rat motor cortex. J. Comp. Neurol. **476**(2), 174–185 (2004)
11. He, K., Zhang, X., Ren, S., Sun, J.: Deep residual learning for image recognition. In: Proceedings of the IEEE Conference on Computer Vision Pattern Recognition, pp. 770–778 (2016)
12. Hou, X., Li, Y., Wang, S.: Disentangled representation for age-invariant face recognition: a mutual information minimization perspective. In: Proceedings of the IEEE International Conference on Computer Vision, pp. 3692–3701 (2021)
13. Hu, J., Shen, L., Sun, G.: Squeeze-and-excitation networks. In: Proceedings of the IEEE Conference Computer Vision Pattern Recognition, pp. 7132–7141 (2018)
14. Kanari, L., et al.: Objective morphological classification of neocortical pyramidal cells. Cereb. Cortex **29**(4), 1719–1735 (2019)
15. Kasper, E.M., et al.: Pyramidal neurons in layer 5 of the rat visual cortex. II. Development of electrophysiological properties. J. Comp. Neurol. **339**(4), 475–494 (1994)
16. Li, Z., et al.: Large-scale exploration of neuronal morphologies using deep learning and augmented reality. Neuroinformatics **16**(3), 339–349 (2018)
17. Li, Z., et al.: Towards computational analytics of 3d neuron images using deep adversarial learning. Neurocomputing **438**, 323–333 (2021)

18. Lin, X., Zheng, J.: A neuronal morphology classification approach based on locally cumulative connected deep neural networks. Appl. Sci. **9**(18), 3876 (2019)
19. Lin, X., Zheng, J., Wang, X., Ma, H.: A neuronal morphology classification approach based on deep residual neural networks. In: Proceedings of the International Conference on Neural Information Processing, pp. 336–348 (2018)
20. Mihaljević, B., et al.: Comparing basal dendrite branches in human and mouse hippocampal ca1 pyramidal neurons with Bayesian networks. Sci. Rep. **10**(1), 1–13 (2020)
21. Radenović, F., Tolias, G., Chum, O.: Fine-tuning CNN image retrieval with no human annotation. IEEE Trans. Pattern Anal. Mach. Intell. **41**(7), 1655–1668 (2018)
22. Schaefer, A.T., et al.: Coincidence detection in pyramidal neurons is tuned by their dendritic branching pattern. J. Neurophysiol. **89**(6), 3143–3154 (2003)
23. Spruston, N.: Pyramidal neurons: dendritic structure and synaptic integration. Nat. Rev. Neurosci. **9**(3), 206–221 (2008)
24. Vasques, X., et al.: Morphological neuron classification using machine learning. Front. Neuroanat. **10**, 102 (2016)
25. Wang, Y., et al.: A simplified morphological classification scheme for pyramidal cells in six layers of primary somatosensory cortex of juvenile rats. IBRO Reports **5**, 74–90 (2018)
26. Zhang, T., et al.: Neuron type classification in rat brain based on integrative convolutional and tree-based recurrent neural networks. Sci. Rep. **11**(1), 1–14 (2021)
27. Zhang, Y., et al.: Pinpointing morphology and projection of excitatory neurons in mouse visual cortex. Front. Neurosci. 912 (2019)
28. Zhao, L., et al.: Learning view-disentangled human pose representation by contrastive cross-view mutual information maximization. In: Proceedings of the IEEE Conference on Computer Vision Pattern Recognition, pp. 12793–12802 (2021)
29. Zhou, M., et al.: Mutual information-driven pan-sharpening. In: Proceedings of the IEEE Conference Computer Vision Pattern Recognition, pp. 1798–1808 (2022)

DermoSegDiff: A Boundary-Aware Segmentation Diffusion Model for Skin Lesion Delineation

Afshin Bozorgpour[1], Yousef Sadegheih[1], Amirhossein Kazerouni[2], Reza Azad[3], and Dorit Merhof[1,4(✉)]

[1] Institute of Image Analysis and Computer Vision, Faculty of Informatics and Data Science, University of Regensburg, Regensburg, Germany
[2] School of Electrical Engineering, Iran University of Science and Technology, Tehran, Iran
[3] Faculty of Electrical Engineering and Information Technology, RWTH Aachen University, Aachen, Germany
[4] Fraunhofer Institute for Digital Medicine MEVIS, Bremen, Germany
`dorit.merhof@ur.de`

Abstract. Skin lesion segmentation plays a critical role in the early detection and accurate diagnosis of dermatological conditions. Denoising Diffusion Probabilistic Models (DDPMs) have recently gained attention for their exceptional image-generation capabilities. Building on these advancements, we propose DermoSegDiff, a novel framework for skin lesion segmentation that incorporates boundary information during the learning process. Our approach introduces a novel loss function that prioritizes the boundaries during training, gradually reducing the significance of other regions. We also introduce a novel U-Net-based denoising network that proficiently integrates noise and semantic information inside the network. Experimental results on multiple skin segmentation datasets demonstrate the superiority of DermoSegDiff over existing CNN, transformer, and diffusion-based approaches, showcasing its effectiveness and generalization in various scenarios. The implementation is publicly accessible on GitHub.

Keywords: Deep learning · Diffusion models · Skin · Segmentation

1 Introduction

In medical image analysis, skin lesion segmentation aims at identifying skin abnormalities or lesions from dermatological images. Dermatologists traditionally rely on visual examination and manual delineation to diagnose skin lesions, including melanoma, basal cell carcinoma, squamous cell carcinoma, and other benign or malignant growths. However, the accurate and rapid segmentation of these lesions plays a crucial role in early detection, treatment planning, and

---

A. Bozorgpour, Y. Sadegheih, and A. Kazerouni—Contributed equally.

© The Author(s), under exclusive license to Springer Nature Switzerland AG 2023
I. Rekik et al. (Eds.): PRIME 2023, LNCS 14277, pp. 146–158, 2023.
https://doi.org/10.1007/978-3-031-46005-0_13

monitoring of disease progression. Automated medical image segmentation methods have garnered significant attention in recent years due to their potential to enhance diagnosis result accuracy and reliability. The success of these models in medical image segmentation tasks can be attributed to the advancements in deep learning techniques, including convolutional neural networks (CNNs) [12,20] and vision transformers [3,26].

Lately, Denoising Diffusion Probabilistic Models (DDPMs) [10] have gained considerable interest due to their remarkable performance in the field of image generation. This newfound recognition has led to a surge in interest and exploration of DDPMs, propelled by their exceptional capabilities in generating high-quality and diverse samples. Building on this momentum, researchers have successfully proposed new medical image segmentation methods that leverage diffusion models to tackle this challenging task [13]. EnsDiff [27] utilizes ground truth segmentation as training data and input images as priors to generate segmentation distributions, enabling the creation of uncertainty maps and an implicit ensemble of segmentations. Kim et al. [14] propose a novel framework for self-supervised vessel segmentation. MedSegDiff [28] introduces DPM-based medical image segmentation with dynamic conditional encoding and FF-Parser to mitigate high-frequency noise effects. MedSegDiff-V2 [29] enhances it with a conditional U-Net for improved noise-semantic feature interaction.

Boundary information has proven crucial in the segmentation of skin images, particularly when it comes to accurately localizing and distinguishing skin lesions from the surrounding healthy tissue [17,26]. Boundary information provides spatial relationships between different regions within the skin and holds greater significance compared to other areas. By emphasizing these regions during the training phase, we can achieve more accurate results by encouraging the model to focus on intensifying boundary regions while reducing the impact of other areas. However, most diffusion-based segmentation methods overlook this importance and designate equal importance to all regions. Another critical consideration is the choice of a denoising architecture, which directly impacts the model's capacity to learn complex data relationships. Most methods have followed a baseline approach [10,19], neglecting the fact that incorporating semantic and noise interaction within the network more effectively.

To address these shortcomings, we propose a novel and straightforward framework called **DermoSegDiff**. Our approach tackles the abovementioned issues by considering the importance of boundary information during training and presenting a novel denoising network that facilitates a more effective understanding of the relationship between noise and semantic information. Specifically, we propose a novel loss function to prioritize the distinguishing boundaries in the segmentation. By incorporating a dynamic parameter into the loss function, we increase the emphasis on boundary regions while gradually diminishing the significance of other regions as we move further away from the boundaries. Moreover, we present a novel U-Net-based denoising network structure that enhances the integration of guidance throughout the denoising process by incorporating a carefully designed dual-path encoder. This encoder effectively combines noise

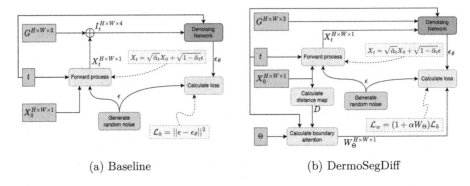

(a) Baseline   (b) DermoSegDiff

Fig. 1. (a) illustrates the architecture of the baseline, and (b) presents our proposed DermoSegDiff framework.

and semantic information, extracting complementary and discriminative features. Our model also has a unique bottleneck incorporating linear attention [23] and original self-attention [9] in parallel. Finally, the decoder receives the output, combined with the two outputs transferred from the encoder, and utilizes this information to estimate the amount of noise. Our experimental results demonstrate the superiority of our proposed method compared to CNN, transformer, and diffusion-based state-of-the-art (SOTA) approaches on ISIC 2018 [8], PH^2 [18], and HAM10000 [24] skin segmentation datasets, showcasing the effectiveness and generalization of our method in various scenarios. Contributions of this paper are as follows: ❶ We highlight the importance of incorporating boundary information in skin lesion segmentation by introducing a novel loss function that encourages the model to prioritize boundary areas. ❷ We present a novel denoising network that significantly improves noise reduction and enhances semantic interaction, demonstrating faster convergence compared to the baseline model on the different skin lesion datasets. ❸ Our approach surpasses state-of-the-art methods, including CNNs, transformers, and diffusion-based techniques, across four diverse skin segmentation datasets.

2   Method

Figure 1 provides an overview of our baseline DDPM model and presents our proposed **DermoSegDiff** framework for skin lesion segmentation. While traditional diffusion-based medical image segmentation methods focus on denoising the noisy segmentation mask conditioning by the input image, we propose that incorporating boundary information during the learning process can significantly improve performance. By leveraging edge information to distinguish overlapped objects, we aim to address the challenges posed by fuzzy boundaries in difficult cases and cases where lesions and backgrounds have similar colors. We begin by presenting our baseline method. Subsequently, we delve into how the inclusion of boundary information can enhance skin lesion segmentation and propose a novel approach to incorporate this information into the learning process. Finally, we introduce our network structure, which facilitates the integration of guidance through the denoising process more effectively.

2.1 Baseline

The core architecture employed in this paper is based on DDPMs [10,27] (see Fig. 1a). Diffusion models primarily utilize T timesteps to learn the underlying distribution of the training data, denoted as $q(x_0)$, by performing variational inference on a Markovian process. The framework consists of two processes: *forward* and *reverse*. During the forward process, the model starts with the ground truth segmentation mask ($x_0 \in \mathbb{R}^{H \times W \times 1}$) and adds a Gaussian noise in successive steps, gradually transforming it into a noisy mask:

$$q\left(x_t \mid x_{t-1}\right) = \mathcal{N}\left(x_t; \sqrt{1 - \beta_t} \cdot x_{t-1}, \beta_t \cdot \mathbf{I}\right), \forall t \in \{1, \ldots, T\}, \tag{1}$$

in which $\beta_1, \ldots, \beta_{t-1}, \beta_T$ represent the variance schedule across diffusion steps. We can then simply sample an arbitrary step of the noisy mask conditioned on the ground truth segmentation as follows:

$$q\left(\mathbf{x}_t \mid \mathbf{x}_0\right) = N\left(\mathbf{x}_t; \sqrt{\bar{\alpha}_t}\mathbf{x}_0, (1 - \bar{\alpha}_t)\mathbf{I}\right) \tag{2}$$

$$x_t = \sqrt{\bar{\alpha}_t}x_0 + \sqrt{1 - \bar{\alpha}_t}\epsilon, \tag{3}$$

where $\alpha_t := 1 - \beta_t$, $\bar{\alpha}_t := \prod_{j=1}^{t} \alpha_j$ and $\epsilon \sim \mathcal{N}(0, \mathbf{I})$. In the reverse process, the objective is to reconstruct the original structure of the mask perturbed during the diffusion process given the input image as guidance ($g \in \mathbb{R}^{H \times W \times 3}$), by leveraging a neural network to learn the underlying process. To achieve this, we concatenate the x_t and g, and denote the concatenated output as $I_t := x_t \| g$, where $I_t \in \mathbb{R}^{H \times W \times (3+1)}$. Hence, the reverse process is defined as

$$p_\theta\left(\mathbf{x}_{t-1} \mid \mathbf{x}_t\right) = \mathcal{N}\left(\mathbf{x}_{t-1}; \mu_\theta\left(I_t, t\right), \Sigma_\theta\left(I_t, t\right)\right), \tag{4}$$

where Ho et al. [10] conclude that instead of directly predicting μ_θ using the neural network, we can train a model to predict the added noise, ϵ_θ, leading to a simplified objective as $\mathcal{L}_b = \|\epsilon - \epsilon_\theta\left(I_t, t\right)\|^2$.

2.2 Boundary-Aware Importance

While diffusion models have shown promising results in medical image segmentation, there is a notable limitation in how we treat all pixels of a segmentation mask equally during training. This approach can lead to saturated results, undermining the model's performance. In the case of segmentation tasks like skin lesion segmentation, it becomes evident that boundary regions carry significantly more importance than other areas. This is because the boundaries

delineate the edges and contours of objects, providing crucial spatial information that aids in distinguishing between the two classes. To address this issue,
we present **DermoSegDiff**, which effectively incorporates boundary information
into the learning process and encourages the model to prioritize capturing and
preserving boundary details, leading to a faster convergence rate compared to
the baseline method. Our approach follows a straightforward yet highly effective
strategy for controlling the learning denoising process. It focuses on intensifying
the significance of boundaries while gradually reducing this emphasis as we move
away from the boundary region utilizing a novel loss function. As depicted in
Fig. 1, our forward process aligns with our baseline, and both denoising networks
produce output ϵ_θ. However, the divergence between the two becomes apparent
when computing the loss function. We define our loss function as follows:

$$\mathcal{L}_w = (1 + \alpha W_\Theta) \|\epsilon - \epsilon_\theta (x_t, g, t)\|^2 \tag{5}$$

where $W_\Theta \in \mathbb{R}^{H \times W \times 1}$ is a dynamic parameter intended to increase the weight
of noise prediction in boundary areas while decreasing its weight as we move
away from the boundaries (see Fig. 5). W_Θ is obtained through a two-step process involving the calculation of a distance map and subsequent computation of
boundary attention. Additionally, W_Θ is dynamically parameterized, depending
on the point of time (t) at which the distance map is calculated. It means it
functions as a variable that dynamically adjusts according to the specific characteristics of each image at time step t.

Our distance map function operates by taking the ground truth segmentation
mask as input. Initially, it identifies the border pixels by assigning a value of
one to them while setting all other pixels to zero. To enhance the resolution
of the resulting distance map, we extend the border points horizontally from
both the left and right sides by $\lceil H\% \rceil$ (e.g., for a 256×256 image, each row
would have seven boundary pixels). To obtain the distance map, we employ the
distance transform function [15], which is a commonly used image processing
technique for binary images. This function calculates the Euclidean distance
between each non-zero (foreground) pixel in the image and the nearest zero
(background) pixel. The result is a gray-level image where the intensities of
points within foreground regions are modified to represent the distances to the
closest boundaries from each individual point. To normalize the intensity levels of
the distance map and improve its suitability as a dynamic weighting matrix W_Θ,
we employ the technique of gamma correction from image processing to calculate
the boundary attention. By adjusting the gamma value, we gain control over the
overall intensity of the distance map, resulting in a smoother representation that
enhances its effectiveness in the loss function.

2.3   Network Architecture

Encoder: The overall architecture of our proposed denoising network is depicted
in Fig. 2. We propose a modification to the U-Net network architecture for predicting added noise ϵ_θ to a noisy segmentation mask x_{i-1}^{enc}, guided by the guidance image g_{i-1} and time embedding t, where i refers to the $i - th$ encoder.

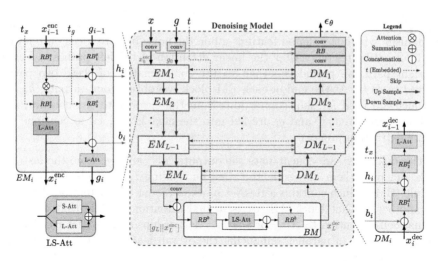

Fig. 2. The overview of the proposed denoising network architecture. The notation L-Att, RB, EM, DM, LS-Att, and S-Att correspond to the Linear Attention, ResNet Block, Encoder Modules, Decoder Modules, Linear Self-Attention, and Self-Attention modules, respectively.

The encoder consists of a series of stacked Encoder Modules (EM), which are subsequently followed by a convolution layer to achieve a four-by-four tensor at the output of the encoder. Instead of simply concatenating x_{i-1}^{enc} and g_{i-1} and feeding into the network [27], our approach enhances the conditioning process by employing a two-path feature extraction strategy in each Encoder Module (EM), focusing on the mutual effect that the noisy segmentation mask and the guidance image can have on each other. Each path includes two ResNet blocks (RB) and is followed by a Linear Attention (L-Att) [23], which is computationally efficient and generates non-redundant feature representation. To incorporate temporal information, time embedding is introduced into each RB. The time embedding is obtained by passing t through a sinusoidal positional embedding, followed by a linear layer, a GeLU activation function, and another linear layer. We use two time embeddings, one for g_{i-1} (t_g) and another for x_{i-1}^{enc} (t_x), to capture the temporal aspects specific to each input. Furthermore, we leverage the knowledge captured by RB_1^x by transferring and concatenating it with the guidance branch, resulting in h_i. By incorporating two paths, we capture specific representations that provide a comprehensive view of the data. The left path extracts noise-related features, while the right path focuses on semantic information. This combination enables the model to incorporate complementary and discriminative features. After applying RB_2^x, we introduce a feedback mechanism that takes a convolution of the RB_2^g output and connects to the RB_2^x input. This feedback allows the resultant features, which contain overall information about both the guidance and noise, to be shared with the noise path. By doing so and multiplying the feature maps, we emphasize important features while attenuating less significant ones. This multiplication operation acts as a form of attention mechanism, where the shared features guide the noise path to focus on relevant and informative regions. After the linear attention of the left path and before the right path, we provide another feature concatenation of these two paths, referred to as b_i. At the end of each EM block, we obtain four outputs: h_i and b_i, which are used for skip connections from the encoder to the decoder, and resultant enriched x_i^{enc} and g_i are fed into the next EM block to continue the feature extraction process.

Bottleneck: Next, we concatenate the outputs, x_L^{enc} and g_L, from the last EM block and pass them alongside the time embedding t_x through a Bottleneck Module (BM), which contains a ResNet block, a Linear Self-Attention (LS-Att), and another ResNet block. LS-Att is a dual attention module that combines original Self-Attention (S-Att) for spatial relationships and L-Att for capturing semantic context in parallel, enhancing the overall feature representation. The output of BM is then fed into the decoder.

Decoder: The decoder consists of stacked Decoder Modules (DM) followed by a convolutional block that outputs ϵ_θ. The number of stacked DMs is the same as the number of EMs in the encoder. Unlike the EM blocks, which are dual-path modules, each DM block is a single-path module. It includes two consecutive RB blocks and one L-Att module. b_i and h_i from the encoder are concatenated with the feature map before and after applying RB_1^d, respectively. By incorporating these features, the decoder gains access to refined information from the encoder, thereby aiding in better estimating the amount of noise added during the forward process and recovering missing information during the learning process. In addition, to preserve the impact of noise during the decoding process, we implement an additional skip connection from x to the final layer of the decoder. This involves concatenating the resulting feature map of the DM_1 with x and passing them together through the last convolutional block to output the estimated noise ϵ_θ.

3   Results

The proposed method has been implemented using the PyTorch library (version 1.14.0) and has undergone training on a single NVIDIA A100 graphics processing unit (80 GB VRAM). The training procedure employs a batch size of 32 and utilizes the Adam optimizer with a base learning rate of 0.0001. The learning rate is decreased by a factor of 0.5 in the event that there is no improvement in the loss function after ten epochs. In all experiments, we established T as 250 and maintained the forward process variances as constants that progressively increased from $\beta_{start} = 0.0004$ to $\beta_{end} = 0.08$ linearly. Furthermore, in the training process, data augmentation techniques have been employed using Albumentations [4], including spatial augmentation methods such as Affine and Flip transforms and CoarseDropout, as well as pixel augmentation methods such as GaussNoise and RGBShift transforms. For each dataset, the network was trained for 40000

Table 1. Performance comparison of the proposed method against the SOTA approaches on skin lesion segmentation benchmarks. Blue indicates the best result, and red displays the second-best.

Methods	ISIC 2018				PH^2				HAM10000			
	DSC	SE	SP	ACC	DSC	SE	SP	ACC	DSC	SE	SP	ACC
U-Net [20]	0.8545	0.8800	0.9697	0.9404	0.8936	0.9125	0.9588	0.9233	0.9167	0.9085	0.9738	0.9567
DAGAN [16]	0.8807	0.9072	0.9588	0.9324	0.9201	0.8320	0.9640	0.9425	–	–	–	–
TransUNet [6]	0.8499	0.8578	0.9653	0.9452	0.8840	0.9063	0.9427	0.9200	0.9353	0.9225	0.9851	0.9649
Swin-Unet [5]	0.8946	0.9056	0.9798	0.9645	0.9449	0.9410	0.9564	0.9678	0.9263	0.9316	0.9723	0.9616
DeepLabv3+ [7]	0.8820	0.8560	0.9770	0.9510	0.9202	0.8818	0.9832	0.9503	0.9251	0.9015	0.9794	0.9607
Att-UNet [21]	0.8566	0.8674	0.9863	0.9376	0.9003	0.9205	0.9640	0.9276	0.9268	0.9403	0.9684	0.9610
UCTransNet [25]	0.8838	0.9825	0.8429	0.9527	0.9093	0.9698	0.8835	0.9408	0.9346	0.9205	0.9825	0.9684
MissFormer [11]	0.8631	0.9690	0.8458	0.9427	0.8550	0.9738	0.7817	0.9050	0.9211	0.9287	0.9725	0.9621
Baseline (EnsDiff) [27]	0.8775	0.8358	0.9812	0.9502	0.9117	0.8752	0.9774	0.9431	0.9277	0.9213	0.9771	0.9625
DermoSegDiff-A	0.9005	0.8761	0.9811	0.9587	0.9450	0.9296	0.9810	0.9637	0.9386	0.9308	0.9814	0.9681
DermoSegDiff-B	0.8966	0.8642	0.9828	0.9575	0.9467	0.9308	0.9814	0.9650	0.9430	0.9326	0.9839	0.9704

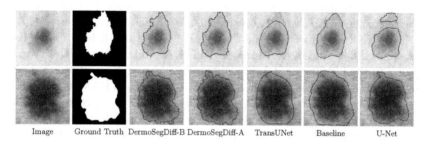

| Image | Ground Truth | DermoSegDiff-B | DermoSegDiff-A | TransUNet | Baseline | U-Net |

Fig. 3. Visual comparisons of different methods on the ISIC 2018 skin lesion dataset. Ground truth boundaries are shown in green, and predicted boundaries are shown in blue. (Color figure online)

iterations. Moreover, we set α empirically as 0.2. The duration of the training process was approximately 1.35 s per sample. Notably, in our evaluation process, we employ a sampling strategy to generate nine different segmentation masks for each image in the test set. To obtain a final segmentation result, we average these generated masks and apply a threshold of 0. The reported results in terms of performance metrics are based on this ensemble strategy.

3.1 Datasets

To evaluate the proposed methodology, three publicly available skin lesion segmentation datasets, ISIC 2018 [8], PH² [18], and HAM10000 [24] are utilized. The same pre-processing criteria described in [2] are used to train and evaluate the first three datasets mentioned. The HAM10000 dataset is also a subset of the

ISIC archive containing 10015 dermoscopy images along with their corresponding segmentation masks. 7200 images are used as training, 1800 as validation, and 1015 as test data. Each sample of all datasets is downsized to 128×128 pixels using the same pre-processing as [1].

3.2   Quantitative and Qualitative Results

Table 1 presents the performance analysis of our proposed DermoSegDiff on all four skin lesion segmentation datasets. The evaluation incorporates several metrics, including Dice Score (DSC), Sensitivity (SE), Specificity (SP), and Accuracy (ACC), to establish comprehensive evaluation criteria. In our notation, the model with the baseline loss function is referred to as DermoSegDiff-A, while the model with the proposed loss function is denoted as DermoSegDiff-B. The results demonstrate that DermoSegDiff-B surpasses both CNN and Transformer-based approaches, showcasing its superior performance and generalization capabilities across diverse datasets. Specifically, our main approach demonstrates superior performance compared to pure transformer-based methods such as Swin-Unet [5], CNN-based methods like DeepLabv3+ [7], and hybrid methods like UCTransNet [25]. Moreover, DermoSegDiff-B exhibits enhanced performance compared to the baseline model (EnsDiff) [27], achieving an increase of +2.18%, +3.83%, and +1.65% in DSC score on ISIC 2018, PH^2, and HAM10000 datasets, respectively. Furthermore, in Fig. 3, we visually compare the outcomes generated by various skin lesion segmentation models. The results clearly illustrate that our proposed approach excels in capturing intricate structures and producing more accurate boundaries compared to its counterparts. This visual evidence underscores the superior performance achieved by carefully integrating boundary information into the learning process.

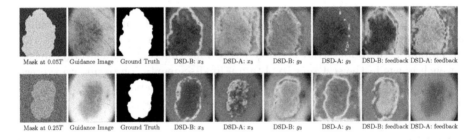

Fig. 4. An illustration of how our proposed loss function concentrates on the segmentation boundary in contrast to the conventional $\mathcal{L}_b$ loss in DermoSegDiff-A. The heatmaps are obtained from the EM_3 using GradCAM [22]. Notably, DSD is an abbreviation of DermoSegDiff.

4   Ablation Studies

Figure 4 illustrates the effects of our innovative loss function. The heatmaps are produced utilizing the GradCAM [22], which visually represents the gradients of the output originating from the EM_3. Incorporating a novel loss function results in a shift of emphasis towards the boundary region, leading to a 0.51% enhancement compared to DermoSegDiff-A in the overall DSC score on the ISIC 2018 dataset. The analysis reveals a distinct behavior within our model. In the noise path, the model primarily emphasizes local boundary information, while in the guidance branch, it aims to capture more global information. This knowledge is then transferred through feedback to the noise branch, providing complementary information. This combination of local and global information allows our model to effectively leverage both aspects and achieve improved results. Figure 5 depicts the evolution of W_Θ with respect to T. In the initial stages of the denoising process, when the effect of noise is significant, the changes in the boundary area are relatively smooth. During this phase, the model focuses on capturing more global information about the image. As the denoising process progresses and it becomes easier to distinguish between the foreground and background in the resulting image, the weight shifts, placing increased emphasis on the boundary region while disregarding the regions that are further away from it. Additionally, as we approach x_0, the emphasis on the boundary information becomes more pronounced. These observations highlight the adaptive nature of W_Θ and its role in effectively preserving boundary details during the denoising process.

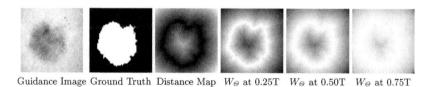

Guidance Image Ground Truth Distance Map W_Θ at 0.25T W_Θ at 0.50T W_Θ at 0.75T

Fig. 5. An illustration of how the W_Θ variable varies dependent on the network's current time step of diffusion.

(a) Annotation limitation   (b) Model limitation

Fig. 6. (a) Illustrates the limitation imposed by annotation of the dataset, and (b) presents some of the limitations of our proposed model. Ground truth boundaries are shown in green, and predicted boundaries are shown in blue. (Color figure online)

5   Limitations

Despite these promising results, there are also some limitations. For example, some annotations within the datasets may not be entirely precise. Figure 6a portrays certain inconsistencies in the annotations of data. However, despite these annotation challenges, our proposed method demonstrates superior precision in the segmentation of skin lesions in comparison to the annotators. The results indicate that with more meticulous annotation of the masks, our proposed approach could have achieved even higher scores across all evaluation metrics. It is worth noting that there were instances where our model deviated from the accurate annotation and erroneously partitioned the area. Figure 6b depicts instances where our proposed methodology fails to segment the skin lesion accurately. The difficulty in accurately demarcating the boundary between the foreground and background in skin images arises from the high similarity between these regions and requires more work that we aim to address in future work.

6   Conclusion

This paper introduced the **DermoSegDiff** diffusion network for skin lesion segmentation. Our approach introduced a novel loss function that emphasizes the importance of the segmentation's boundary region and assigns it higher weight during training. Further, we proposed a denoising network that effectively models the noise-semantic information and results in performance improvement.

References

1. Alom, M.Z., Hasan, M., Yakopcic, C., Taha, T.M., Asari, V.K.: Recurrent residual convolutional neural network based on u-net (r2u-net) for medical image segmentation. arXiv preprint arXiv:1802.06955 (2018)
2. Azad, R., Al-Antary, M.T., Heidari, M., Merhof, D.: Transnorm: transformer provides a strong spatial normalization mechanism for a deep segmentation model. IEEE Access **10**, 108205–108215 (2022)
3. Azad, R., et al.: Advances in medical image analysis with vision transformers: a comprehensive review. arXiv preprint arXiv:2301.03505 (2023)
4. Buslaev, A., Iglovikov, V.I., Khvedchenya, E., Parinov, A., Druzhinin, M., Kalinin, A.A.: Albumentations: fast and flexible image augmentations. Information **11**(2) (2020). https://doi.org/10.3390/info11020125
5. Cao, H., et al.: Swin-unet: unet-like pure transformer for medical image segmentation. arXiv preprint arXiv:2105.05537 (2021)
6. Chen, J., et al.: Transunet: transformers make strong encoders for medical image segmentation. arXiv preprint arXiv:2102.04306 (2021)
7. Chen, L.C., Zhu, Y., Papandreou, G., Schroff, F., Adam, H.: Encoder-decoder with atrous separable convolution for semantic image segmentation. In: Proceedings of the European Conference on Computer Vision (ECCV), pp. 801–818 (2018)
8. Codella, N., et al.: Skin lesion analysis toward melanoma detection 2018: a challenge hosted by the international skin imaging collaboration (ISIC). arXiv preprint arXiv:1902.03368 (2019)

9. Dosovitskiy, A., et al.: An image is worth 16x16 words: transformers for image recognition at scale. arXiv preprint arXiv:2010.11929 (2020)

10. Ho, J., Jain, A., Abbeel, P.: Denoising diffusion probabilistic models. Adv. Neural. Inf. Process. Syst. **33**, 6840–6851 (2020)

11. Huang, X., Deng, Z., Li, D., Yuan, X.: Missformer: an effective medical image segmentation transformer. arXiv preprint arXiv:2109.07162 (2021)

12. Isensee, F., Jaeger, P.F., Kohl, S.A., Petersen, J., Maier-Hein, K.H.: nnu-net: a self-configuring method for deep learning-based biomedical image segmentation. Nat. Methods **18**(2), 203–211 (2021)

13. Kazerouni, A., et al.: Diffusion models in medical imaging: a comprehensive survey. Med. Image Anal. 102846 (2023)

14. Kim, B., Oh, Y., Ye, J.C.: Diffusion adversarial representation learning for self-supervised vessel segmentation. In: The Eleventh International Conference on Learning Representations (2023)

15. Kimmel, R., Kiryati, N., Bruckstein, A.M.: Sub-pixel distance maps and weighted distance transforms. J. Math. Imaging Vis. **6**, 223–233 (1996)

16. Lei, B., et al.: Skin lesion segmentation via generative adversarial networks with dual discriminators. Med. Image Anal. **64**, 101716 (2020)

17. Liu, X., Yang, L., Chen, J., Yu, S., Li, K.: Region-to-boundary deep learning model with multi-scale feature fusion for medical image segmentation. Biomed. Signal Process. Control **71**, 103165 (2022)

18. Mendonça, T., Ferreira, P.M., Marques, J.S., Marcal, A.R., Rozeira, J.: Ph 2-a dermoscopic image database for research and benchmarking. In: 2013 35th Annual International Conference of the IEEE Engineering in Medicine and Biology Society (EMBC), pp. 5437–5440. IEEE (2013)

19. Nichol, A.Q., Dhariwal, P.: Improved denoising diffusion probabilistic models. In: International Conference on Machine Learning, pp. 8162–8171. PMLR (2021)

20. Ronneberger, O., Fischer, P., Brox, T.: U-net: convolutional networks for biomedical image segmentation. In: Navab, N., Hornegger, J., Wells, W.M., Frangi, A.F. (eds.) MICCAI 2015. LNCS, vol. 9351, pp. 234–241. Springer, Cham (2015). https://doi.org/10.1007/978-3-319-24574-4_28

21. Schlemper, J., et al.: Attention gated networks: learning to leverage salient regions in medical images. Med. Image Anal. **53**, 197–207 (2019)

22. Selvaraju, R.R., Cogswell, M., Das, A., Vedantam, R., Parikh, D., Batra, D.: Grad-cam: visual explanations from deep networks via gradient-based localization. In: Proceedings of the IEEE International Conference on Computer Vision, pp. 618–626 (2017)

23. Shen, Z., Zhang, M., Zhao, H., Yi, S., Li, H.: Efficient attention: attention with linear complexities. In: Proceedings of the IEEE/CVF Winter Conference on Applications of Computer Vision, pp. 3531–3539 (2021)

24. Tschandl, P., Rosendahl, C., Kittler, H.: The ham10000 dataset, a large collection of multi-source dermatoscopic images of common pigmented skin lesions. Sci. Data **5**(1), 1–9 (2018)

25. Wang, H., Cao, P., Wang, J., Zaiane, O.R.: Uctransnet: rethinking the skip connections in u-net from a channel-wise perspective with transformer. Proc. AAAI Conf. Artif. Intell. **36**, 2441–2449 (2022)

26. Wang, J., Wei, L., Wang, L., Zhou, Q., Zhu, L., Qin, J.: Boundary-aware transformers for skin lesion segmentation. In: de Bruijne, M., et al. (eds.) MICCAI 2021. LNCS, vol. 12901, pp. 206–216. Springer, Cham (2021). https://doi.org/10.1007/978-3-030-87193-2_20

27. Wolleb, J., Sandkühler, R., Bieder, F., Valmaggia, P., Cattin, P.C.: Diffusion models for implicit image segmentation ensembles. In: International Conference on Medical Imaging with Deep Learning, pp. 1336–1348. PMLR (2022)

28. Wu, J., Fang, H., Zhang, Y., Yang, Y., Xu, Y.: Medsegdiff: medical image segmentation with diffusion probabilistic model. arXiv preprint arXiv:2211.00611 (2022)

29. Wu, J., Fu, R., Fang, H., Zhang, Y., Xu, Y.: Medsegdiff-v2: diffusion based medical image segmentation with transformer. arXiv preprint arXiv:2301.11798 (2023)

Self-supervised Few-Shot Learning for Semantic Segmentation: An Annotation-Free Approach

Sanaz Karimijafarbigloo[1], Reza Azad[2(✉)], and Dorit Merhof[1,3]

[1] Institute of Image Analysis and Computer Vision, Faculty of Informatics and Data Science, University of Regensburg, Regensburg, Germany
[2] Faculty of Electrical Engineering and Information Technology, RWTH Aachen University, Aachen, Germany
rezazad68@gmail.com
[3] Fraunhofer Institute for Digital Medicine MEVIS, Bremen, Germany
dorit.merhof@ur.de

Abstract. Few-shot semantic segmentation (FSS) offers immense potential in the field of medical image analysis, enabling accurate object segmentation with limited training data. However, existing FSS techniques heavily rely on annotated semantic classes, rendering them unsuitable for medical images due to the scarcity of annotations. To address this challenge, multiple contributions are proposed: First, inspired by spectral decomposition methods, the problem of image decomposition is reframed as a graph partitioning task. The eigenvectors of the Laplacian matrix, derived from the feature affinity matrix of self-supervised networks, are analyzed to estimate the distribution of the objects of interest from the support images. Secondly, we propose a novel self-supervised FSS framework that does not rely on any annotation. Instead, it adaptively estimates the query mask by leveraging the eigenvectors obtained from the support images. This approach eliminates the need for manual annotation, making it particularly suitable for medical images with limited annotated data. Thirdly, to further enhance the decoding of the query image based on the information provided by the support image, we introduce a multi-scale large kernel attention module. By selectively emphasizing relevant features and details, this module improves the segmentation process and contributes to better object delineation. Evaluations on both natural and medical image datasets demonstrate the efficiency and effectiveness of our method. Moreover, the proposed approach is characterized by its generality and model-agnostic nature, allowing for seamless integration with various deep architectures. The code is publicly available at GitHub.

Keywords: Few-shot Learning · Medical · Segmentation · Self-supervised

I. Rekik et al. (Eds.): PRIME 2023, LNCS 14277, pp. 159–171, 2023.
https://doi.org/10.1007/978-3-031-46005-0_14

1 Introduction

Computer vision tasks such as localization and segmentation, which require
a detailed understanding of image structure, can achieve good results when
approached with fully-supervised deep learning methods. Although the success
of supervised deep learning methods depends heavily on the availability of a
large amount of well-annotated data [3,5], collecting and annotating such data
is costly and challenging, as it requires to be performed manually by a domain
expert. The other equally problematic challenge with fully-supervised models
is their inflexibility when confronted with new classes of segmentation targets
(e.g., different and novel lesion types) [12,21]. This is a significant challenge,
as training a new model for every new segmentation class is impractical and
time-consuming. To address the aforementioned problems, few-shot semantic
segmentation (FSS) has been proposed. The core concept of FSS is a potent
approach that effectively minimizes the requirement for extensive annotation,
enabling precise predictions of unobserved classes using only a limited number
of guiding examples. By capitalizing on FSS, a model can create a discriminative
representation of a previously unknown class using a small set of labeled examples (support). This acquired representation can then be employed to accurately
predict the outcomes for unlabeled examples (query), without the need for any
model retraining. This approach significantly alleviates the annotation burden
and empowers the model to swiftly generalize and adapt to new unseen classes
(e.g., new lesions)

Several approaches have been proposed to tackle the FSS problem. One approach involves the use of a mask average pooling strategy, which effectively
removes irrelevant features based on information from the support masks [32].
Another improvement proposed by Wang et al. [29] is the introduction of a novel
prototype alignment regularization between support and query images, resulting
in better generability for new classes. Additionally, in other recent works [31],
researchers have utilized deep attention mechanisms to learn attention weights
between support and query images, enabling improved label propagation. In spite
of the promising outcomes observed in applying few-shot learning paradigms to
the segmentation of natural images [33], their utilization in medical image segmentation remains limited. This limitation is due to the scarcity of annotated
classes, which hinders the network's ability to generalize and to prevent over-
fitting [30]. The concept of few-shot segmentation on medical images was initially introduced by [19]. The authors proposed the use of adversarial learning
to segment brain images, leveraging only one or two labeled brain images, drawing inspiration from successful semi-supervised approaches [25]. Feyjie et al. [8]
introduced a novel approach that incorporates a semi-supervised mechanism
within the conventional few-shot learning framework. This approach leverages
the availability of abundant unlabeled datasets to predict skin lesion masks for
previously unseen samples. In recent work, to further benefit from unlabelled
data, Ouyang et al. [21] proposed a self-supervised few-shot semantic segmentation (FSS) framework called SSL-ALPNet to segment medical images by utilizing superpixel-based pseudo-labels as supervision signals. This method also

improved the segmentation accuracy using an adaptive local prototype pooling module. Xiao et al. [30] proposed a Siamese few-shot network for medical image segmentation and they used a grid attention module to enhance semantic information localization. Ding et al. [6] designed a self-supervised few-shot network to segment medical images. They introduced a Cycle-Resemblance Attention module to effectively capture the pixel-wise relations between query and support medical images.

Despite the incorporation of semi-supervised and self-supervised techniques within these strategies to optimize the training procedure of the model, the presence of annotated data remains indispensable during the inference stage for accurate query mask prediction. To mitigate this requirement, we undertake an exploration of the role played by self-supervised techniques in facilitating the acquisition of object representation within a conventional few-shot context. Specifically, we draw inspiration from the accomplishments of few-shot segmentation methods in natural images, which rely on the episodic training paradigm. In our approach (depicted in Fig. 1), ❶ we aim to eliminate the need for extensive annotation by leveraging the eigenvectors of the Laplacian matrix derived from the feature affinity matrix of self-supervised networks. This allows us to effectively capture the global representation of the object of interest in the Support image. By integrating this concept into the standard few-shot segmentation framework, ❷ we propose an end-to-end network that leverages support guidance to predict the query mask. In order to enhance the decoding process of the query image by leveraging the information from the support image, ❸ we propose to incorporate large kernel attention along with multi-scale attention gate modules. These modules effectively highlight pertinent features and intricate details, resulting in an enhanced segmentation process.

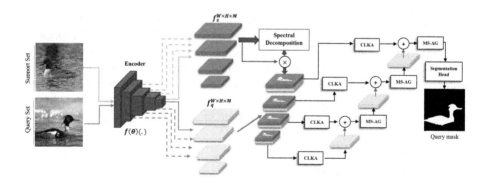

Fig. 1. The overview of our annotation-free FSS model.

2   Proposed Method

2.1   Problem Formulation

In the context of standard FSS, our approach involves three main datasets: a training set denoted as $D_{train} = \{(X_i^t, Y_i^t)\}_{i=1}^{N_{train}}$, a support set denoted as $D_{support} = \{(X_i^s, Y_i^s)\}_{i=1}^{N_{support}}$, and a test set denoted as $D_{test} = \{(X_i^q)\}_{i=1}^{N_{test}}$. Here, X_i and Y_i represent the input image and corresponding binary mask, respectively. Each dataset contains a total of N images, specified by N_{train}, $N_{support}$, and N_{test}, involving C distinct classes. Notably, the classes are shared between the support and test sets but are disjoint with the training set, denoted as $\{C_{train}\} \cap \{C_{support}\} = \emptyset$.

The objective of few-shot learning is to train a neural network $f_{(\theta,\gamma)}(\cdot)$ on the training set, enabling it to accurately segment a new class $c \notin C_{train}$ in the test set based on k reference samples from $D_{support}$. Here, θ and γ represent the learnable parameters of the encoder and decoder respectively. To reproduce this procedure, training on the base dataset D_{train} follows the episodic learning paradigm introduced in [27], where each episode entails a c-way k-shot learning task. Specifically, each episode is created by sampling two components. Firstly, we construct a support training set for each class c, denoted as $D_{train}^{\mathcal{S}} = \{(X_s^t, Y_s^t(c))\}_{s=1}^k \subset Dtrain$, where $Y_s^t(c)$ represents the binary mask corresponding to the support image X_s^t for class c. Secondly, we create a query set $D_{train}^{\mathcal{Q}} = \{(X_q^t, Y_q^t(c))\} \subset D_{train}$, where X_q^t is the query image and $Y_q^t(c)$ is the corresponding binary mask for class c. In order to estimate the segmentation mask of a given class c in the query image, the model leverages the support training set and the query image. This process can be expressed as $\hat{Y}_q^t(c) = f_{(\theta,\gamma)}(D_{train}^{\mathcal{S}}, X_q^t)$.

More specifically, in our approach we utilize an encoder module to encode the support and query images, resulting in feature representations denoted as $f_s \in \mathbb{R}^{W \times H \times M}$ and $f_q \in \mathbb{R}^{W \times H \times M}$, respectively. Here, W, H, and M represent the width, height, and feature dimensionality in the feature space, respectively. In the subsequent step, we employ a hierarchical approach to acquire the class prototypes, employing a self-supervision strategy in contrast to the prevailing literature [2,10], which utilizes the support mask Y_s to filter out the support prototype. We will provide a full explanation of our hierarchical prototype estimation process in the next sections.

2.2   Hierarchical Prototypes

In the realm of few-shot learning, the support prototype assumes a pivotal role as a representative reference for a specific class, greatly influencing the model's ability to generalize and accurately predict unseen instances. By encapsulating the fundamental characteristics of a class, the support prototype empowers the model with the capacity to make informed predictions. Our study introduces a novel approach for generating a hierarchical support prototype using spectral decomposition, eliminating the need for a support mask.

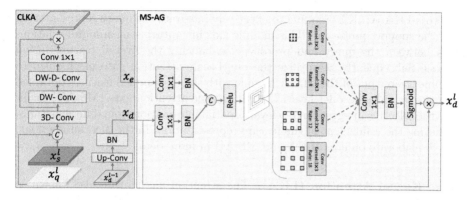

Fig. 2. The overview of the proposed **CLKA** and **MS-AG** modules. In each block of the decoder network, we include both CLKA and MS-AG for conditioning the query representation based on the support prototype.

Initially, we extract the support representation denoted as $f_s \in \mathbb{R}^{W \times H \times M}$ by leveraging an encoder module $f_{(\theta)}(\cdot)$. This support representation is derived from different parts of the encoder module, including combinations of various layers such as hyper-columns [10]. Our experimental findings, consistent with previous research [2], reveal that incorporating features from both shallow and deep layers of the encoder network produces favorable results. This approach captures multi-level and multi-scale representations while preserving global contextual object features.

Subsequently, we construct an affinity matrix based on pixel correlations. By setting the affinity threshold to zero, our focus lies on aggregating similar features rather than anti-correlated ones. The resulting feature affinities, denoted as $W_s \in \mathbb{R}^{HW \times HW}$, encompass semantic information at both coarse and low-level resolutions. Utilizing W_s, we compute the eigenvectors of its Laplacian matrix $L = D^{-1/2}(D-W)D^{-1/2}$ to decompose an image into soft segments, represented as $y_0, \cdots, y_{n-1} = \text{eigs}(L)$. Among these eigenvectors, we pay particular attention to the remaining ones $y_{>0}$ since the first eigenvector y_0 is constant, corresponding to an eigenvalue $\lambda_0 = 0$.

To identify the support object, akin to prior studies [16], we examine the Fiedler eigenvector y_1 of L and discretize it by considering its sign, resulting in binary image segmentation. By creating a bounding box around the smaller region, which is more likely to represent the foreground object rather than the background, we establish an alternative to the support mask. This bounding box serves the purpose of hierarchically filtering the support representation to generate support prototype f_s'.

2.3 Decoder

In our network architecture, we incorporate a decoder module consisting of four blocks. Each block follows a specific sequence of operations. Firstly, we employ the cross-LKA (CLKA) module to effectively integrate the query representation with the support prototype. This module aids in capturing meaningful relationships between the query and prototype, enhancing the overall feature fusion process. Subsequently, we utilize the multi-scale attention gate mechanism to combine the output of the CLKA module with the up-sampled features obtained from the previous decoder layer. The multi-scale attention gate (MS-AG) facilitates the selective integration of relevant spatial information from different scales, promoting the refinement of the feature representation. In the next subsections, we will elaborate on cross-LKA and MS-AG in more detail.

Large Kernel Attention (LKA). The attention mechanism, also known as an adaptive selection process, has the ability to identify discriminative features while disregarding noisy responses with respect to the input features. Generating an attention map that signifies the importance of various parts is one of the key roles of the attention mechanism. There are two well-known attention mechanisms and each one has its own pros and cons. The first one is the self-attention mechanism [7] which has the potential to discover long-range dependencies however it has some drawbacks (e.g., ignoring channel adaptability, high quadratic complexity for high-resolution images, neglecting the 2D structure of images). The second one is large kernel convolution [22] which can establish relevance and produce an attention map. Nevertheless, employing large-kernel convolutions introduces substantial computational overhead and increases the number of parameters. To address the mentioned limitations and leverage the advantages of both self-attention and large kernel convolutions, the large kernel attention (LKA) approach is proposed in [9], which decomposes a large kernel convolution operation to capture long-range relationships. In our study, we extend the idea of the LKA for distilling discriminative representation derived from the support prototype into a query representation to condition the prediction of the query mask based on support distribution. To this end, we first fuse the support prototype f'_S and the query representation f_q with learnable parameters (modeled as 3D convolution) followed by a non-linear activation function. This operation enables the network to encode the prior knowledge obtained from the support representation into query features for estimating the object of interest's representation and eliminating the background noise. Next, to capture long-range dependency in an efficient way, we follow the LKA approach. Regarding C as the number of channels, then a $C \times C$ convolution can be decomposed into a $[\frac{c}{d}] \times [\frac{c}{d}]$ depth-wise dilation convolution (a spatial long-range convolution) with dilation d, a $(2d - 1) \times (2d - 1)$ depth-wise convolution (a spatial local convolution) and a 1×1 convolution (a channel convolution). Therefore, long-range relationships can be extracted within a feature space and the attention map is generated with a few computational complexity and parameters. The large kernel attention (LKA) module is written as

$$\text{Attention} = \text{Conv}_{1 \times 1}(\text{DW} - \text{D} - \text{Conv}(\text{DW} - \text{Conv}(\text{F}(f'_s, f_q)))) \tag{1}$$

$$\text{Output} = \text{Attention} \otimes \text{F}(f'_s, f_q) \tag{2}$$

where $F(f'_s, f_q) \in R^{C \times H \times W}$ and *Attention* $\in R^{C \times H \times W}$ denote the 3D convolutional operation for support and query aggregation and the attention map, respectively. Also, $\otimes$ indicates the element-wise product and the value of the attention map represents the importance of each feature. Unlike conventional attention methods, the LKA approach does not use an additional normalization function such as sigmoid or SoftMax. The overall process is depicted in Fig. 2

Multi-scale Attention Gate (MS-AG). The main purpose of AGs is to mitigate irrelevant features in background regions by employing a grid-attention technique that considers the spatial information of the image [20]. To achieve this objective, we initiate the fusion process by combining the feature representation obtained from the decoder block x_d^{l-1} with the output of the CLKA module x_e^l. This fusion is accomplished using a 1×1 convolution operation, which combines the two sets of information into a unified representation. Next, to model multi-scale representation we employ Atrous convolution in our attention gate module. Atrous convolution, also referred to as dilated convolution, is a technique that expands the kernel size of a filter without increasing the parameter count or computational load. By introducing $r - 1$ zeros between consecutive filter values, the kernel size of a $k \times k$ filter is effectively enlarged to $k_{Atrous} = k + (k-1)(r-1)$. Using this multi-scale attention mechanism allows the model to more precisely determine the importance of each region and effectively manage their impact on the final outcome. The multi-scale attention gate $MS-AG(\cdot)$ can be formulate as follows:

$$q_{att}(x_e, x_d) = C_{at}(\sigma_1 (BN (C_e(x_e) + BN (C_d(x_d))))) \quad (3)$$

$$MS-AG(x_e, x_d) = x_d * \sigma_2 (BN (C (q_{att}(x_e, x_d)))) \quad (4)$$

where $\sigma_1(\cdot)$ refers to ReLU, and $\sigma_2(\cdot)$ corresponds to the Sigmoid activation function. $C_e(\cdot), C_d(\cdot)$, and $C(\cdot)$ indicate the channel-wise 1×1 convolution operation. $BN(\cdot)$ denotes the batch normalization operation and $C_{at}(\cdot)$ shows the Atrous convolution operation. x_d and x_e represent the up-sampled and skip connection features, respectively. Figure 2 illustrates the overall process.

3 Experiments

3.1 Dataset

In this study, the FSS-1000 dataset is utilized to assess the effectiveness of our method in analyzing natural images. Additionally, to examine the network's ability to generalize to medical images, we evaluate its performance on the publicly accessible (PH^2) dataset, specifically designed for skin lesion segmentation.

FSS-1000: The FSS-1000 class dataset [14] is a significantly large-scale dataset specifically tailored for few-shot segmentation tasks. It encompasses a total of 1000 classes, with each class consisting of 10 images accompanied by their corresponding pixel-level ground truth annotations. The official training split, comprising 760 classes, is utilized as the primary dataset for training purposes. On the other hand, the testing set, comprising 240 classes, is used for inference.

PH^2 **Dataset:** The PH^2 dataset [17] consists of 200 RGB dermoscopic images of melanocytic lesions including 80 common nevi, 80 atypical nevi, and 40 melanomas. The dataset was provided at the Dermatology Service of Hospital Pedro Hispano in Matosinhos, Portugal. The resolution of images is 768×560 pixels, but in our work we resized them to 224×224 pixels. In our experimental setup, we follow the same setting suggested in [8] to evaluate our method.

3.2   Implementation Details

In our implementation, ResNet50 backbone network with ImageNet pre-trained weights is used. Feature extraction is performed by extracting features from the last convolutional layer at each encoder block of the backbone network. This feature extraction approach yields four pyramidal layers ($P = 4$). To ensure consistency, we set the spatial sizes of both support and query images to 400×400 pixels, resulting in $H, W = 400$. Consequently, we obtain the following spatial sizes for each pyramidal layer: $H_1, W_1 = 100$, $H_2, W_2 = 50$, $H_3, W_3 = 25$, and $H_4, W_4 = 13$. As a result, our decoder component consists of four blocks, where each block involves fusing the support prototype with the query representation, as illustrated in Fig. 1. The entire network is implemented using the PyTorch framework and optimized using the Adam optimizer, with a learning rate of $1e-3$. To prevent the pre-trained backbone networks from learning class-specific representations from the training data, we freeze the encoder weight.

3.3   Evaluation Metrics

For FSS-1000 benchmark, we adopt the mean intersection over union (mIoU) as our evaluation metric. To assess the performance of our network on the skin dataset, we compare our method against the unsupervised k-means clustering method, as well as SOTA self-supervised methods such as DeepCluster [4], IIC [11], and spatial guided self-supervised strategy (SGSCN) [1]. Our evaluation methodology follows the guidelines outlined in [1]. To evaluate the efficacy of our network, we employ three evaluation metrics: the Dice similarity coefficient (DSC), the Hammoud distance (HM), and the XOR metric.

3.4   Results

FSS-1000: We commence our evaluation of the proposed model on the FSS-1000 dataset, considering two distinct settings. In the first setting, the inference process incorporates the support mask to guide the network. We compare our results with recent few-shot methods, including DoG [2], PFENet [26], HSNet [18] and etc. The results for 1-shot and 5-shot scenarios are summarized in Table 1b. Remarkably, our models, set new benchmarks in terms of performance while maintaining a minimal number of learnable parameters. With including the support annotation on the inference time, our 1-shot and 5-shot results exhibit substantial improvements of 15.3% and 14.9% in mIoU, respectively, compared to the baseline OSLSM method. Furthermore, compared to the recent SOTA approaches, HSNet [18] and DAN [28], our strategy achieves promising results.

In the second setting, we conduct additional experiments without including support annotation. As outlined in our proposed method, we estimate the support distribution through spectral decomposition. Notably, our model performs exceptionally well even without annotation, as evident from Table 1a. In the 1-shot scenario, our model achieves a notable mIoU improvement of 19.7% over the FSS-baseline method. In addition using the same setting, our method is abale to obtain superior performance than HSNet [18]. Some challenging cases are visualized in Fig. 3.

PH^2: We present a comparative results in Table 1b. The comparative results highlight the superiority of our approaches over SOTA methods across all evaluation metrics, affirming the effectiveness of our self-supervised few-shot learning strategy. Notably, by employing the episodic training paradigm, a noticeable enhancement of approximately 19.1% is observed compared to the few-shot baseline model suggested in [8]. In contrast to the semi-supervised strategy [8] that integrates additional samples through the utilization of unsupervised methodologies, the proposed models demonstrate a superior level of performance by employing a self-supervised strategy. Moreover, our strategy differentiates itself from the self-supervised approach [1,13] that generates a supervisory signal solely based on image content. Instead, we leverage a support sample to incorporate prior knowledge, effectively guiding the network and elevating its performance. From a qualitative standpoint, we provide a visual comparison in Fig. 3.

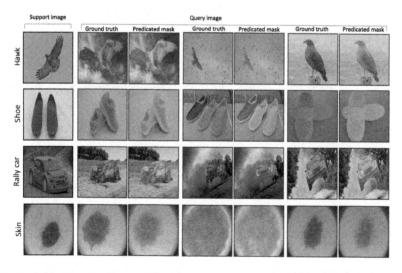

Fig. 3. Sample of prediction results of the proposed method on the FSS-1000 and PH^2 datasets, employing a one-shot setting.

3.5 Ablation Study

The proposed architecture incorporates two key modules: the CLKA, and the MS-AG module in the decoding path. These modules are designed to facilitate the feature representation and adaptively fuse support information into the query representation. In order to assess the impact and contribution of each module on the generalization performance, we conducted experiments where we selectively removed individual modules, as outlined in Table 1c. The experimental results highlight the significance of each module in the overall architecture. Specifically, removing any of the modules from the network leads to a noticeable decrease in performance. Notably, when the CLKA module is removed, the impact of support prior knowledege diminishes, resulting in a clear drop in performance. Similarly, replacing the MS-AG with simple concatenation results in a performance drop. However, by including the MS-AG module, our model tends to reduce the number of wrong predictions and isolated false positives.

Table 1. (a) Comparison of IoU on the FSS-1000 dataset. (b) Comparative performance of the proposed method against the SOTA approaches on the PH^2 dataset. (c) Contribution of each module on the model performance.

(a) Results on FSS-1000 Dataset

Setting	Methods	mIoU 1-shot	5-shot
With Annotation	OSLSM [24]	70.2	73.0
	co-FCN [23]	71.9	74.2
	FSS-1000 [14]	73.4	80.1
	DoG [2]	80.8	83.3
	PFENet [26]	80.8	81.4
	MemoryFSS [15]	83.0	85.7
	DAN [28]	85.2	87.1
	HSNet [18]	85.5	87.8
	Proposed Method	**85.7**	**87.9**
Without Annotation	FSS baseline [8]	65.3	67.9
	HSNet [18]	84.3	86.1
	Proposed Method	**85.0**	**86.8**

(b) Results on PH2 dataset

Methods	PH^2 DSC ↑	HM ↓	XOR ↓
FSS-baseline	68.13	-	-
Semi-supervised FSS [8]	74.77	-	-
k-means	71.3	130.8	41.3
DeepCluster [4]	79.6	35.8	31.3
IIC [11]	81.2	35.3	29.8
SGSCN[1]	83.4	32.3	28.2
MSS-Former[1]	86.0	23.1	25.9
Our Method	**87.3**	**21.2**	**23.5**

(c) Modules effect

CLKA	MS-AG	mIoU (FSS-1000)
✗	✗	83.8
✓	✗	84.1
✗	✓	84.0
✓	✓	85.0

4 Conclusion

Our study presents a novel approach for addressing few-shot semantic segmentation on medical images in the absence of annotated data. We reframe the problem as a graph partitioning task and leverage the eigenvectors of the Laplacian matrix derived from self-supervised networks to effectively model the Support representation and capture the underlying distribution. Within the standard FSS framework, we predict the query mask by utilizing the learned support distribution. Furthermore, we introduce the hierarchical LKA module to enrich the feature representation and improve the decoding process.

Acknowledgment. This work was funded by the German Research Foundation (Deutsche Forschungsgemeinschaft, DFG)- project number 455548460.

References

1. Ahn, E., Feng, D., Kim, J.: A spatial guided self-supervised clustering network for medical image segmentation. In: de Bruijne, M., et al. (eds.) MICCAI 2021. LNCS, vol. 12901, pp. 379–388. Springer, Cham (2021). https://doi.org/10.1007/978-3-030-87193-2_36

2. Azad, R., Fayjie, A.R., Kauffmann, C., Ben Ayed, I., Pedersoli, M., Dolz, J.: On the texture bias for few-shot CNN segmentation. In: Proceedings of the IEEE/CVF Winter Conference on Applications of Computer Vision, pp. 2674–2683 (2021)

3. Azad, R., et al.: Advances in medical image analysis with vision transformers: a comprehensive review. arXiv preprint arXiv:2301.03505 (2023)

4. Caron, M., Bojanowski, P., Joulin, A., Douze, M.: Deep clustering for unsupervised learning of visual features. In: Proceedings of the European Conference on Computer Vision (ECCV), pp. 132–149 (2018)

5. Chaitanya, K., Erdil, E., Karani, N., Konukoglu, E.: Contrastive learning of global and local features for medical image segmentation with limited annotations. Adv. Neural Inf. Process. Syst. **33**, 12546–12558 (2020)

6. Ding, H., Sun, C., Tang, H., Cai, D., Yan, Y.: Few-shot medical image segmentation with cycle-resemblance attention. In: Proceedings of the IEEE/CVF Winter Conference on Applications of Computer Vision, pp. 2488–2497 (2023)

7. Dosovitskiy, A., et al.: An image is worth 16x16 words: transformers for image recognition at scale. arXiv preprint arXiv:2010.11929 (2020)

8. Feyjie, A.R., Azad, R., Pedersoli, M., Kauffman, C., Ayed, I.B., Dolz, J.: Semi-supervised few-shot learning for medical image segmentation. arXiv preprint arXiv:2003.08462 (2020)

9. Guo, M.H., Lu, C.Z., Liu, Z.N., Cheng, M.M., Hu, S.M.: Visual attention network. arXiv preprint arXiv:2202.09741 (2022)

10. Hariharan, B., Arbeláez, P., Girshick, R., Malik, J.: Hypercolumns for object segmentation and fine-grained localization. In: Proceedings of the IEEE Conference on Computer Vision and Pattern Recognition, pp. 447–456 (2015)

11. Ji, X., Henriques, J.F., Vedaldi, A.: Invariant information clustering for unsupervised image classification and segmentation. In: Proceedings of the IEEE/CVF International Conference on Computer Vision, pp. 9865–9874 (2019)

12. Karimijafarbigloo, S., Azad, R., Kazerouni, A., Ebadollahi, S., Merhof, D.: Mmcformer: missing modality compensation transformer for brain tumor segmentation. In: Medical Imaging with Deep Learning (2023)

13. Karimijafarbigloo, S., Azad, R., Kazerouni, A., Merhof, D.: Ms-former: multi-scale self-guided transformer for medical image segmentation. In: Medical Imaging with Deep Learning (2023)

14. Li, X., Wei, T., Chen, Y.P., Tai, Y.W., Tang, C.K.: Fss-1000: a 1000-class dataset for few-shot segmentation. In: Proceedings of the IEEE/CVF Conference on Computer Vision and Pattern Recognition, pp. 2869–2878 (2020)

15. Lu, H., Wei, C., Deng, Z.: Learning with memory for few-shot semantic segmentation. In: 2021 IEEE International Conference on Image Processing (ICIP), pp. 629–633. IEEE (2021)
16. Melas-Kyriazi, L., Rupprecht, C., Laina, I., Vedaldi, A.: Deep spectral methods: a surprisingly strong baseline for unsupervised semantic segmentation and localization. In: Proceedings of the IEEE/CVF Conference on Computer Vision and Pattern Recognition, pp. 8364–8375 (2022)
17. Mendonça, T., Ferreira, P.M., Marques, J.S., Marcal, A.R., Rozeira, J.: Ph 2-a dermoscopic image database for research and benchmarking. In: 2013 35th Annual International Conference of the IEEE Engineering in Medicine and Biology Society (EMBC), pp. 5437–5440. IEEE (2013)
18. Min, J., Kang, D., Cho, M.: Hypercorrelation squeeze for few-shot segmentation. In: Proceedings of the IEEE/CVF International Conference on Computer Vision, pp. 6941–6952 (2021)
19. Mondal, A.K., Dolz, J., Desrosiers, C.: Few-shot 3d multi-modal medical image segmentation using generative adversarial learning. arXiv preprint arXiv:1810.12241 (2018)
20. Oktay, O., et al.: Attention u-net: learning where to look for the pancreas. arXiv preprint arXiv:1804.03999 (2018)
21. Ouyang, C., Biffi, C., Chen, C., Kart, T., Qiu, H., Rueckert, D.: Self-supervised learning for few-shot medical image segmentation. IEEE Trans. Med. Imaging 41(7), 1837–1848 (2022)
22. Park, J., Woo, S., Lee, J.Y., Kweon, I.S.: Bam: bottleneck attention module. arXiv preprint arXiv:1807.06514 (2018)
23. Rakelly, K., Shelhamer, E., Darrell, T., Efros, A., Levine, S.: Conditional networks for few-shot semantic segmentation (2018)
24. Shaban, A., Bansal, S., Liu, Z., Essa, I., Boots, B.: One-shot learning for semantic segmentation. arXiv preprint arXiv:1709.03410 (2017)
25. Souly, N., Spampinato, C., Shah, M.: Semi supervised semantic segmentation using generative adversarial network. In: Proceedings of the IEEE International Conference on Computer Vision, pp. 5688–5696 (2017)
26. Tian, Z., Zhao, H., Shu, M., Yang, Z., Li, R., Jia, J.: Prior guided feature enrichment network for few-shot segmentation. IEEE Trans. Pattern Anal. Mach. Intell. 44(2), 1050–1065 (2020)
27. Vinyals, O., et al.: Matching networks for one shot learning. Adv. Neural Inf. Process. Syst. 29 (2016)
28. Wang, H., Zhang, X., Hu, Y., Yang, Y., Cao, X., Zhen, X.: Few-shot semantic segmentation with democratic attention networks. In: Vedaldi, A., Bischof, H., Brox, T., Frahm, J.-M. (eds.) ECCV 2020. LNCS, vol. 12358, pp. 730–746. Springer, Cham (2020). https://doi.org/10.1007/978-3-030-58601-0_43
29. Wang, K., Liew, J.H., Zou, Y., Zhou, D., Feng, J.: Panet: few-shot image semantic segmentation with prototype alignment. In: Proceedings of the IEEE/CVF International Conference on Computer Vision, pp. 9197–9206 (2019)
30. Xiao, G., Tian, S., Yu, L., Zhou, Z., Zeng, X.: Siamese few-shot network: a novel and efficient network for medical image segmentation. Appl. Intell. 1–13 (2023)

31. Zhang, C., Lin, G., Liu, F., Yao, R., Shen, C.: Canet: class-agnostic segmentation networks with iterative refinement and attentive few-shot learning. In: Proceedings of the IEEE/CVF Conference on Computer Vision and Pattern Recognition, pp. 5217–5226 (2019)
32. Zhang, X., Wei, Y., Yang, Y., Huang, T.S.: Sg-one: similarity guidance network for one-shot semantic segmentation. IEEE Trans. Cybernet. **50**(9), 3855–3865 (2020)
33. Zhou, H., Zhang, R., He, X., Li, N., Wang, Y., Shen, S.: Mceenet: multi-scale context enhancement and edge-assisted network for few-shot semantic segmentation. Sensors **23**(6), 2922 (2023)

Imputing Brain Measurements Across Data Sets via Graph Neural Networks

Yixin Wang[1], Wei Peng[2], Susan F. Tapert[3], Qingyu Zhao[2],
and Kilian M. Pohl[2,4(✉)]

[1] Department of Bioengineering, Stanford University, Stanford, CA, USA
[2] Department of Psychiatry and Behavioral Sciences, Stanford University, Stanford, CA, USA
kpohl@stanford.edu
[3] Department of Psychiatry, University of California, San Diego, CA, USA
[4] Center for Biomedical Sciences, SRI International, Menlo Park, CA, USA

Abstract. Publicly available data sets of structural MRIs might not contain specific measurements of brain Regions of Interests (ROIs) that are important for training machine learning models. For example, the curvature scores computed by Freesurfer are not released by the Adolescent Brain Cognitive Development (ABCD) Study. One can address this issue by simply reapplying Freesurfer to the data set. However, this approach is generally computationally and labor intensive (e.g., requiring quality control). An alternative is to impute the missing measurements via a deep learning approach. However, the state-of-the-art is designed to estimate randomly missing values rather than entire measurements. We therefore propose to re-frame the imputation problem as a prediction task on another (public) data set that contains the missing measurements and shares some ROI measurements with the data sets of interest. A deep learning model is then trained to predict the missing measurements from the shared ones and afterwards is applied to the other data sets. Our proposed algorithm models the dependencies between ROI measurements via a graph neural network (GNN) and accounts for demographic differences in brain measurements (e.g. sex) by feeding the graph encoding into a parallel architecture. The architecture simultaneously optimizes a graph decoder to impute values and a classifier in predicting demographic factors. We test the approach, called *D*emographic *A*ware *G*raph-based *I*mputation (*DAGI*), on imputing those missing Freesurfer measurements of ABCD (N=3760; minimum age 12 years) by training the predictor on those publicly released by the National Consortium on Alcohol and Neurodevelopment in Adolescence (NCANDA, N=540). 5-fold cross-validation on NCANDA reveals that the imputed scores are more accurate than those generated by linear regressors and deep learning models. Adding them also to a classifier trained in identifying sex results in higher accuracy than only using those Freesurfer scores provided by ABCD.

Keywords: Brain measurements · Feature imputation · Graph representation learning

© The Author(s), under exclusive license to Springer Nature Switzerland AG 2023
I. Rekik et al. (Eds.): PRIME 2023, LNCS 14277, pp. 172–183, 2023.
https://doi.org/10.1007/978-3-031-46005-0_15

1   Introduction

Neuroscience heavily relies on ROI measurements extracted from structural magnetic resonance imaging (MRI) to encode brain anatomy [24]. However, public releases of brain measurements might not contain those that are important for a specific task. For example, the Freesurfer scores [6] publicly released by the ABCD study do not contain curvature measurements of cortical regions [3], which might be useful for identifying sex differences. While one could theoretically reapply the Freesurfer pipeline to generate those missing measurements, it requires substantial computational resources and manual labor, as, for example, the Freesurfer scores from thousands of MRIs would have to be quality controlled. A more efficient solution is to learn to impute missing brain measurements from the existing ones.

Imputation involves estimating or filling in missing or incomplete data values based on the available data, thereby creating a complete dataset suitable for further analysis or modeling. Examples of popular approaches for imputing measurements are MICE [26] and k-nearest neighbors [8]. The state-of-the-art in this domain relies on deep learning models, such as using generative autoencoders [25] or graph convolutional networks [23,28]. However, such methods assume that missing values are randomly distributed within a matrix capturing all measurements of a data set (refer to Fig. 1 (a)). If each column now represents a measurement, estimating missing values in a column then partly relies on rows (or samples) for which that measurement exists. Here we aim to solve the issue that the entire column does not contain any values (Fig. 1 (b)), i.e., some specific measurements are absent throughout an entire dataset. One could address this issue by combining the data set with the missing values with one that contains them, which then relates to the scenario in Fig. 1 (a). However, the imputation now explicitly depends on the data set with the missing scores so if that data set is updated (e.g., ABCD yearly releases) so do all imputations, which could result in scores conflicting with those imputed based on earlier versions of the data set. We instead address this challenge by re-framing the imputation problem as a prediction task on a single (public) data set, such as NCANDA [1], that contains the missing measurements and shares some ROI measurements with the data set of interest. A deep learning model can then be trained on NCANDA to predict the curvature scores from the measurements that are shared with ABCD. Afterwards, the trained model is applied to ABCD (or other data sets that share those scores) to predict the missing curvature scores on ABCD. Consequently, our primary objective is to determine the most accurate mapping from the currently available shared measurements to the missing ones.

Measurements of the same ROI (e.g., cortical thickness and volume) are highly dependent, and measurements of adjacent regions are more likely to be correlated than those from distant regions [10,16]. To explicitly account for such dependencies, our prediction model is based on a graph neural network (GNN) [22] called Graph Isomorphism Network [29]. In our graph, each node represents an ROI and adjacent ROIs are connected via edges. In addition to modeling adjacency of ROIs, our prediction model also accounts for the dependencies between

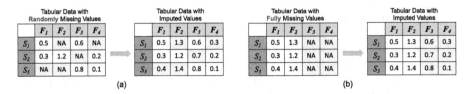

Fig. 1. Scenarios of missing values : (a) missing values are being randomly distributed across the data set or (b) specific measurements are absent from a data set, which is the problem we aim to solve here.

demographic factors and ROI measurements [11,21]. For example, women tend to have higher gyrification in frontal and parietal regions than men, which results in the curvature of those ROIs being different between the sexes [13]. We account for this difference by feeding the GNN encodings into a parallel architecture that simultaneously optimizes a graph decoder for imputing values and a classifier for identifying sex.

We apply our approach, called *Demographic Aware Graph-based Imputation* (*DAGI*), to impute Freesurfer measurements that are available in the NCANDA data set but are missing in ABCD (i.e., "mean curvature" and "Gaussian curvature") by explicitly taking advantage of those that are shared among them (i.e., "average thickness", "surface area" and "gray matter volume"). Using 5-fold cross-validation, we then show on NCANDA that the accuracy of the imputed scores is significantly higher than those generated by linear regressors and deep learning models. Furthermore, We identify the brain ROIs important in the imputation task by visualizing the learned graph structure via GNNExplainer [30]. On the ABCD data set, adding the scores to a classifier in identifying sex results in significantly higher accuracy than only using those provided by ABCD or using those imputed by combing the ABCD with the NCANDA data set (Fig. 1 (a)).

2   Method

Let's assume that the first data set is represented by a matrix $X^1 \in \mathbb{R}^{v \times d}$ containing the cortical measurements of v regions, where d cortical measurements $X_i \in \mathbb{R}^d$ are extracted from each region i. Furthermore, let $X^2 \in \mathbb{R}^{v \times p}$ be the data matrix of the second data set, which is based on the same parcellation but contains a different set of measurements for each region, of which $p(< d)$ are those also found in X^1. Let $X_i^o \in \mathbb{R}^{1 \times p}$ be the p shared measures across datasets, and $X_i^m \in \mathbb{R}^{1 \times q}$ be the remaining q measurements only available in X^1. Thus, X^1 can be divided into $X^O = [X_1^o, ..., X_v^o]^T$ and $X^M = [X_1^m, ..., X_v^m]^T$. Our goal is to learn an imputation mapping $X^O \rightarrow X^M$ so that we can impute the missing measurements on the second data set. To generate an accurate mapping, we first design a GNN implementation that accounts for dependencies among brain ROI measurements and in parallel consider demographic variations (e.g. sex) within those ROI measurements via a classifier.

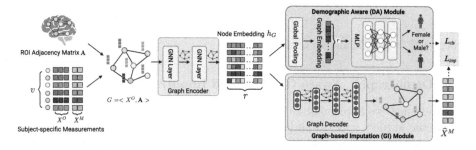

Fig. 2. Overview of our model: A GNN encodes both adjacency and measurements of brain ROIs into node embeddings, which are utilized by a graph decoder to impute missing values X^M. The parallel (upper) branch refines the node representations by differentiating between the sexes.

2.1 Graph-Based Imputation

We view the v regions as the nodes of a graph with X^O as node features. To capture adjacency among cortical ROIs and simplify training, we construct a sparse graph by adding an edge between two brain regions if they share a boundary on the cortical surface. This undirected graph with v nodes is then encoded by an "adjacency matrix" $\mathbf{A} \in \mathbb{R}^{v \times v}$, where $\mathbf{A}_{ij}$ is 1 if and only if nodes i and j are connected. As $\mathbf{A}$ does not change across subjects, then each subject is encoded by the graph $G = <X^O, \mathbf{A}>$, whose node features are the subject-specific measurements X^O.

Given a graph G, we aim to learn its encoding into node embeddings $h_G \in \mathbb{R}^{v \times r}$ that is optimized for imputing missing ROI measurements and predicting the label, i.e., demographic factor sex (see Fig. 2). The node embeddings are learned by a Graph Isomorphism Network (GIN) [29], which compares favorably to conventional GNNs such as GCN [9] in capturing high-order relationships across features of neighboring ROIs [29]. Each layer of a GIN learns the relationships between neighboring ROIs by first summing up the feature vectors of adjacent nodes. These new vectors are then mapped to hidden vectors via a multi-layer perceptron (MLP). The hidden vector h_i^k of a particular node i at the k-th layer is then defined as :

$$h_i^k := \text{MLP}\left((1 + \varepsilon) \cdot h_i^{k-1} + \sum_{j \in \mathcal{N}_i} h_j^{k-1}\right), \tag{1}$$

where $\mathcal{N}_i$ denotes nodes adjacent to node i (according to $\mathbf{A}$) and the weight ε of a node compared to its neighbors is learned.

The node embeddings of the last layer $h_G := \{h_i\}_{i \in v}$ are then fed into a graph decoder, which again is a GIN. The decoder is trained to reconstruct the missing measurements X^M using h_G obtained from "shared measurements" X^O by deriving the mapping function $f(\cdot)$ so that the predicted value $\widehat{X}^M := f(h_G)$ minimizes the loss function

$$\mathcal{L}_{imp} := \left\| X^M - f(h_G) \right\|^2, \tag{2}$$

where $\| \cdot \|$ is the Euclidean distance.

2.2 Demographic Aware Graph-Based Imputation

As mentioned, we implement a classifier in parallel to the graph decoder (Fig. 2). Given the subject-specific node embedding h_G and label y_G (e.g., female or male), this classifier aims to learn a function $g(\cdot)$ that maps the node embeddings of G to label y_G, i.e., $\widehat{y}_G := g(h_G)$. As shown in Fig. 2, our model first applies a global mean pooling operation to h_G in order to extract the graph embedding required for the MLP to perform the classification [7]. The loss function optimized by the classifier is then

$$\mathcal{L}_{cls} := y_G \log\left(g(h_G)\right) + (1 - y_G)\log\left(1 - g(h_G)\right). \tag{3}$$

To minimize this loss, the node embeddings h_G are optimized with respect to representing demographic differences.

Explicitly accounting for demographic differences then improves the accuracy of the imputation task as the demographic factors (i.e., sex) estimated by the classifier provide additional information further constraining the search space. Thus, the overall loss function minimized by DAGI combines imputation and classification loss, i.e.,

$$\mathcal{L}_{total} := \mathcal{L}_{imp} + \mathcal{L}_{cls}. \tag{4}$$

2.3 Implementation

We implement the model in PyTorch using the Adam optimizer with a learning rate of 0.01. The batch size is set to 32 and the number of epochs is 300. The dimension of node embedding r is 32. Our graph encoder is composed of two GIN layers, each containing an MLP with two fully-connected layers. Our graph decoder contains one GIN layer with four fully-connected layers. Following each GIN layer, we apply ReLU functions and batch normalization to enhance stability. Codes will be available at https://github.com/Wangyixinxin/DAGI

3 Experimental Results

In this section, we evaluate DAGI on the NCANDA and ABCD data sets (described in Sect. 3.1). On NCANDA (Sect. 3.2), we determine the accuracy of the imputed measurements by our and other approaches by comparing them with real measurements via 5-fold cross-validation. We highlight the crucial role of explicitly accounting for the relationship between ROIs and the demographic factor sex in the imputation process by visualizing the learned embeddings and examining the discrepancy in the imputed measurements across the sexes. In an out-of-sample test on ABCD (Sect. 3.3), the curvature scores are not provided so we infer the accuracy from a classifier identifying sex just based on ABCD measurements, by including also our imputed ones, and by adding those imputed by alternative approaches that combine NCANDA and ABCD dataset in the training process.

Table 1. Imputation accuracy based on 5-fold cross-validation on NCANDA. GI refers to the implementation of DAGI without the classifier. The best results are shown in **bold**. Compared to DAGI, all error scores are significantly higher ($p \leq 0.05$ based on two-sided paired t-test) with the exception of the MSE and MAE associated with the mean curvature scores produced by GIN.

	Mean Curvature			Gaussian Curvature		
	MSE (e^{-3})	MAE (e^{-2})	MRE	MSE (e^{-4})	MAE (e^{-2})	MRE
Linear Regression [18]						
Direct	9.40	2.95	40.36	3.15	1.63	15.68
ROI-based	8.52	2.12	31.77	2.24	1.12	9.58
Multi-layer Perceptron [2]	8.89	2.56	35.65	2.99	1.58	12.90
GI						
GCN [9]	9.80	3.01	45.29	3.05	1.60	14.51
GIN [29]	7.87	1.99	28.65	1.88	1.05	7.22
DAGI (Proposed)	**7.71**	**1.92**	**26.77**	**1.19**	**0.81**	**5.41**

3.1   Dataset

We utilize two publicly available datasets to evaluate our proposed model. The first data set (Release: NCANDA_PUBLIC_BASE_STRUCTURAL_V01 [20]) consists of baseline Freesurfer measurements of all 540 participants (270 females and 270 males) of NCANDA [1] that are between the ages 12–18 years and report no-to-low alcohol drinking in the past year. The Freesurfer score for each of the 34 bilateral cortical regions defined according to the Desikan-Killiany Atlas [5] consists of 5 regional measurements: average thickness, surface area, gray matter volume, mean curvature, and Gaussian curvature. The second public data release is the Data Release 4.0 of ABCD dataset [3], from which we use data from all 3760 adolescents (1682 females and 2078 males) collected between ages 12 to 13.8 years for our analysis. In addition to the average thickness, surface area and gray matter volume, ABCD released the "sulcal depth" but does not contain the two curvature scores released by NCANDA. Imputing those curvature scores from the three shared ones is the goal here.

3.2   Experiments on NCANDA

Quantitative Comparison. In NCANDA, we measure the accuracy of our imputed measurements by performing 5-fold cross-validation and then record for each measurement type the average Mean Squared Error (MSE) and Mean Absolute Error (MAE) across all subjects. Based on MAE, we also compute the Mean Relative Error (MRE) to have an error score that is indifferent to the scale of the inferred measurements. To put those accuracy scores into context, we repeat the 5-fold cross-validation for other approaches. Specifically, we impute the measurements via an MLP [2] and a linear regression model [18] (a.k.a., direct linear regression). As not all measurements across ROIs necessarily have a direct relationship with one another, the "ROI-based Linear Regression" separately fits a linear model to each ROI so that it imputes missing measurements as the linear combinations of observed measures within each individual region. We investigate our modeling choices by imputing scores without the classifier (referring to as Graph Imputation, or GI) and by replacing the GIN with a GCN [9]. We apply two-sided paired t-tests between the error scores recorded for the proposed DAGI and each alternative approach and label p-values ≤ 0.05 as being significantly different.

According to Table 1, the two approaches oblivious to ROIs, i.e., linear regression and MLP, received relatively high error scores indicating the importance of accounting for ROI-specific characteristics in the imputation process. This observation is further supported as their error scores are significantly higher (p<0.0017 across all scores) than those of the ROI-based linear regression. Significantly lower MRE scores than the ROI-based linear regression are recorded for GIN (p<0.0001), which supports our choice for encoding adjacency between ROIs in a graph structure. This encoding of the graph structure is significantly more accurate (p<0.0085 across all scores) than the alternative based on the GCN model. The MRE is further significantly reduced (p<0.0001) by guiding the training of the imputation model using the sex classifier, i.e., produced by DAGI. In summary, DAGI reported the lowest error scores across all metrics, which supports our modeling choices.

The Importance of the Classifier for Imputation. To gain a deeper understanding of the importance of modeling demographic factors (i.e., sex) for imputing each curvature score, Fig. 3 (a) plots the Wasserstein distance [27] between the sex-specific distributions of the imputed measurements for DAGI and GI (i.e., DAGI with GIN and without classifier). We choose the Wasserstein distance as it is a fairly robust metric that ignores outliers by comparing the overall shape of distributions. While for both curvature scores the distance for DAGI is higher for the majority of ROIs (20 out of 34 ROIs for "mean curvature" and 19 ROIs for "Gaussian curvature"), the difference compared to GIN across all regions is significant (p = 0.03, two-sided paired t-test) only with respect to the "Gaussian curvature". This finding supports that sex is important for imputations for both curvature scores but more so for the "Gaussian curvature", which would also explain why in Table 1 all error scores of DAGI are significantly lower for this curvature score (than GI) but for the mean curvature it is only the MRE that is significantly lower.

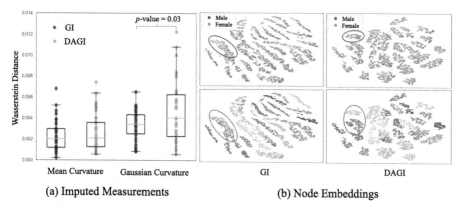

(a) Imputed Measurements   (b) Node Embeddings

Fig. 3. The importance of the classifier for imputation. (a) Wasserstein distance between sexes with respect to imputed ROI curvature scores. The distances are higher for DAGI (vs. GI) and that difference is significant with respect to the Gaussian Curvature according to the two-sided paired t-test; (b) t-SNE visualization of node embeddings color-coded by sex (first row) and by ROIs (second row). Embeddings of DAGI (right column) have clearer sex differences (e.g., highlighted by red circles) and larger separation between ROIs (e.g., blue circles) compared to embeddings of GI. (Color figure online)

Visualizing the Node Embeddings. Next we investigate the importance of modeling sex and ROI adjacency for the imputation task by visualizing the node embeddings of the two implementations. Shown in Fig. 3 (b) are the t-SNE plots [15] of those embeddings, where each dot represents an imputed ROI measurement of an NCANDA subject and in the top row the color refers to a specific ROI. While the embeddings by GI are clearly separated by region (Fig. 3 (b) left, first row), they fail to distinguish measurements by sex, i.e., blue and orange dots overlap with each other (Fig. 3 (b) left, second row). Our approach, (Fig. 3 (b) right), effectively distinguishes the sexes in the latent space (first row) while also keeping separate clusters for the ROIs (second row) as highlighted by the red circles. This separation is important for imputing the ROI measurements according the to error scores reported in Table 1.

Visualizing the Brain Graph. We investigate the importance of specific ROIs in imputing the measurements by visualizing the graph structure via the GNNExplainer [30]. GNNExplainer defines the subgraph most important for the task at hand as the one whose predicted distribution maximizes the mutual information with the one derived from the original graph. Figure 4 visualizes this subgraph with red edges (i.e., the connection between ROIs). The importance of individual nodes (i.e., ROI) is encoded by their radius. It is striking that the subgraph of DAGI (Fig. 4 (c)) is a combination of the graphs of the other two models, i.e., the importance of nodes is similar to those of the approach with solely Demographic Aware module, referring to as DA (Fig. 4 (a)) while the

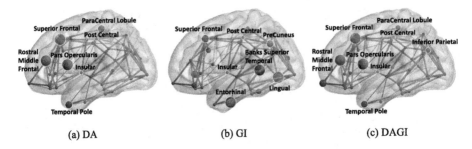

(a) DA   (b) GI   (c) DAGI

Fig. 4. Graph node and edge importance according to GNNExplainer [30]. Each node corresponds to an ROI. Larger nodes represent higher contributions with the most influential ones highlighted by a yellow circle. Red edges are those of the subgraph deemed most important for the task at hand. According to the figure, individual ROIs are more important for sex classification ((a) and (c)), while the relationship between ROIs is more important for imputation ((b) and (c)).

importance of edges agrees with the model that only relies on the imputation model, i.e., GI in Fig. 4 (b). This suggests that individual ROIs are more important for classification while the interaction between ROIs is more important for imputation. Based on those plots, we conclude that identifying sex is mostly driven by pars opercularis, rostral middle frontal, and superior frontal regions, which is in line with the literature [12,14]. However, imputation heavily relies on the interaction between neighboring regions (such as between post central and insula regions).

3.3   Out-of-Sample Test on ABCD

Using DAGI trained on NCANDA (i.e., the most accurate model according to Table 1), we now impute the missing curvature scores on ABCD. Given the lack of "ground truth" with respect to the missing ABCD measurements, we indirectly evaluate the quality of the imputed values by comparing the accuracy of a classifier identifying sex on the 3760 ABCD participants with and without utilizing the imputed measurements. This experimental setup is based on the observation that if the imputed measurements are accurate then they should hold pertinent and discriminatory details that could be utilized for downstream tasks, such as sex classification.

The sex classifier is a three-layer MLP model, whose balanced test accuracy is measured via 5-fold cross-validation. In order to remove the confounding effect of brain size on sex classification, we normalize the "average thickness", "surface area" and "gray matter volume" measurements by the supratentorial volume [19,20]. Note, the imputed curvature scores are left unchanged since they are not confounded by brain size as their Pearson correlation [4] with the supratentorial volume is insignificant for all regions (maximum correlation is 0.053, p<0.01).

According to Table 2, the balanced accuracy of the classifier just on the ABCD measurements is 83.8 %, which then significantly improves (p=0.008,

Table 2. Balanced accuracy of an MLP classifying sex based on ABCD with and without imputed brain measurements. The best results are shown in **bold**. All accuracies are significantly lower than DAGI (p-value ≤ 0.01 according to McNemar's test).

Measurements Used by Classifier		Accuracy
Only ABCD scores		0.838
Including imputed curvature scores	MICE [26] (trained on NCANDA & ABCD)	0.811
	GINN [23] (trained on NCANDA & ABCD)	0.832
	DAGI (trained on NCANDA only)	**0.845**

McNemar's test [17]) to 84.5 % once the imputed scores are added. To put the improvement into context, we also record the classification accuracy with respect to curvature scores generated by the traditional imputation methods MICE [26] and the deep learning-based GINN [23]. Since these methods are originally designed for randomly missing values (Fig. 1 (a)) and thus cannot work on the ABCD dataset alone, we train them to impute missing values on matrices containing both the NCANDA and ABCD measurements. Surprisingly, the inclusion of the curvature measurements imputed by MICE and GINN results in significantly lower classification accuracy than DAGI (p<0.01, McNemar's test). The accuracy is even worse than the classifier solely based on ABCD scores. This suggests that they fail to accurately impute the curvature scores and instead mislead the classifier by making the data more noisy. This might be attributed to the fact that these methods are typically designed for randomly distributed missing values, and thus may not be suitable for our specific scenario where specific measurements are entirely missing in a dataset (Fig. 1 (b)). For this scenario, the significant improvement achieved via the curvature scores predicted by DAGI demonstrates the utility of imputing brain measurements for enhancing downstream tasks.

4   Conclusion

The accuracy of classifiers (e.g. identifying sex from brain ROI measurements) applied to publicly available data can be negatively impacted by the absence of entire measurements from that data set. Instead of imputing the scores by merging the data set with ones that contain the measurements, we propose to rephrase the problem as a prediction task in which we learn to predict missing measurements from those that are shared across data sets. We do so by coupling a graph neural network capturing the relationship between brain regions and a classifier to model demographic differences in ROI brain measurements. Compared to existing technology, our proposed method is significantly more accurate in imputing curvature scores on NCANDA. Imputing the measurements on ABCD and then feeding them into a classifier also result in more accurate sex identification than solely relying on the ROI measurements provided by ABCD. Overall, our framework provides a novel and effective approach for imputing missing measurements across data sets as it is only trained once on the data set that contains the values. This might also have important implications for generalizing neuroscientific findings of deep learning approach across data sets as they could now rely on the same set of measurements.

Acknowledgments. This work was partly supported by funding from the National Institute of Health (DA057567, AA021697, AA017347, AA010723, AA005965, and AA028840), the DGIST R&D program of the Ministry of Science and ICT of KOREA (22-KUJoint-02), Stanford School of Medicine Department of Psychiatry and Behavioral Sciences Faculty Development and Leadership Award, and by the Stanford HAI Google Cloud Credit.

References

1. Brown, S.A., et al.: The national consortium on alcohol and neurodevelopment in adolescence (NCANDA): a multisite study of adolescent development and substance use. J. Stud. Alcohol Drugs **76**(6), 895–908 (2015). https://doi.org/10.15288/jsad.2015.76.895
2. Buitinck, L., et al.: API design for machine learning software: experiences from the scikit-learn project. In: ECML PKDD Workshop: Languages for Data Mining and Machine Learning, pp. 108–122 (2013)
3. Casey, B.J., et al.: The adolescent brain cognitive development (ABCD) study: imaging acquisition across 21 sites. Dev. Cogn. Neurosci. **32**, 43–54 (2018)
4. Cohen, I., et al.: Pearson correlation coefficient. Noise reduction in speech processing (2009)
5. Desikan, R.S., et al.: An automated labeling system for subdividing the human cerebral cortex on MRI scans into gyral based regions of interest. Neuroimage **31**(3), 968–980 (2006)
6. Fischl, B.: Freesurfer. NeuroImage **62**(2), 774–781 (2012)
7. Grattarola, D., et al.: Understanding pooling in graph neural networks. CoRR abs/2110.05292 (2021), https://arxiv.org/abs/2110.05292
8. Hastie, T., Tibshirani, R., Friedman, J.: The Elements of Statistical Learning. SSS, Springer, New York (2009). https://doi.org/10.1007/978-0-387-84858-7
9. Kipf, T.N., Welling, M.: Semi-supervised classification with graph convolutional networks. arXiv preprint arXiv:1609.02907 (2016)
10. Lisowska, A., Rekik, I.: Joint pairing and structured mapping of convolutional brain morphological multiplexes for early dementia diagnosis. Brain Connect. **9**(1), 22–36 (2019). https://doi.org/10.1089/brain.2018.0578, https://doi.org/10.1089/brain.2018.0578
11. Llera, A., Wolfers, T., Mulders, P., Beckmann, C.F.: Inter-individual differences in human brain structure and morphology link to variation in demographics and behavior. **8**, e44443 (2019). https://doi.org/10.7554/eLife.44443
12. Luders, E., Narr, K.L., Zaidel, E., Thompson, P.M., Toga, A.W.: Gender effects on callosal thickness in scaled and unscaled space. Neuroreport **17**(11), 1103–1106
13. Luders, E., Thompson, P.M., Narr, K., Toga, A.W., Jancke, L., Gaser, C.: A curvature-based approach to estimate local gyrification on the cortical surface. Neuroimage **29**(4), 1224–1230 (2006)
14. Lv, B., et al.: Gender consistency and difference in healthy adults revealed by cortical thickness. NeuroImage **53**(2), 373–382 (2010). https://doi.org/10.1016/j.neuroimage.2010.05.020

15. Van der Maaten, L., Hinton, G.: Visualizing data using t-SNE. J. Mach. Learn. Res. **9**(11), 2579–2605 (2008)
16. Mahjoub, I., et al.: Brain multiplexes reveal morphological connectional biomarkers fingerprinting late brain dementia states. Sci. Rep. **8**(1), 1–14 (2018)
17. McNemar, Q.: Note on the sampling error of the difference between correlated proportions or percentages. Psychometrika **12**(2), 153–157 (1947)
18. Montgomery, D.C., Peck, E.A., Vining, G.G.: Introduction to Linear Regression Analysis. Wiley (2021)
19. O'Brien, J.: Encyclopedia of gender and society, vol. 1. Sage (2009)
20. Pfefferbaum, A., et al.: Adolescent development of cortical and white matter structure in the NCANDA sample: role of sex, ethnicity, puberty, and alcohol drinking. Cereb. Cortex **26**(10), 4101–4121 (2016)
21. Ruigrok, A.N., et al.: A meta-analysis of sex differences in human brain structure. Neurosci. Biobehav. Rev. **39**, 34–50 (2014)
22. Scarselli, F., Gori, M., Tsoi, A.C., Hagenbuchner, M., Monfardini, G.: The graph neural network model. IEEE Trans. Neural Netw. **20**(1), 61–80 (2008)
23. Spinelli, I., Scardapane, S., Uncini, A.: Missing data imputation with adversarially-trained graph convolutional networks. Neural Netw. **129**, 249–260 (2020). https://doi.org/10.1016/j.neunet.2020.06.005
24. Symms, M., et al.: A review of structural magnetic resonance neuroimaging. J. Neurol. Neurosurg. Psychiatry **75**(9), 1235–1244 (2004)
25. Talukder, S., et al.: Deep neural imputation: A framework for recovering incomplete brain recordings. arXiv preprint arXiv:2206.08094 (2022)
26. Van Buuren, S., Groothuis-Oudshoorn, K.: MICE: multivariate imputation by chained equations in R. J. Stat. Softw. **45**(3), 1–67 (2011). https://doi.org/10.18637/jss.v045.i03
27. Villani, C.: Optimal transport - Old and new, vol. 338, p. 973 (2008). https://doi.org/10.1007/978-3-540-71050-9
28. Vivar, G., et al.: Simultaneous imputation and classification using multigraph geometric matrix completion (MGMC): application to neurodegenerative disease classification. Artif. Intell. Med. **117**, 102097 (2021). https://doi.org/10.1016/j.artmed.2021.102097, https://doi.org/10.1016/j.artmed.2021.102097
29. Xu, K., et al.: How powerful are graph neural networks? In: 7th International Conference on Learning Representations, ICLR 2019, New Orleans, LA, USA, 6–9 May 2019. OpenReview.net (2019). https://openreview.net/forum?id=ryGs6iA5Km
30. Ying, Z., et al.: GNNExplainer: generating explanations for graph neural networks. In: NeurIPS 2019, 8–14 December 2019, Vancouver, BC, Canada, pp. 9240–9251 (2019), https://proceedings.neurips.cc/paper/2019/hash/d80b7040b773199015de6d3b4293c8ff-Abstract.html

Multi-input Vision Transformer with Similarity Matching

Seungeun Lee[1], Sung Ho Hwang[2], Saelin Oh[2], Beom Jin Park[2],
and Yongwon Cho[2,3(✉)]

[1] Department of Mathematics, Korea University, Seoul, Republic of Korea
duneag2@korea.ac.kr
[2] Department of Radiology, Korea University Anam Hospital, Seoul,
Republic of Korea
dragon1won@gmail.com
[3] AI center, Korea University Anam Hospital, Seoul, Republic of Korea

Abstract. Multi-input models for image classification have recently gained considerable attention. However, multi-input models do not always exhibit superior performance compared to single models. In this paper, we propose a multi-input vision transformer (ViT) with similarity matching, which uses original and cropped images based on the region of interest (ROI) as inputs, without additional encoder architectures. Specifically, two types of images are matched on the basis of their cosine similarity in descending order, and they serve as inputs for a multi-input model with two parallel ViT-architectures. We conduct two experiments using a dataset of pediatric orbital wall fracture and chest X-rays. Consequently, the multi-input models with similarity matching outperform the baseline models and achieve balanced results. Furthermore, it is feasible that our method provides both global and local features, and the Grad-CAM results demonstrate that two different inputs of the proposed mechanism can help complementarily study the image. The code is available at https://github.com/duneag2/vit-similarity.

Keywords: Multi-input Learning · X-Ray Classification · Similarity

1 Introduction

The department of radiology presents research results related to various medical image analysis. [3] Significant interest has been shown in the development of computer-aided diagnosis schemes for X-rays, which can improve the work efficiency of radiologists and enhance their performance. [2–5] Deep learning models that are based on convolutional neural networks (CNNs) have achieved encouraging results for X-ray classification. Recently, owing to the advent of vision transformers (ViTs), more promising results have been obtained. [6,7]

Specifically, multi-input learning for medical images has recently received considerable attention. It has been applied to various tasks, including image

I. Rekik et al. (Eds.): PRIME 2023, LNCS 14277, pp. 184–193, 2023.
https://doi.org/10.1007/978-3-031-46005-0_16

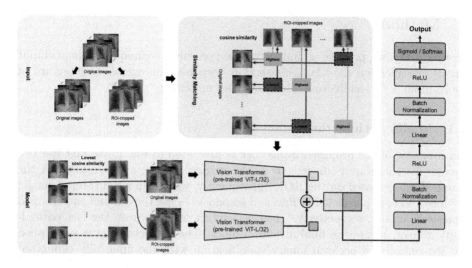

Fig. 1. Our proposed framework for multi-input vision transformer with similarity matching.

classification, segmentation, or restoration. [1,8,10,11] These multi-input models synchronously analyze different formats, such as modalities or resolutions. A multi-modal fusion method [10] is designed to jointly examine images, graphs, and genomic data. Likewise, a multi-resolution fusion model [8] analyzes the same object at different views. However, it is not always possible to concurrently obtain different data types, because of cost or time-related issues. To overcome these data limitations, there have been studies aiming to enhance performance by employing cropping techniques on individual image data. Some previous studies [15,16] propose a two-stage network that first learns from small random patches of the original input images, then conducts transfer learning with whole images. Nevertheless, it requires two separate steps and a large amount of time for training because a sufficient number of patches are needed to achieve meaningful performance.

In addition, these multi-input models usually have preceding architectures that are specialized for feature fusion. Previous works [1,8–10] introduce Siamese networks, new blocks that integrate features in the extraction stage, and the Kronecker products for multi-input image analysis. However, these models do have a drawback of increased complexity compared to single models. Therefore, in this paper, we present a novel approach to designing a straightforward multi-input model that surpasses single models with the utilization of similarity matching.

We build a multi-input model by using two parallel ViTs without any specially designed feature fusion encoders, except for one concatenation layer to improve the performance and time efficiency of existing single models. Experiments on two X-ray classification tasks validate that multi-input models with similarity matching outperform single and multi-input models without similarity matching.

2   Method

In this study, we propose a similarity-based learning technique for multi-input image classification models. This section describes the overall architecture of multi-input ViT-architecture with similarity matching.

2.1   Model Architecture

An overview of the proposed framework is presented in Fig. 1. We first use two images for each input image: one is the original image, and the other is the cropped image based on the ROI. Subsequently, we design a multi-input model with two ViTs in parallel. The first and second ViTs use the original and cropped images as inputs, respectively. Then we extract features from the last normalization layer, before the final attention block. The extracted features are piled up sequentially to perform binary classification with the final fully connected layers.

2.2   Multi-input Vision Transformer with Similarity Matching

---

Algorithm 1. Similarity Matching (for train)

---

procedure TRAIN($X_{tr}, Xc_{tr}, y_{tr} = yc_{tr}$)

    split X_{tr} and Xc_{tr} **with respect to** $y_{tr} = yc_{tr}$

    $X_{tr} = \bigcup_{p=0}^{n-1}\{X_{tr}\}^p, Xc_{tr} = \bigcup_{p=0}^{n-1}\{Xc_{tr}\}^p$

    for $i = 0...n - 1$ **do**

        for $j = 1...\# of \{X_{tr}\}^i$ **do**

            for $k = 1...\# of \{Xc_{tr}\}^i$ **do**

                compute $cosine\ similarity(\{X_{tr}\}_j^i, \{Xc_{tr}\}_k^i)$

                where $\{X_{tr}\}_j^i \in \{X_{tr}\}^i, \{Xc_{tr}\}_k^i \in \{Xc_{tr}\}^i$

            end for

            $\mu \leftarrow \underset{t}{\operatorname{argmin}}(cosine\ similarity(\{X_{tr}\}_j^i, \{Xc_{tr}\}_t^i))$

            aggregate $\{X_{tr}\}_j^i$ and $\{Xc_{tr}\}_\mu^i$

            $cosine\ similarity(\{X_{tr}\}_r^i, \{Xc_{tr}\}_\mu^i) \leftarrow \infty \quad \forall r$

        end for

    end for

end procedure

Training Process. We need pairs of original images X_{tr} and their corresponding ROI-cropped images Xc_{tr}. First, X_{tr} and Xc_{tr} are split with respect to their classes, $y_{tr} = yc_{tr}$, and let n denote the number of classes. ($\{X_{tr}\}^0$ stands for the collections of original training images that are labeled as 0 (e.g. normal), and $\{X_{tr}\}^1$ stands for those of 1 (e.g. abnormal)) This step guarantees that the given classes of the input pairs aren't mixed. Within the sets of images with the same classes, $cosine\,similarity(\{X_{tr}\}_j^i, \{Xc_{tr}\}_k^i)$ are computed. (let $\{X_{tr}\}_j^i$ denote the jth original training image of ith class) For the experiments, three different similarity functions, namely, L1-norm, L2-norm, and cosine similarity are conducted. The cosine similarity is finally chosen for training. After calculating the similarities for every pair, we find the index of the ROI-cropped images having the lowest cosine similarity with each original image. It aims to simultaneously train pairs with the lowest closeness possible, thereby increasing the diversity between inputs.

$$\left\|\{X_{tr}\}_j^i - \{Xc_{tr}\}_k^i\right\|_1 = \left|\{X_{tr}\}_j^i - \{Xc_{tr}\}_k^i\right| \tag{1}$$

$$\left\|\{X_{tr}\}_j^i - \{Xc_{tr}\}_k^i\right\|_2 = \left(\left|\{X_{tr}\}_j^i - \{Xc_{tr}\}_k^i\right|^2\right)^{\frac{1}{2}} \tag{2}$$

$$cosine\,similarity\left(\{X_{tr}\}_j^i, \{Xc_{tr}\}_k^i\right) = \frac{\{X_{tr}\}_j^i \cdot \{Xc_{tr}\}_k^i}{\left\|\{X_{tr}\}_j^i\right\|_2 \times \left\|\{Xc_{tr}\}_k^i\right\|_2} \tag{3}$$

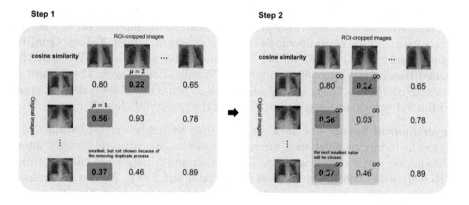

Fig. 2. Details of multi-input ViT with similarity matching.

Details of Similarity Matching. *Step 1:* Find the index of the cropped image with the lowest cosine similarity for each original image (i.e. the index having the lowest cosine similarity in a row-wise manner). *Step 2 (Removing duplicate process):* From top to bottom, assign ∞ to all the entries in the corresponding column of the indices with the lowest cosine similarity selected in Step 1. Step 2 is introduced to prevent the selected cropped images from being chosen again, thereby increasing the variation among the entire input.

Finally, we aggregate two matched images as inputs for the multi-input classification models. Each ViT receives the original and ROI-cropped images as inputs. Subsequently, we concatenate two extracted features of the last normalization layer from two separate ViTs sequentially. The final classification is performed using the merged features.

Validation and Test Process. Unlike the training process, there is no need to implement similarity matching for the validation and test processes. It simply aggregates the original and ROI-cropped images with the same indexes as pairs and uses them as inputs for multi-input classification models. We split the training, validation, and test processes to guarantee patient-based classification in the final real world.

3   Experiments and Results

3.1   Experimental Details

Dataset. Our experiments use the following datasets. **Pediatric Orbital Wall Fracture X-Ray Classification:** This consists of 594 training and 141 test images. We then split the original training set into 534 training and 60 validation images. The dataset is obtained from Korea University Anam Hospital and Korea University Ansan Hospital. It has two classes, namely, abnormal and normal, which are classified in terms of fractures. Previous work in radiology [14] shows that computed tomography is the golden standard to examine the orbit, whereas X-rays have limitations in diagnosis related to fracture. **Chest X-Ray Quality Assessment:** This consists of 744 training and 83 test images. We split the original training set into 669 training and 75 validation images. The dataset is obtained from Korea University Anam Hospital. It has two classes, namely, good and limited, which are classified in terms of the quality of chest X-rays.

Experimental Setup. For data preprocessing, we apply standard scaling. All images, including cropped ones, are resized to 384×384, with the Lanczos interpolation over 8×8 neighborhoods. The ROI-cropped images are cut according to ROI from the top to the bottom of the skull and chest. We use pre-trained ViT-L/32, which is a large variant of ViT with a patch size of 32×32, as our backbone network. The goal is to reduce the binary cross entropy loss, with a batch size of 64 and a learning rate of 0.001, then adjust the rate depending on the number of epochs. We use the Adam optimizer [21] and all the experiments are performed using stratified 10-fold cross validation under a GPU server with Ubuntu 20.04, CUDA 11.2, and three 24 GB Titan RTX graphics cards. All models are implemented using PyTorch 1.8.0 [17] and packages containing PyTorch image models [18] and are assessed with accuracy, area under the curve (AUC), sensitivity, and specificity.

Before implementing similarity matching, we experimentally verify that the cosine similarity between the original and corresponding ROI-cropped images from the same patient origin is the highest among all the other pairs with different indexes.

3.2 Discussion on the Results of Pediatric Orbital Wall Fracture X-Ray Classification and Chest X-Ray Quality Assessment

Motivation. We devise a method to increase the efficiency of studying two different images by constructing entire and ROI-cropped images. The first model that is built (Proposed*-ViT) uses the original and cropped images as inputs. However, this model deteriorates or maintains the performance compared with the single model for some tasks. Thereafter, we assume that the reason for the failure is that the features from two different models are too similar. When concatenated, the model is not capable of learning various features, thus hindering performance enhancement. Then we introduce the idea of changing the order between the original and ROI-cropped images with similarity functions or standards.

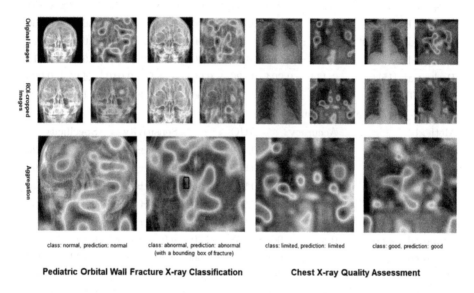

class: normal, prediction: normal   class: abnormal, prediction: abnormal (with a bounding box of fracture)   class: limited, prediction: limited   class: good, prediction: good

Pediatric Orbital Wall Fracture X-ray Classification   **Chest X-ray Quality Assessment**

Fig. 3. Grad-CAM results with similarity matching (Proposed-ViT)

Results and Discussions. The proposed multi-input ViT-architecture with similarity matching achieves meaningful results in terms of accuracy, AUC, and balanced performance concerning sensitivity and specificity. Experiments have supported the effectiveness of similarity matching. First, similarity matching outperforms the single model using only the original as inputs and the multi-input model without similarity matching. Among the various similarity functions and standards, including the L1-norm, L2-norm, random matching, and cosine similarity, cosine similarity shows a noticeable performance. In addition, we confirm that it's better to use each cropped image only once in the training. Finally, matching the original and ROI-cropped images with the highest cosine similarity yields unsatisfactory performance, thereby solidifying our proposed learning

Table 1. Pediatric Orbital Wall Fracture X-Ray Classification and Chest X-Ray Quality Assessment Results.

Pediatric Orbital Wall Fracture X-Ray Classification				
Method	Accuracy	AUC	Sensitivity	Specificity
Single-ViT[a]	0.670 ± 0.002	0.658 ± 0.001	0.806 ± 0.000	0.448 ± 0.001
Proposed*-ViT[b]	0.671 ± 0.009	0.713 ± 0.007	0.642 ± 0.010	0.760 ± 0.016
Proposed-ViT[b]	0.701 ± 0.004	0.730 ± 0.001	0.684 ± 0.019	0.705 ± 0.007
Proposed-random[c]	0.679 ± 0.015	0.709 ± 0.007	0.642 ± 0.010	0.730 ± 0.018
Proposed-L1-norm[d]	0.664 ± 0.013	0.726 ± 0.004	0.677 ± 0.000	0.736 ± 0.000
Proposed-L2-norm[d]	0.664 ± 0.013	0.726 ± 0.004	0.677 ± 0.000	0.736 ± 0.000
Proposed-duplicates[e]	0.556 ± 0.018	0.676 ± 0.025	0.545 ± 0.098	0.763 ± 0.076
Proposed-max[f]	0.449 ± 0.086	0.551 ± 0.044	0.681 ± 0.129	0.384 ± 0.138
Single-RES50[a]	0.678 ± 0.005	0.713 ± 0.002	0.697 ± 0.021	0.673 ± 0.000
Proposed*-RES50[b]	0.643 ± 0.017	0.715 ± 0.002	0.742 ± 0.000	0.615 ± 0.022
Proposed-RES50[b]	0.585 ± 0.014	0.654 ± 0.003	0.748 ± 0.013	0.539 ± 0.019
Park et al. [15]	0.484 ± 0.004	0.526 ± 0.096	0.584 ± 0.010	0.447 ± 0.003
LocalViT [23]	0.602 ± 0.027	0.550 ± 0.065	0.874 ± 0.065	0.118 ± 0.088
Chest X-Ray Quality Assessment				
Method	Accuracy	AUC	Sensitivity	Specificity
Single-ViT[a]	0.866 ± 0.013	0.949 ± 0.004	0.946 ± 0.009	0.808 ± 0.022
Proposed*-ViT[b]	0.857 ± 0.004	0.958 ± 0.002	0.917 ± 0.009	0.813 ± 0.000
Proposed-ViT[b]	0.911 ± 0.006	0.956 ± 0.000	0.914 ± 0.000	0.908 ± 0.010
Proposed-random[c]	0.892 ± 0.005	0.951 ± 0.001	0.937 ± 0.011	0.858 ± 0.008
Proposed-L1-norm[d]	0.890 ± 0.006	0.957 ± 0.000	0.943 ± 0.000	0.852 ± 0.011
Proposed-L2-norm[d]	0.890 ± 0.006	0.958 ± 0.000	0.943 ± 0.000	0.852 ± 0.011
Proposed-duplicates[e]	0.864 ± 0.008	0.955 ± 0.000	0.963 ± 0.018	0.792 ± 0.000
Proposed-max[f]	0.855 ± 0.009	0.949 ± 0.003	0.886 ± 0.009	0.831 ± 0.011
Single-RES50[a]	0.802 ± 0.006	0.923 ± 0.000	0.874 ± 0.014	0.750 ± 0.000
Proposed*-RES50[b]	0.828 ± 0.006	0.931 ± 0.000	0.923 ± 0.018	0.758 ± 0.010
Proposed-RES50[b]	0.858 ± 0.007	0.933 ± 0.001	0.886 ± 0.000	0.838 ± 0.012
Park et al. [15]	0.900 ± 0.029	0.965 ± 0.004	0.994 ± 0.011	0.831 ± 0.053
LocalViT [23]	0.636 ± 0.034	0.720 ± 0.007	0.486 ± 0.130	0.846 ± 0.046

[a] Single: Single model only with original images.
[b] Proposed*/Proposed: without/with similarity matching.
[c] Match original and ROI-cropped images randomly.
[d] Proposed-L1-norm/L2-norm: L1-norm/L2-norm as a similarity function.
   Assign $-\infty$ and match index with $argmax$ for L1-norm and L2-norm.
   The lowest cosine similarity corresponds to the highest L1-norm and L2-norm.
[e] Similarity matching without removing duplicate process.
[f] Match indexes with the largest cosine similarity with removing duplicate process.
   Proposed-random, L1-norm, L2-norm, duplicates, max are conducted with ViT.
   "-ViT" refers to the use of ViT and "-RES50" refers to that of ResNet50.

technique. We also conduct experiments using a previously proposed network. Our work achieves similar or better results than those of Park et al. [15]. In particular, Park et al. [15] uses a two-stage architecture and spends approximately 5 d for the entire training and test process, and does not achieve meaningful performance with a dataset of pediatric orbital wall fracture. In contrast, multi-input ViT-architecture with similarity matching has an end-to-end architecture and takes only a few hours. The proposed framework also achieves notable results on both datasets.

From the experiments, we also verify the contributions of similarity matching with ResNet50 [19] as a representative CNN. Overall, similarity matching using ViT outperforms ResNet50. ViT is introduced as a global feature extractor with multiheaded self-attention, by utilizing patches from images. However, the limitation of ViT is that it has less locality than CNN. The locality is related to the structures or objects of images [23], which can be significant for diagnosis with medical images. We believe that our similarity matching yields both global and local features. ViT architecture and similarity matching contribute to global attributes. ROI-cropped images and feature concatenation layers provide local features, thus leading to desirable performance compared to baseline models. We also confirm that similarity matching outperforms LocalViT [23], an existing method that adds locality to ViT, which introduce a local mechanism via a depth-wise convolution. In addition, similarity matching provides meaningful results even with data augmentation [20] for every experiment. Data augmentation usually transforms images randomly, which can degrade accurate diagnosis by omitting the target-relevant region in medical images. We also consider that similarity matching can reduce unintended randomness and provide significant information regarding the ROI. Furthermore, current data augmentation techniques are performed serially, whereas similarity matching can analyze whole images and image patches in parallel.

For Grad-CAM [12,13], we first produce Grad-CAM results for Proposed-ViT with the original and ROI-cropped images separately. We then combine these two results. In more detail, for a dataset of pediatric orbital wall fracture, abnormal images have a predetermined location of lesions, whereas normal images require a comprehensive examination of the entire image. For a dataset of chest X-rays, the location of lesions is not predetermined, necessitating a whole-image inspection. The aggregated images demonstrate that similarity matching can help the model to focus on learning the entire images. In addition, the parts in which two different inputs are concentrated are complementary. This illustrates that both the original and ROI-cropped images are useful for analyzing various regions.

4 Conclusions

In this study, we propose multi-input ViT-architecture with similarity matching, which matches the original and ROI-cropped images with the lowest cosine similarity for multi-input image classification. Experiments with two datasets verify our proposed framework and demonstrate the possibility of using similarity matching to enhance the performance of the multi-input models both quantitatively and qualitatively. Furthermore, a research [22] introduces the concept of center-neighbor similarity into GNN (Graph Neural Network), aiming to enhance the performance by regulating the embedding of nodes to be as dissimilar as possible from their aggregating neighbors. As part of future work, we plan to extend our research to incorporate GNN. In addition, we plan to develop a learnable similarity function instead of a cosine similarity function and to generate cropped images of various sizes from the original images with multiple parallel architectures.

Acknowledgements. This research was supported by a grant of the Korea Health Technology R&D Project through the Korea Health Industry Development Institute (KHIDI), funded by the Ministry of Health & Welfare, Republic of Korea (grant number: HR22C1302). The authors received funding for this study through the Basic Science Research Program of the National Research Foundation of Korea, funded by the Ministry of Education (2020R1I1A1A01071600). We would like to thank the Advanced Medical Imaging Institute in the Department of Radiology, Korea University Anam Hospital in Republic of Korea, and the researchers for providing software, datasets, and various forms of technical support.

References

1. Oktay, O., et al.: Multi-input cardiac image super-resolution using convolutional neural networks. In: Ourselin, S., Joskowicz, L., Sabuncu, M.R., Unal, G., Wells, W. (eds.) MICCAI 2016. LNCS, vol. 9902, pp. 246–254. Springer, Cham (2016). https://doi.org/10.1007/978-3-319-46726-9_29
2. Çallı, E., et al.: Deep learning for chest X-ray analysis: A survey. Med. Image Anal. **72**, 102125 (2021)
3. Mondal, S., et al.: Deep learning approach for automatic classification of x-ray images using convolutional neural network. In: 2019 Fifth International Conference on Image Information Processing (ICIIP), IEEE (2019)
4. Yu, Ke, et al.: Anatomy-guided weakly-supervised abnormality localization in chest x-rays. In: MICCAI 2022: 25th International Conference on Medical Image Computing and Computer Assisted Intervention, Part V. Springer Nature Switzerland , Cham(2022). https://doi.org/10.1007/978-3-031-16443-9_63
5. Mishra, S., et al.: Data-Driven Deep Supervision for Skin Lesion Classification. In: MICCAI 2022: 25th International Conference on Medical Image Computing and Computer Assisted Intervention, Part I. Springer Nature Switzerland, Cham (2022). https://doi.org/10.1007/978-3-031-16431-6_68
6. Dosovitskiy, A., Beyer, L., Kolesnikov, A., et al.: An image is worth 16 x 16 words: Transformers for image recognition at scale. In: Proceedings of the IEEE/CVF International Conference on Computer Vision. IEEE, Venice (2020)
7. Chetoui, M., Akhloufi, M.A.: Explainable vision transformers and radiomics for Covid-19 detection in chest x-rays. J. Clin. Med. **11**(11), 3013 (2022)
8. Duarte, D., et al.: Multi-resolution feature fusion for image classification of building damages with convolutional neural networks. Remote Sensing **10**(10), 1636 (2018)
9. Zamir, S.W., et al.: Multi-stage progressive image restoration. In: Proceedings of the IEEE/CVF Conference on Computer Vision and Pattern Recognition (2021)

10. Chen, R.J., et al.: Pathomic fusion: an integrated framework for fusing histopathology and genomic features for cancer diagnosis and prognosis. IEEE Trans. Med. Imaging **41**(4), 757–770 (2020)
11. Yang, S., et al.: Knowledge matters: Radiology report generation with general and specific knowledge. arXiv preprint arXiv:2112.15009 (2021)
12. Selvaraju, R.R., et al.: Grad-cam: visual explanations from deep networks via gradient-based localization. In: Proceedings of the IEEE International Conference on Computer Vision (2017)
13. Radford, A., et al.: Learning transferable visual models from natural language supervision. In: International Conference on Machine Learning, PMLR (2021)
14. Lee, J.Y., et al.: Pediatric orbital fractures. Facial Trauma Surgery, 296–303 (2020)
15. Park, B., et al.: A curriculum learning strategy to enhance the accuracy of classification of various lesions in chest-PA X-ray screening for pulmonary abnormalities. Sci. Rep. **9**(1), 1–9 (2019)
16. Cho, Y., et al.: Optimal number of strong labels for curriculum learning with convolutional neural network to classify pulmonary abnormalities in chest radiographs. Comput. Biol. Med. **136**, 104750 (2021)
17. Paszke, A., et al.: PyTorch: An imperative style, high-performance deep learning library. In: Advances in Neural Information Processing Systems 32 (2019)
18. PyTorch image models Homepage. https://github.com/rwightman/pytorch-image-models. (Accessed 15 Feb 2023)
19. He, K., et al.: Deep residual learning for image recognition. In: Proceedings of the IEEE Conference on Computer Vision and Pattern Recognition (2016)
20. Wang, J., Perez, L.: The effectiveness of data augmentation in image classification using deep learning. Convolut. Neural Netw. Vis. Recognit. **11**, 1–8 (2017)
21. Kingma, D.P., Ba, J.: Adam: a method for stochastic optimization. In: 3rd International Conference for Learning Representations (2015)
22. Xie, Y., et al.: When do GNNs work: understanding and improving neighborhood aggregation. In: Proceedings of the Twenty-Ninth International Joint Conference on Artificial Intelligence (2020)
23. Li, Y., et al.: Localvit: bringing locality to vision transformers. arXiv preprint arXiv:2104.05707 (2021)

Federated Multi-domain GNN Network for Brain Multigraph Generation

Chun Xu and Islem Rekik$^{(\boxtimes)}$ ⓘ

BASIRA Lab, Imperial-X and Department of Computing, Imperial College London,
London, UK
i.rekik@imperial.ac.uk
https://basira-lab.com/

Abstract. Brain multigraph (i.e. multi-view or multi-domain) is a set of
brain graphs also called brain connectomes, where each brain graph represents a unique view of pairwise relationships between brain regions
(nodes) like morphology. Several works based on Graph Generative
Adversarial Networks (GANs) have been recently proposed to predict
brain multigraph from a single graph with the aim of early detection
of anomalous changes in the human brain connectome. However, such
frameworks exhibit some drawbacks. *First*, there is a lack of generalis-
ability, as they did not consider the case of predicting varying domains
of brain graphs from a single domain as different hospitals may have
different targets. *Second*, they merely consider data-sharing situations
and build a robust model from the cooperation of different hospitals. To
overcome these limitations, we propose a Federated Multi-Domain GNN
model (**FMDGNN**), which not only predicts multiple brain graphs with
a varying number of domains from a single brain graph, but also preserves data privacy when different hospitals. Our core contributions are
as follows: (i) We are the first to propose federated multi-domain GNN
models for generating *varying domains* of brain graphs across hospitals
while preserving data privacy. For instance, while hospital i can generate
one domain, hospital j can generate a few domains (ii) We introduce a
residual connection in the graph autoencoders to further improve the
prediction performance. (iii) We propose and simplify a domain-specific
GNN decoder to predict a specific brain graph domain and enhance the
prediction efficiency. Our results outperform its variants, preserve data
privacy and tackle statistical heterogeneity in non-IID data distribution
across hospitals, thereby showing its potential in brain multigraph prediction with varying number of domains from a single graph. Our source
code is available at https://github.com/basiralab/FMDGNN.

Keywords: brain multigraph prediction · federated multi-domain ·
heterogeneity · graph neural network

1 Introduction

A brain graph is an undirected graph represented in a symmetric connectivity
matrix where each element (i.e., edge connecting two nodes) measures the con-

© The Author(s), under exclusive license to Springer Nature Switzerland AG 2023
I. Rekik et al. (Eds.): PRIME 2023, LNCS 14277, pp. 194–205, 2023.
https://doi.org/10.1007/978-3-031-46005-0_17

nectivity strength between pairs of regions of interest (ROIs) [1]. It can be derived from medical imaging techniques like Magnetic Resonance Imaging (MRI) and can be used for early detection and identification of anomalous changes within the human brain connectome such as Alzheimer's Disease [1]. Due to the high clinical scan costs and time-consuming processing steps [2], graph neural network (GNN) models have emerged as the core of a nascent field focusing on various graph-related tasks such as graph classification and graph prediction, where graphs are Non-Euclidean data [3]. A brain multigraph is a set of brain graphs, each representing a unique view of pairwise relationships between brain regions (nodes) like morphology or function. Predicting a brain multigraph from a single brain graph is becoming more important to help better understand how a specific disorder can change the connectional attributes of the brain. Several works based on GANs were proposed for brain multigraph prediction [2]. Multi-GraphGAN [4] was first proposed for jointly predicting the brain multigraph from a single graph using the GAN model while maintaining the topological structure. TopoGAN [1] further improved the prediction performance. However, such methods demand very high computational resources and they do not sufficiently consider the scenario of predicting a *varying number* of brain graph domains from a single domain across different hospitals, which may fail to generalized well.

The collaboration between different hospitals, each predicting varying numbers of domains, could potentially result in a more robust and generalized GNN model for predicting a brain multigraph from a single graph. However, this might raise issues on data privacy when sharing sensitive brain data, as well as statistical heterogeneity, which is a common issue when data is distributed non-identically among hospitals [5,6]. Federated Learning, or *FedAvg*, is a paradigm designed to address the challenges associated with data sharing, with a specific focus on preserving data privacy [7]. However, *FedAvg* shows its limitation in solving heterogeneous problems when the data distribution of each client is non-IID. Inspired by the principles of federated learning, [8] proposed a Ψ-Net, which is composed of *non-grouped shared layers* and *grouped layers*, to tackle heterogeneous problems in federated learning, specifically on non-IID data distribution. This approach outperforms other heterogeneous federated learning frameworks such as FedMA [9] and FedProx [10]. However, they are not considering multi-domain generation tasks and non-IID graph data. Consequently, their utilities in the context of brain multigraph prediction are limited.

To address these challenges, we propose **FMDGNN**, the first for generating brain multigraphs with a varying number of domains across hospitals. For example, hospital i can generate one domain while hospital j can generate several domains. We draw inspiration primarily from brain multigraph prediction methods [1,4], as well as multi-task learning methods [11] and the heterogeneous federated learning method in [12–15]. Our contributions are the following: (i) To the best of our knowledge, we are the first to propose federated multi-domain GNN models (**FMDGNN**) specifically designed for predicting brain multigraph with a varying number of domains. (ii) We introduce a residual connection in the graph autoencoders, a modification to further improve the prediction performance. (iii) We propose a domain-specific GNN decoder for predicting a specific brain graph domain and improving the prediction efficiency. Mainly, a more generalized and robust model can be derived, which is capable of predicting brain multigraph with a varying number of domains across different hospitals while preserving data privacy and tackling the non-IID data distribution heterogeneity.

2   Proposed Methods

In the following, we present the main steps for our brain multigraph prediction from a single graph with varying domains across hospitals while maintaining data privacy and tackling heterogeneous problems caused by non-IID brain graph data across hospitals. Fig. 1 gives an overview of the brain multigraph prediction task: **A)** The construction of a graph population for each source and target domains and extraction of multi-domain brain features, and **B)** the prediction of a brain multigraph by the proposed GNN models. Fig. 2 shows the federated multi-domain GNN framework for generating brain multigraphs with a varying number of domains across hospitals from a single shared domain. The data in the source domain is assumed to be more affordable to acquire compared to the target domains. The details of the symbols used in the context are shown in Table 2.

A - Construction of Graph Population using Multi-domain Brain Graphs. Given a set of hospitals (i.e., clients), denoted as $\{C_i\}_{i=1}^t$, where t is the total number of hospitals. Each hospital is associated with a set of subjects and each subject is a brain graph. For hospital C_i, the subjects can be denoted as $\{S_j\}_{j=1}^{n_i}$ where n_i is the number of subjects in hospital C_i. For each subject S_j, it consists of one connectivity matrix referred to as source domain, denoted as $V_S^j \in \mathbb{R}^{r \times r}$, and multiple sets of connectivity matrices as target views (i.e., graphs), denoted as $\{V_{T_v}^j\}_{v=1}^k \in \mathbb{R}^{r \times r}$, where S represents the source domain, r is the number of brain regions (ROIs), T_v is the target view v and k is the total number of target domains. The source and target views of connectivity matrices can be stacked as a tensor $\mathbb{V}^j \in \mathbb{R}^{r \times r \times v}$.

To map the source brain graph to its corresponding target brain multigraph, we extract the connectivity features from the stacked connectivity matrix tensors $\{\mathbb{V}^j\}_{j=1}^{n_i}$. Fig. 1-**A)** shows the process of the construction of the graph population and extraction of features. Considering that the connectivity matrix is symmetric, we flatten each graph by extracting the feature vector from its connectivity matrix, where the off-diagonal upper-triangular part of the matrix is retained. For each hospital, following the vectorization of the feature vectors of all connectivity matrices, we vertically stack all vectors into a feature matrix. The set of source feature matrix is denoted as $\mathbf{F}_S \in \mathbb{R}^{n_i \times f}$ and the multiple sets of target feature matrices are denoted as $\{\mathbf{F}_{T_v}\}_{v=1}^k \in \mathbb{R}^{n_i \times f}$ of the target view T_v, where n_i is the number of subjects in hospital C_i and f is the number of features

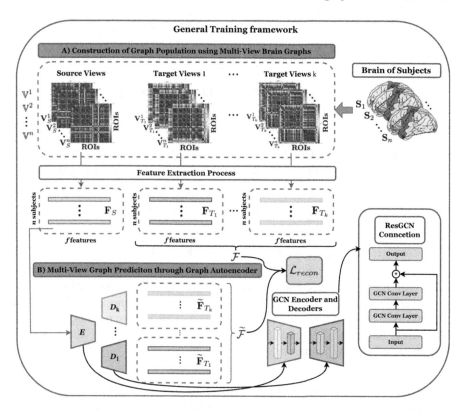

Fig. 1. *Proposed federated multi-domain GNN model* **A) Construction of graph populations using multi-domain brain graphs.** We construct connectivity tensors, including one single source domain and k target domains. Next, we extract feature vectors from each connectivity matrix and stack them into feature matrices. **B) Multi-view brain graph prediction through graph autoencoders.** Source feature matrices serve as an input to the graph autoencoder model to predict multi-domain target brain graphs. The graph autoencoder consists of the source encoder and *domain-specific* decoders, each contains two GCN layers. During the training process, the reconstruction loss $\mathcal{L}_{recon}$ is computed. To further enhance the performance of the model, a residual connection is added in the graph autoencoder.

extracted from one brain graph. These constructed feature matrices of source graphs serve as the input to a graph convolutional network (GCN) model, which is trained to predict multiple target graphs (i.e., domains).

B - Multi-view Graph Prediction using Through Graph Autoencoders.

We propose a graph autoencoder structure for predicting a brain multigraph spanning multiple domains from a source graph. This design leads to a significant reduction in computational resources and an enhancement in efficiency. Fig. 1-**B)** shows the general brain multigraph prediction process through the graph autoencoder, which consists of one GCN encoder and various GCN *domain-specific* decoders. Both of the encoder and decoder networks consist of two GCN layers. The graph convolution function used in each layer is:

$$\mathbf{Z} = f_\phi\left(\mathbf{F}, \mathbf{A} \mid \boldsymbol{\Theta}\right) = \phi\left(\widetilde{\mathbf{D}}^{-\frac{1}{2}}\widetilde{\mathbf{A}}\widetilde{\mathbf{D}}^{-\frac{1}{2}}\mathbf{F}\boldsymbol{\Theta}\right) \tag{1}$$

where $\mathbf{Z}$ is the graph representation learned from a specific GCN layer, ϕ is the activation function such as ReLU or LeakyReLU. $\boldsymbol{\Theta}$ denotes the graph convolutional weights. $\widetilde{\mathbf{A}} = \mathbf{A} + \mathbf{I}$ is the adjacency matrix of the undirected graph and $\mathbf{I}$ is the identity matrix; $\widetilde{\mathbf{D}}_{ii} = \sum_j \widetilde{\mathbf{A}}_{ij}$ is a diagonal degree matrix [16].

The predicted feature matrices are denoted as $\widetilde{\mathcal{F}} = \{\widetilde{\mathbf{F}}_{T_v}\}_{v=1}^k$ and the ground truth feature matrices are $\mathcal{F} = \{\mathbf{F}_{T_v}\}_{v=1}^k$. The reconstruction loss is computed using:

$$\mathcal{L}_{recon} = \|\widetilde{\mathcal{F}} - \mathcal{F}\|_1 = \sum_{v=1}^k \|\widetilde{\mathbf{F}}_{T_v} - \mathbf{F}_{T_v}\|_1 \tag{2}$$

In addition, to preserve the topological structure of the original brain graph and further improve the model performance, a residual connection [17] is added in the GCN source encoder and target decoders. This simple modification could significantly improve the prediction performance, especially in the federated multi-domain learning framework.

C - Federated Multi-domain Learning Framework. To predict a brain multigraph from a single brain graph with varying domains across hospitals, we propose **FMDGNN** consisting of one server and multiple hospitals (i.e., clients). There are t hospitals, each undertaking entirely different tasks, which is to generate varying domains from a single source domain. Within each hospital, target views are randomly sampled in ascending order, represented as $\{\mathbf{V}_v\}_{v=1}^{\delta(n_v)}$ where $\delta(n_v)$ is a random number denoting the number of target domains this hospital can generate. Every hospital has one source encoder E_{V_S} and multiple decoders D_{V_v} where V_v is the target domains this hospital can generate. Despite the varying domains, hospitals are sharing decoders for the same domain. For instance, in the scenario shown in Fig. 2, Hospitals 1 and 2 will share the decoder D_{V_1}. The server contains a global model which consists of all domain-specific GCN decoders for all domains $\{D_{V_v}\}_{v=1}^k$. In the federated multi-domain graph generation, each hospital trains its own local graph autoencoder model with its local dataset where the data distribution of local datasets in all hospitals are non-IID to simulate statistical heterogeneity. In each round of federation, the local models are trained for E local epochs, the global model in the server aggregates the updates from every hospital's GCN and computes its average layers after E local epochs. The updates can be computed as:

$$w_v^{t+1} = \frac{1}{k}\sum_{i=1}^k w_{v,i}^t \tag{3}$$

where v is a specific domain, k is the total number of decoders in domain v, and w_v^t is the update at t^{th} round federation. The averaged update w_v^{t+1} is broadcasted back to each hospital to build personalized local models and a robust global model.

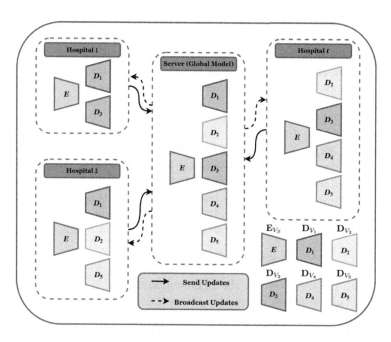

Fig. 2. *Federated multi-domain learning framework on brain multigraph prediction with a varying number of domains.* Hospitals can generate a varying number of brain graph domains from a single brain graph drown from a source domain shared across hospitals. The goal is to train a generalized and robust global model and personalized local models.

3   Results and Discussion

Multi-domain Brain Graph Dataset. The dataset used in the **FMDGNN** model is derived from the Brain Genomics Superstruct Project (GSP) dataset [18,19]. A subset of 678 healthy participants is used, of which 382 are male subjects and 296 are female subjects. None of them exhibit any signs of brain disorders nor have they had any history of mental illness. Each subject is derived from a structural T1-weighted (T1-w) Magnetic Resonance (MR) image. These images undergo several preprocessing steps, including motion and topology correction, normalization of T1-w intensity, and segmentation of the subcortical white and deep grey matter volumetric structures [20]. In this paper, we utilize the left hemisphere of the brain, which is partitioned into $r = 35$ cortical regions of interest (ROIs) using the Desikan-Killiany Atlas [21] and FreeSurfer software package [22]. Finally, each brain graph encapsulates 6 views, which are extracted from the following cortical measurement: maximum principal curvature, mean cortical thickness, mean sulcal depth, average curvature, cortical surface area and minimum principle area [23–26].

Model Structure and Parameter Setting. To simulate the federated learning scenario, we initialize three virtual hospitals which can generate a varying number of domains. In the local models of hospitals, each GCN encoder consists of two GCN convolutional layers of dimension 595×32 and 32×16 respectively. The GCN domain-specific decoders consist of two GCN convolutional layers of dimension 16×32 and 32×595, respectively. The final layer outputs a feature vector with a size of 595, which is calculated as $r \times (r-1)/2$ where $r = 35$ is the number of ROIs. The activation function LeakyReLU and a dropout layer are added between two GCN convolutional layers. The local models are trained using the Adam local optimizer, with a batch size of 32, a learning rate of 0.001, $\beta_1 = 0.5$ and $\beta_2 = 0.999$. They are trained for 10 rounds with each round composed of 10 local epochs. We use 4-fold cross-validation training, where each training fold is assigned to a hospital and the left-out test fold is used for testing all hospitals.

Evaluation. First, we recover the brain connectivity tensor (i.e., brain multi-graph) from the predicted brain feature matrix through *anti-vectorization*. Then we evaluate the different methods by computing the mean absolute error (MAE) between the predicted and the ground truth brain multigraphs in multi-domains. The prediction performance is better when the MAE value is lower. Moreover, the predicted graph and the residual error are presented graphically shown in Fig. 3

Table 1. Numerical results of average MAE under different methods

	Average MAE ± std			
	Hospital 1	Hospital 2	Hospital 3	Global
GCN standalone	0.0412 ± 0.0018	0.2571 ± 0.0052	0.3126 ± 0.0116	0.2017 ± 0.0057
ResGCN standalone	0.0531 ± 0.0026	0.1836 ± 0.0032	0.2205 ± 0.0042	0.1586 ± 0.0025
GCN + Fed	0.0234 ± 0.0012	0.1901 ± 0.0108	0.2603 ± 0.0058	0.1596 ± 0.0027
FMDGNN	**0.0232 ± 0.0010**	**0.1578 ± 0.0018**	**0.2182 ± 0.0021**	**0.1331 ± 0.0016**

In the experiments, we predict a brain multigraph with varying domains across hospitals from a single graph (Fig. 2). We evaluate and compare our **FMDGNN** and its variants: **GCN standalone, ResGCN standalone** and **GCN+Fed**. Fig. 3 shows the results of the ground truth graph, predicted graph and residual error in Hospital 3 (Fig. 2). This hospital can generate graphs in domains of 2, 3, 4 and 5 from the source graph. From the graphical comparisons

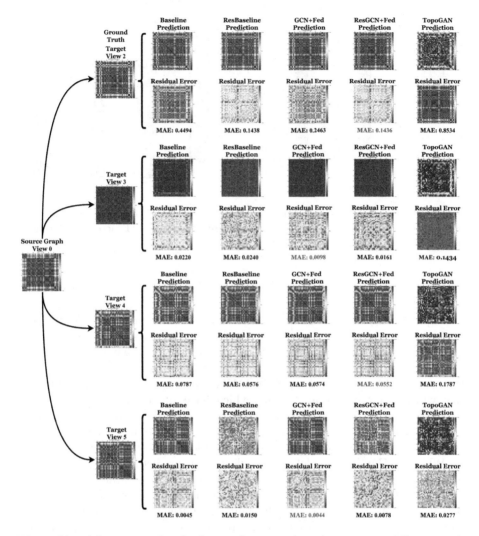

Fig. 3. *Visual Inspection of multi-domain brain graph prediction using different methods.* This figure shows the multigraph prediction for Hospital 3 in Fig. 2. This hospital aims to predict the multi-domains of 2, 3, 4 and 5 from the source graph (view 0). With the experiments of different methodologies, the federated GNNs consistently generate the best predictions of target multi-domain brain graphs compared to standalone variants.

in Fig. 3, **FMDGNN** outperforms other methods in predicting domains 2 and 4 while **GCN+Fed** is better in predicting domains 3 and 5. However, when comparing the performance across different hospitals, as shown in Table 1 and Fig. 4, **FMDGNN** outperforms other methods in predicting a varying number of brain domains, thereby showing the benefits of the federation in predicting a

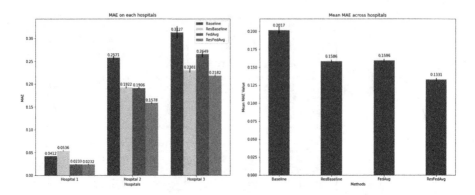

Fig. 4. *MAE on each hospital and Mean MAE on different methods* **Left**: The MAE on each hospital using different methods. **Right**: Average MAE across all hospitals using different methods

varying number of domains across hospitals while maintaining data privacy and tackling heterogeneity.

Figure 3 compares the results of different methods. Clearly, **FMDGNN** outperforms other methods in predicting most target domains, but it falls short for predicting domain 5. This can be attributed to the fact that domain 5 has a much lower connectivity strength than other target domains. As a result, even though the MAE value is low, **FMGDNN** may lose some structure information when predicting brain domains which have small values of connectivity strength. However, the general performance of predicting multi-domains across hospitals, shown in Table 1 and Fig. 4, demonstrates the effectiveness of the federated GNNs in outperforming standalone models in a consistent way.

While **FMDGNN** model proves effective in predicting a varying number of brain domains across hospitals, there are still some limitations. *First*, the brain graph dataset used in the experiments is not sufficiently large, which could potentially limit the model generalizability. To mitigate this, we may introduce more brain graph datasets from more sources to construct a more comprehensive federated multi-domain scenario. *Second*, the data may be susceptible to reverse interpretation attacks during the update broadcasting process. To address this and further improve data privacy, random noise could be introduced into the updates during communication.

Table 2. Mathematical Notations

Symbols	Dimension	Definition
r	N	Number of brain regions (ROIs)
v	N	The view or domain number
n_i	N	Number of training subjects in hospital C_i
k	N	Number of target views or domains
f	N	Number of features extracted from brain graph
t	N	Number of hospitals
C_i		Each hospital where $i = \{1, ..., t\}$
S		Source domain of brain graph
$\mathbf{T}_i$		Target domain of brain graph, $i \in \{0, ...n\}$
E_S		GCN encoder
D_{V_v}		GCN decoders for target view v
$\mathbf{V}_S$	$\mathbb{R}^{r \times r}$	Brain connectivity matrix of the brain graph in the source domain
$\mathbf{V}_{T_v}$	$\mathbb{R}^{r \times r}$	Brain connectivity matrix of the brain graph in the target domain T_v
$\mathbb{V}$	$\mathbb{R}^{r \times r \times k}$	A brain tensor of a subject stacking one source domain and k target domains
$\mathbf{S}_j$		Training subjects in hospital C_i, $j = \{1, ...n_i\}$
$\mathbf{F}_S$	$\mathbb{R}^{n_i \times f}$	Feature matrix stacking feature vectors from source brain graph
$\mathbf{F}_{T_v}$	$\mathbb{R}^{n_i \times f}$	Ground truth feature matrix stacking feature vectors from brain graph with target view T_v
$\widetilde{\mathbf{F}}_{T_v}$	$\mathbb{R}^{n_i \times f}$	Predicted feature matrix stacking feature vectors from brain graph with target view T_v
$\mathcal{F}$	$\mathbb{R}^{n_i \times f \times k}$	The ground truth feature matrix, $\mathcal{F} = \{\mathbf{F}_{T_1}, ..., \mathbf{F}_{T_k}\}$
$\widetilde{\mathcal{F}}$	$\mathbb{R}^{n_i \times f \times k}$	The predicted feature matrix, $\widetilde{\mathcal{F}} = \{\widetilde{\mathbf{F}}_{T_1}, ..., \widetilde{\mathbf{F}}_{T_k}\}$

4   Conclusion

In this paper, we propose the first generative **FMDGNN** to generate brain multigraph from a single brain graph while federating hospitals with a varying number of domains (i.e., GNN architectures). The model effectively predicts the brain multigraph while preserving data privacy and security during communication among hospitals and also addressing the challenges of non-IID data distribution. Additionally, we introduce the residual connection in GCN graph autoencoders to further improve the prediction performance. Moreover, the proposed method significantly enhances prediction efficiency by conserving computational resources, therefore showing its potential for future applications in predicting brain multigraphs with a varying number of domains across different hospitals. However, limitations of this work are the training data size and potential data leakage. In our future work, we plan to utilize more datasets and incorporate differential privacy techniques to address these limitations.

References

1. Bessadok, A., Mahjoub, M.A., Rekik, I.: Brain multigraph prediction using topology-aware adversarial graph neural network. Med. Image Anal. **72**, 102090 (2021)
2. Goodfellow, I., et al.: Generative adversarial networks. Commun. ACM **63**, 139–144 (2020)
3. Bessadok, A., Mahjoub, M.A., Rekik, I.: Graph neural networks in network neuroscience. IEEE Trans. Pattern Anal. Mach. Intell. **45**, 5833–5848 (2022)
4. Bessadok, A., Mahjoub, M.A., Rekik, I.: Topology-aware generative adversarial network for joint prediction of multiple brain graphs from a single brain graph (2020)
5. Roski, J., Bo-Linn, G.W., Andrews, T.A.: Creating value in health care through big data: opportunities and policy implications. Health Aff. **33**, 1115–1122 (2014)
6. Heitmueller, A., Henderson, S., Warburton, W., Elmagarmid, A., Pentland, A., Darzi, A.: Developing public policy to advance the use of big data in health care. Health Aff. **33**, 1523–1530 (2014)
7. McMahan, B., Moore, E., Ramage, D., Hampson, S., y Arcas, B.A.: Communication-efficient learning of deep networks from decentralized data. In: Artificial intelligence and statistics, PMLR, pp. 1273–1282 (2017)
8. Yu, F., et al.: Heterogeneous federated learning. arXiv preprint arXiv:2008.06767 (2020)
9. Wang, H., Yurochkin, M., Sun, Y., Papailiopoulos, D., Khazaeni, Y.: Federated learning with matched averaging. arXiv preprint arXiv:2002.06440 (2020)
10. Li, T., Sahu, A.K., Zaheer, M., Sanjabi, M., Talwalkar, A., Smith, V.: Federated optimization in heterogeneous networks (2020)
11. Caruana, R.: Multitask learning: a knowledge-based source of inductive bias1. In: Proceedings of the Tenth International Conference on Machine Learning, Citeseer, pp. 41–48 (1993)
12. Gao, D., Yao, X., Yang, Q.: A survey on heterogeneous federated learning (2022)
13. Ghosh, A., Chung, J., Yin, D., Ramchandran, K.: An efficient framework for clustered federated learning. Adv. Neural Inf. Process. Syst. **33**, 19586–19597 (2020)
14. Jiang, Y., Konečný, J., Rush, K., Kannan, S.: Improving federated learning personalization via model agnostic meta learning. arXiv preprint arXiv:1909.12488 (2019)
15. Wang, K., Mathews, R., Kiddon, C., Eichner, H., Beaufays, F., Ramage, D.: Federated evaluation of on-device personalization. arXiv preprint arXiv:1910.10252 (2019)
16. Kipf, T.N., Welling, M.: Semi-supervised classification with graph convolutional networks. arXiv preprint arXiv:1609.02907 (2016)
17. He, K., Zhang, X., Ren, S., Sun, J.: Deep residual learning for image recognition (2015)
18. Holmes, A.J., et al.: Brain genomics superstruct project initial data release with structural, functional, and behavioral measures. Sci. Data **2**, 1–16 (2015)

19. Buckner, R., et al.: The brain genomics superstruct project. Harvard Dataverse Network (2012)
20. Nebli, A., Rekik, I.: Gender differences in cortical morphological networks. Brain Imaging Behav. **14**, 1831–1839 (2020)
21. Fischl, B., et al.: Automatically parcellating the human cerebral cortex. Cereb. Cortex **14**, 11–22 (2004)
22. Fischl, B.: Freesurfer. Neuroimage **62**, 774–781 (2012)
23. Chaari, N., Akdağ, H.C., Rekik, I.: Estimation of gender-specific connectional brain templates using joint multi-view cortical morphological network integration. Brain Imaging Behav. **15**, 2081–2100 (2021)
24. Mahjoub, I., Mahjoub, M.A., Rekik, I.: Brain multiplexes reveal morphological connectional biomarkers fingerprinting late brain dementia states. Sci. Rep. **8**, 4103 (2018)
25. Soussia, M., Rekik, I.: High-order connectomic manifold learning for autistic brain state identification. In: Wu, G., Laurienti, P., Bonilha, L., Munsell, B.C. (eds.) CNI 2017. LNCS, vol. 10511, pp. 51–59. Springer, Cham (2017). https://doi.org/10.1007/978-3-319-67159-8_7
26. Soussia, M., Rekik, I.: Unsupervised manifold learning using high-order morphological brain networks derived from T1-w MRI for autism diagnosis. Front. Neuroinformatics **12**, 70 (2018)

An Ambient Intelligence-Based Approach for Longitudinal Monitoring of Verbal and Vocal Depression Symptoms

Alice Othmani[(✉)] and Muhammad Muzammel

Université Paris-Est Créteil (UPEC), LISSI, 94400 Vitry sur Seine, France
{alice.othmani,muhammad.muzammel}@u-pec.fr

Abstract. Automatic speech recognition (ASR) technology can aid in the detection, monitoring, and assessment of depressive symptoms in individuals. ASR systems have been used as a tool to analyze speech patterns and characteristics that are indicative of depression. Depression affects not only a person's mood but also their speech patterns. Individuals with depression may exhibit changes in speech, such as slower speech rate, longer pauses, reduced pitch variability, and decreased overall speech fluency. Despite the growing use of machine learning in diagnosing depression, there is a lack of studies addressing the issue of relapse. Furthermore, previous research on relapse prediction has primarily focused on clinical variables and has not taken into account other factors such as verbal and non-verbal cues. Another major challenge in depression relapse research is the scarcity of publicly available datasets. To overcome these issues, we propose a one-shot learning framework for detecting depression relapse from speech. We define depression relapse as the similarity between the speech audio and textual encoding of a subject and that of a depressed individual. To detect depression relapse based on this definition, we employ a Siamese neural network that models the similarity between of two instances. Our proposed approach shows promising results and represents a new advancement in the field of automatic depression relapse detection and mental disorders monitoring.

Keywords: Ambient Intelligence · Automatic speech recognition (ASR) · one-shot learning · depression relapse · clinical depression

1 Introduction

Major Depressive Disorder (MDD) is a mood disorder that has detrimental effects on an individual's cognition, emotions, and daily functioning. It is primarily characterized by persistent feelings of sadness, anger, and loss of interest in activities. MDD is among the most prevalent mental disorder, impacting over 300 million people globally [14]. Furthermore, recent studies have indicated a significant rise in mental health issues, including anxiety, stress, and depression, during the COVID-19 pandemic [27].

© The Author(s), under exclusive license to Springer Nature Switzerland AG 2023
I. Rekik et al. (Eds.): PRIME 2023, LNCS 14277, pp. 206–217, 2023.
https://doi.org/10.1007/978-3-031-46005-0_18

Depression relapse refers to the re-occurrence of depressive symptoms after a period of partial or complete remission. It means that a person who previously experienced an episode of depression and showed improvement or recovery from their symptoms subsequently experiences a return or worsening of those symptoms [16]. Relapse can happen during or after treatment for depression, and it is often characterized by a recurrence of the emotional, cognitive, and behavioral manifestations associated with depression. Relapse and recurrence rates are high in MDD patients with a percentage of 60% after 5 years, 67% after 10, and 85% after 15 [10]. Thus, there is a pressing need for automatic monitoring systems which can be employed to detect depression relapse or recurrence at an early stage, thereby facilitating timely intervention.

Despite the increasing utilization of machine learning (ML) for analyzing Major Depressive Disorder (MDD) and other mental health issues, and its potential to enhance decision-making for mental health practitioners, [6,7,19,28], there is a noticeable lack of studies utilizing ML to address the issue of depression relapse. Additionally, previous research on relapse prediction primarily relies on clinical variables such as age, gender, medication types, number of episodes, symptom severity, cognitive markers, and medical image data [1,4,25,26]. However, these approaches have overlooked other important attributes, such as the analysis of speech patterns and facial expressions.

On the other hand, a big limitation to depression research studies is the lack of public datasets. Moreover, due to privacy, safety, expense, and ethical concerns [29], acquiring examples to train a model for depression relapse is a difficult task. This motivates research for approaches that take into account the data scarcity problem in this area. Few-shot learning is a subfield of machine learning that deals with the challenge of learning new concepts or tasks with limited labeled training data. In traditional machine learning approaches, a large amount of labeled data is typically required to train models effectively. However, in few-shot learning, the goal is to develop algorithms that can generalize and learn from only a few examples or instances of a particular class or task.

In this paper, we propose a robust approach that deals with depression relapse data scarcity. The proposed approach is based on one-shot learning. We define depression relapse as the closeness of the speech encoding of a subject to that of a depressed subject. By modeling the similarity between two instances, Siamese neural network is chosen as a suitable candidate for depression relapse detection following the proposed definition. The proposed approach investigates the predictive power of audio and textual encodings of the speech for depression relapse prediction using Siamese neural network architecture. Three Siamese networks built using (1) MFCC audio features, (2) VGGish audio features, and (3) audio-textual fusion features are compared and investigated for the relapse identification task. To our knowledge, this work is the first to tackle the prediction of depression relapse based on verbal and non-verbal cues in a speech, and to employ one-shot learning for this task.

The paper is structured as follows. In the following section, a literature review is conducted to identify major previous works done to predict depression relapse

and recurrence. An overview of n-shot learning and Siamese networks is also
included (Sect. 2). In Sect. 3, the different steps of our methodology are described.
Finally, the obtained results and discussion of the performed tests are presented
in Sect. 4.

2 Related Work

Relapse and recurrence can be attributed to various factors. It is suggested that
recurrence is ascribed to a genetic vulnerability [2]. Likewise, some findings suggest that inflammation can issue a possible mechanism for recurrent depression
[13]. Another factor can be neuropsychological functioning [25]. Factors trigger-
ing depression relapse may vary among individuals. Moreover, in many cases it is
difficult to underpin the trigger factors leading to a depression relapse episode.
This motivates the development of automatic monitoring systems capable of
detecting relapse.

Researcher for predicting depression relapse often relies on n clinical variables
such as medication type, episode number, symptom severity, cognitive markers,
and occasionally medical imaging data. For example, Borges et al. (2018) [1] have
explored the use of machine learning algorithms in predicting relapse in bipolar
patients based on their clinical data, with Random Forests showing promising
results (68% for the Relapse Group and 74% for the No Relapse Group). Another
study by Chanda et al. (2020) [4] aimed to develop a recurrence classification
platform based on gender, age, medication, and treatment time, where K-Nearest
Neighbor outperformed SVM and RF with an 83% accuracy. Emotional biases
were investigated by Ruhe et al. (2019) [25], as potential biomarkers for depression relapse, resulting in a linear SVM model with a 75% accuracy. Moreover, a
multimodal approach proposed by Cearns et al. (2019) [3] incorporating various
modalities, including clinical, blood-biomarker, genetic, bio-electrical impedance,
electrocardiography, and structural imaging, achieved an accuracy of 65.72%
using SVM. Further, a holistic approach involving the analysis of depression
scores trajectories and predicting individual treatment outcomes was proposed
using smoothing splines, K-means clustering, and collaborative modeling [12].

Just recently, three research studies have emerged that propose utilizing video
data for the prediction of depression relapse [17,21,22]. In [22] along with CNN,
a Model of Normality (MoN) was utilize to detect depression and relapse. While,
the other approach [17] proposed a preliminary study based one-shot learning
due to capacity to learn instantly. Both of these state of the art modalities relies
on audio and visual features for monitoring depression relapse. In [21], a deep
learning-based approach is proposed for depression recognition and depression
relapse prediction using videos of clinical interviews. Their approach is based on
a correlation-based anomaly detection framework and a measure of similarity to
depression where depression relapse is detected when the deep audiovisual patterns of a depression-free subject become close to the deep audiovisual patterns
of depressed subjects. Thus, the correlation between the audiovisual encoding

of a test subject and a deep audiovisual representation of depression is computed and used for monitoring depressed subjects and for predicting relapse after depression.

3   Methodology

Depression relapse is defined in this work as the similarity (dissimilarity) between the audio-textual speech encoding of a subject and the speech encoding of a diagnosed depressed (non-depressed) subject. One-shot learning based Siamese network is chosen in this work for modeling depression relapse, as it models the similarity (dissimilarity) between two samples. The proposed framework is composed of four stages: (1) pre-processing audio data augmentation (Sect. 3.1), (3) audio-textual features extraction (Sect. 3.2), and (4) one-shot learning-based depression relapse detection (Sect. 3.3). Each of these steps are detailed in the following.

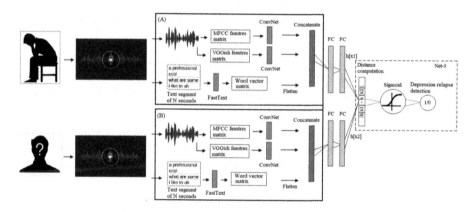

Fig. 1. Proposed multimodal-based Siamese networks for depression relapse detection.

3.1   Pre-processing and Data Augmentation

Audio Preprocessing. In the pre-processing step, unvoiced segments are first filtered and the speech of the subject is extracted from the audio signal. The speech signal is then divided into $n = 7.6$ seconds speech segments. To increase the number of data samples and the system's robustness to noise, data augmentation is performed. The signals are perturbed using two audio augmentation techniques [18,20,23]:

1) *Noise Injection*: the audio signal is perturbed through the injection of random noise. Let x be an audio signal and α a noise factor, the noise perturbed signal x_N is given by: $x_N = x - \alpha \times rand(x)$, with $\alpha = 0.01$, 0.02 and 0.03.
2) *Pitch Augmentation*: pitch is lowered by factors of 0.5, 2, and 2.5 (in semitones).

Text Preprocessing. The clinical interviews are recorded and accompanied by transcriptions of the conversations between the participant and the interviewer. Unlike the audio data, we analyze both the transcriptions of the interviewer and the participant. This is because the verbal reactions of the interviewer following the participant's responses can contain valuable information about the participant's emotions. For example, when the participant responds negatively, the interviewer may express phrases like "that sucks" or "I'm sorry to hear that," which provide insight into the participant's depressive state. Our decision to focus solely on the audio patterns of the participant is based on the fact that the interviewer's audio patterns do not exhibit signs of depression. However, the words used by the interviewer can indicate sympathy when the patient is depressed.

3.2   Audio-Textual Features Extraction

Following data augmentation, audio-textual features are extracted. These constitute MFCC and Vggish audio features, and textual word2Vec features.

MFCC Features Extraction from Audio Signal. MFCC features represent the audio cepstrum in the non-linear Mel scale. Such representation is said to approximate the human auditory system. Below is the detailed description of the MFCC feature extraction steps.

Windowing: The signal is split into 60 ms frames. A Hamming window is then applied on each frame to taper the signal towards the frame boundaries. Given a signal $s[n]$ of length n and a hamming window $w[n]$, the sliced frame is given by:

$$x[n] = w[n]s[n] \quad with \quad w[n] = \alpha - \beta \cos\left(2\pi\frac{n}{N-1}\right) \tag{1}$$

where $\alpha = 0.54$, $\beta = 0.46$, N is the window length such that $0 \leq n \leq N$.

DFT Spectrum: Discrete Fourier Transform (DFT) is then performed on each windowed frame to get the magnitude spectrum:

$$X[k] = \sum_{n=0}^{N-1} x[n]e^{-j\frac{2\pi}{N}kn}; \quad 0 \leq k \leq N - 1 \tag{2}$$

Mel Spectrum: Triangular Mel-scale filter banks are then multiplied by the magnitude spectrum to compute the Mel spectrum.

$$Y_t[m] = \sum_{k=0}^{N-1} W_m[k]|X_t[k]|^2; \quad 0 \leq m \leq M - 1 \tag{3}$$

where W_m represents the mth triangular Mel-scale filter bank, M is total number of filters, and k corresponds to the DFT bin number.

Discrete Cosine Transform (DCT): The Mel spectrum is then represented on a log scale and DCT is applied generating a set of cepstral coefficients. MFCC is thus calculated as:

$$c[n] = \sum_{m=0}^{M-1} log_{10}\left(Y_t[m]\right) cos\left(n(m-0.5)\frac{\pi}{M}\right) \quad (4)$$

For this work, 60 dimensional MFCC features are extracted leading to a matrix of 378×60 for each 7.6 s signal.

Vggish Features Extraction from Audio Signal. In this work, VGGish features [11] are extracted from the audio segments. VGGish converts audio features into semantically significant compact high-level 128 dimensional embedding. This embedding can be then fed to a shallow or deep classification model.

To compute the VGGish features, first a one-sided Short-Time Fourier Transform (STFT) is applied to the audio clip using a 25 ms periodic Hann window with 10 ms hop, and 512-point DFT. The complex spectral values are then converted to magnitude and phase information is discarded. The one-sided magnitude spectrum are passed to a 64-band mel-spaced filter bank, and the magnitudes in each band are then summed. The obtained mel spectrograms are then converted into a log scale and buffered into overlapped segments consisting of 96 spectrums each. These mel spectrograms are passed through VGGish network to obtain a 14×128 matrix [8,11].

The VGGish feature matrix contained zero values. To resolve this issue, the VGGish model was released with a precomputed principal component analysis (PCA) matrix [8,11]. First, we subtract the precomputed 1×128 PCA mean vector from the 14×128 feature matrix, and then premultiply the result by the precomputed 128×128 PCA matrix.

Textual Features Extraction. For each audio segment (7.6*sec*) of the clinical interviews, the words spoken by both the participant and the interviewer are converted into sequences of vectors using word embedding as a textual features. Word embedding is a technique that transforms words into dimensional vectors, where words with similar meanings or words that frequently occur together in context are represented by vectors that are close to each other in the dimensional space. In particular, each frame transcript is represented by a matrix $E = (e_1, \ldots, e_k, \ldots e_{nw})$ where e_k is the word vector corresponding to the kth word and nw is the number of words in the frame transcript.

For word embedding, we utilize the fastText pretrained network [15], which was trained on Common Crawl[1] and incorporates sub-word information. This network produces word vectors of size 300. In cases where certain words are not present in the pretrained model, we replace them with their synonyms. Additionally, the resulting word vector matrix for each transcript frame is resized to

---

[1] https://commoncrawl.org/2017/06.

60 × 9, where 60 represents the size of MFCC coefficients and 9 represents the minimum number of words present in a single frame.

3.3 One-Shot Learning Framework for Depression Relapse Detection

In this work, 1D convolutional Siamese networks are proposed for depression relapse detection based on audio-textual cues. The proposed architectures are summarized in Fig. 1.

One-Shot Learning. One-shot learning refers to the classification task where the number of available instances per class is limited. In some cases, a class may have only a single example during the model training phase. The objective of one-shot learning is to train models that can determine the similarity between a pair of inputs and identify whether they belong to the same class or not.

Siamese neural networks, also known as twin neural networks, are a type of one-shot learning model that aim to learn a distance function between pairs of input vectors. In the architecture of a Siamese neural network, two identical sub-networks with shared weights are employed. Each sub-network takes in a distinct pair of inputs and produces output representations. The network then computes a distance metric, such as Euclidean distance or cosine similarity, between the outputs of the sub-networks. This distance metric reflects the similarity between the two input vectors [5]. The training can be done on different pairs of inputs from all possible classes. To obtain a prediction for an instance, a comparison between the instance and reference instances of all classes should be performed. The final prediction is then obtained based on the different similarity scores.

For training a Siamese network, dataset pre-processing is required. A pairing procedure is performed where pairs of data points are created: similar samples pair, and dissimilar samples pair. Similar samples are then assigned positive labels, while dissimilar samples are assigned negative labels. The pairs are then fed to the Siamese architecture. The pairing procedure employed in this paper is detailed in Sect. 4.1.

Proposed Siamese Architectures. We propose two Siamese networks built using (1) MFCC audio features, (2) VGGish audio features, and (3) audio-textual fusion features.

Audio Based Siamese Network. The proposed MFCC and VGGish Siamese models have similar architectures. The architecture consists of two blocks of convolutional, Relu, dropout, and flatten layers. Two fully connected layers are used to compute encodings and an euclidean distance is measured between the two encodings. In other words, both Net-1 (A and B) from Fig. 1 are connected with Net-3 through the fully connected layers. A last layer of size two is added with a sigmoid activation function for binary prediction of relapse.

Audio-Textual Based Siamese Network. In Fig. 1, the 60 MFCC features are fed to a Convolutional Neural Network composed of two blocks of 1D convolutional and Relu layers, followed by dropout and flatten layers. Similarly 14 VGGish features are fed to a similar Convolutional Neural Network consisting of two blocks of 1D convolutional and Relu layers, followed by dropout and flatten layers. These high level MFCC and VGGish features are then concatenated with the textual features into a features vector of size 540 and fed to two fully connected layers to obtain the audio-textual encoding. Afterwords, an euclidean distance is computed between the two encodings: one of non-diagnosed subject and one of a reference depressed subject. A last layer of size two is also added for binary prediction of relapse.

4 Results and Discussion

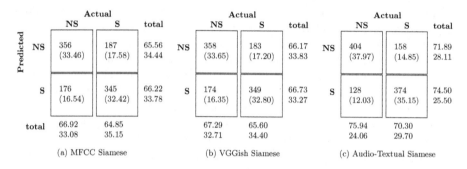

| | | Actual | | | | | Actual | | | | | Actual | | |
		NS	S	total			NS	S	total			NS	S	total
Predicted	NS	356 (33.46)	187 (17.58)	65.56 34.44	NS		358 (33.65)	183 (17.20)	66.17 33.83	NS		404 (37.97)	158 (14.85)	71.89 28.11
	S	176 (16.54)	345 (32.42)	66.22 33.78	S		174 (16.35)	349 (32.80)	66.73 33.27	S		128 (12.03)	374 (35.15)	74.50 25.50
total		66.92 33.08	64.85 35.15				67.29 32.71	65.60 34.40				75.94 24.06	70.30 29.70	
		(a) MFCC Siamese					(b) VGGish Siamese					(c) Audio-Textual Siamese		

Fig. 2. Confusion matrices of Siamese networks for depressive state similarity detection. NS: Non-Similar, S: Similar.

4.1 Dataset

We use the Distress Analysis Interview Corpus Wizard-of-Oz dataset (DAIC-WOZ) [9]. This dataset was introduced in AVEC 2017 challenge [24]. 189 subjects took part in the data collection, where they were interviewed by a virtual agent manipulated in a wizard-of-oz setting. The subject's speech and interviews transcripts were saved and publicly made available for research. The average length of the audio samples is 15 min, sampled at 16 kHz. The dataset includes depression scores in two formats: binary and severity level. Binary depression and severity labels were collected via a self-report Patient Health Questionnaire (PHQ) [30]. Only 182 subjects were used in the evaluation. We use a percentage split strategy where the dataset is randomly divided into 80% training, 10% validation, and 10% testing. Out of the 182 subjects, the training dataset included 146 subjects, while the validation and test sets included 18 subjects each.

Pairing. Features pairs are then generated to train, test and validate the one-shot learning model. Samples from the train set are randomly paired with each others to form the training pairs. No sample was paired with itself. To generate the test and validation pairs, samples from these sets are paired with the samples from the training set. The binary depression score provided in DAIC-WOZ consists of two classes: depressed and non-depressed. Binary depression relapse is defined to be the paired feature groups of the couple (Non-Depressed, Depressed). Also, in both classes (i.e., Depressed, Non-Depressed) 50% features matrix groups are paired with the same class, while the remaining 50% features matrix groups are paired with the other class. Also pairs are created for PhQ-score provided in DAIC-WOZ dataset. For all 24 classes 50% features matrix groups are paired with the same class, while the remaining 50% features matrix groups are paired with the other classes.

4.2 Network Implementation Details

A ReLU activation function with 64 filters is used for the convolutional layers in the presented CNN architectures. The stride and filter sizes are set to 1 and 3, respectively. The dropout fraction value is set to 0.01%. The dense layers' sizes are set to 1024 and hyperbolic tangent (tanh) is used as an activation function. To predict the similarity between two feature sets for depression relapse detection based on PHQ-binary, the output layer is a dense layer with a sigmoid activation function and a size of 2. To predict the similarity based on PHQ-score pairs, the output dense layer has a size of 25. To train the models, an initial learning rate of 10^{-5} and a decay of 10^{-6} is used. The batch size and epochs are set to 100 and 300, respectively. For both models, Root Mean Square Error is used as a loss function and trained with RMSProp optimizer. An early stopping is used if the loss function stops decreasing after 10 epochs.

Table 1. Performance of proposed Siamese networks for depressive state similarity in terms of accuracy, Root Mean Square Error (RMSE) and CC

Network	Acc. (%)	RMSE	CC
MFCC Siamese	65.88	0.4841	0.3177
VGGish Siamese	66.45	0.4792	0.3290
Audio-Textual Siamese	**73.12**	**0.4585**	**0.4631**

4.3 Performance Analysis of Siamese Networks

The proposed Siamese networks are evaluated using accuracy, Root Mean Square Error (RMSE), and Pearson Correlation Coefficient (CC) metrics. As shown in Table 1, the proposed framework reaches an accuracy of 65.88% and 66.45% when using only the MFCC features and VGGish features, respectively. The fusion of MFCC, VGGish and textual features notably increases the performance where an accuracy of 73.12% is obtained. A minor decrease in RMSE and a minor increase in CC is noted for the VGGish model compared to the MFCC based one. Further, the CC value of MFCC and VGGish based Siamese networks are 0.3177 and 0.3290, which increases to 0.4631 with the fusion of audio and textual features.

Figure 2 shows the confusion matrices of MFCC, VGGish and Audio-textual based Siamese networks. From the figure, one can notice that the fusion of textual features with audio features network adequately improves the performance of one shot learning Siamese network. For non-similar feature pairs classification, the audio-textual based fusion network achieved 9.02% and 8.65% better results compared to MFCC and VGGish based networks. Also for non-similar feature pairs, a notable decrement in false positives has been reported for audio-textual based fusion network.

For similar feature pairs (i.e., when both features sets in pair belong to the same class) classification the Audio-Textual based fusion network obtained 5.45% and 4.70% better results compared to MFCC and VGGish based networks. Also a considerable decrement in false positives has been reported for Audio-Textual based fusion network compared to MFCC and VGGish based Siamese networks. Furthermore, We also investigate the pair matching for PhQ-Score using multi-class Audio-Textual based Siamese network and we obtained an RMSE value of 4.025 (Normalized RMSE of 0.161).

5   Conclusion and Future Work

In this work, an ASR framework is proposed for depression relapse detection, modeling the similarity of audio and textual speech encoding between a new subject and a diagnosed depressed subject using one-shot learning. The proposed model gave reliable results using the speech's audio and textual cues. The fusion of audio and textual features enhanced the one-shot learning model performance, which made it reliable for detecting depression relapse. Further, the proposed ASR system could help depression patients to monitor their recovery. Lastly, in future work we plan to consider also visual cues in the proposed framework.

Acknowledgments. This work is funded under grant number IF040-2021 (MATCH2021: Malaysia France Bilateral Research Grant).

References

1. Borges-Júnior, R., Salvini, R., Nierenberg, A.A., Sachs, G.S., Lafer, B., Dias, R.S.: Forecasting depressive relapse in bipolar disorder from clinical data. In: 2018 IEEE International Conference on Bioinformatics and Biomedicine (BIBM), pp. 613–616. IEEE (2018)
2. Burcusa, S.L., Iacono, W.G.: Risk for recurrence in depression. Clin. Psychol. Rev. **27**(8), 959–985 (2007)

3. Cearns, M., et al.: Predicting rehospitalization within 2 years of initial patient admission for a major depressive episode: a multimodal machine learning approach. Transl. Psychiatry **9**(1), 1–9 (2019)
4. Chanda, K., Bhattacharjee, P., Roy, S., Biswas, S.: Intelligent data prognosis of recurrent of depression in medical diagnosis. In: 2020 8th International Conference on Reliability, Infocom Technologies and Optimization (Trends and Future Directions) (ICRITO), pp. 840–844. IEEE (2020)
5. Chicco, D.: Siamese neural networks: an overview, pp. 73–94
6. Dwyer, D.B., Falkai, P., Koutsouleris, N.: Machine learning approaches for clinical psychology and psychiatry. Annu. Rev. Clin. Psychol. **14**, 91–118 (2018)
7. Gao, S., Calhoun, V.D., Sui, J.: Machine learning in major depression: from classification to treatment outcome prediction. CNS Neurosci. Therapeutics **24**(11), 1037–1052 (2018)
8. Gemmeke, J.F., et al.: Audio set: an ontology and human-labeled dataset for audio events. In: 2017 IEEE International Conference on Acoustics, Speech and Signal Processing (ICASSP), pp. 776–780. IEEE (2017)
9. Gratch, J., et al.: The distress analysis interview corpus of human and computer interviews. In: Proceedings of the International Conference on Language Resources and Evaluation, pp. 3123–3128 (2014)
10. Hardeveld, F., Spijker, J., De Graaf, R., Nolen, W., Beekman, A.: Prevalence and predictors of recurrence of major depressive disorder in the adult population. Acta Psychiatr. Scand. **122**(3), 184–191 (2010)
11. Hershey, S., et al.: CNN architectures for large-scale audio classification. In: 2017 IEEE International Conference on Acoustics, Speech and Signal Processing (ICASSP), pp. 131–135. IEEE (2017)
12. Lin, Y., Huang, S., Simon, G.E., Liu, S.: Analysis of depression trajectory patterns using collaborative learning. Math. Biosci. **282**, 191–203 (2016)
13. Liu, C.H., et al.: Role of inflammation in depression relapse. J. Neuroinflammation **16**(1), 1–11 (2019)
14. Marcus, M., Yasamy, M.T., van van Ommeren, M., Chisholm, D., Saxena, S.: Depression: a global public health concern (2012). https://doi.org/10.1037/e517532013-004
15. Mikolov, T., Grave, E., Bojanowski, P., Puhrsch, C., Joulin, A.: Advances in pre-training distributed word representations. In: Proceedings of the International Conference on Language Resources and Evaluation (2018)
16. Monroe, S.M., Harkness, K.L.: Recurrence in major depression: a conceptual analysis. Psychol. Rev. **118**(4), 655 (2011)
17. Muzammel, M., Othmani, A., Mukherjee, H., Salam, H.: Identification of signs of depression relapse using audio-visual cues: a preliminary study. In: 2021 IEEE 34th International Symposium on Computer-Based Medical Systems (CBMS), pp. 62–67. IEEE (2021)
18. Muzammel, M., Salam, H., Hoffmann, Y., Chetouani, M., Othmani, A.: Audvowelconsnet: a phoneme-level based deep CNN architecture for clinical depression diagnosis. Mach. Learn. Appl. **2**, 100005 (2020)
19. Muzammel, M., Salam, H., Othmani, A.: End-to-end multimodal clinical depression recognition using deep neural networks: a comparative analysis. Comput. Methods Programs Biomed. **211**, 106433 (2021)
20. Othmani, A., Kadoch, D., Bentounes, K., Rejaibi, E., Alfred, R., Hadid, A.: Towards robust deep neural networks for affect and depression recognition from speech. In: Del Bimbo, A., et al. (eds.) ICPR 2021. LNCS, vol. 12662, pp. 5–19. Springer, Cham (2021). https://doi.org/10.1007/978-3-030-68790-8_1

21. Othmani, A., Zeghina, A.O.: A multimodal computer-aided diagnostic system for depression relapse prediction using audiovisual cues: a proof of concept. Healthc. Anal. **2**, 100090 (2022)
22. Othmani, A., Zeghina, A.O., Muzammel, M.: A model of normality inspired deep learning framework for depression relapse prediction using audiovisual data. Comput. Methods Programs Biomed. **226**, 107132 (2022)
23. Rejaibi, E., Komaty, A., Meriaudeau, F., Agrebi, S., Othmani, A.: MFCC-based recurrent neural network for automatic clinical depression recognition and assessment from speech. arXiv preprint arXiv:1909.07208 (2019)
24. Ringeval, F., et al.: AVEC 2017: real-life depression, and affect recognition workshop and challenge. In: Proceedings of the 7th Annual Workshop on Audio/Visual Emotion Challenge, pp. 3–9. ACM (2017)
25. Ruhe, H.G., et al.: Emotional biases and recurrence in major depressive disorder. Results of 2.5 years follow-up of drug-free cohort vulnerable for recurrence. Front. Psychiatry **10**, 145 (2019)
26. Sato, J.R., Moll, J., Green, S., Deakin, J.F., Thomaz, C.E., Zahn, R.: Machine learning algorithm accurately detects fMRI signature of vulnerability to major depression. Psychiatry Res. Neuroimaging **233**(2), 289–291 (2015)
27. Shah, S.M.A., Mohammad, D., Qureshi, M.F.H., Abbas, M.Z., Aleem, S.: Prevalence, psychological responses and associated correlates of depression, anxiety and stress in a global population, during the coronavirus disease (COVID-19) pandemic. Community Ment. Health J. **57**(1), 101–110 (2021)
28. Su, C., Xu, Z., Pathak, J., Wang, F.: Deep learning in mental health outcome research: a scoping review. Transl. Psychiatry **10**(1), 1–26 (2020)
29. Thelisson, E., Sharma, K., Salam, H., Dignum, V.: The general data protection regulation: an opportunity for the HCI community? In: Extended Abstracts of the 2018 CHI Conference on Human Factors in Computing Systems, pp. 1–8 (2018)
30. Williams, L.S., et al.: Performance of the PHQ-9 as a screening tool for depression after stroke. Stroke **36**(3), 635–638 (2005)

Dynamic Depth-Supervised NeRF for Multi-view RGB-D Operating Room Videos

Beerend G. A. Gerats[1,3]([✉]) [iD], Jelmer M. Wolterink[2] [iD],
and Ivo A. M. J. Broeders[1,3] [iD]

[1] Centre for Artificial Intelligence, Meander Medisch Centrum,
Amersfoort, The Netherlands
{bga.gerats,iamj.broeders}@meandermc.nl
[2] Department of Applied Mathematics and Technical Medical Center,
University of Twente, Enschede, The Netherlands
j.m.wolterink@utwente.nl
[3] Robotics and Mechatronics, University of Twente, Enschede, The Netherlands

Abstract. The operating room (OR) is an environment of interest for the development of sensing systems, enabling the detection of people, objects, and their semantic relations. Due to frequent occlusions in the OR, these systems often rely on input from multiple cameras. While increasing the number of cameras generally increases algorithm performance, there are hard limitations to the number and locations of cameras in the OR. Neural Radiance Fields (NeRF) can be used to render synthetic views from arbitrary camera positions, virtually enlarging the number of cameras in the dataset. In this work, we explore the use of NeRF for view synthesis of dynamic scenes in the OR, and we show that regularisation with depth supervision from RGB-D sensor data results in higher image quality. We optimise a dynamic depth-supervised NeRF with up to six synchronised cameras that capture the surgical field in five distinct phases before and during a knee replacement surgery. We qualitatively inspect views rendered by a virtual camera that moves 180° around the surgical field at differing time values. Quantitatively, we evaluate view synthesis from an unseen camera position in terms of PSNR, SSIM and LPIPS for the colour channels and in MAE and error percentage for the estimated depth. We find that NeRFs can be used to generate geometrically consistent views, also from interpolated camera positions and at interpolated time intervals. Views are generated from an unseen camera pose with an average PSNR of 18.2 and a depth estimation error of 2.0%. Our results show the potential of a dynamic NeRF for view synthesis in the OR and stress the relevance of depth supervision in a clinical setting.

Keywords: Neural radiance fields · RGB-D imaging · Operating room videos

Supplementary Information The online version contains supplementary material available at https://doi.org/10.1007/978-3-031-46005-0_19.

I. Rekik et al. (Eds.): PRIME 2023, LNCS 14277, pp. 218–230, 2023.
https://doi.org/10.1007/978-3-031-46005-0_19

1   Introduction

The operating room (OR) is an environment of interest for the development of sensing systems, with tasks ranging from person detection and human pose estimation [4] to domain modeling and role identification [9]. These sensing systems could automatically register adverse events and distractions [3] or monitor X-ray radiation exposure [10] to enhance patient and staff safety. Due to frequent occlusions by large devices, hanging monitors and a crowded space, detection systems often rely on video input from multiple cameras. Typically, the underlying algorithms perform better when the number of cameras is increased [2]. However, there are limitations to the number and locations of cameras in the OR due to sterility concerns and limited available space.

Neural Radiance Fields (NeRF) [7] is a powerful technology for the reconstruction of a 3D scene from a set of images that capture the scene from various camera positions. Although the introduction of this technology has caused an explosion of interest in the field of computer vision, with many follow-up studies [20], NeRF-based methods for clinical use remain largely unexplored [16]. The use of NeRF could help to overcome the limited availability of camera placement in the OR, by virtually increasing the number of cameras with view synthesis from new camera locations. Subsequently, renders of OR scenes from arbitrary camera angles could be used to improve detection algorithms.

In this paper, we explore the use of NeRF for view synthesis of dynamic scenes in the OR and we show that regularisation with depth supervision [1] increases the render quality and reduces the need for many camera positions. We find that a depth-supervised NeRF optimised with only six synchronised camera views is able to generate images of the surgical intervention from a range of camera angles. In contrast to existing depth supervision in NeRF, we directly optimise our model using measured RGB-D sensor data instead of estimated depth from a structure from motion (SfM) algorithm. Additionally, we extend the method with a notion of scene dynamics by optimising with an extra time variable enabling the reconstruction of the surgical scene at specific time intervals. We show how the dynamic NeRF could be used for region-of-interest localisation through unsupervised segmentation of objects and people in the OR.

2   Related Work

2.1   Neural Radiance Fields

NeRF is a method for volume rendering, based upon the *implicit representation* of a 3D scene in the weights of a neural network F_Θ [7]. This network is generally a standard multi-layer perceptron (MLP) that takes a 5D vector (x, y, z, θ, ϕ) as input and that outputs a 4D vector (RGB, σ). An input vector consists of a 3D location (x, y, z) in the captured scene and an orientation (θ, ϕ) from which this location is viewed. F_Θ returns for each vector a colour RGB and a volume density σ. With this simple setup, NeRF can reconstruct images by casting a viewing ray from each pixel, sampling points along that ray, asking the MLP to find the colours and densities for these points and to sum over these results. In this way, it is possible to use a discrete set of sampled points in the 3D scene, while representing the scene in continuous form. Reconstructed images are compared with ground truth images that are taken from the same camera positions. The rendering function that sums over the colours and densities is differentiable such that the MLP can be optimised by stochastic gradient descent. The loss function is often a mean squared error between the colours of the rendered and the ground truth images.

2.2   NeRF with Depth Priors

Although NeRF has the ability to synthesise photo-realistic images from unseen camera perspectives, the method does not guarantee to capture 3D geometry accurately. This limitation becomes visible when rendering poorly textured areas that often occur in indoor scenes [18]. It is likely that this problem will play a role when NeRF is applied to the OR.

Several solutions are proposed that involve regularisation with depth priors. Nerfing MVS [18] provides a guided optimisation scheme, where points are sampled along a viewing ray only around depth values found earlier. A sparse set of depth values is found by applying the COLMAP SfM algorithm [14] on multi-view images. The sparse sets are used to train a depth completion network that provides full sets of depth values. A more common approach is to use a depth loss that enforces NeRF to represent a large amount of volume density around ground truth depth values [12], or that enforces NeRF to terminate rays close to depth observations, provided by a depth completion network [13], the COLMAP algorithm or RGB-D data [1].

2.3   NeRF for Dynamic Scenes

While the original NeRF has been developed to represent static scenes, several adaptations have been proposed to give NeRF a sense of scene dynamics. D-NeRF [11] uses an additional deformation network that models point translation to a canonical configuration. With this network, it is possible to render 3D objects that change in shape over time. However, it is less suitable for the clinical setting, where people and objects can appear and disappear in the reconstructed scene. Li et al., [5] add temporal latent codes to the input vectors for video synthesis. To speed up training, they propose hierarchical frame selection and importance sampling of camera rays.

2.4   NeRF for Clinical Interventions

Although NeRF has inspired several works in medical image computing [15,19], it has not been widely adopted in the field of computer-assisted interventions. To the best of our knowledge, the technology has thus far only been used for 3D

reconstruction of soft tissues in robotic surgery videos [16]. Because the laparo-
scopic view is a single view, their method uses time-dependent modelling of neural radiance and displacement fields, based on D-NeRF. Using the stereoscopic
camera of the surgical robot, the method finds depth maps along the coloured
image frames. The depth information is used to constrain NeRF optimisation
with an additional loss function.

3   Methods

3.1   Dynamic Depth-Supervised NeRF

We use the depth-supervised NeRF (DS-NeRF) by Deng *et al.* [1] for building 3D
reconstructions of OR scenes. This method regularises the training with an additional depth loss such that a model can be optimised with relatively few camera
positions. The key idea in DS-NeRF is that most viewing rays terminate at the
closest surface, which is often opaque. Therefore, most volume density should
be found close to the distance of this surface along the viewing ray. DS-NeRF
enforces such a distribution of volume density by minimising the KL divergence
between the volume density distribution $h_i(s)$ and a normal distribution around
the ground truth depth d_i of keypoint $x_i \in X$:

$$KL[\mathbb{N}(d_i, \hat{\sigma}_i) \| h_i(s)], \tag{1}$$

where X is the set of all keypoints in an image for which the depth is known and s
is the far endpoint of the viewing ray. The variance $\hat{\sigma}_i$ is set to the uncertainty of
the depth estimation for keypoint x_i. When depth is estimated with COLMAP,
the uncertainty is calculated by re-projecting the keypoint to and from another
camera position in which the keypoint is visible. In RGB-D data, however, the
depth values are measurements rather than estimations. Therefore, we set $\hat{\sigma}_i =
1.0$ for all keypoints such that each depth value is weighted equally. We sample
100K depth values in each ground truth image at random positions, where pixels
that have zero depth are never included.

The OR is a dynamic environment, where objects and people move around
in a controlled manner. Training NeRF with a notion of these dynamics over
time is a natural choice for the synthesis of video. Inspired by DyNeRF [5], we
extend DS-NeRF to generate views dependent on a time variable t. Our Dynamic
DS-NeRF takes a 6D vector $(x, y, z, \theta, \phi, t)$ as input and outputs the same 4D
vector (RGB, σ). In contrast to the other input variables, we do not encode the
time variable. We concatenate the scalar to the positional embeddings of the
locations.

3.2   Dataset

The 4D-OR dataset [9] from the Technical University of Munich contains RGB-D
images and camera poses from ten simulated knee replacement surgeries. We use
this dataset to train the method in the reconstruction of five surgical phases (see

Fig. 1). In this way, we can evaluate the quality of synthesised views for different OR activities. The dataset contains synchronised images from six cameras that have fixed locations in the OR. Three cameras are located above the surgical field, each rotated approximately 90° around the yaw axis (the red dots in Fig. 2). Two of the three other cameras capture the OR from a wide perspective, while the sixth camera records from a position that is closer to the ground (the green dots).

Empty OR   Patient in   Draping   Cleaning   Procedure

Fig. 1. Five distinct phases during or before the surgery.

Fig. 2. Locations of the RGB-D cameras are indicated by a red or green dot. The viewing angle is directed by the arrows. Red dots indicate three cameras located above the surgical field, whereas the green dots capture the OR from very different perspectives. The scene is a coloured point cloud formed by camera projection using depth values. (Color figure online)

3.3   Experimental Setup

First, we train Dynamic DS-NeRF with images from all six camera positions and qualitatively inspect a set of synthesised views. To obtain this set, we ask the algorithm to synthesise views from the three camera locations above the surgical field as well as from interpolated poses that together form a 180° rotation around the surgical field. Second, we train the method with five camera positions and evaluate view synthesis from the remaining unseen sixth position (the circled camera pose in Fig. 2). We evaluate the resulting images in terms of peak signal-to-noise ratio (PSNR), structural similarity index measure (SSIM) and learned perceptual image patch similarity (LPIPS). These metrics indicate image reconstruction quality in comparison to real images, where PSNR is derived from a pixel-wise mean squared error, SSIM indicates the inter-dependency of pixels that are spatially close [17], and LPIPS is based upon similarity in the deep representations of a convolutional neural network [21]. We evaluate the quality of depth perception in terms of mean absolute error (MAE) and in percentage of the ground truth depth value. Depth values equal to zero in the ground truth images are not evaluated, since these values are inaccurate measurements.

For each surgical phase, we optimise the method with $t = \{-2, -1, 0, 1, 2\}$ and evaluate the reconstructed scene at $t = 0$ such that we can compare the results with non-dynamic methods. All models are trained to synthesise images of 512×384 pixels with the following hyperparameters: 768 neurons in each network layer, 4096 selected rays per batch, 192 points sampled per ray, 50K iterations and depth loss weighting factor λ_D set to 0.1. This number of iterations takes around 20 h of training time on a single NVIDIA A40 (48 GB) GPU. At inference, the rendering of a single frame requires 22 s.

4   Results

4.1   Qualitative Analysis

The synthesised views for three surgical phases are given in Fig. 3. When comparing the top-row synthesised views with the ground truth images, it can be seen that Dynamic DS-NeRF is able to reconstruct the scenes independently of the surgical phase. Lighting conditions, such as reflections on the floor and shadows, are realistically rendered. However, the reconstructed scene looks smoothed with missing details, e.g., in the keyboard of the mobile monitor.

Synthesised views from the interpolated camera poses (images without red borders) correctly grasp the geometry of the scenes and find realistic lighting conditions. For the "patient in" in phase, we interpolate the time values at $t = -0.5$ and $t = 0.5$. The moving patient bed is correctly positioned in these frames, at an interpolated location. However, the interpolated camera positions and time values induce a number of artefacts. First, various objects seem to be misaligned. For example, the tape on the floor and the instrument table are not always represented correctly. Second, fine-grained details, such as the surgical instruments in the hands of the left physician, are missing.

4.2   Quantitative Analysis

Results of the quantitative analysis can be found in Table 1. On average, Dynamic DS-NeRF is able to synthesise views from the unseen camera pose

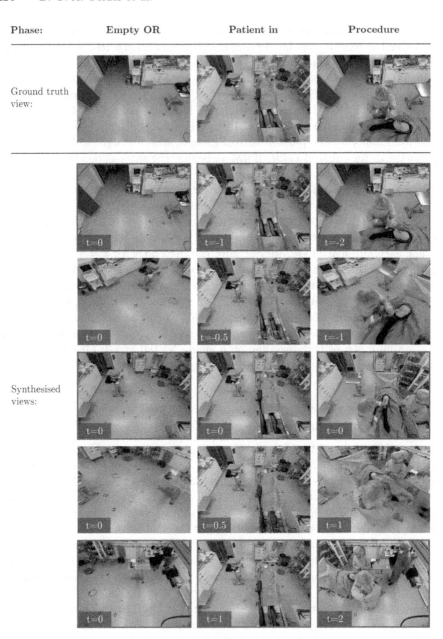

Fig. 3. Dynamic DS-NeRF synthesised views for three phases in the OR at time intervals t. For "empty OR", the virtual camera rotates 180° around the surgical field. For "patient in", the camera position is static, but the time intervals are interpolated. For "procedure", the images differ in camera location and time value. The top row displays the ground truth images for the starting camera pose. Views with a red border are generated from camera poses with which the algorithm is trained, corresponding to the red camera positions in Fig. 2. (Color figure online)

with 18.2 PSNR, 0.61 SIMM and 0.41 LPIPS. The image quality of the rendered views on the 4D-OR dataset differs per phase and ranges in PSNR from 17.5 for "patient in" to 19.6 for "empty OR". This shows that the image quality is dependent on the complexity of the surgical scene. Table 2 provides a comparison with a naive baseline method for view synthesis that uses the projection of pointclouds to reconstruct the images. In this method, the five training images are projected into a single pointcloud, which is reprojected to the sixth camera position. Figure 4 shows a left-right comparison between the baseline images and Dynamic DS-NeRF for two surgical phases. It can be seen that our method is able to generate proper colours for locations where the pointcloud has no presence. This results in more realistic-looking images and better image quality scores.

Table 1. Evaluation metrics comparing Dynamic DS-NeRF synthesised views with unseen ground truth RGB-D images.

Surgery phase	Colour Image			Depth Map	
	PSNR ↑	SSIM ↑	LPIPS ↓	MAE (in cm) ↓	Error (in %) ↓
Empty OR	19.6	0.70	0.35	2.5	0.86
Patient in	17.5	0.59	0.39	3.2	1.28
Draping	18.4	0.62	0.43	4.3	1.76
Cleaning	17.7	0.58	0.42	5.6	2.66
Procedure	17.7	0.58	0.44	5.5	3.43
Average	**18.2**	**0.61**	**0.41**	**4.2**	**2.00**

Table 2. Ablation of Dynamic DS-NeRF where dynamics and depth supervision are disabled consecutively. The last row gives the performance of a baseline method.

Method	Colour Image			Depth Map	
	PSNR ↑	SSIM ↑	LPIPS ↓	MAE (in cm)↓	Error (in %)↓
Dynamic DS-NeRF	**18.2**	**0.61**	0.41	**4.2**	2.00
DS-NeRF	18.1	**0.61**	**0.39**	4.3	**1.98**
NeRF	13.9	0.45	0.59	48.4	18.91
Pointcloud (baseline)	12.0	0.41	0.59	10.8	4.38

An ablation study is provided in Table 2, where dynamics and depth supervision are disabled consecutively. It can be seen that the dynamic extension does not negatively affect view synthesis performance. The presence of depth supervision has a large positive impact on image quality, with PSNR increasing from 13.9 to 18.1. The depth estimation error decreases drastically from 18.91

to 1.98%. Figure 5 displays the estimated depth for an unseen camera position in the "procedure" phase in comparison with the ground truth depth channel captured from the same camera pose. It can be seen that Dynamic DS-NeRF is able to grasp the geometry of the captured scene accurately. Moreover, the algorithm is able to generate depth values that are not present in the ground truth image due to the depth sensor's hexagon shape or sensor artefacts (e.g., the zero-valued "shadows"). These results show that depth supervision helps NeRF to reconstruct the scene's 3D geometry accurately, resulting in a higher quality of synthesised images.

Draping   Cleaning

Fig. 4. Left-right comparison between the pointcloud projection as baseline method (left) and output of Dynamic DS-NeRF (right) for an unseen camera pose in two surgical phases.

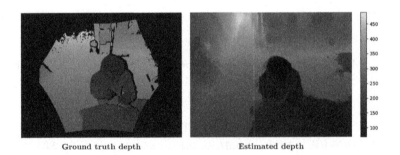

Ground truth depth   Estimated depth

Fig. 5. Depth estimation output of Dynamic DS-NeRF for the "procedure" phase (right) in comparison with the ground truth depth channel (left). Color bar displays distance in cm. (Color figure online)

4.3   Dynamic NeRF for Segmentation

Besides the modelling of consecutive video frames, a dynamic NeRF could also represent the scene at distinct moments in time. We use the algorithm to reconstruct an empty OR at $t = 0$ and the other phases at $t = \{1, 2, 3, 4\}$. Hence, a single model is optimised to represent these five distinct phases jointly. The top row in Fig. 6 displays the model output at four time intervals. To demonstrate that Dynamic DS-NeRF could be used for tasks other than view synthesis, we use this model configuration for unsupervised segmentation of objects and people. The representation of NeRF at $t = 0$ is considered the base image. This image consists of an empty OR, and we assume that its materials are not of interest as long as they do not move. At this time interval, we sample points along camera rays as usual and store the densities $\sigma^{(0)}$. For the other phases, we sample the densities $\sigma^{(t)}$ of the same point locations at the corresponding time interval. To segment the point locations, we subtract the density of the base image from the density of each other phase: $\sigma^{(t)} - \sigma^{(0)}$. The resulting densities correspond to material that is present at t, but that was not present in the empty OR. We used these resulting densities to render the segmented views. It can be seen that the static floor and left counter disappear from the segmented view, while the surgeons, patient and the anaesthetic tower remain present. Note that we do not simply obtain a difference image, but use the 3D estimated density of the Dynamic DS-NeRF model.

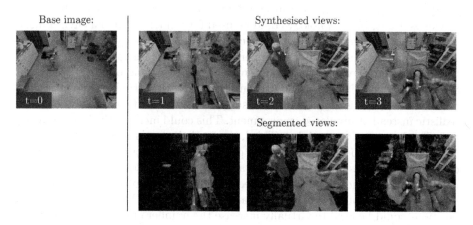

Fig. 6. Top row: synthesised views by Dynamic DS-NeRF, where each surgical phase is reconstructed at a specific time interval t. Bottom row: segmented views, constructed by subtracting the volume densities at $t = 0$ from the densities at t.

5   Discussion

In this work, we explored the use of NeRF for reconstructing surgical scenes in the OR with multi-view RGB-D images from the 4D-OR dataset [9]. We showed that the original NeRF does not provide optimal reconstruction results and that the use of depth supervision benefits image quality and removes the necessity to train the algorithm with tens of camera positions, which are difficult to obtain during a surgical procedure. With an additional time variable at the input vector, we showed the possibility of rendering views with a notion of scene dynamics without affecting image quality. When virtually rotating around the surgical field, the synthesised images remain geometrically consistent, even at interpolated camera locations and time values. On the other hand, the images miss fine details and contain artefacts. Training with larger image resolutions or geometric priors can potentially help to produce views with higher quality.

Dynamic DS-NeRF can generate views from an unseen position above the surgical field with 18.2 PSNR, 0.61 SSIM, 0.41 LPIPS and an average depth error of 2.0%. The method provides better results in comparison to a baseline method that is based on pointcloud projection. Besides a baseline model, we compared three configurations of NeRF: the original NeRF, DS-NeRF and a dynamic DS-NeRF. From the wide range of NeRF architectures available [20], we hypothesis that depth supervision and dynamics are most relevant to the clinical environment. Nevertheless, the exploration of other models, such as pixelNeRF and RegNeRF, would be an interesting follow-up. Other developments in this field are of interest as well, such as methods for speeding up the training of NeRF algorithms [8].

We envision several potential uses for NeRF in the synthesis of OR images or videos. First, the technology could be used for rendering virtual environments displaying real surgeries in 3D. A spectator could watch a video-recorded procedure while moving the virtual camera to arbitrary camera positions in order to obtain a better view. This could enhance the reviewing or learning process. Second, when combining the 3D reconstruction with virtual reality, one could construct a training exercise for new surgeons or OR staff that shows a photo-realistic instead of simulated environment. This could increase the immersiveness and effectiveness of the training. Third, the implicit neural representations of the NeRF-model can be used for further processing. We showed briefly how these can be used for unsupervised segmentation of relevant objects and people. The resulting pointcloud could help to reduce the number of candidate locations for the detection of objects and human poses. Last, renders from new camera positions could be used to virtually increase the number of cameras in a dataset. This is particularly relevant for OR video datasets, due to limitations for camera placement.

In conclusion, Dynamic DS-NeRF is able to synthesise views of a dynamic surgical field in which the 3D geometry is captured accurately. Depth supervision with RGB-D sensing data increases render quality drastically while requiring fewer camera positions, making the technology applicable to clinical environments.

Declarations. This work was sponsored by Johnson & Johnson MedTech. Jelmer M. Wolterink was supported by NWO domain Applied and Engineering Sciences VENI grant (18192).

References

1. Deng, K., Liu, A., Zhu, J.Y., Ramanan, D.: Depth-supervised NERF: fewer views and faster training for free. In: Proceedings of the IEEE/CVF Conference on Computer Vision and Pattern Recognition, pp. 12882–12891 (2022)
2. Gerats, B.G., Wolterink, J.M., Broeders, I.A.: 3D human pose estimation in multi-view operating room videos using differentiable camera projections. Comput. Methods Biomech. Biomed. Eng. Imaging Visual. 1–9 (2022)
3. Goldenberg, M.G., Jung, J., Grantcharov, T.P.: Using data to enhance performance and improve quality and safety in surgery. JAMA Surg. **152**(10), 972–973 (2017)
4. Hansen, L., Siebert, M., Diesel, J., Heinrich, M.P.: Fusing information from multiple 2D depth cameras for 3D human pose estimation in the operating room. Int. J. Comput. Assist. Radiol. Surg. **14**(11), 1871–1879 (2019)
5. Li, T., et al.: Neural 3D video synthesis from multi-view video. In: Proceedings of the IEEE/CVF Conference on Computer Vision and Pattern Recognition, pp. 5521–5531 (2022)
6. Mildenhall, B., et al.: Local light field fusion: practical view synthesis with prescriptive sampling guidelines. ACM Trans. Graph. **38**(4), 1–14 (2019)
7. Mildenhall, B., Srinivasan, P.P., Tancik, M., Barron, J.T., Ramamoorthi, R., Ng, R.: NeRF: representing scenes as neural radiance fields for view synthesis. In: Vedaldi, A., Bischof, H., Brox, T., Frahm, J.-M. (eds.) ECCV 2020. LNCS, vol. 12346, pp. 405–421. Springer, Cham (2020). https://doi.org/10.1007/978-3-030-58452-8_24
8. Müller, T., Evans, A., Schied, C., Keller, A.: Instant neural graphics primitives with a multiresolution hash encoding. ACM Trans. Graph. **41**(4), 1–15 (2022)
9. Özsoy, E., Örnek, E.P., Czempiel, T., Tombari, F., Navab, N.: 4D-or: semantic scene graphs for or domain modeling. In: Wang, L., Dou, Q., Fletcher, P.T., Speidel, S., Li, S. (eds.) MICCAI 2022. LNCS, vol. 13437, pp. 475–485. Springer, Cham (2022). https://doi.org/10.1007/978-3-031-16449-1_45
10. Padoy, N.: Machine and deep learning for workflow recognition during surgery. Minimally Invasive Therapy Allied Technol. **28**(2), 82–90 (2019)
11. Pumarola, A., Corona, E., Pons-Moll, G., Moreno-Noguer, F.: D-NeRF: neural radiance fields for dynamic scenes. In: Proceedings of the IEEE/CVF Confernce on Computer Vision and Pattern Recognition, pp. 10318–10327 (2021)
12. Rematas, K., et al.: Urban radiance fields. In: Proceedings of the IEEE/CVF Conference on Computer Vision and Pattern Recognition, pp. 12932–12942 (2022)
13. Roessle, B., Barron, J.T., Mildenhall, B., Srinivasan, P.P., Nießner, M.: Dense depth priors for neural radiance fields from sparse input views. In: Proceedings of the IEEE/CVF Conference on Computer Vision and Pattern Recognition, June 2022
14. Schonberger, J.L., Frahm, J.M.: Structure-from-motion revisited. In: Proceedings of the IEEE Conference on Computer Vision and Pattern Recognition, pp. 4104–4113 (2016)
15. Sun, Y., Liu, J., Xie, M., Wohlberg, B., Kamilov, U.S.: Coil: coordinate-based internal learning for tomographic imaging. IEEE Trans. Comput. Imaging **7**, 1400–1412 (2021)
16. Wang, Y., Long, Y., Fan, S.H., Dou, Q.: Neural rendering for stereo 3D reconstruction of deformable tissues in robotic surgery. In: Wang, L., Dou, Q., Fletcher, P.T., Speidel, S., Li, S. (eds.) MICCAI 2022. LNCS, vol. 13437, pp. 431–441. Springer, Cham (2022). https://doi.org/10.1007/978-3-031-16449-1_41

17. Wang, Z., Bovik, A.C., Sheikh, H.R., Simoncelli, E.P.: Image quality assessment: from error visibility to structural similarity. IEEE Trans. Image Process. **13**(4), 600–612 (2004)
18. Wei, Y., Liu, S., Rao, Y., Zhao, W., Lu, J., Zhou, J.: Nerfingmvs: guided optimization of neural radiance fields for indoor multi-view stereo. In: Proceedings of the IEEE/CVF International Conference on Computer Vision, pp. 5610–5619 (2021)
19. Wolterink, J.M., Zwienenberg, J.C., Brune, C.: Implicit neural representations for deformable image registration. In: International Conference on Medical Imaging with Deep Learning, pp. 1349–1359. PMLR (2022)
20. Xie, Y., et al.: Neural fields in visual computing and beyond. Comput. Graph. Forum **41**, 641–676 (2022). Wiley Online Library
21. Zhang, R., Isola, P., Efros, A.A., Shechtman, E., Wang, O.: The unreasonable effectiveness of deep features as a perceptual metric. In: Proceedings of the IEEE Conference on Computer Vision and Pattern Recognition, pp. 586–595 (2018)

Revisiting N-CNN for Clinical Practice

Leonardo Antunes Ferreira[1]([✉])(iD), Lucas Pereira Carlini[1](iD),
Gabriel de Almeida Sá Coutrin[1](iD), Tatiany Marcondes Heideirich[1](iD),
Marina Carvalho de Moraes Barros[2](iD), Ruth Guinsburg[2](iD),
and Carlos Eduardo Thomaz[1](iD)

[1] FEI University Center, Sao Bernardo do Campo, SP 09850-901, Brazil
{leferr,cet}@fei.edu.br
[2] Federal University of Sao Paulo, Sao Paulo SP 04024–002, Brazil

Abstract. This paper revisits the Neonatal Convolutional Neural Network (N-CNN) by optimizing its hyperparameters and evaluating how they affect its classification metrics, explainability and reliability, discussing their potential impact in clinical practice. We have chosen hyperparameters that do not modify the original N-CNN architecture, but mainly modify its learning rate and training regularization. The optimization was done by evaluating the improvement in F1 Score for each hyperparameter individually, and the best hyperparameters were chosen to create a Tuned N-CNN. We also applied soft labels derived from the Neonatal Facial Coding System, proposing a novel approach for training facial expression classification models for neonatal pain assessment. Interestingly, while the Tuned N-CNN results point towards improvements in classification metrics and explainability, these improvements did not directly translate to calibration performance. We believe that such insights might have the potential to contribute to the development of more reliable pain evaluation tools for newborns, aiding healthcare professionals in delivering appropriate interventions and improving patient outcomes.

Keywords: Neonatal pain · AI · Explainability · Reliability

1 Introduction

In recent years, Artificial Intelligence (AI) models capable of automatically detecting pain through facial expression analysis have gained significant attention, addressing the issues of human subjectivity and untreated pain [4]. Among these models, the Neonatal Convolutional Neural Network (N-CNN) stands out as the first end-to-end Deep Learning model specifically designed and trained for neonatal pain detection based on facial expressions [14]. In fact, the N-CNN offers a lightweight architecture, that requires less memory and lower computational resources, making it suitable for embedding into mobile or clinical devices within neonatal intensive care units (NICU), ensuring faster training and recall capabilities.

Models intended for clinical practice must exhibit qualities such as accuracy, explainability and reliability [4,8,9]. While the N-CNN has already proven to be accurate [14], limited research has been conducted regarding its hyperparameters, explainability and reliability. Hyperparameter optimization, or tuning, is often used to improve model performance without altering its architecture. Although this performance improvement can be verified by traditional classification metrics and eXplainable Artificial Intelligence (XAI) methods, less attention has been given to model reliability. Being reliable, or calibrated, is a highly desirable property in automatic medical diagnosis, as it enables the estimation of associated risks during clinical practice [8,9]. For instance, high-confidence predictions made by an AI model should exactly match the likelihood of that event occurring, otherwise, overconfident predictions can potentially lead to harmful consequences. In this context, this paper investigates the effects of hyperparameter optimization on classification metrics, explainability and reliability discussing their potential impact in clinical practice.

2   Materials and Methods

For training and testing the N-CNN, we utilized two facial image datasets: iCOPE [1] and UNIFESP [7]. In this way, the model was trained from scratch. The iCOPE dataset comprised 60 images labeled as *"Pain"* and 63 images labeled as *"No Pain"* from 26 newborns (NBs). The UNIFESP dataset included 164 *"Pain"* images and 196 *"No Pain"* images from 30 NBs. To ensure robust evaluation, we employed a leave-sample-subjects-out cross-validation method [3] with 10 folds, using the same 10 folds in all evaluations. Data augmentation was applied to training images in each fold, generating 20 new images with varied parameters such as width and height shift (0.20), rotation (30°), shear (0.15), brightness (0.50–1.10), zoom (0.70–1.50), and horizontal flip.

2.1   N-CNN Performance Evaluation

We selected hyperparameters according to Table 1 that do not modify the original N-CNN architecture [14], primarily affecting learning rate and training regularization. However, a slight modification was required in the N-CNN output activation function to accommodate the Label Smoothing Regularizer (LSR) [13] applied here. Specifically, we replaced the single output neuron activated by a sigmoid function with two neurons activated by a softmax function, being each neuron responsible for providing normalized probabilities for the respective classes. We exclusively focused on the *"Pain"* neuron output, where a threshold of 50% was set to consider a prediction belonging to this class.

Since we separately evaluated each hyperparameter, only those that demonstrated an improvement in F1 Score were selected to make the Tuned N-CNN. To assess the performance of the final model, we employed standard evaluation metrics including Accuracy, F1 Score, Precision, and Sensibility. We also used Grad-CAM (GC) [11] and Integrated Gradients (IG) [12]. Both are considered to be attribution methods and provide further insights into the model's decision-making process, but GC focuses on regions of the images deemed discriminant to classification, whereas IG assigns to each pixel an importance value to the final classification. Regarding the GC, we generated the attribution mask based on the last convolutional layer of the N-CNN, where the model should capture high-level features and semantic information [11].

Additionally, we employed calibration curves to validate whether the confidence scores yielded by the N-CNN are aligned with the frequency of the *"Pain"* class occurrences. The calibration curve plots the frequency of the positive class against the model's confidence scores. A perfectly calibrated model is represented by a 45° diagonal line, that is, the confidence is exactly equal to the actual frequency of events [6]. Points below the diagonal indicate overconfidence, where the model assigns higher probabilities to the occurrence of events than what is observed in reality. Conversely, points above the diagonal indicate a lack of confidence, where the model's confidence is lower than expected despite correctly identifying most of the positive class samples. To quantify if a model is calibrated, we used the Expected Calibration Error (ECE) [10]. This metric divides predictions confidences into K equally-spaced bins, here $K = 10$, and calculates the weighted average of the differences between the frequency of the positive class and the confidence within each bin, providing a quantification of the model's miscalibration [10]. It is important to note that the calibration curve focuses solely in the positive class, considered here as the *"Pain"* class.

2.2 NFCS as Soft Label

One of the studied hyperparameters is the value ϵ of the LSR [13]. It involves adjusting the ground truth labels during training by introducing a small amount of smoothing. Instead of assigning a hard label (binary target) of 0 or 1 to a particular class, LSR assigns a slightly softened label (non-binary target), such as [0.1, 0.9]. This regularization technique helps prevent the model from becoming overconfident and overfitting [13]. Nonetheless, applying the same smoothing value for all labels can potentially result in information loss as we increase ϵ, encouraging the model to be less confident about the true class. Therefore, we propose a novel approach for establishing independent class membership probabilities for each image using the Neonatal Facial Coding System (NFCS) [5], as it is widely used and available in the UNIFESP dataset [7].

The NFCS aims to quantify the presence of 8 facial action units (FAUs) related to pain facial expressions [5]. However, the UNIFESP dataset considered only 5 FAUs due to acquisition limitations [7]. A $NFCS \geq 3$ indicates a facial expression of pain [5], which is easily mapped to a hard label as seen in Fig. 1b. For mapping to a soft label, the sigmoid in Eq. 1 was used, as it offers a degree of smoothness in the probability distribution and provides normalized probabilities between 0 and 1. To assure the sigmoid stays in the range (0–5) of the NFCS scores available in the UNIFESP dataset we added the value 2.5:

$$S(NFCS) = (1 + e^{-NFCS+2.5})^{-1}. \tag{1}$$

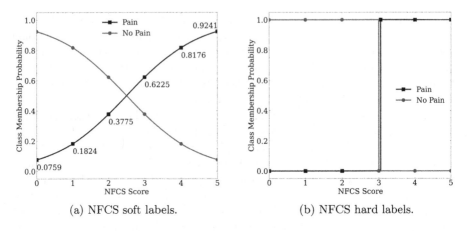

(a) NFCS soft labels.   (b) NFCS hard labels.

Fig. 1. NFCS mapping to soft and hard labels.

Equation 1 maps the NFCS score to the *"Pain"* class membership probability, while the complement is used for the *"No Pain"* class. The final soft label is made of $[1 - S(NFCS), S(NFCS)]$ (Fig. 1a).

Using the NFCS as a soft label, we encourage the output neuron of the *"Pain"* class to be more confident in images with more FAUs of pain. In contrast, the output neuron of the *"No Pain"* class will be more confident when there are few or no FAUs of pain. It is important to acknowledge that the availability of NFCS scores was limited to the UNIFESP dataset. Therefore, to ensure consistency in our evaluations and fair comparisons with other hyperparameters, we excluded the iCOPE images from the original 10 training folds. However, the iCOPE images remained a part of the test folds.

3 Results

As we evaluated each hyperparameter individually, some were kept fixed when not being assessed, based on [14]: learning rate ($1e^{-4}$), total number of epochs (100), and batch size (16). Model checkpoints were created if the test loss value decreased, and we only selected the lowest loss value checkpoint for evaluation.

3.1 Metrics

Changing image size and optimizer did not improve F1 Score. The LSR improved F1 Score in +4.21% when using $\epsilon = 0.3$. Cosine Annealing presented the best results to the learning rate schedulers, with an improvement of +0.84%. Furthermore, increasing the number of epochs led to a notable improvement of +2.99%. Surprisingly, even with 30% fewer images for training, the proposed NFCS soft label achieved the same F1 Score as the Original N-CNN 74.10%, demonstrating the positive impact of integrating probabilities during training.

Table 2 presents the classification metrics of the test folds for the Original and Tuned N-CNN, with standard deviations. All metrics are statistically significant by the *t-test* ($p < 0.05$), highlighting that hyperparameter optimization alone can lead to improvements in classification results without altering the N-CNN architecture.

Table 1. Hyperparameters search space and selected values.

Hyperparameter	Search Space	Selected	F1 Score	Δ
Image Size	64 × 64, 120 × 120, 224 × 224	120 × 120	74.10%	0%
Optimizer	Adam, Adagrad, RMSProp, SGD	RMSprop	74.10%	0%
Epochs	50 to 120	120	77.09%	+2.99%
Label Smoothing	0.1, 0.3, 0.5 and NFCS Soft Label	0.3	78.31%	+4.21%
Schedulers	Step, Exponential, Cosine Annealing	Cosine Annealing	74.94%	+0.84%

Table 2. Classification metrics for Original and Tuned N-CNN.

Model	Accuracy	F1 Score	Precision	Recall
Original	78.69% ± 5%	74.10% ± 6%	83.17% ± 8%	68.96% ± 9%
Tuned	82.97% ± 5%	79.74% ± 6%	85.63% ± 8%	75.43% ± 9%
Δ	+4.28%	+5.64%	+2.46%	+6.47%

3.2 Reliability

Despite achieving higher classification metrics, the Tuned N-CNN did not exhibit the same level of calibration as the Original N-CNN. Specifically, the calibration curve of the Tuned N-CNN displayed an "S" shape, indicating overestimation of predictions with low confidences and underestimation of predictions with high confidences (Fig. 2a). This difference in calibration is confirmed by the ECE metric [10], with the Tuned N-CNN yielding an $ECE = 0.091$, approximately three times greater than the Original N-CNN's $ECE = 0.035$.

As shown in Fig. 2a, of the predicted samples for which the model exhibits confidence around 20%, less than 10% of them were actually in the *"Pain"* class.

On the other hand, almost all samples with 80% confidence were of the *"Pain"* class, indicating that the Tuned N-CNN has a lower confidence in this interval. Conversely, when considering the Original N-CNN, the model exhibits limited confidence in the 50% to 60% range, indicating challenges in confidently classifying samples within the threshold region of the *"Pain"* class.

The low confidence phenomenon in Tuned N-CNN, is further depicted in Fig. 2b, showing how the percentage of samples with confidences over 90%, from Original N-CNN, shifted to a less confident range due to the LSR technique which tends to reduce model overconfidence.

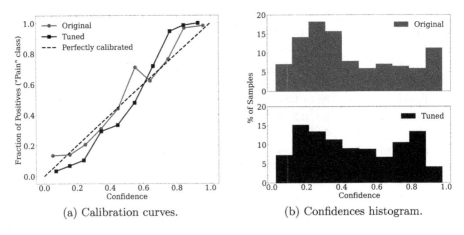

(a) Calibration curves.   (b) Confidences histogram.

Fig. 2. Calibration results of the Original and Tuned N-CNN.

3.3   Explainability

Figures 3 and 4 depict images correctly classified by both models, providing insights into the explainability improvements when accessing the Tuned N-CNN. For example, the Tuned N-CNN focused on regions of the NBs face, ignoring artifacts such as clothing (Fig. 3d). In addition, it was found that the IG_{Tuned} acquired a more uniform distribution across the NBs face, unlike the $IG_{Original}$, which gave more attention to the eyes and mouth. As for the *"No Pain"* images, GC_{Tuned} concentrated on the forehead and cheeks (Fig. 3e), contrasting with $GC_{Original}$, which did not obtain a central area of focus.

Our results revealed a correlation between XAI and the predicted confidence in both Original and Tuned N-CNNs. Confidences ranging from 40% to 60% were observed to explain features not related to the NB face, as it can be seen in Fig. 3c and 3f, that is, an overconfidence in the *"Pain"* class. This interpretation was also observed for images that both models incorrectly classified. In contrast, confidences above 80% or below 20% in the *"Pain"* class that were correctly classified presented an attribution mask deemed more relevant to clinical practice.

Moreover, both *IG* and *GC* results mainly gave more importance to the mouth region, which agrees with one of the observed regions by neonatologists [2].

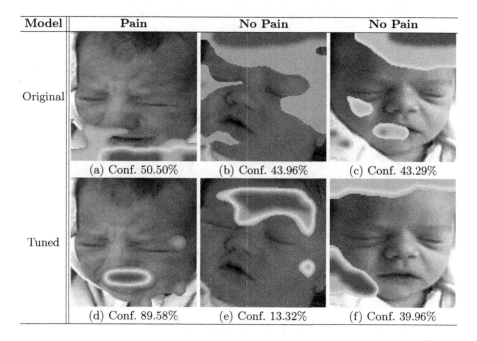

Model	Pain	No Pain	No Pain
Original	(a) Conf. 50.50%	(b) Conf. 43.96%	(c) Conf. 43.29%
Tuned	(d) Conf. 89.58%	(e) Conf. 13.32%	(f) Conf. 39.96%

Fig. 3. *GC* attribution masks and predictions confidence in the *"Pain"* class.

4   Discussion

Based on our observations, training with soft labels instead of hard labels proved beneficial to the N-CNN classification metrics, which has not been extensively explored in the existing literature. We believe that the NFCS soft label proposed here can surpass the best LSR result found if iCOPE NFCS scores were available, emphasizing the necessity for standardization across neonatal pain scales in datasets, promoting consistency and comparability in future research. This technique can also be applied to various clinical pain scales that quantify the presence or absence of pain, not only to NFCS.

Regarding reliability, calibrated predictions are essential to accurately estimate the associated risks in critical settings like in NICU. For instance, predictions with 90% confidence in the *"Pain"* class should prompt immediate action as the NB has a real 90% chance of being in pain, while predictions with 60% confidence require more careful analysis by healthcare professionals, as the AI model exhibits uncertainty in its prediction for the specific situation of the NB. The fact that the calibration of the Tuned N-CNN has worsened raises an important

Model	Pain	No Pain	No Pain
Original			
	(a) Conf. 50.50%	(b) Conf. 43.96%	(c) Conf. 43.29%
Tuned			
	(d) Conf. 89.58%	(e) Conf. 13.32%	(f) Conf. 39.96%

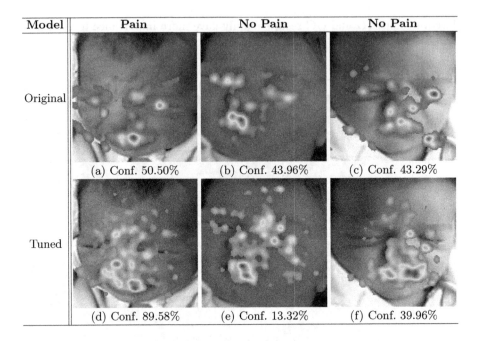

Fig. 4. *IG* attribution masks and predictions confidence in the *"Pain"* class.

question: to what extent does improving classification metrics benefit clinical practice? While a +5% increase in the Tuned N-CNN metrics may lead to more accurate automatic predictions, healthcare professionals may only rely on these predictions if the model's decision-making process is explainable and aligned with the actual probability of event occurrence.

The use of *IG* on the Tuned N-CNN revealed that more pixels contributed to the final prediction. We believe that this increase in relevant pixels were a contributing factor to the Tuned N-CNN achieving higher metrics. However, the N-CNN still has some explainability limitations when compared to other Deep-Learning models [3], due to the shallow architecture which may limit its capacity to capture complex patterns and nuances in neonatal pain assessment. Nevertheless, by visualizing these attribution masks, healthcare professionals can better understand the model's reasoning and gain trust in its predictions.

5   Conclusion

In this work, we revisited the N-CNN model by optimizing its hyperparameters and evaluating how tuning affects its classification metrics, explainability and reliability. Although we observed improvements in classification metrics and explainability, these improvements did not simply translate to calibration performance. An uncalibrated model applied in clinical practice can lead to a lack of trust by the health professional in the model's predictions, resulting in the rejection of the technology. While enhancements in traditional metrics are notable, achieving reliability and explainability in any AI model intended for the health sector is imperative to ensure reliable and actionable predictions.

We believe that the new approach proposed here of using the NFCS as a soft label might disclose a new paradigm in training classification models for neonatal pain analysis based on facial expressions. As future work, we intend to explore soft labels based on clinical pain scales and calibration methods, ensuring that confidences align with the actual frequency of both pain and no-pain events. Overall, we understand that it is crucial to address the issue of uncalibrated confidences as risk estimators in the medical field, not only to prevent erroneous automatic decision-making and foster trust among healthcare professionals, but also to facilitate the responsible and effective use of AI in clinical practice.

Acknowledgments. This study was financed in part by CAPES (Finance Code 001) and FAPESP (2018/13076-9).

References

1. Brahnam, S., Chuang, C.F., Shih, F.Y., Slack, M.R.: Machine recognition and representation of neonatal facial displays of acute pain. Artif. Intell. Med. **36**(3), 211–222 (2006)
2. Carlini, L.P., et al.: A visual perception framework to analyse neonatal pain in face images. In: Campilho, A., Karray, F., Wang, Z. (eds.) ICIAR 2020. LNCS, vol. 12131, pp. 233–243. Springer, Cham (2020). https://doi.org/10.1007/978-3-030-50347-5_21
3. Coutrin, G.Ã., et al.: Convolutional neural networks for newborn pain assessment using face images: a quantitative and qualitative comparison. In: Proceedings of the 3rd International Conference on Medical Imaging and Computer-Aided Diagnosis, MICAD 2022. LNEE. Springer, Cham (2024). ISSN: 1876-1100
4. Gkikas, S., Tsiknakis, M.: Automatic assessment of pain based on deep learning methods: a systematic review. Comput. Methods Programs Biomed. **231**, 107365 (2023)
5. Grunau, R.V., Craig, K.D.: Pain expression in neonates: facial action and cry. Pain **28**(3), 395–410 (1987)
6. Guo, C., Pleiss, G., Sun, Y., Weinberger, K.Q.: On calibration of modern neural networks. In: International Conference on Machine Learning, pp. 1321–1330. PMLR (2017)
7. Heiderich, T.M., Leslie, A.T.F.S., Guinsburg, R.: Neonatal procedural pain can be assessed by computer software that has good sensitivity and specificity to detect facial movements. Acta Paediatr. **104**(2), e63–e69 (2015)
8. Jiang, X., Osl, M., Kim, J., Ohno-Machado, L.: Calibrating predictive model estimates to support personalized medicine. J. Am. Med. Inform. Assoc. **19**(2), 263–274 (2012)
9. Kompa, B., Snoek, J., Beam, A.L.: Second opinion needed: communicating uncertainty in medical machine learning. NPJ Digit. Med. **4**(1), 4 (2021)
10. Naeini, M.P., Cooper, G., Hauskrecht, M.: Obtaining well calibrated probabilities using Bayesian binning. In: Proceedings of the AAAI Conference on Artificial Intelligence, vol. 29 (2015)

11. Selvaraju, R.R., Cogswell, M., Das, A., Vedantam, R., Parikh, D., Batra, D.: Grad-cam: visual explanations from deep networks via gradient-based localization. In: Proceedings of the IEEE International Conference on Computer Vision, pp. 618–626 (2017)
12. Sundararajan, M., Taly, A., Yan, Q.: Axiomatic attribution for deep networks. In: International Conference on Machine Learning, pp. 3319–3328. PMLR (2017)
13. Szegedy, C., Vanhoucke, V., Ioffe, S., Shlens, J., Wojna, Z.: Rethinking the inception architecture for computer vision. In: Proceedings of the IEEE Conference on Computer Vision and Pattern Recognition, pp. 2818–2826 (2016)
14. Zamzmi, G., Paul, R., Goldgof, D., Kasturi, R., Sun, Y.: Pain assessment from facial expression: neonatal convolutional neural network (n-CNN). In: 2019 International Joint Conference on Neural Networks (IJCNN), pp. 1–7. IEEE (2019)

Video-Based Hand Pose Estimation for Remote Assessment of Bradykinesia in Parkinson's Disease

Gabriela T. Acevedo Trebbau[1]([✉]), Andrea Bandini[2], and Diego L. Guarin[1]

[1] Department of Applied Physiology and Kinesiology, University of Florida, Gainesville,
FL 32611, USA
d.guarinlopez@ufl.edu
[2] Interdisciplinary Research Center "Health Science" – Scuola Superiore Sant'Anna, Pisa, Italy

Abstract. There is a growing interest in using pose estimation algorithms for video-based assessment of Bradykinesia in Parkinson's Disease (PD) to facilitate remote disease assessment and monitoring. However, the accuracy of pose estimation algorithms in videos recorded from video streaming services during Telehealth appointments has not been studied. In this study, we used seven off-the-shelf hand pose estimation models to estimate the movement of the thumb and index fingers in videos of the finger-tapping (FT) test recorded from Healthy Controls (HC) and participants with PD and under two different conditions: *streaming* (videos recorded during a live Zoom meeting) and *on-device* (videos recorded locally with high-quality cameras). The accuracy and reliability of the models were estimated by comparing the models' output with manual results. Three of the seven models demonstrated good accuracy for *on-device* recordings, and the accuracy decreased significantly for *streaming* recordings. We observed a negative correlation between movement speed and the model's accuracy for the *streaming* recordings. Additionally, we evaluated the reliability of ten movement features related to bradykinesia extracted from video recordings of PD patients performing the FT test. While most of the features demonstrated excellent reliability for *on-device* recordings, most of the features demonstrated poor to moderate reliability for *streaming* recordings. Our findings highlight the limitations of pose estimation algorithms when applied to video recordings obtained during Telehealth visits, and demonstrate that *on-device* recordings can be used for automatic video-assessment of bradykinesia in PD.

Keywords: Telehealth · Machine Leaning · Parkinson's Disease

1 Introduction

There is a growing interest in developing methods for automatic, video-based quantification of motor symptoms in Parkinson's Disease; in particular, many studies have proposed methodologies for assessing bradykinesia from videos of the finger tapping (FT)

Supplementary Information The online version contains supplementary material available at https://doi.org/10.1007/978-3-031-46005-0_21.

test. [1–4]. Bradykinesia is a cardinal motor symptom of PD characterized by slowness of movement, decrease in movement amplitude, hesitations/halts during movement, and progressive decrease in movement speed [5, 6]. The FT test is a clinical motor assessment used to evaluate upper-limb bradykinesia, and many studies have developed machine learning algorithms to assess bradykinesia severity using videos of the FT tests. Most of these studies use markerless hand pose estimation algorithms to estimate the subjects' hand movements during the FT test and quantify the degree of bradykinesia [1–4, 7–10].

Available methods automatically assess bradykinesia from standard videos of the FT test, making them potentially useful tools to support remote assessment during Tele-health appointments. However, most studies employ high-quality videos recorded in controlled laboratory or clinical settings where technical components related to video quality, frame rate, and image resolution were tightly controlled throughout the recordings. Such conditions are not common during Telehealth appointments as Telehealth platforms prioritize connection latency over image quality and frame rate [11]. It is not known to what extent aspects related to image quality, information loss, and variable frame rate affect the accuracy of markerless hand pose estimation algorithms and negatively impact the automatic assessment of bradykinesia. There is a need to validate the accuracy of hand pose estimation algorithms in videos recorded under conditions similar to those encountered in Telehealth appointments.

This study aims to evaluate the accuracy and reliability of automatically estimated hand movements from videos of the FT test recorded during two conditions: (1) *streaming* (i.e., Zoom recordings), and (2) *on-device* (high-quality recordings). We performed two experiments to explore the effects of the recording conditions on the accuracy and reliability of hand pose estimation algorithms. For the first experiment, we investigated the accuracy of seven off-the-shelf hand pose estimation algorithms for tracking hand movements during the FT test in healthy subjects for both recording conditions. We compared the results provided by the algorithms against manual annotations. For this experiment, we employed videos of healthy controls demonstrating a wide range of movement speeds and amplitudes. For the second experiment, we investigated the reliability of video-based kinematic features related to bradykinesia derived from videos of subjects previously diagnosed with PD and under stable deep brain stimulation (DBS).

1.1 Previous Work

Multiple studies have used machine learning algorithms for automatic assessment of bradykinesia from videos of the FT test. A common approach involves using hand pose estimation algorithms to track the movement of the index and thumb fingers during the test, and then compute movement and velocity-based features that can be used to identify persons with PD from healthy controls and to estimate disease severity by predicting a clinical score such as the Movement Disorder Society – Unified Parkinson's Disease Rating Scale (MDS-UPDRS) score for the FT test (ranging from 0 to 4). H. Li et al. proposed a method that estimates hand pose features (location of 21 joints in the hand), motion features (temporal inter-frame variation of the hand skeleton data), and geometry features (inter-joint relationship of hand skeleton data) to automatically classify the motor severity based on the MDS-UPDRS score for the FT test [1]. Their proposed method for automatic scoring achieved an accuracy of 72.4%, demonstrating accurate and reliable results [1]. Z. Li, et al. proposed using one-dimensional time series data of velocity and movement range of the finger movements as input features to predict the MDS-UPDRS score for FT [2]. Using a fivefold cross-validation method, they achieved an average prediction accuracy of 79.7% [2]. In addition, they analyzed each feature set individually to investigate the importance of range and velocity information for predicting the MDS-UPDRS score and found that the accuracy obtained using the movement range data was higher than the accuracy obtained using the velocity data (68.4% and 46.8%, respectively) [2]. N. Yang, et al. proposed using tapping rate, tapping frozen times, and tapping amplitude variation as input features to predict the FT test severity [4]. They evaluated their method for each hand separately; for the left hand they obtained a micro average of precision, recall, and f1-score of 88%, 89%, and 88%, respectively, and for the right hand they obtained a micro average of precision, recall, and f1-score of 85%, 85%, and 84%, respectively [4]. Y. Liu, et al., proposed using four parameters related to finger movement amplitude and velocity, and their variabilities to automatically predict the MDS-UPDRS score for the FT test [7]. They achieved an average accuracy of 89.7% [7]. K. W. Park, et al., employed pose estimation algorithms to extract features related to speed, amplitude, and fatigue during the FT task. They obtained good agreement (Intra Class Correlation = 0.8) and an absolute agreement rate of 70% between the predicted and the clinician scores [10]. Finally, G. Morinan et al. proposed a computer-vision-based approach to extract features relevant to bradykinesia and predict the MDS-UPDRS ratings for the limb-based bradykinesia items [9]. The features proposed described the main aspects evaluated during the MDS-UPDRS; amplitude, speed, hesitations and halts, and decrementing amplitude and speed [9]. They obtained an acceptable accuracy (the percentage of estimates for which the prediction error was zero or ±1) of 84%, for the prediction of the MDS-UPDRS score for the FT test [9].

2   Methods

2.1   Participants

Experiment 1. Ten healthy subjects participated in this study (6 females, 4 males; age range 19–57). Participants were included if they: (1) were fluent in English; (2) have no self-reported history of neurological or movement disorders; and (3) did not demonstrate any signs of cognitive impairments as measured by a score of 26 or higher in the Montreal Cognitive Assessment (MoCA) [12]. All participants were recorded during one session at Florida Institute of Technology in Melbourne, Florida, U.S. The study was approved by the institutional Research Ethics Board and participants signed an informed consent form according to the declaration of Helsinki.

Experiment 2. Six patients previously diagnosed with Parkinson's Disease (PD) participated in this study (1 female, 5 males; age range 64–71). Participants were included if they: (1) were fluent in English; (2) have been previously diagnosed with Parkinson's Disease by a movement disorders specialist using the UK PD Brain Bank diagnostic criteria [13]; (3) were under stable DBS; and (4) did not demonstrate signs of moderate cognitive impairments as measured by a score of 18 or higher in the MoCA [14]. All participants were recorded during one session at the University of Florida, Gainesville, Florida, U.S. Participants were in the OFF-medication state, they had not taken any medication to control their Parkinsonism for at least 12h before starting the recording. The study was approved by the institutional Research Ethics Board and Participants signed an informed consent form according to the declaration of Helsinki.

2.2 Recordings

Experiment 1. The recording sessions were held in a quiet, well-illuminated room. Participants sat down comfortably facing a Logitech BRIO camera positioned on a tripod and the webcam of a Dell XPS laptop positioned on a table. A Zoom meeting was held between the laptop and a computer workstation set up in an office nearby the recording room. The workstation was connected to the internet through ethernet, and the laptop was connected to the local Wi-Fi network. The camera and laptop's webcam were adjusted to record the same view, which included the subjects' torso and head. One researcher was in the recording room guiding the participants, while another researcher was supervising the Zoom meeting. We acquired videos using two recording setups: (1) high-speed Logitech BRIO camera, recording at 100 fps with a resolution of 1280x720 pixels (px) (*on-device*); and (2) built-in webcam from a Dell XPS laptop computer streaming through a Zoom meeting (*streaming*), the Zoom meeting was recorded at 25 fps with a resolution of 640x360 px on the computer workstation.

During the recording session, participants were asked to tap their index and thumb as fast as possible, fully separating the fingers after each tap for fifteen seconds. Subjects were requested to start the task with the fingers fully separated. We collected a total of four videos from each participant: one video for each hand (right and left) and with each camera (on-*device* and *streaming*).

Experiment 2. The recording sessions were held in a well-illuminated clinical examination room. Participants sat down facing an iPhone 12 and an iPad that were set up on two tripods. A Zoom meeting was held between the iPad and a computer workstation set up in an office nearby to the recording room. The workstation, iPad, and iPhone were connected to the local Wi-Fi network. The iPhone and iPad cameras were adjusted to record the same view, which included the participant's whole body. One researcher was in the examination room guiding the participants, while another researcher was supervising the Zoom meeting. We acquired videos using two recording setups: (1) iPhone 12 camera, recording at 60 fps with a resolution of 1080×1920 px (*on-device*); and (2) iPad front camera, streaming through a Zoom meeting (*streaming*), the Zoom meeting was recorded at 25 fps with a resolution of 640×360 px on the computer workstation.

Participants with PD arrived at the recording room with the Deep Brain Stimulators (DBS) turned ON and performed an initial recording session of the FT test (DBS ON). Then, the DBS was turned OFF and the recording session was repeated (DBS OFF). A total of eight videos were collected from each participant with PD, one video for each hand (right and left), each camera (*on-device* and *streaming*) and with the DBS turned ON and OFF (DBS ON and DBS OFF).

2.3 Video Analysis

Manual Annotations. A single annotator manually localized the (x, y) coordinates of the tip of the thumb and index fingers and calculated the Euclidian distance in each video frame, resulting in a distance time series with the same length as the video. The distance signals were smoothed using a Savitzky-Golay filter and normalized between 0 and 1, indicating the minimum and maximum distance between the fingers. These signals were considered as the ground truth for the remainder of the study.

Pose Estimation

Experiment 1. Table 1. describes the seven off-the-shelf hand pose estimation models used in this study. The open-source models are available in two Python libraries: MediaPipe and MMPose. The models' input was a video frame containing one or two hands, and the output was the (x, y) coordinates of 21 hand landmarks for each hand, corresponding to the base of the hand, the carpometacarpal, metacarpophalangeal, and interphalangeal joints, and tip of the thumb, and the metacarpophalangeal, proximal interphalangeal, and distal interphalangeal joins, and tip of the remainder fingers. We extracted the (x, y) coordinates for the tip of the thumb and index fingers and calculated the Euclidean distance between these two landmarks for each video frame, resulting in a distance time series with the same duration as the video recording. Signals were smoothed and normalized as the ground truth signals.

Experiment 2. We selected the best-performing model from the results of Experiment 1 to analyze the video from participants with PD. We followed the same protocol as Experiment 1 to extract, smooth, and normalize the distance signals.

Feature Extraction. From the distance signals obtained in Experiment 2, we extracted ten movement features related to bradykinesia, mean and coefficient of variation (cv) of movement frequency, mean and cv of movement amplitude, mean and cv of movement speed, range of period duration, roughness, decrement in amplitude, and decrement in speed. These features have been used previously for video-based assessment of Bradykinesia [9]. These features are based on the peaks (maximum opening) and valleys (maximum closing) of the distance signal; we identify the peaks and valleys manually from the videos to guarantee consistency among the different recording environments. A description of the features is presented in the supplementary material. Features extracted from the manually annotated, *on-device* videos were considered as the ground truth for the remainder of this study.

2.4 Statistical Analyses

Experiment 1. We calculated the coefficient of determination (R^2 score) to evaluate the similarity between the ground truth and automatically estimated distance signals. We performed the Shapiro-Wilk test of the R^2 scores to test for normality and compared R^2 scores obtained from the *on-device* and *streaming* recordings using a t-test or a Mann-Whitney U test in case of non-normal distributions. We also performed a Spearman Correlation analysis between the subjects' maximum speed and R^2 score. The level of statistical significance was set at 0.05.

Table 1. Description of the Seven Hand Pose Estimation Models Used in this Study.

Model Name	Python Library	Training Database	Architecture
model 1	MediaPipe	Google's Database	BlazePose
model 2	MMPose	COCO Hands [19]	HRNet [20]
model 3			MobileNet [22]
model 4			ResNet [21]
model 5		OneHand10k [18]	HRNet [20]
model 6			MobileNet [22]
model 7			ResNet [21]

Experiment 2. We calculated the Intraclass correlation coefficient (ICC (2,1); single random rater, absolute agreement) to assess the reliability between the ground truth features and the features estimated using a hand pose estimation algorithm. Values with negative ICC were set to 0.0 as suggested by J. J. Bartko [15]. ICC values < 0.50 indicated poor reliability, values between 0.50 to 0.74 indicated moderate reliability, values between 0.75 to 0.9 indicated good reliability, and values > 0.9 indicated excellent reliability [16]. The level of statistical significance was set at 0.05.

3   Results

3.1   Experiment 1: Pose Estimation for Automatic Movement Tracking

Figure 1 presents two frames from the *streaming* and *on-device* recordings from a HC demonstrating the maximum opening and closing of the fingers during the FT test. Figure 2 presents the manually and automatically derived distance signals for the right hand of two HC demonstrating the lowest and highest movement speeds.

Table 2. shows the results of the statistical analysis comparing the R^2 score between the manual and automatically derived distance signals for the *on-device* and *streaming* recordings. *Model 1, model 5,* and *model 7* achieved the highest average R^2 score for *streaming* and *on-device* recordings. All other models demonstrated R^2 score values lower than 0.9 for *streaming* and *on-device* recordings, with some models demonstrating negative R^2 score values. The last column of Table 2. presents the statistical comparison between the R^2 score obtained for *on-device* and *streaming* recordings. For most models, the *on-device* recordings demonstrated significantly higher R^2 scores when compared to the *streaming* recordings. *Model 3* and *model 4* did not show significantly different R^2 scores between the recording conditions.

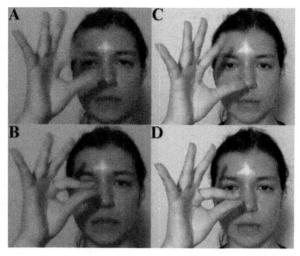

Fig. 1. Frames from a video recording of the FT test. A and B are frames from the *streaming* recording A) maximum opening (peak), and B) maximum closing (valley). C and D are frames from the *on-device* recording, C) maximum opening (peak), and D) maximum closing (valley)

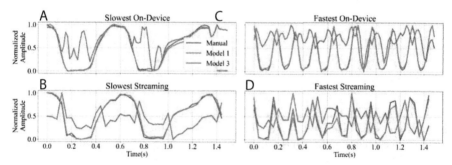

Fig. 2. Blue lines show the manually derived distance signals between the tip of the index and thumb fingers of the right hand for the HC participants with the lowest (left column, maximum speed of 8.35/s) and highest (right column, maximum speed of 22.3/s) maximum speeds. Orange and green lines show the distance signals between the tip of the index and thumb fingers yielded by the best and worst performing models (Model 1 and Model 3, respectively). First and second row present the results obtained with *on-device* and *streaming* recordings respectively.

Figure 3 shows the results obtained for the correlation analysis between R^2 scores and the maximum speed for the best performing models. For the *streaming* recordings, there was a significant negative correlation between the subjects' maximum speeds and R^2 scores for *models 1, 5,* and *7*. The correlation results and respective p-values are presented in the supplementary materials.

Table 2. Statistical Analyses Results for Experiment 1

Model	R^2 score Mean $\pm$ Std		P-value
	Streaming	On-Device	
model 1	0.90 ± 0.10	0.98 ± 0.02	< 0.001A
model 2	0.23 ± 0.78	0.73 ± 0.44	0.005A
model 3	-0.78 ± 0.91	-0.32 ± 0.84	0.105B
model 4	-0.17 ± 1.14	0.31 ± 0.66	0.102A
model 5	0.73 ± 0.25	0.97 ± 0.04	< 0.001A
model 6	0.53 ± 0.52	0.88 ± 0.19	0.002A
model 7	0.67 ± 0.36	0.95 ± 0.11	< 0.001A

A Mann Whitney U Test
B T-test

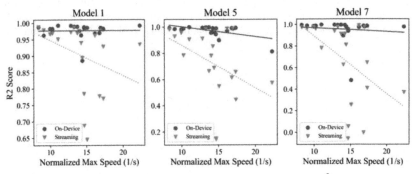

Fig. 3. Scatter plot showing the relation between maximum speed and R^2 scores for *model 1, 5* and *7*. The blue and orange results represent the *on-device* and *streaming* recordings, respectively. The lines represent the fest fit results obtained via least mean squares minimization.

3.2 Experiment 2: Reliability of Automatic Pose Estimation-Based Features

On-device **Recordings:** For the *on-device* recordings (see supplemental material), most of the features achieved excellent reliability for DBS ON and DBS OFF (ICC > 0.90). Only *Roughness* demonstrated poor reliability for DBS OFF (ICC = 0.37) and moderate reliability for DBS ON (ICC = 0.72).

Streaming Recordings: For the *streaming* recordings (see supplemental material), most features achieved poor or moderate reliability for DBS ON and DBS OFF (ICC from 0.0 to 0.71). Only measures related to movement frequency and period duration achieved good or excellent reliability (ICC => 75).

4   Discussion

In this study, we used hand pose estimation algorithms to automatically track the movements of the hand and extract movement features from videos of the FT test, a widely used motor task for assessment of upper limbs bradykinesia in PD. We explored the effects of various recording conditions, including *on-device* and *streaming* recordings, on the accuracy of pose estimation models. The *streaming* recordings are similar to those observed during Telehealth appointments, so that our results are relevant to understand the limitations of hand pose estimation algorithm in the remote assessment of bradykinesia. Additionally, we explored the impact of both recording conditions on the reliability of ten video-based movement features related to bradykinesia.

4.1   Accuracy of Hand Pose Estimation Models

The first part of this study evaluated the performance of different hand pose estimation models during the FT test. Our results indicate that *model 1* is the best-performing model for pose estimation, demonstrating R^2 scores of at least 0.90 for all recording settings. This model is part of Google's MediaPipe and was trained with a private dataset consisting of 30.000 natural and artificial images [17]. Regarding the other models, we observed that models trained with the OneHand10k dataset demonstrated better performance compared to those trained with the COCO database. This observation might be explained because the OneHand10K dataset includes single hand images covering a wide range of hand poses [18], whereas the COCO dataset contains full body images [19]. Thus, models trained with the OneHand10K dataset are optimized for hand pose estimation, while the models trained with the COCO dataset are optimized for whole-body pose estimation. Moreover, HRNet outperformed all other architectures, achieving the highest R2 scores with the given dataset. This result might be attributed to HRNet's ability to maintain the frame's resolution throughout the process, resulting in more spatially precise representations [20]. In contrast, ResNet and MobileNet initially encode the input frame as low-resolution representations [21, 22], leading to reduced accuracy. Our results also demonstrated that *on-device* recordings yielded significantly higher R^2 scores than *streaming* recordings for most models. Zoom adjusts the true frame rate and image compression based on the internet connectivity, resulting in video with variable video quality and repeated frames. During the streaming recordings we observed images with high pixelization and blurring, especially during high-speed movement - see for example Fig. 1A -, which negatively affected the accuracy of hand pose estimation algorithms. In contrast, *on-device* recordings have constant frame rate and compression throughout the video, resulting in overall high accuracy.

Our result also showed that the movement maximum speed significantly impacted the model's performance for the *streaming* recordings. We link this phenomenon with the blurring effect observed in the *streaming* recording, where the shape of the fingers was lost for high-speed movements, causing the hand pose estimation model to misplace the finger. These results are important because inconsistent rhythm and the sequence effect can appear early in PD, while slowness of movement will appear later as the disease progresses. Based on this observation, we argue that *streaming* recordings with variable video quality and rate are not adequate for assessing bradykinesia from videos of the FT test as assessment will be influenced by the movement speed.

4.2 Reliability of Automatically Estimated Movement Features

The second part of this study investigated the reliability of video-based movement features used to quantify bradykinesia across different recording conditions. When considering *on-device* recordings, most of the features resulted in good to excellent reliability. In contrast, *Roughness'* reliability was poor for DBS OFF (ICC = 0.37) and moderate for DBS ON (ICC = 0.72). The low reliability is likely because *Roughness* relies on acceleration and jerk, the second and third-order derivatives of the distance signal, and derivatives are known to amplify the signal's noise [23]. Our findings suggest that features based on the distance signal and its first-order derivative (velocity) can be reliably estimated from *on-device* videos recorded at 60 fps with a resolution of 1080 $\times$ 1920 px but features based on higher-order derivatives require different recording conditions to the ones explored in this study.

When considering *streaming* recordings, most of the features demonstrated poor to moderate reliability. Features that did not depend on the results provided by the hand pose estimation algorithm provided excellent or good reliability, including *MeanFreq*, *CovarFreq*, and *PeriodRange*. The low reliability can be explained by errors in the distance signal caused by the low video quality. These findings suggest that there is a clear impact of the streaming recordings' video quality in the estimation of pose estimation-based features and highlights the limitations of using streaming recordings for automatic assessment of bradykinesia from videos of the FT test.

4.3 Limitations

Several limitations should be considered when interpreting the results. First, the small sample size restricts the generalizability of the findings and limits the statistical power of the analyses. Future studies with larger sample sizes are needed to validate and strengthen our findings. Second, the setup for the streaming video recordings was standardized for all subjects, which does not capture the variations in connectivity, lighting conditions, and background noise commonly encountered in real-world Telehealth appointments. These variations could potentially impact the streaming quality and may influence the performance of pose estimation models. Future work should explore different streaming setups, proving a wider range of situations encountered in Telehealth visits. Third, the investigation focused solely on one streaming platform, Zoom, which does not represent the technical capacities and quality offered by other platforms. Exploring multiple streaming platforms would provide a broader perspective on the influence of streaming conditions in automatic movement tracking applications. Another limitation is that for this study we manually selected the peaks and valleys in the distance signal, which might not be efficient in real-world applications. Consequently, the impact of low-quality conditions was not appreciated for features that depend on movement frequency and period duration. Future works should include algorithms for the automatic detection of peaks and valleys to investigate the impacts of streaming conditions in fully automated systems for feature extraction.

5   Conclusion

In conclusion, this study focused on evaluating the accuracy and reliability of pose estimation-based movement data estimated from videos of the FT test recorded on-device and streaming settings. Our results demonstrated that Google MediaPipe and other off-the-shelf hand pose estimation algorithms provide accurate and reliable hand movement tracking and movement features for *on-device* recordings. These findings suggest that is feasible to use *on-device* recordings in combination with hand pose estimation algorithms for automatic, remote assessment of bradykinesia in PD. In contrast, the models' performance of the algorithms significantly decreased when applied to *streaming* video recordings. In particular, the model's performance was severely affected by the movement speed, with higher speed resulting in significantly worst performance. Moreover, clinically relevant movement features automatically estimated from streaming videos demonstrated poor reliability when compared to manually derived measures. These findings suggest that *streaming* recordings might not be adequate for automatic assessment of bradykinesia in PD.

References

1. Li, H., Shao, X., Zhang, C., Qian, X.: Automated assessment of Parkinsonian finger-tapping tests through a vision-based fine-grained classification model. Neurocomputing **441**, 260–271 (2021). https://doi.org/10.1016/j.neucom.2021.02.011
2. Li, Z., et al.: An automatic evaluation method for Parkinson's Dyskinesia using finger tapping video for small samples. (2022, in Review). https://doi.org/10.21203/rs.3.rs-1207003/v1
3. Vignoud, G., et al.: Video-based automated assessment of movement parameters consistent with MDS-UPDRS III in Parkinson's disease. J. Park. Dis. **12**(7), 2211–2222 (2022). https://doi.org/10.3233/JPD-223445
4. Yang, N., et al.: Automatic detection pipeline for accessing the motor severity of Parkinson's disease in finger tapping and postural stability. IEEE Access **10**, 66961–66973 (2022). https://doi.org/10.1109/ACCESS.2022.3183232
5. Goetz, C.G., et al.: Movement disorder society-sponsored revision of the unified Parkinson's disease rating scale (MDS-UPDRS): scale presentation and clinimetric testing results: MDS-UPDRS: clinimetric assessment. Mov. Disord.Disord. **23**(15), 2129–2170 (2008). https://doi.org/10.1002/mds.22340
6. Berardelli, A.: Pathophysiology of bradykinesia in Parkinson's disease. Brain **124**(11), 2131–2146 (2001). https://doi.org/10.1093/brain/124.11.2131
7. Liu, Y., et al.: Vision-based method for automatic quantification of Parkinsonian bradykinesia. IEEE Trans. Neural Syst. Rehabil. Eng.Rehabil. Eng. **27**(10), 1952–1961 (2019). https://doi.org/10.1109/TNSRE.2019.2939596

8. Williams, S., et al.: The discerning eye of computer vision: can it measure Parkinson's finger tap bradykinesia? J. Neurol. Sci. **416**, 117003 (2020). https://doi.org/10.1016/j.jns.2020.117003

9. Morinan, G., et al.: Computer vision quantification of whole-body Parkinsonian bradykinesia using a large multi-site population. NPJ Park. Dis. **9**(1), 10 (2023). https://doi.org/10.1038/s41531-023-00454-8

10. Park, K.W., et al.: Machine learning-based automatic rating for cardinal symptoms of Parkinson disease. Neurology **96**(13), e1761–e1769 (2021). https://doi.org/10.1212/WNL.0000000000011654

11. Fatehi, F., Armfield, N.R., Dimitrijevic, M., Gray, L.C.: Technical aspects of clinical video-conferencing: a large scale review of the literature. J. Telemed. TelecareTelemed. Telecare **21**(3), 160–166 (2015). https://doi.org/10.1177/1357633X15571999

12. Nasreddine, Z.S., et al.: The montreal cognitive assessment, MoCA: a brief screening tool for mild cognitive impairment: MOCA: a brief screening tool for MCI. J. Am. Geriatr. Soc.Geriatr. Soc. **53**(4), 695–699 (2005). https://doi.org/10.1111/j.1532-5415.2005.53221.x

13. Hughes, A.J., Daniel, S.E., Kilford, L., Lees, A.J.: Accuracy of clinical diagnosis of idiopathic Parkinson's disease: a clinico-pathological study of 100 cases. J. Neurol. Neurosurg. Psychiatr. **55**(3), 181–184 (1992). https://doi.org/10.1136/jnnp.55.3.181

14. Hobson, J.: The Montreal cognitive assessment (MoCA). Occup. Med.. Med. **65**(9), 764–765 (2015). https://doi.org/10.1093/occmed/kqv078

15. J. J. Bartko, "On Various Intraclass Correlation Reliability Coefficients"

16. Koo, T.K., Li, M.Y.: A guideline of selecting and reporting intraclass correlation coefficients for reliability research. J. Chiropr. Med.Chiropr. Med. **15**(2), 155–163 (2016). https://doi.org/10.1016/j.jcm.2016.02.012

17. Zhang, F., et al.: MediaPipe Hands: On-device Real-time Hand Tracking, 17 June 2020. http://arxiv.org/abs/2006.10214. Accessed 19 Jun 2023

18. Wang, Y., Peng, C., Liu, Y.: Mask-pose cascaded CNN for 2D hand pose estimation from single color image. IEEE Trans. Circuits Syst. Video Technol. **29**(11), 3258–3268 (2019). https://doi.org/10.1109/TCSVT.2018.2879980

19. Jin, S., et al.: Whole-Body Human Pose Estimation in the Wild, 23 July 2020. http://arxiv.org/abs/2007.11858. Accessed 19 Jun 2023

20. Wang, J., et al.: Deep high-resolution representation learning for visual recognition. IEEE Trans. Pattern Anal. Mach. Intell.Intell. **43**(10), 3349–3364 (2021). https://doi.org/10.1109/TPAMI.2020.2983686

21. He, K., Zhang, X., Ren, S., Sun, J.: Deep residual learning for image recognition. In: 2016 IEEE Conference on Computer Vision and Pattern Recognition (CVPR), Las Vegas, NV, USA, pp. 770–778. IEEE, June 2016. https://doi.org/10.1109/CVPR.2016.90

22. Sandler, M., Howard, A., Zhu, M., Zhmoginov, A., Chen, L.-C.: MobileNetV2: inverted residuals and linear bottlenecks. In: 2018 IEEE/CVF Conference on Computer Vision and Pattern Recognition, Salt Lake City, UT, pp. 4510–4520. IEEE, June 2018. https://doi.org/10.1109/CVPR.2018.00474

23. Winter, D., Sidwall, G., Hobson, D.: Measurement and reduction of noise in kinematic locomotion. J. Biomech.Biomech. **7**(2), 157–159 (1974)

More Than Meets the Eye: Analyzing Anesthesiologists' Visual Attention in the Operating Room Using Deep Learning Models

Sapir Gershov[1(✉)], Fadi Mahameed[2,3], Aeyal Raz[3], and Shlomi Laufer[2]

[1] Technion Autonomous Systems Program, Israel Institute of Technology, Technion City, Haifa 3200003, Israel
sapirgershov@campus.technion.ac.il
[2] The Faculty of Data and Decision Sciences, Israel Institute of Technology, Technion City, Haifa 3200003, Israel
[3] Rambam Health Care Campus, Haifa 3109601, Israel

Abstract. Patient's vital signs, which are displayed on monitors, make the anesthesiologist's visual attention (VA) a key component in the safe management of patients under general anesthesia; moreover, the distribution of said VA and the ability to acquire specific cues throughout the anesthetic, may have a direct impact on patient's outcome. Currently, most studies employ wearable eye-tracking technologies to analyze anesthesiologists' visual patterns. Albeit being able to produce meticulous data, wearable devices are not a sustainable solution for large-scale or long-term use for data collection in the operating room (OR). Thus, by utilizing a novel eye-tracking method in the form of deep learning models that process monitor-mounted webcams, we collected continuous behavioral data and gained insight into the anesthesiologist's VA distribution with minimal disturbance to their natural workflow. In this study, we collected OR video recordings using the proposed framework and compared different visual behavioral patterns. We distinguished between baseline VA distribution during uneventful periods to patterns associated with active phases or during critical, unanticipated incidents. In the future, such a platform may serve as a crucial component of context-aware assistive technologies in the OR.

Keywords: Visual attention · Monitoring · Human activity recognition · Webcam · Anesthesia · Operating room · context awareness

---

S. Gershov and F. Mahameed—Equal contribution.

1 Introduction

1.1 Situation Awareness and Visual Attention

Situation awareness (SA) has been recognized as a crucial element in various domains, including aviation and sports, and has remained a subject of consistent interest in recent decades. [4, 15]. Endsley defined the concept of SA as "the perception of elements in the environment within a volume of time and space, the comprehension of their meaning, and the projection of their status in the near future." [3] It can be understood that SA is composed of three discrete hierarchies that are interdependent, with the first hierarchy-"perception", serving as the cornerstone of the structure. Throughout the following years, Endsley's work and research were adopted by various medical fields; anesthesiology pioneered its incorporation into the training process of residents. [6,14] While under anesthesia, there is a multitude of clinical information pertaining to the patient that the anesthesiologist must monitor and oversee. Given that most of the information is presented visually, anesthesiologists' visual attention(VA) is essentially the method by which their perception is achieved, and on that rest, clinical decisions that affect patient care and safety; moreover, the way anesthesiologists distribute their VA both spatially and temporally in order to acquire specific cues along the provision of anesthesia may have a direct impact on the ability to provide better care. From an observer's standpoint, such a phenomenon might even offer insight into the situation in which the provider is present and even divulge a part of his cognitive process. [6]

1.2 Monitoring Anesthesiologists Visual Behavior

Anesthesiologists' VA has been the subject of many studies in the past. Schulz et al. [13] used a head-mounted eye-tracking camera system to assess Anesthesiologists' distribution of VA to monitors, patients, and the environment. It was found that 20% of visual attention was directed to the patient monitor during an uneventful procedure, with an increase to 30% during critical incidents; they concluded that there is a correlation between visual attention and critical events requiring interventions. White et al. [18] and Roche et al. [12] also examined the visual patterns of expert physicians; however, they used mobile eye-tracking glasses in simulated and actual resuscitation cases. Both studies reported similar results where expert physicians seemed to maintain situational awareness by using their ability to fixate on the monitor and vital signs temporarily, meanwhile, managing a specific task during the resuscitation. Furthermore, a study by Szulewski et al. [16], which also employed gaze-tracking glasses, reported evidence of visual patterns associated with better performance during simulated resuscitation scenarios. Studies such as these lay the foundations for the claim that it is possible to utilize VA and SA for Anesthesiology residents' training and assess their advancement by analyzing their visual patterns. However, these studies assessed anesthesiologists' gaze using wearable eye-tracking devices. Although these devices produce highly accurate data, they have an inherent flaw as they are not a sustainable and ecological solution for long-term data collection in an environment such as the operating room (OR). Due to the devices' limited battery life, using them during lengthy procedures may be challenging. Moreover, based on what was reported, they require calibration before use, which typically requires additional staff and might impede workflow in the OR. In addition, these devices are inconvenient for the anesthesiologists who need to wear them during their long and intensive working hours [17]. Our study presents an alternative approach that utilizes advanced Deep Learning techniques that provide continuous, day-to-day visual behavioral data with minimal interference in the daily workflow. If successful, such a system will facilitate the collection of vast amounts of data, enable in-depth analysis of the anesthesiologists' work, and potentially lay the cornerstone for developing context-aware assistive technologies in the OR. Implementing a webcam-based eye contact recognition model suitable for medical simulations and real-life OR settings. The presented framework will facilitate empirical comparisons between visual behaviors and patterns, whether uneventful or active for one individual during the procedure or between two individuals' patterns in a similar scenario (e.g., a resident and his attending). In the future, this may help determine the VA effect on patient care.

1.3   Challenges in Gaze Pattern Detection

There are two primary inquiries regarding the gaze of Anesthesiologists: whether they have inspected the patient's monitor and at what point this examination took place. This differentiation will determine if the physician noticed the critical cue displayed on the patient's monitor. We addressed these questions using the "Onfocus" detection, which identifies whether the individual's focus is on the camera [20]. Onfocus detection in unconstrained capture conditions presents numerous challenges arising from complex image scenes, inevitable occlusions, varied face orientations, continuous changes in frame focus, multiple objects appearing, and factors such as blur and over-exposure. Zhang et al. [20] introduced a model and dataset to assess onfocus detection under these challenges; however, certain components were lacking to make it suitable for clinical usage. In the present study, we enhanced and adapted the model proposed by Zhang et al. to be suitable for implementation in the OR. Once we achieved a functional system, we applied our model to a newly generated dataset consisting of webcam videos capturing the gaze of anesthesiologists during medical simulations and real-life OR scenarios. To summarize, the objectives of this study are twofold: to advance gaze detection methodology and enhance healthcare training and assessment via gaze pattern analysis. By employing unobtrusive equipment to detect gaze within the dynamic and demanding OR environment, and subsequently analyzing the context-specific VA patterns of anesthesiologists, this research presents an exciting opportunity to enhance deep learning models for detecting focus. Furthermore, it offers valuable insights into the intricate work patterns involved in anesthesia delivery without compromising patient safety and potentially even improving it.

2   Material

2.1   Onfocus Detection in the Wild Dataset

Zhang et al. [20] presented a significant contribution to onfocus detection by introducing the large-scale 'OFDIW' dataset. The OFDIW dataset has unique videos featuring face-to-camera communication, a single camera perspective, fully visible faces, and minimal frame-to-frame variations. However, the dataset's limitations, including using a single camera with fixed camera-face orientation, result in the absence of crucial characteristics necessary for comprehensive VA analysis in the OR.

2.2   Eye-Context Interaction Inferring Network

Zhang et al.'s [20] work provided a novel end-to-end model for onfocus detection. The model, named "Eye-Context Interaction Inferring Network" (ECIIN), is a deep learning architecture composed of a convolution neural network (CNN) context capsule network (CAP) [10]. Given an input frame, the ECIIN model begins by localizing the eye regions, which are then processed with conventional convolution layers adopted to extract feature maps (Eye CNN). In parallel, context features from the original image are extracted using another CNN (Context CNN). The feature vectors are passed to the CAPs trained to reflect the context and eye status, respectively; furthermore, CAPs model the interaction between the eye and context regions. Eventually, the model classifies the eye-context interaction as "onfocus" or "out of focus". As it shows, Zhang et al.'s model does not take advantage of Yang et al.'s publicly available dataset for face detection [19], which is rich with labeled data suitable for training a model for such a task. They also do not employ a well-known, state-of-the-art detection model that can be more accurate and robust using transfer learning techniques. Finally, their model does not support detecting multiple objects in the same image.

2.3   WIDER FACE Dataset

The WIDER FACE dataset [19] is one of the most extensive publicly available datasets for face detection. It contains 32,203 images and 393,703 labels of faces with a wide range of scale, poses, and occlusion variability. Each recognizable face in the WIDER FACE dataset is labeled by bounding boxes, which must tightly contain facial landmarks (FL) (e.g., forehead, chin, and cheek). In the case of occlusion, the face is labeled with an estimated bounding box.

2.4   YOLOv7 for Face Detection

YOLO, which stands for "You Only Look Once", is a popular family of real-time object detection algorithms. The original YOLO object detector was published by Redmon et al. [11]. Since then, different versions and variants of YOLO have been proposed, each providing a significant increase in performance and efficiency. Previously, Qi et al. [9] published a modification of the YOLO architecture, YOLO5Face, which treats face detection as a general object detection task. In their work, they designed a face detector model capable of achieving state-of-the-art performance in varying image sizes by adding a five-point landmark regression head into the original architecture and using the Wing loss function [5].

FL detection can be achieved by Dlib-ml [7], a cross-platform, open-source software library with pre-trained detectors for FL. The Dlib detector estimates the location of 68 coordinates (x, y) that map the facial points on a person's face. Though newer algorithms leverage a dense "face mesh" with machine learning to infer the 3D facial surface from single camera input, these models fail to produce superior results when the acquired images have disturbances and motion [2].

2.5   Spatiotemporal Gaze Architecture

Most works that tackled the task of detecting gaze target prediction constructed 2D representations of the gaze direction, which fails to encode whether the person of interest is looking onward, backward, or sideward. Chong et al. [1] proposed using a deep-learning network to construct a 3D gaze representation and incorporate it as an additional feature channel. The input to their network was the video frame scene, the heads' position in the frame, and the reciprocal cropped head images; however, they did not provide a face-detection model to generate this input automatically. In addition, Chong et al.'s work applied α - a learned scalar that evaluates whether the person's object of attention is inside or outside the frame, with higher values indicating in-frame attention. Yet, when the person's object of attention was outside the frame, they did not examine the cases in which the object of attention was the camera itself.

3   Methods

3.1   Pipeline Construction

For face detection, we trained YOLOv7 on the WIDER FACE dataset [19]. For each detected bounding box prediction, an FL algorithm was applied [7]. We used only the coordinates visible in the collected data - eyes, nose, and mouth. The coupling of YOLOv7 trained for face detection with an FL detector is a suitable replacement for Zhang et al.'s. [20] ECIIN-designed network modules. Our modifications harness the benefits of well-trained object detectors and large datasets. Thus, produce superior results. Once the region of interest is located, we apply the process described in Zhang et al.'s. work to generate the onfocus detection. Lastly, we modified Chong et al. spatiotemporal model [1] by introducing the ECIIN component. This modification has improved Chong et al. model performance in cases where the object of attention is "out-of-frame". The complete end-to-end pipeline is depicted in Fig. 1.

Applying the end-to-end pipeline to video footage produced a new video with labeled bounding boxes around faces, indicating whether they were classified as "onfocus". A text file was also generated, documenting the model predictions for each frame. Since multiple "onfocus" labels with varying confidence levels could appear in each frame, we established a threshold of 0.72 to exclude predictions with low confidence. This value was achieved via hyperparameter tuning of the framework. Addressing the output text file as a time series enabled various statistical measurements to be applied.

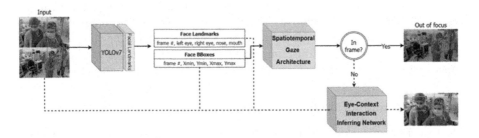

Fig. 1. End-to-end framework pipeline. The Spatiotemporal prediction is indicated by a bounding box over the allocated head and a heatmap over the object of attention. If the attention is on an object inside the frame, we automatically classify the image as "out of focus". Otherwise, we pass the frame to the ECIIN model. The ECIIN network classification confidence is indicated by color, where green is for high confidence and red is for low confidence. The score next to the bounding box is the prediction probability. (Color figure online)

3.2   Data Acquisition

Simulation Data. In order to adjust the proposed framework to the OR settings, we began with a small-scale dataset of residents' VA during simulated

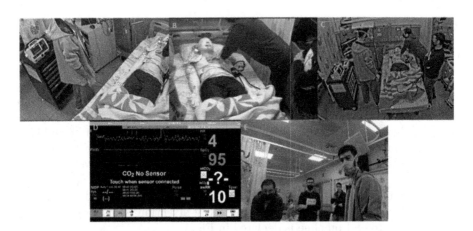

Fig. 2. Data acquisition system.(A) Nurse working area; (B) Physician working area; (C) Overview of the simulation area; (D) Patient monitor; (E) Patient monitor point-of-view. The participants gave their approval for publishing these images.

medical scenarios. A webcam was attached to a patient monitor, which recorded the anesthesiologists' VA patterns. Additional vantage points were added in order to offer a broader clinical context (see Fig. 2).

The Video and audio data collecting was managed via StreamPix digital video recording software developed by NorPix Inc.. The dataset included 20-minute video recordings of 31 simulations performed by 33 residents, from which over 1200 frames were extracted. The appearing faces were manually labeled with bounding boxes suitable for the YOLO network. An independent human observer marked the events of direct eye contact with the monitor; these events were classified as "Onfocus" or "Out of focus" while maintaining a balanced and diverse dataset (see Fig. 3). The labeled frames were used for fine-tuning the proposed framework, which was then applied to video recordings from the OR.

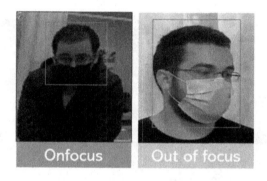

Fig. 3. Zoom-in examples of the labeled frames.

OR Data. After analyzing the preliminary data and acquiring the approval of the Rambam Health Care Campus Institutional Review Board (IRB), we installed a similar, larger-scale RGB camera system in the institution's OR. The system included more vantage points, see Fig. 4, such as the anesthesia cart (containing most medications and equipment), additional monitors (anesthesia machine/ventilator monitors), and different workstations. The collected data was analyzed and labeled by the proposed framework.

A separate labeling of the OR dataset was performed; different tasks, behaviors, and monitor interactions of anesthesiologists were manually labeled by an independent researcher(also an anesthesiologist) using the event logging software for video/audio coding and live observations BORIS. The labeled data was then cross-referenced between those labeled manually and those labeled using the deep learning model. Using this combination, we validated the applicability of the proposed framework in a real-life clinical environment.

4   Results

4.1   Evaluation of the Proposed Framework

We evaluated the different models' performance on our labeled simulation frames. The dataset was randomly divided into 80% train, 10% validation, and 10% test, followed by 5-fold cross-validation. We used our YOLOv7 model for face detection to provide the input for the Spatiotemporal model [1] and then assessed the model's heatmaps. Theoretically, the Spatiotemporal model will not generate heatmaps in cases where the anesthesiologist has direct eye contact with the monitor. Thus, we can address the calculated heatmaps as binary classifications (i.e., the object of attention is inside the frame or outside). Table 1 shows the performance of the different models regarding the task of onfocus detection.

Fig. 4. Main angles of the OR RGB camera system set-up

Table 1. Models onfocus detection results on medical simulations frames.

Model	Dataset	Accuracy	F1-Score
ECIIN		63.98% ± 2.53%	0.64 ± 0.03
Spatiotemporal	Medical simulations	71.03% ± 1.87%	0.72 ± 0.11
Complete pipeline		**89.22% ± 1.26%**	**0.87 ± 0.02**

4.2   VA Analysis in the OR

We conducted a detailed analysis of 12 anesthesia procedures, of which ten were conducted by residents, one by an attending doctor, and one by an attending doctor in collaboration with a resident. We applied the proposed framework to assess gaze frequency, length, and cumulative time during the induction phase of anesthesia. This phase typically commences with the acquisition of baseline vital sign measurements, drug administration to achieve sedation, management and securing of the patient's airway, and patient positioning in preparation for surgery. Additional camera angles were used to categorize almost all activities related to the anesthesia induction phase, including interactions with the monitor, among other tasks. Detection of monitor interactions using each approach is compared in Table 2. Figure 5 outlines the different tasks labeled by a human evaluator during a resident-conducted induction of a procedure.

Table 2. Comparative results of the anesthesiologist VA - displayed as mean±SD, the total time displayed as the percentage of time throughout the induction phase.

Monitor	Detector	Freq. $[(5min)^{-1}]$	Duration [s]	Total time (%)	P-value
Patient	Framework	14±3.78	4.59±1.23	27.23%±3.14%	0.0167
	Human observer	11±5.96	4.33±2.14	23.81%±5.41%	
Ventilator	Framework	24±3.93	6.13±1.24	34.59%±11.83%	0.271
	Human observer	23±6.89	10.19±3.11	47.39%±4.70%	

Table 3. Comparative results of the anesthesiologist VA - displayed as the percentage of time spent observing monitors throughout the airway manipulation tasks.

Monitor	Detector	Total time (%)	P-value
Patient	Framework	38.72% ± 9.04%	0.0238
	Human observer	40.19% ± 3.65%	
Ventilator	Framework	49.22% ± 8.54%	0.0946
	Human observer	53.07% ± 6.11%	

Manual labeling served a dual purpose. On the one hand, it offered a "ground truth" for the data labeled by the proposed framework, specifically concerning monitor interactions. When comparing the monitor interaction data from both analytical approaches, the results were reasonably consistent regarding time spent interacting with the patient's monitor, as indicated in Table 2. However, frequency, duration, and total time results did not align well for ventilator monitor interactions. This discrepancy can be partly attributed to the camera angle. On the other hand, overlapping manually labeled events with monitor interactions detected by the proposed framework provided the procedural context for these interactions. For example, during the Airway manipulation task, which includes multiple steps such as Mask ventilation, endotracheal tube or laryngeal mask placement, and verification of adequate placement, significant findings were noted: the overall time dedicated to patient monitor interaction was considerably higher compared to other segments of the induction phase, as demonstrated in Table 3.

5   Discussion

Considering the significance of visual attention (VA) in healthcare quality and patient safety, there is a growing belief that eye-tracking technology can provide valuable insights in these areas. As technology has advanced, researchers have increasingly employed eye-tracking devices to study VA and examine the activities of healthcare professionals in their natural work settings. This is particularly relevant in the field of anesthesiology. However, many of these devices have been intrusive and disrupted the natural workflow.

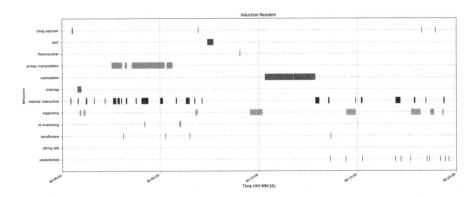

Fig. 5. Human evaluator mapping of tasks distribution and duration along the time course of an uneventful induction. The provider is an anesthesia attending.

To address this issue, we conducted a study utilizing webcams to record the eye contact of anesthesiologists with the operating room (OR) monitors. This unobtrusive approach allowed us to gather continuous visual behavioral data without interfering with the workflow of the anesthesiologists. Furthermore, we analyzed the context in which such eye contact occurred.

The findings of our study using the proposed framework have significant implications for clinical research by providing insights into the relationship between interventions, behaviors, and patient outcomes. Additionally, assessing and providing feedback on anesthesiologists' performance without compromising behavior or workflow could usher in a new era in clinical training and assessment.

We presented preliminary data analyses based on a small sample, focusing on VA during the induction phase of anesthesia procedures. Our findings align with previous reports by Schulz et al. [13], showing similar VA allocation patterns during increased activity phases (30% of VA directed towards patient monitor). Moreover, the frequency and duration of VA exhibited comparable values to those reported in the work of Manser et al. [8]. Thus, our proposed framework, combined with manual labeling of the different activities of an anesthesiologist in the OR environment, offers a more robust and non-intrusive method for analyzing OR data.

Acknowledgment. This study was funded by The Bernard M. Gordon Center for Systems Engineering at the Technion.

Ethical Consideration. First, we assert that all procedures contributing to this work comply with the ethical standards of the national and institutional committees on human experimentation and with the Helsinki Declaration.

Second, participants presented in un-blurred images provided explicit permission for these images.

Third, the framework we describe only documents the medical personnel without disturbing the daily workflow or harming the patient.

References

1. Chong, E., Wang, Y., Ruiz, N., Rehg, J.M.: Detecting attended visual targets in video. In: Proceedings of the IEEE Computer Society Conference on Computer Vision and Pattern Recognition, pp. 5395–5405 (2020). https://doi.org/10.1109/CVPR42600.2020.00544,https://github.com/ejcgt/attention-target-detection
2. Deng, J., Guo, J., Ververas, E., Kotsia, I., Zafeiriou, S.: Retinaface: single-shot multi-level face localisation in the wild. In: Proceedings of the IEEE Computer Society Conference on Computer Vision and Pattern Recognition, pp. 5202–5211 (2020). https://doi.org/10.1109/CVPR42600.2020.00525
3. Endsley, M.R.: Design and evaluation for situation awareness enhancement. Proc. Human Factors Soc. Ann. Meeting. **32**(2), 97–101 (1988). https://doi.org/10.1177/154193128803200221, http://journals.sagepub.com/doi/10.1177/154193128803200221
4. Endsley, M.R.: Toward a theory of situation awareness in dynamic systems. Human Error Aviat. **37**(December), 217–249 (2017)
5. Feng, Z.H., Kittler, J., Awais, M., Huber, P., Wu, X.J.: Wing loss for robust facial landmark localisation with convolutional neural networks. In: Proceedings of the IEEE Conference on Computer Vision and Pattern Recognition, pp. 2235–2245 (2018)
6. Gaba, D.M., Howard, S.K., Small, S.D.: Situation awareness in anesthesiology (1995). https://doi.org/10.1518/001872095779049435
7. King, D.E.: DLIB-ML: a machine learning toolkit. J. Mach. Learn. Res. **10**, 1755–1758 (2009)
8. Manser, T., Wehner, T.: Analysing action sequences: variations in action density in the administration of anaesthesia. Cogn. Technol. Work **4**, 71–81 (2002)
9. Qi, D., Tan, W., Yao, Q., Liu, J.: YOLO5Face: Why Reinventing a Face Detector(2021). https://www.github.com/deepcam-cn/yolov5-face, http://arxiv.org/abs/2105.12931
10. Ramasinghe, S., Athuraliya, C.D., Khan, S.H.: A context-aware capsule network for multi-label classification. In: Leal-Taixé, L., Roth, S. (eds.) ECCV 2018. LNCS, vol. 11131, pp. 546–554. Springer, Cham (2019). https://doi.org/10.1007/978-3-030-11015-4_40
11. Redmon, J., Divvala, S., Girshick, R., Farhadi, A.: You only look once: unified, real-time object detection. In: Proceedings of the IEEE Computer Society Conference on Computer Vision and Pattern Recognition, vol. 2016-Decem, pp. 779–788 (2016). https://doi.org/10.1109/CVPR.2016.91,http://pjreddie.com/yolo/

12. Roche, T.R., et al.: Anesthesia personnel's visual attention regarding patient monitoring in simulated non-critical and critical situations, an eye-tracking study. BMC Anesthesiol. **22**(1), 167 (2022). https://doi.org/10.1186/s12871-022-01705-6

13. Schulz, C.M., et al.: Visual attention of anaesthetists during simulated critical incidents. Br. J. Anaesth. **106**(6), 807–813 (2011). https://doi.org/10.1093/bja/aer087,www.anvil-software.de

14. Schulz, C., Endsley, M., Kochs, E., Gelb, A., Wagner, K.: Situation awareness in anesthesia. Anesthesiology **118**(3), 729–742 (2013). https://doi.org/10.1097/aln.0b013e318280a40f

15. Stanton, N.A., Salmon, P.M., Walker, G.H., Salas, E., Hancock, P.A.: State-of-science: situation awareness in individuals, teams and systems. Ergonomics. **60**, 449–466 (2017). https://doi.org/10.1080/00140139.2017.1278796

16. Szulewski, A., et al.: A new way to look at simulation-based assessment: the relationship between gaze-tracking and exam performance. Can. J. Emerg. Med. **21**(1), 129–137 (2019). https://doi.org/10.1017/cem.2018.391

17. Wagner, M., et al.: Video-based reflection on neonatal interventions during COVID-19 using eye-tracking glasses: an observational study. Archives of disease in childhood. Fetal Neonatal Edn. **107**(2), 156–160 2022).https://doi.org/10.1136/archdischild-2021-321806, https://fn.bmj.com/content/107/2/156https://fn.bmj.com/content/107/2/156.abstract

18. White, M.R., et al.: getting inside the expert's head: an analysis of physician cognitive processes during trauma resuscitations. Ann. Emerg. Med. **72**(3), 289–298 (2018). https://doi.org/10.1016/j.annemergmed.2018.03.005

19. Yang, S., Luo, P., Loy, C.C., Tang, X.: WIDER FACE: a face detection benchmark. In: Proceedings of the IEEE Computer Society Conference on Computer Vision and Pattern Recognition. vol. 2016-Decem, pp. 5525–5533 (2016). https://doi.org/10.1109/CVPR.2016.596, http://mmlab.ie.cuhk.edu.hk/projects/

20. Zhang, D., et al.: Onfocus detection: identifying individual-camera eye contact from unconstrained images. Sci. China Inf. Sci. **65**(6), 1–12 (2022). https://doi.org/10.1007/s11432-020-3181-9

Pose2Gait: Extracting Gait Features from Monocular Video of Individuals with Dementia

Caroline Malin-Mayor[1,2]([✉]), Vida Adeli[1,2], Andrea Sabo[2], Sergey Noritsyn[1],
Carolina Gorodetsky[3], Alfonso Fasano[1,2,4,5,6], Andrea Iaboni[1,2,7],
and Babak Taati[1,2]

[1] University of Toronto, Toronto, ON, Canada
[2] KITE Research Institute, Toronto Rehabilitation Institute,
University Health Network, Toronto, ON, Canada
caroline.malinmayor@mail.utoronto.ca
[3] The Hospital for Sick Children, Toronto, ON, Canada
[4] Morton and Gloria Shulman Movement Disorders Clinic,
Toronto Western Hospital, University Health Network, Toronto, ON, Canada
[5] Krembil Brain Institute, University Health Network, Toronto, ON, Canada
[6] Center for Advancing Neurotechnological Innovation to Application, Toronto, ON,
Canada
[7] Centre for Mental Health, University Health Network, Toronto, ON, Canada

Abstract. Video-based ambient monitoring of gait for older adults with dementia has the potential to detect negative changes in health and allow clinicians and caregivers to intervene early to prevent falls or hospitalizations. Computer vision-based pose tracking models can process video data automatically and extract joint locations; however, publicly available models are not optimized for gait analysis on older adults or clinical populations. In this work we train a deep neural network to map from a two dimensional pose sequence, extracted from a video of an individual walking down a hallway toward a wall-mounted camera, to a set of three-dimensional spatiotemporal gait features averaged over the walking sequence. The data of individuals with dementia used in this work was captured at two sites using a wall-mounted system to collect the video and depth information used to train and evaluate our model. Our Pose2Gait model (Code available at https://github.com/TaatiTeam/pose2gait_public) is able to extract velocity and step length values from the video that are correlated with the features from the depth camera, with Spearman's correlation coefficients of .83 and .60 respectively, showing that three dimensional spatiotemporal features can be predicted from monocular video. Future work remains to improve the accuracy of other features, such as step time and step width, and test the utility of the predicted values for detecting meaningful changes in gait during longitudinal ambient monitoring.

Keywords: Gait Analysis · Pose Estimation · Dementia

Supplementary Information The online version contains supplementary material available at https://doi.org/10.1007/978-3-031-46005-0_23.

I. Rekik et al. (Eds.): PRIME 2023, LNCS 14277, pp. 265–276, 2023.
https://doi.org/10.1007/978-3-031-46005-0_23

1 Introduction

Ambient monitoring of gait has the potential to be a powerful tool for improving quality of life for individuals with dementia. Not only do individuals with dementia fall at a rate at least two times higher than cognitively healthy individuals [8], but changes in gait can reflect injuries or illnesses that individuals with dementia have trouble communicating to caregivers. Daily ambient monitoring of gait features such as velocity and step length could quickly and automatically detect changes that indicate serious underlying issues, allowing early intervention and treatment. While historically gait analysis has required costly motion capture systems, recent advances in computer vision research have made it possible to reconstruct two-dimensional or three-dimensional poses from a simple monocular video. These computer vision-based pose tracking models open up the possibility for new clinical applications to detect fall risk or gait anomalies based on ambient monitoring of gait with an inexpensive wall-mounted video camera.

Yet generic computer vision research does not optimize pose trackers for gait analysis, which has a small range of common poses but requires precise lower body joint placement. Additionally, there is a gap between having joint locations from a pose estimator and knowing clinically relevant gait features such as step time, step length, and velocity. With knowledge of heel down and toe off times, one can heuristically extract gait features from pose sequences, but automatic heel strike detection is highly dependent on the quality of the pose sequences. Therefore, small errors in pose estimation can cause large errors in step time and extracted gait features. Training a neural network to predict gait features from pose sequences provides a more flexible approach. This work shows how a neural network can be trained to predict three-dimensional gait features from two-dimensional pose sequences extracted from monocular video of individuals with dementia with open-source pose estimators.

2 Related Work

Monocular human pose estimation and tracking in two and three dimensions is an active area of computer vision research, with increasingly many methods and benchmark datasets. Surveys [9,19] provide an overview of the field. With the increasing capability of these methods to extract pose information from a single image or video, there is also increasing research on applying them to clinical use cases, both extracting gait features and predicting downstream clinical values.

Previous work has validated the use of computer vision-based pose tracking to extract temporal and spatiotemporal gait features from monocular video. Stenum et al. [17] validate gait features extracted from saggital plane videos using OpenPose against motion capture values and find high correlation for step time, stance time, swing time, double support time, and step length. They also indicate that positioning of the person with respect to the camera affected the accuracy of results, with highest accuracy when the person was directly in front of the camera and lower accuracy when they were approaching or past the camera. Sabo et al. [14] validate gait features extracted from a variety of pose tracking models against a Zeno^{TM} Instrumented Walkway during clinical analysis of individuals with Parkinson's disease. The videos in this dataset had a frontal view of the body, with the participant walking toward or away from the camera. The analysis showed a moderate to strong positive correlation for number of steps, cadence, and step width between the Zeno^{TM} Walkway and the two-dimensional pose tracking models with automated heel strike detection. Correlations were low for step time, and features such as step length and velocity could not be computed using this extraction method from two-dimensional poses. The results from these validation studies illustrate that while pose tracking has promise for gait analysis, further work is required to extract features with high accuracy in challenging clinical conditions.

Lonini et al. [10] and Cotton et al. [3] address these challenges by training an additional model to extract gait features from pose sequences. Lonini et al. [10] use DeepLabCut to train a custom pose tracker focusing on lower body keypoints in below-waist videos of stroke survivors. They then trained a convolutional neural network to predict the mean value over the walk for temporal gait features including cadence and per-leg swing and stance time, and compare the accuracy to a GAITRite® walkway, achieving correlations of greater than .9 for all features except swing time. Cotton et al. [3] also use a neural network to predict gait features from pose sequences on a diverse clinical dataset with a median age of 11 years and cerebral palsy and spina bifida as the most common conditions. The authors first use open-source pose tracking models to extract three-dimensional pose sequences from video. They then train a transformer neural network to predict hip and knee flexion angle, forward position of foot relative to pelvis, forward velocity of feet and pelvis, and step timing information. They compare this neural network to a motion capture and force plate system and achieve high correlations for cadence (0.98), step time (0.95), step length (0.70), velocity (0.88), single support time (0.71), and double stance time (0.91).

In addition to prior work extracting gait features from monocular video, there is also significant literature on predicting clinical outcomes from gait features. Gait features computed from monocular video using OpenPose are used to predict UPDRS scores and detect anti-psychotic induced Parkinsonism in individuals with dementia [16]. Gait features can also be used to predict short-term fall risk in high-risk individuals from 2D video [13] and depth camera data [12]. Aich et al. [1] use gait features extracted from accelerometer data to predict freezing of gait in individuals with Parkinson's disease. These clinical tools were validated using gait features from a variety of sources, such as motion capture systems, wearable accelerometers, and depth cameras, each of which is more expensive and less accessible than a simple video camera. Accurately predicting gait features from monocular video will increase access to these clinical tools beyond labs with specialized equipment.

3   Methods

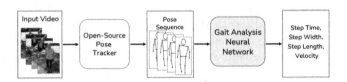

Fig. 1. Pipeline for predicting gait features from monocular video. The input is a frontal video of an individual walking toward the camera. An open-source two-dimensional pose estimator is used to predict joint locations for each frame in the video. After interpolation and smoothing, the two-dimensional pose sequences are fed into a gait feature predictor neural network, which outputs a set of four gait features for the walk, representing the mean value over all steps in the walk.

The overall pipeline from frontal view video of a walk to mean gait features is shown in Fig. 1. We take as input a monocular video of an individual walking toward the camera. We then apply a two-dimensional pose estimator to get a sequence of joint locations. We choose to use a two-dimensional pose estimator because we have found them to be more reliable than three-dimensional pose trackers on diverse clinical datasets, with less instances of catastrophic failure where the poses are meaningless. During training, we use the output of three different pose estimators [2,7,18] as a form of data augmentation, but at test time we use AlphaPose [7], as this model achieved the best performance in prior work [14]. We then apply our gait analysis neural network, the architecture of which is shown in Fig. 2.

This model predicts four gait features which have been shown to be clinically relevant in prior work: step length [5], step width [11,13,16], step time [5,13], and velocity [5,16]. For each of these features, we predict the mean value over the walk, as the data used to train the model does not contain the information about the value of each feature for individual steps. Gait feature values are usually averaged before being fed into downstream clinical applications, so predicting the mean does not greatly limit clinical applicability of the features.

3.1   Dataset

The data used in this project was collected by the AMBIENT system as described by Dolatabadi et al. [6]. The system automatically detects participants walking down a hallway and records the walk with the video camera and the depth camera of a Kinect sensor. We use data collected from two sites to train and evaluate our model. Dataset 1 (DS1) was collected in a hospital setting, while Dataset 2 (DS2) was captured in a long term care facility. Data collection and analysis plans at each location were approved by the institutional ethics review boards. Gait features to be used as ground truth were extracted from the three

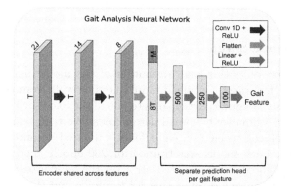

Fig. 2. Architecture of the gait feature predictor neural network. It consists of two sections, an encoder which is shared by all gait features, and a separate prediction head for each gait feature. The encoder uses multiple layers of 1D convolutions to incorporate information over the time dimension, while the prediction head uses simple linear layers. Here, T represents the number of input frames in the pose sequence, while J is the number of joints. Additional metadata of length M is also added before the prediction head. This includes one-hot encodings representing the two-dimensional pose tracker used to generate the sequence and the dataset that the sequence is from. In our experiments, $T = 120$ (4 s), $J = 12$, and $M = 5$.

dimensional depth data as done in a prior validation study that showed high agreement with values from the GAITRite® electronic walkway [4]. Specifically, the derivative of the ankle keypoint trajectories was used to detect stance and swing times of each foot, based on the knowledge that a foot in contact with the ground is stationary. Once steps were detected, distance information for each step was then computed from the location of the ankle keypoints at each heelstrike event. Table 1 summarizes the number of participants and walks captured in each location and summary statistics about the selected gait features for each dataset. While most gait features show similar distributions across datasets, step length and velocity are higher for DS2, as participants in the long term care facility tended to be healthier and walk faster than those in the hospital setting.

Table 1. Summary of datasets used to train and evaluate the gait feature prediction neural network. Number of walks and participants are recorded, along with the mean value of each gait feature with the coefficient of variation in parentheses.

Dataset	Walks	Participants	Step Time	Step Width	Step Length	Velocity
DS1	2216	37	.60 s (.21)	17 cm (.27)	30 cm (.32)	50 cm/s (.31)
DS2	989	12	.61 s (.43)	17 cm (.27)	32 cm (.29)	65 cm/s (.33)
Total	3205	49	.60 s (.30)	17 cm (.27)	31 cm (.31)	55 cm/s (.34)

4   Results

4.1   Experimental Setup

We performed the validation and evaluation of the model using 10-fold cross validation. As each dataset contained more than one walk from the same participant, we randomly assigned participants to one of the folds such that individuals from each dataset were evenly spread across folds. We then trained ten models, where each model was trained on eight folds, validated on one fold, and evaluated on one fold. Each model was trained for 200 epochs, and the model with the minimum weighted mean squared error on the validation set was used for evaluation. Results are aggregated over all the folds and then summary statistics are computed. We report Spearman's correlation coefficients (ρ) and mean average error (MAE) for each feature, and present results on each dataset individually as well as in aggregate to see if performance varies across the datasets. The Spearman's correlation coefficient shows if the predictions are consistent with the ground truth in terms of rank, while the mean average error shows how accurate the features are. A model with high correlation but lower mean average error likely has a bias, predicting higher or lower values than the ground truth. We compare our model with the Transforming Gait model (TG) from Cotton et al. [3], using the pre-trained model from that publication without any fine tuning. While retraining or fine tuning would be optimal, it requires per-step features which are much more difficult to obtain from our data than those averaged over the walk. Therefore, we use the model trained by the original authors on a diverse clinical dataset with a median age of 11 years and cerebral palsey and spina bifida as the most common conditions. The Transforming Gait model does not predict step width, so we compare on velocity, step length, and step time only.

4.2   Model Training

We train our Pose2Gait model for 200 epochs. Each epoch uses all three versions of each walk predicted with each pose tracker as a form of data augmentation, randomizing the order over all sequences, with a batch size of 20 sequences. We use the Adam optimizer with learning rate 1^{-5} and apply the mean squared error loss with hand-crafted weights applied to each feature. The weights are necessary because the range of values for each feature varies, with step length being consistently larger than step width, for example. We chose weights to get the means of all features to be around 1, as shown in Table 2. We normalize the input pose sequences by shifting and scaling to center the mid-hip point at $(0, 0)$ and have a hip width of 1 at the center frame of the sequence. We choose 120 frames (4 s) as the input sequence length. We have seen that pose sequence quality is better when the participant closer to the camera, so rather than cropping randomly, we crop the full video to the portion at the end where the subject is closest to the camera as they are walking towards it.

Table 2. Weights used when balancing loss across gait features. The weights were chosen to balance the contribution of the features to the overall loss. Without weighting, features with larger values, such as step length, would overpower features with smaller values, such as step width, when computing the gradient or determining the best model from the validation performance.

Gait Feature	Step Time	Step Width	Step Length	Velocity
Weight in Loss	0.5	2.0	1.25	1.0

4.3 Results

The overall results for our model Pose2Gait (P2G) and the Transforming Gait (TG) model [3] are reported in Table 3, with correlation plots for the common features shown in Fig. 3. The Transforming Gait model failed to detect steps for 12.5% of videos. The Transforming Gait model predicts the quadrature encoding of the gait phase and extracts the step times from zero crossing detection; therefore, if the predicted gait phase encodings did not cross zero (or a multiple of 2π after Kalman smoothing), no steps were detected. In the following tables and analysis, Transforming Gait results are presented only for the 87.5% of videos where the model successfully obtained an output, potentially inflating results compared to Pose2Gait which obtained results for all videos.

When examining the results aggregated across both datasets, the Pose2Gait model shows a high correlation with ground truth gait features for velocity (.81), a medium correlation for step length (.60), and low correlations for step time (.35) and step width (.27). Conversely, the Transforming Gait model achieves highest correlation for step time (.55), with low correlations on step length (.28) and velocity (.36). Similar trends are shown by the mean average error metric, with the Transforming Gait model showing lower error than Pose2Gait for step time and higher error for step length and velocity. Examination of the correlation plots in Fig. 3 shows different failure modes between the models. The Pose2Gait model predicts a relatively constant step time of around 0.6 s, failing to capture the variability of the data. The Transforming Gait model tends to overpredict the velocity, likely due to higher walking speeds in the population used to train the model.

The Pose2Gait results are surprising, as our input is two-dimensional pose sequences with individuals walking toward the camera, which we would expect to contain more information about the step width than the velocity and step length. These results show that the Pose2Gait neural network can extract three-dimensional gait information from a two-dimensional pose sequence, likely by examining the difference in size of the poses over time as the individual gets closer to the camera. However, our model struggles to extract step width, perhaps because we normalize the size of the pose sequence and do not provide the height of the participant, making it difficult to infer real world coordinates for features that are perpendicular to the camera.

Table 3. Spearman's correlation coefficient (ρ) and mean absolute error (MAE) for the Pose2Gait (P2G) and Transforming Gait (TG) models aggregated across all folds and datasets. The p-values associated with all Spearman's correlation coefficients in this table are less than 0.01, indicating statistical significance. Best result for each metric and feature is in bold.

Metric	Model	Step Time	Step Width	Step Length	Velocity
ρ	P2G	.35	.27	**.60**	**.81**
	TG	**.55**	—	.28	.36
MAE	P2G	93 ms	3.4 cm	**6.0 cm**	**8.0 cm/s**
	TG	**88 ms**	—	8.8 cm	28.1 cm/s

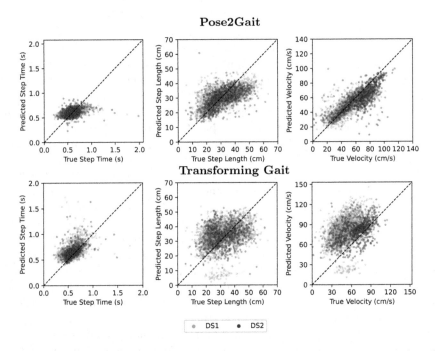

Fig. 3. Correlation plots between true and predicted values for step time, step length, and velocity. Top row shows Pose2Gait predictions, while bottom row shows Transforming Gait predictions. Dataset membership is indicated by color of the point, and the equality line is plotted for reference.

In addition to examining the overall results, we show the correlation coefficients for DS1 only in Table 4, and DS2 in Table 5. As our datasets come from two locations with potentially different walking gaits, as shown by the difference in gait features between populations in Table 1, we additionally include Pose2Gait models trained on each dataset individually (P2G-DS1 and P2G-DS2, respectively) to determine if training one global model or two separate models performs better. In each case, the Pose2Gait model trained on both datasets achieves the highest correlation for step length and velocity, while the Transforming Gait baseline performs best on step time, although the difference is slight for DS1. For both datasets, step width correlations improve slightly for the model trained on that dataset only. Mean average error results show similar trends to the correlation coefficients; these values are included in Appendix A for completeness.

Table 4. Spearman's correlation coefficients for DS1 only. The p-values associated with all coefficients in this table are less than 0.01, indicating statistical significance. Best result for each feature is in bold.

Model	Step Time	Step Width	Step Length	Velocity
P2G	.35	.30	**.60**	**.83**
P2G-DS1	.32	**.32**	.59	.82
TG	**.36**	—	.29	.36

4.4 Ablation Study

We change various aspects of our architecture and data augmentation and preprocessing to determine the effect on the accuracy of gait features predicted. In addition to the Pose2Gait architecture described in this work, we tested the architecture from Lonini et al. [10] which incorporates batch normalization and max pooling layers in the convolutional architecture. As these features are standard for convolutional neural networks and the model accurately predicted temporal gait features from pose sequences in the original work, we were surprised to see that performance decreased significantly, with negative correlations for step time and step width, and only a .30 correlation for velocity. As such, we did not adopt this architecture and focused on variations of the Pose2Gait model described below.

Table 5. Spearman's correlation coefficients for DS2 only. The p-values associated with all coefficients in this table are less than 0.01, indicating statistical significance. Best result for each feature is in bold.

Model	Step Time	Step Width	Step Length	Velocity
P2G	.35	.18	**.58**	**.75**
P2G-DS2	.22	**.20**	.39	.61
TG	**.53**	—	.25	.50

First, many prior publications have used mirroring poses as a simple method of increasing the size of the training data. We trained the Pose2Gait+Mirror model with twice as many training samples by laterally reflecting each pose sequence. In addition, upper body joints tended to be noisier in our datasets due to some individuals walking with hands behind their backs. Since our gait features focus on the lower body, we trained a model with only the hips, knees, and ankles (Pose2Gait+Lower) to determine if removing the potentially extraneous upper body information improved performance. Previous work has shown that normalizing the pose sequences per frame, rather than per video as we have done in our main model, can be effective for predicting UPDRS scores [15]. While we suspected that normalizing per frame would remove crucial information about velocity and step length that is provided by the scale of the person as the move toward the camera, we trained the Pose2Gait+PerFrame model to test this normalization method. Spearman's correlation coefficients for all these augmentations are shown in Table 6, with the main Pose2Gait model shown for reference. Mean average error values are available in Appendix B. Although the mirror augmentation produced the best step time correlations and the lower body only model had the highest step width correlations, these positive effects came at the cost of other features. Per-frame normalization is the only augmentation that had an overall beneficial impact on all features, although the effect is slight.

5   Discussion

This paper presents a neural network that can predict velocity and step length from monocular video of individuals with dementia walking collected via environmental monitoring in a clinical setting. Results from the ablation study show that standard practices in computer vision for training convolutional networks, such as batch normalization, max pooling, and data augmentation, do not have a strictly positive effect when using convolutions to process joint locations instead of images. Similarly, the performance of the pre-trained Transforming Gait model suggests that gait analysis neural networks will not naturally generalize between different clinical populations, and fine-tuning or retraining is likely required. Additionally, architectures or data preprocessing techniques that work well for one gait analysis task might not be suitable for others, as shown by the architecture from Lonini et al. [10] working very well for temporal features in the original work but less well for spatiotemporal features here, as well as the inclusion of only lower body joints in the Pose2Gait model helping step width accuracy while hurting step length and velocity.

Table 6. Spearman's correlation coefficients for variations on the main Pose2Gait model. The p-values associated with all coefficients in this table are less than 0.01, indicating statistical significance. Best result for each feature is in bold.

Model	Step Time	Step Width	Step Length	Velocity
P2G	.35	.27	**.60**	.81
P2G+Mirror	**.41**	.25	**.60**	.80
P2G+Lower	.37	**.44**	.53	.80
P2G+PerFrame	.37	.29	**.60**	**.83**

Future work remains to boost the accuracy of predictions for step time and step width. Because we have shown that different architecture and preprocessing approaches perform better for different features, training separate models for each feature could yield more accurate results, although it is much less efficient than sharing a single model. To improve performance on a specific dataset, for example before deployment in an ambient monitoring setting, it would make sense to fine-tune the general Pose2Gait model on the target dataset only. Finally, while this work shows a proof of concept that three dimensional spatiotemporal gait features can be predicted from monocular video using computer vision techniques, gait features are only a proxy for the health of an individual. Further work must be done to collect longitudinal data from ambient monitoring and to develop and validate clinical models that can detect sudden changes in gait that indicate high risk of negative health outcomes such as fall risk or hospitalization.

References

1. Aich, S., Pradhan, P.M., Park, J., Sethi, N., Vathsa, V.S.S., Kim, H.C.: A validation study of freezing of gait (FoG) detection and machine-learning-based fog prediction using estimated gait characteristics with a wearable accelerometer. Sensors **18**(10), 3287 (2018). https://doi.org/10.3390/s18103287

2. Cao, Z., Hidalgo, G., Simon, T., Wei, S.E., Sheikh, Y.: OpenPose: realtime multi-person 2D pose estimation using part affinity fields. IEEE Trans. Pattern Anal. Mach. Intell. **43**(1), 172–186 (2021). https://doi.org/10.1109/TPAMI.2019.2929257

3. Cotton, R.J., McClerklin, E., Cimorelli, A., Patel, A., Karakostas, T.: Transforming gait: video-based spatiotemporal gait analysis. In: 2022 44th Annual International Conference of the IEEE Engineering in Medicine & Biology Society (EMBC), pp. 115–120, July 2022. https://doi.org/10.1109/EMBC48229.2022.9871036

4. Dolatabadi, E., Taati, B., Mihailidis, A.: Concurrent validity of the microsoft kinect for windows v2 for measuring spatiotemporal gait parameters. Med. Eng. Phys. **38**(9), 952–958 (2016). https://doi.org/10.1016/j.medengphy.2016.06.015

5. Dolatabadi, E., Van Ooteghem, K., Taati, B., Iaboni, A.: Quantitative mobility assessment for fall risk prediction in dementia: a systematic review. Dement. Geriatr. Cogn. Disord. **45**(5–6), 353–367 (2018). https://doi.org/10.1159/000490850

6. Dolatabadi, E., Zhi, Y.X., Flint, A.J., Mansfield, A., Iaboni, A., Taati, B.: The feasibility of a vision-based sensor for longitudinal monitoring of mobility in older adults with dementia. Arch. Gerontol. Geriatr. **82**, 200–206 (2019). https://doi.org/10.1016/j.archger.2019.02.004

7. Fang, H.S., et al.: AlphaPose: Whole-Body Regional Multi-Person Pose Estimation and Tracking in Real-Time, November 2022. https://doi.org/10.48550/arXiv.2211.03375

8. Härlein, J., Dassen, T., Halfens, R.J.G., Heinze, C.: Fall risk factors in older people with dementia or cognitive impairment: a systematic review. J. Adv. Nurs. **65**(5), 922–933 (2009). https://doi.org/10.1111/j.1365-2648.2008.04950.x

9. Liu, W., Bao, Q., Sun, Y., Mei, T.: Recent advances of monocular 2D and 3D human pose estimation: a deep learning perspective. ACM Comput. Surv. **55**(4), 80:1–80:41 (2022). https://doi.org/10.1145/3524497

10. Lonini, L., et al.: Video-based pose estimation for gait analysis in stroke survivors during clinical assessments: a proof-of-concept study. Digital Biomark. **6**(1), 9–18 (2022). https://doi.org/10.1159/000520732
11. Mehdizadeh, S., et al.: Vision-based assessment of gait features associated with falls in people with dementia. J. Gerontol. Ser. A **75**(6), 1148–1153 (2020). https://doi.org/10.1093/gerona/glz187
12. Mehdizadeh, S., et al.: Predicting short-term risk of falls in a high-risk group with dementia. J. Am. Med. Dir. Assoc. **22**(3), 689-695.e1 (2021). https://doi.org/10.1016/j.jamda.2020.07.030
13. Ng, K.D., Mehdizadeh, S., Iaboni, A., Mansfield, A., Flint, A., Taati, B.: Measuring gait variables using computer vision to assess mobility and fall risk in older adults with dementia. IEEE J. Transl. Eng. Health Med. **8**, 1–9 (2020). https://doi.org/10.1109/JTEHM.2020.2998326
14. Sabo, A., Gorodetsky, C., Fasano, A., Iaboni, A., Taati, B.: Concurrent validity of Zeno instrumented walkway and video-based gait features in adults with Parkinson's disease. IEEE J. Transl. Eng. Health Med. **10**, 1–11 (2022). https://doi.org/10.1109/JTEHM.2022.3180231
15. Sabo, A., Mehdizadeh, S., Iaboni, A., Taati, B.: Estimating Parkinsonism Severity in Natural Gait Videos of Older Adults with Dementia, October 2021. http://arxiv.org/abs/2105.03464
16. Sabo, A., Mehdizadeh, S., Ng, K.D., Iaboni, A., Taati, B.: Assessment of Parkinsonian gait in older adults with dementia via human pose tracking in video data. J. Neuroeng. Rehabil. **17**(1), 97 (2020). https://doi.org/10.1186/s12984-020-00728-9
17. Stenum, J., Rossi, C., Roemmich, R.T.: Two-dimensional video-based analysis of human gait using pose estimation. PLoS Comput. Biol. **17**(4), e1008935 (2021). https://doi.org/10.1371/journal.pcbi.1008935
18. Wu, Y., Kirillov, A., Massa, F., Lo, W.Y., Girshick, R.: Detectron2 (2019). https://github.com/facebookresearch/detectron2
19. Zhang, F., Zhu, X., Wang, C.: Single person pose estimation: a survey, September 2021. https://doi.org/10.48550/arXiv.2109.10056

Self-Supervised Learning of Gait-Based Biomarkers

R. James Cotton[1,2(✉)] [ID], J. D. Peiffer[1,3] [ID], Kunal Shah[1], Allison DeLillo[1], Anthony Cimorelli[1], Shawana Anarwala[1], Kayan Abdou[1], and Tasos Karakostas[1,2]

[1] Shirley Ryan AbilityLab, Chicago, USA
[2] Department of Physical Medicine and Rehabilitation, Northwestern University, Evanston, USA
rcotton@sralab.org
[3] Northwestern University, Department of Biomedical Engineering, Evanston, USA

Abstract. Markerless motion capture (MMC) is revolutionizing gait analysis in clinical settings by making it more accessible, raising the question of how to extract the most clinically meaningful information from gait data. In multiple fields ranging from image processing to natural language processing, self-supervised learning (SSL) from large amounts of unannotated data produces very effective representations for downstream tasks. However, there has only been limited use of SSL to learn effective representations of gait and movement, and it has not been applied to gait analysis with MMC. One SSL objective that has not been applied to gait is contrastive learning, which finds representations that place similar samples closer together in the learned space. If the learned similarity metric captures clinically meaningful differences, this could produce a useful representation for many downstream clinical tasks. Contrastive learning can also be combined with causal masking to predict future timesteps, which is an appealing SSL objective given the dynamical nature of gait. We applied these techniques to gait analyses performed with MMC in a rehabilitation hospital from a diverse clinical population. We find that contrastive learning on unannotated gait data learns a representation that captures clinically meaningful information. We probe this learned representation using the framework of biomarkers and show it holds promise as both a diagnostic and response biomarker, by showing it can accurately classify diagnosis from gait and is responsive to inpatient therapy, respectively. We ultimately hope these learned representations will enable predictive and prognostic gait-based biomarkers that can facilitate precision rehabilitation through greater use of MMC to quantify movement in rehabilitation.

Keywords: rehabilitation · self-supervised learning · contrastive learning · gait analysis · gait biomarkers · markerless motion capture

Supplementary Information The online version contains supplementary material available at https://doi.org/10.1007/978-3-031-46005-0_24.

I. Rekik et al. (Eds.): PRIME 2023, LNCS 14277, pp. 277–291, 2023.
https://doi.org/10.1007/978-3-031-46005-0_24

1 Introduction

The development of markerless motion capture (MMC) has greatly lowered the barrier to the biomechanical analysis of movement. With this technology, it is now feasible to perform routine gait analysis on individuals undergoing rehabilitation for gait impairments, and even longitudinally during treatment. This presents a new set of challenges, as each gait analysis produces a huge amount of data including spatiotemporal gait parameters and whole-body joint kinematics down to individual fingers. To effectively utilize this technology in clinical care, it is essential to reduce each gait analysis into a much smaller set of summary statistics that can be reviewed by treating clinicians. Ideally, these statistics should be interpretable, valid, reliable and robust, sensitive to clinically meaningful change, and clinically actionable. Biomarkers provide a useful framework to consider such statistics. For example, some types of biomarkers identified by an NIH workgroup are diagnostic biomarkers, which signal the presence of a disease, and response biomarkers, which measure the response to interventions [17].

This raises the question of how to identify these gait-based biomarkers. One approach for learning useful representations is self-supervised learning (SSL). SSL establishes a pretext task that does not require data manual labeling, where training a system to solve this task produces a representation is effective for other downstream tasks. This has been successful for a range of applications, including natural language processing, image categorization, scene segmentation, and mapping between images and language. There are many potential pretext tasks used in SSL. For example, predicting the next word is commonly used for SSL in language with great success. This can naturally be extended to gait by predicting a future trajectory from a set of observations.

Winner et al. [35] used a recurrent neural network to predict the next time step from marker-based gait analysis, which produced individualized gait signatures clustered by whether participants had a history of stroke or not and separated by degree of impairment. They also showed this network could autoregressively generate sample trajectories, which made the gait signatures more interpretable as a change in gait signatures could be visualized through a change in sampled kinematics. Endo et al. [16] used a transformer with an encoder-decoder architecture trained to predict a block of future timesteps movements estimated using human pose estimation from monocular videos. They pretrained the network on a large existing dataset from able-bodied individuals containing multiple actions, before fine-tuning it on a small dataset of videos from individuals with Parkinson's disease. In addition to the prediction pretext task, they trained a classification head on the input trajectory to predict the activity being performed in the pretext task and then fine-tuned this to predict clinical gait impairment scores.

Several other pretext tasks have shown success on a range of tasks that, to our knowledge, have not been applied to clinical gait analysis. Contrastive learning involves taking different augmentations of samples that should not change the underlying meaning (positive samples) and learning a representation that makes those augmented views close together in an embedding space while being far away from other samples [28]. The learned representation should embed more similar samples more closely together, despite never receiving explicit labels, which can produce a representation useful for downstream tasks. This has been applied with great success to learn visual representations that perform well on object classification [9]. The augmentations to produce positive samples should be designed to not change the relevant information in the sample. In the case of gait, temporal crops that take different observations of the same walking condition provide a natural approach. Another pretext task is similar to future prediction but involves masking some of the inputs and forcing the system to predict those missing samples [15]. This commonly uses bidirectional transformers, which are challenging to integrate with causal prediction. However, Forgetful Causal Masking (FCM) can combine masking input tokens with a causal mask that predicts future tokens and substantially improves language model performance for downstream tasks [23].

MMC can enable much greater use of gait analysis in clinical care and research, but using SSL to learn representations from this data has not been explored. The works described above used marker-based motion capture and human pose estimation applied to monocular video [16,35]. Several pretext tasks have not been explored for gait representation learning. This work aimed to use SSL to learn a good representation from gait data acquired with MMC in a rehabilitation hospital from a dataset that contains a mixture of diagnoses with a high representation of stroke survivors and lower limb prosthesis users. We also wanted to explore the influence of different neural network architectures and SSL objectives, including using contrastive learning. The utility of a learned representation is its performance on downstream tasks. We tested the performance of the learned representations on three downstream tasks: diagnosis, laterality of impairments, and monitoring changes in gait impairments during rehabilitation.

In short, the contributions of this work include:

- We show that contrastive learning, using different time windows from a given gait trial as positive examples, is a powerful objective for learning gait representations. Without any explicit annotation, it learns embeddings that are similar for different trials from a given participant.
- By fine-tuning a simple linear decoder on these embeddings we can classify diagnoses (diagnostic biomarker). The embeddings of stroke survivors undergoing inpatient therapy also shift closer to control participants after therapy (response biomarker). These show how much health information can be inferred with gait analysis powered by SSL.
- We show that SSL can be successfully applied to gait analysis data collected with MMC.
- We explore a range of hyperparameters including network architecture, augmentations, input masking, pretraining on other datasets, and loss functions on the contrastive loss and downstream task performance.

2   Methods

2.1   Data Collection

The participants, acquisition system, and methods to perform inverse kinematic fits to estimate joint angles are described in the appendix. In short, gait analysis was performed with markerless motion capture on 75 individuals seen during inpatient and outpatient therapy as well as healthy controls. Of these, 18 were controls, 22 had a history of stroke, and 26 were lower limb prosthesis users, with the remainder having a variety of conditions. Walking over 7 m was collected in a variety of conditions, such as different speeds and assistive devices. The dataset included 712 walking trials. Keypoints detected from multiple views were reconstructed with an implicit representation mapping from time to 87 3D marker locations [11] and then inverse kinematic fits with a biomechanical model were performed on these markers to extract joint angles [4,12,34]. For this study, we used the sagittal plane joint angles from the hip, knee, and ankles and also included back and elbow flexion.

2.2   Network Architecture, Losses, and Training

Gait trajectories were processed with a transformer [33], specifically a decoder-only architecture based on GPT-2 [30], which consists of multiple self-attention and feed-forward neural network layers. Each layer in the network consists of a multi-head self-attention mechanism followed by a position-wise feed-forward neural network. The feed-forward network used a 4-time expansion of the hidden dimension. The self-attention mechanism used 4 attention heads. We performed tests with both learned positional embeddings and rotary encoding [32]. This was implemented in Jax using Equinox [22]. We used Haliax [2] with named tensor dimensions and an architecture like GPT2 [30], based on the implementation from Levanter [3].

The input sequence length was 90. The output sequence tokens were mapped to future predictions, through a final linear layer. We used causal masking, which was sometimes combined with FCM. To decode the overall gait representation, we either extracted the last temporal token or used an additional token appended to the end of the sequence, called a [CLS] token. The input joint trajectory space was projected into the token embedding dimension with a linear layer. They were optionally augmented by adding noise proportional to the standard deviation of each joint over the entire training dataset (typically 10% of the standard deviation). The network was trained with the AdamW optimizer from Optax for 1000 epochs with a learning rate of 2e-3 [5,24]. The network batch size was 32.

Losses. For the contrastive loss, we projected the gait representation (using either the last token or an additional [CLS] token) into a 16-dimensional space with a linear layer. Like prior work, this was normalized to a length of one before and after projection [9]. Positive samples were two 90-frame (3 s) trajectories sampled from the same walking trial, which could potentially overlap. Negative samples were drawn from any other trial, including potentially another from the same session. We did not treat multiple trials from the same person and condition as positive examples, as we were trying to avoid using labels. The contrastive loss was computed as in Eq. (1), where z_i and z_j are the embeddings of the positive samples and z_k are the embeddings of the negative samples. τ is the temperature, which was fixed at 0.1. The similarity function was the cosine similarity. N is the batch size before generating the two temporal crops from each trial.

$$\mathcal{L}_{contrastive} = -\log \frac{\exp(\mathrm{sim}(z_i, z_j)/\tau)}{\sum_{k=1}^{2N} \mathbb{1}_{[k \neq i]} \exp(\mathrm{sim}(z_i, z_k)/\tau)} \tag{1}$$

For the next timestep prediction loss, embeddings from the last layer were projected via a linear layer into the original joint space to produce predictions of the next time step, t, for each joint, j, $\hat{y}_{t,j} \in \mathbb{R}$. We used a mean-squared error loss on these predictions against the ground truth one sample into the future, $y_{t,j}$, Eq. (2). Note because of the future prediction, $y_{t,j} = x_{t-1,j}$ where $x_{t,j}$ is the input trajectory. Because $y_{t,j}$ is not defined for $i = 0$ this time step was not included in the loss. Throughout this work, we used a constant sequence length of $T = 90$ (3 s), and J was the number of joints.

$$\mathcal{L}_{prediction} = \frac{1}{(T-1)J} \sum_{t=2}^{T} \sum_{j=1}^{J} (\hat{y}_{t,j} - y_{t,j})^2 \tag{2}$$

The contrastive loss was always included during training and the prediction loss was only included in some of the runs with a weighting producing a total loss in Eq. (3) using a λ of either 1.0 or 0.0.

$$\mathcal{L} = \mathcal{L}_{contrastive} + \lambda \mathcal{L}_{prediction} \tag{3}$$

We pretrained our network on the gait laboratory dataset for 1000 epochs using these losses before fine tuning for the tasks described below. When fine tuning, we discarded the contrastive projection head and joint angle prediction head.

Hyperparameter Testing. The dataset was split for 3-fold cross-validation based on subject identities (i.e., subjects in the validation test were never seen during training). For each hyperparameter (HP) setting, we trained the model and then the downstream classifiers for diagnosis and laterality. We then computed the prediction loss, contrastive loss, and performance on downstream tasks on the validation data. For each HP setting, we recorded the average cross-validated performance.

HPs adjusted included the number of layers, the transformer embedding dimensionality, the use of an additional [CLS] token for the contrastive loss, the use of a prediction loss, the use of noise augmentation, the use of forgetful causal masking,1 fixed sinusoidal positional encoding versus rotary encoding, and the number of epochs of pretraining. Experiments were tracked with Weights and Biases [6].

We initially experimented with automated HP optimization, but as discussed later, did not find that improving the contrastive loss translated into downstream task performance. Thus we opted for more of a semi-systematic exploration of different HP parameters.

2.3   Downstream Tasks

Diagnosis Classification. To quantify the clinically relevant information contained in the SSL representation, we trained a linear readout for a logistic classifier to predict diagnosis and laterality. This received the input from the layer before the contrastive projection, similar to other works [9]. Because the hidden dimensionality was substantially larger than the number of samples, we also included L1 regularization. We performed inner 4-fold cross-validation over subjects in the training set while sweeping logarithmically over an L1 regularization weight from -6 to -3 to find the optimal regularization parameter. We then trained the classifier with this optimized regularization value on the learned embeddings from the whole training set before finally testing on the corresponding outer 3-folded validation set.

To be explicit, in each case, both the gait representation *and* classifier were trained on only the training data, before first embedding the validation trajectories and scoring them. No subjects in the validation data were included in the training data (i.e., this was not cross-validation over trials). The classification was performed on only 3 s of data from a trial and for the validation trials, this was selected from the middle of a walking segment.

We used this approach to fit logistic regression classifiers for stroke versus control, lower-limb prosthesis user versus control, and impairment laterality. Given our sample size, this typically resulted in 6 to 9 people with each diagnosis in each validation set. We report absolute accuracy and did not adjust for any imbalances between training and validation sets.

Biomarker for Progress. To explore whether this learned representation produces a meaningful topology, we tested its ability to quantify and detect changes during inpatient rehabilitation. We performed this analysis on a subset of our participants (n=11) with a recent history of stroke who were undergoing inpatient rehabilitation and had an MMC gait analysis both early and later during treatment. Due to the limited population size for this analysis, using a single model we computed the gait embeddings for the subjects who were both in the validation and training set.

We computed the geometric median embedding over all the control participants. For each trial for our participants with stroke, we then computed the cosine similarity between their gait and the median control embedding. This analysis used embeddings after being passed through the contrastive projection into the 16-dimensional space. We took the median similarity scores for all trials on a given day as the score for their gait at that point in rehabilitation.

3 Results

3.1 Hyperparameter Testing

Our HP search was a semi-structured exploration. We found the contrastive loss worked robustly on our MMC data for a wide range of network architectures. The contrastive loss on the validation data was responsive to several training parameters consistent with studies for other modalities. Specifically, a large hidden dimension, a greater number of layers, and a longer period of pretraining all tended to improve the contrastive loss. Rotary encoding also seemed to outperform learned positional encoding. While this seemed to be the trend, in a statistical analysis using multivariate analysis on the contrastive loss, two features were statistically significantly associated with an improved contrastive loss: including an additional [CLS] token and also including a next timestep prediction loss. Concerning hidden dimension size, while the contrastive loss tended to be lower with a larger hidden dimension, the next timestep prediction validation error was statistically significantly lower for smaller dimensional models. Using FCM and adding noise augmentation did not have a strong impact, and in general, seemed to worsen performance. A complete table of all the HP runs, the losses, and the downstream task performance is available in the supplementary materials (Fig. 3).

3.2 Downstream Task Performance

The scores on the SSL losses did not seem to predict performance on diagnosis or for laterality classification performance. The only HP that was statistically significantly linked to better classification performance was not including an addition [CLS] token, which was also statistically significantly associated with greater contrastive losses. We found across a wide range of settings that the learned representations performed well on the downstream tasks (Table 1). Thus, we report the aggregate statistics for classifying stroke versus control, lower-limb prosthesis user (LLPU) versus control, and laterality over all our 50 HP experiments. In general, laterality was the worst-performing task and stroke diagnosis was the best-performing task. We did not find a single best architecture that we would recommend, with many values performing well, and the raw scores are available in the supplementary materials (Fig. 3).

3.3 Example Embeddings

To explore the learned representations, we computed the cosine similarity between the learned embeddings from different trials, ordered by participant

Table 1. Performance statistics on downstream tasks

Metric	Stroke	LLPU	Laterality
Mean	0.879	0.774	0.657
Std	0.034	0.043	0.037
Max	0.941	0.842	0.728

and diagnosis (Fig. 1). This visualization only includes the subset of trials from healthy controls and participants with a stroke or prothesis, our three largest groups. Despite never being supervised with subject identity, trials from the same individual were more similar than trials from different individuals. The control participants are also in the lower right and show a region that has higher overall similarity than the other regions.

3.4 Longitudinal Embeddings

We measured how the embedding of individuals with a recent stroke undergoing inpatient rehabilitation changed over time by measuring how aligned it was to the average control participant (Fig. 2). In most cases, the gait representation became more aligned with the average control embedding. Participants who started further from the control embedding tended to have a greater shift towards the control embedding.

There are two outliers where their embedding did not monotonically shift towards the control embedding over time. There was one participant who started fairly closely aligned to the healthy control embedding and then appeared to move away over time. In this case, they had a particularly unusual and impaired gait during the initial session with arms held fairly wide, and their gait was substantially improved at the follow-up assessment in contradiction to measuring their distances to control participants. In the second case, there was an overall trend to improvement, but an additional intermediate assessment where their gait was more aligned to control representation than at baseline or discharge. In this case, it was less apparent to which biomechanical features the gait representation was responding.

4 Discussion

To the best of our knowledge, the efficacy of contrastive learning of gait representations from MMC data has not been explored, although prior work showing SSL works for gait analyzed using marker-based motion capture and using HPE from monocular video suggested it was likely to be successful. Our main finding is that self-supervised learning applied to MMC-based gait analysis, using contrastive learning and next timestep prediction as pretext tasks, can learn gait representations that show promise as both diagnostic and response biomarkers.

Averaged over all our models, we obtained a cross-validated accuracy of 88% for classifying stroke versus able-bodied control, 77% for classifying lower-limb prosthesis users versus able-bodied control, and 66% for identifying the laterality of their impairment. The best scores were 94%, 84%, and 73% respectively. All these findings hinged on only 3 s of gait data, highlighting how much meaningful information SSL allows us to extract about an individual's health status from only a glimpse of their gait. The fact stroke is more easily decoded than a prosthesis user is not surprising, as in general they have a more pronounced

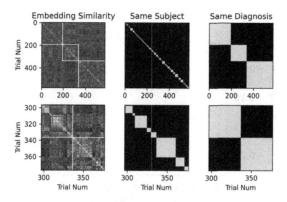

Fig. 1. Example similarity measured between embeddings from different trials, where each row and trial within an image is a trial. The left column shows the embedding similarity between pairs of trials. The next column shows yellow on the pairs of trials that are from the same individual. The blocks on this diagonal structure are also visible in the similarity between the embeddings from trials, showing the SSL objective learns an embedding where different trials from the same individual are similar. The last column shows whether the diagnosis was the same, with these block positions overlaid on the left column with white lines. Controls are in the bottom right corner. The second row is zoomed into the diagonal at the transition from stroke to control participants. (Color figure online)

and visible gait deviation. It is perhaps surprising that laterality is not robustly decoded and we hypothesize it is not linearly disentangled in the embedding space.

A goal of this study was to optimize the hyperparameters of SSL training to produce the best gait biomarker representation; however, this was only partially successful, because SSL loss did not robustly predict downstream task performance. The learned representations of all our models did well on the downstream task of decoding the diagnosis. The difference between models was often not much larger than the standard deviation over cross-validation folds. There was a trend towards models with smaller numbers of dimensions and not including an addition [CLS] token to have better diagnosis and laterality decoding. We anticipate the accelerating use of MMC during clinical care will produce larger datasets with richer clinical information for testing gait representations and will clarify which representations contain the most clinically meaningful information.

We saw a more consistent influence of hyperparameters on the validation contrastive loss. The most important decision was to include an additional [CLS] token at the end of the sequence, which was fed into the contrastive loss projection layer. Including a secondary SSL loss to predict the joint angles at the next time step also improved performance. This is rather interesting as it is an entirely different loss, and this finding likely speaks to how important the dynamics of walking are to learning and understanding it. Averaged over all our experiments, pretraining on our gait laboratory dataset produced slightly lower

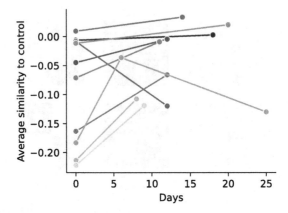

Fig. 2. The similarity between the average embedding of participants with a recent stroke undergoing inpatient rehabilitation and the average control participant embedding. In most cases, the average embedding for the stroke participants at each assessment becomes more aligned with the average control embedding (not visualized) throughout their rehabilitation.

contrastive losses, and fairly unsurprisingly, this became more pronounced for larger models. Rotary encoding with fixed frequencies generally outperformed learned positional encoding. Motivated by the success of masked modeling, we used FCM [23] with 20% masking in the majority of our experiments but ultimately found it seemed to worsen performance. This might improve with higher masking levels in the future. Augmenting trajectories with noise did not seem to help, possibly because accurate biomechanical trajectories should be fairly smooth, and so noise augmentation produces a domain shift between the training and validation data. Other features we did not systematically vary may influence performance, such as the learning rate, batch size, contrastive loss temperature, and the relative weighting of the prediction loss and contrastive loss. We found the prediction loss was substantially lower for smaller hidden dimensions, although the contrastive loss tended to be lower for large hidden dimensions. We defer investigating the tradeoff between these pretext tasks on downstream tasks to future work contingent on finding a more robust performance metric for the downstream task.

Different losses might improve the learned gait representation. We generated positive samples from temporal crops of a given walking trial, which could include overlaps. Alternatively, we could define positive samples from one session from an individual or specific walking conditions using a supervised contrastive learning [21]. This could make the contrastive loss align more with the downstream task and improve on the weak association we saw between the contrastive loss and downstream task performance, but would restrict the approach to carefully annotated datasets. It is also possible to combine supervised and SSL for gait representation, such as GaitForeMer [16]. During pretraining on videos from healthy controls, they combined a future prediction SSL loss with an activity recognition head and then fine-tuned the activity recognition head on a clinical impairment score as well as the prediction of future activity. There are also opportunities for multimodal SSL, and our dataset also includes electromyography and inertial measurements. Recent works have shown that large pretrained language models can also be combined with motion understanding in novel ways [37]. Other future directions include integrating physics and biomechanical simulations into the SSL objectives, and developing algorithms that can process variable durations extending longer than 3 s, which is necessary to characterize gait variability. Endo et al. [16] demonstrated the benefit of clinically interpreting gait patterns from pretraining on a large monocular video dataset of mixed activities from able-bodied individuals. In addition to motion from video, there are also large datasets of movement such as AMASS [25]. We hope future work will extend SSL to learn from disparate datasets including control and clinical populations with movement estimated with different modalities to ultimately result in a Foundation Model for gait [8].

From a clinical standpoint, determining the diagnosis or laterality of impairment of an individual seen in a rehabilitation setting is of minimal practical benefit, because this is already known. Linking observational gait analysis to diagnosis and functional outcomes is routinely done by clinicians, and our experience with this motivated this study. Replicating this clinical skill with MMC gait analysis demonstrates that SSL produces gait representation that captures clinically meaningful information about the individual's health status and enables a novel diagnostic biomarker. Finding that the distance in the learned embedding space from individuals with a stroke to the average control embedding shifts towards the control embedding during inpatient rehabilitation demonstrates its potential utility as a response biomarker.

Here, we focused on both diagnostic and response biomarkers. Tantalizingly, the shape of the response biomarker resembles the proportional recovery rule in the upper extremity, where more severely impaired individuals make a large proportional recovery [36]. We also note that the idea there is a single representation of a 'healthy control gait' is a dramatic oversimplification, that serves as a simple proxy for the question of how far and individual is from their premorbid gait pattern. Additionally, more work is required to determine what biomechanical features of gait the representation is sensitive to. Ultimately, we would like to disentangle this representation into interpretable features including traditional gait measures (velocity, cadence, spatiotemporal gait parameters), diagnoses, clinical assessments, and additional holistic features capturing overall walking quality that are not captured by these prior other measures. A clear next step is to extend this work to probe for all of these features using the clinical data associated with our dataset. Mapping the learned gait representation to more interpretable features will be important for this to be useful in clinical practice and to move towards more trustworthy, explainable artificial intelligence [26]. It will also be important to thoroughly evaluate the psychometric properties of any such response biomarkers, including reliability, validity, and sensitivity, with careful testing for any biases.

One advantage of the gait signatures approach [35] over our approach, is that they used autoregressive generation from their long-short term memory (LSTM) to make changes in gait signatures biomechanically interpretable. Our transformer architecture can also produce kinematics autoregressively, but must be conditioned on an entire kinematic sequence and cannot be conditioned on the contrastively learned overall gait representation. In the future, we could train a generative component conditioned on our gait representation to produce a representative gait. It will also be important to directly compare the LSTM trained with a future prediction as the SSL loss from Winner et al. [35] to the transformer architecture used here to compare their performance decoding gait-based biomarkers. An LSTM has the advantage of autoregressive generation from an initial state, but transformers typically achieve state-of-the-art performance when training on large datasets. In preliminary studies, we also found that a temporal convolutional neural network worked well with contrastive learning, although we did not evaluate this extensively.

Finally, we hope to extend the learned gait representation to other types of biomarkers including prognostic and predictive biomarkers. The distinction between these is that a prognostic biomarker anticipates future outcomes, whereas a predictive biomarker informs the counterfactual question about outcomes based on different treatments. These are both critical for the development of precision rehabilitation [14,18]. To develop prognostic gait-based biomarkers, we could train additional layers on these learned representations to predict future clinical outcomes. For example, predicting the discharge walking speed from the gait analysis during early rehabilitation. The development of predictive biomarkers will require additional training on data from randomized controlled trials or combining gait analysis and longitudinal, observational data with causal inference methods [29], an exciting future direction.

5 Conclusion

We showed that self-supervised learning from gait data with both contrastive learning and next timestep prediction produces a representation of gait that perform well on clinically relevant downstream tasks. We also found this approach works for gait analysis performed with markerless motion capture. MMC makes gait analysis much more accessible, and we envision this soon being integrated into routine clinical care, including outpatient medical visits, physical therapy visits, and at multiple points during inpatient rehabilitation. Finally, we showed that a linear layer fine-tuned on these gait representations, using only a fairly small dataset, already enables both diagnostic and response gait-based biomarkers.

6 Ethical Considerations

The motivation for this work is to extend gait-based biomarkers to allow more precise and frequent clinical analysis, to ultimately improve outcomes through precision rehabilitation approaches. However, developing algorithms that can infer health information from movement also carries potential risks. For example, the algorithms might be used to infer health information without the consent of the individual, or the algorithms might be used to discriminate against individuals. While the US has strict protections around sharing of health information by healthcare organizations through HIPAA, it is not clear there are yet sufficient regulations on how such ambiently sensed information could be used. An additional possible risk is that the algorithm might be used to identify individuals from their walking patterns to enable surveillance and monitoring without the consent of the individuals. As such, a concern we have around the sharing of clinical gait datasets, even if only kinematics, is that individualized gait patterns could be deanonymized and risk patient privacy. In addition, like most other artificial intelligence tools, the algorithm is not guaranteed to be 100% correct and in fact, our current work shows this is not the case. We also have not yet investigated whether any biases influence its accuracy. We believe the benefits of this work outweigh the risks and will ultimately lead to tools that will advance rehabilitation, but strongly believe they should not be used to infer anything about an individual without their consent.

Acknowledgements. This work was generously supported by the Research Accelerator Program of the Shirley Ryan AbilityLab and with funding from the Restore Center P2C (NIH P2CHD101913). We thank the participants and staff of the Shirley Ryan AbilityLab for their contributions to this work.

We would like to thank the creators of Jax, Equinox, Haliax, Levanter, Optax and WandB that made it a pleasure to implement and train these models. Large language models were used in this work. Copilot was used during code development. Some portions of the text were reviewed by ChatGPT. Grammarly was also used.

References

1. Easymocap (2021). https://github.com/zju3dv/EasyMocap
2. Haliax (2022). https://github.com/stanford-crfm/haliax/
3. Levanter (2022). https://github.com/stanford-crfm/levanter/
4. Nimblephysics (2022). https://github.com/keenon/nimblephysics
5. Babuschkin, I., et al.: The DeepMind JAX Ecosystem (2020). http://github.com/deepmind
6. Biewald, L.: Experiment tracking with weights and biases (2020). https://www.wandb.com/
7. Bilney, B., Morris, M., Webster, K.: Concurrent related validity of the GAITRite walkway system for quantification of the spatial and temporal parameters of gait. Gait Posture **17**(1), 68–74 (2003)
8. Bommasani, R., et al.: On the Opportunities and Risks of Foundation Models, July 2022
9. Chen, T., Kornblith, S., Norouzi, M., Hinton, G.: A Simple Framework for Contrastive Learning of Visual Representations, February 2020
10. Cotton, R.J.: PosePipe: Open-Source Human Pose Estimation Pipeline for Clinical Research. arXiv:2203.08792 [cs, q-bio], March 2022

11. Cotton, R.J., Cimorelli, A., Shah, K., Anarwala, S., Uhlrich, S., Karakostas, T.: Improved Trajectory Reconstruction for Markerless Pose Estimation, March 2023
12. Cotton, R.J., et al.: Markerless Motion Capture and Biomechanical Analysis Pipeline, March 2023
13. Cotton, R.J., McClerklin, E., Cimorelli, A., Patel, A., Karakostas, T.: Transforming gait: video-based spatiotemporal gait analysis. In: 2022 44th Annual International Conference of the IEEE Engineering in Medicine & Biology Society (EMBC), pp. 115–120 (Jul 2022)
14. Cotton, R.J., et al.: Letter to the editor: precision rehabilitation: optimizing function, adding value to health care. Arch. Phys. Med. Rehabil. **103**(9), 1883–1884 (2022)
15. Devlin, J., Chang, M.W., Lee, K., Toutanova, K.: BERT: Pre-training of Deep Bidirectional Transformers for Language Understanding, May 2019
16. Endo, M., Poston, K.L., Sullivan, E.V., Fei-Fei, L., Pohl, K.M., Adeli, E.: GaitForeMer: self-supervised pre-training of transformers via human motion forecasting for few-shot gait impairment severity estimation. In: Wang, L., Dou, Q., Fletcher, P.T., Speidel, S., Li, S. (eds.) Medical Image Computing and Computer Assisted Intervention. MICCAI 2022. LNCS, vol. 13438, pp. 130–139. Springer, Cham (2022). https://doi.org/10.1007/978-3-031-16452-1_13
17. FDA-NIH Biomarker Working Group: FDA-NIH Biomarker Working Group. Food and Drug Administration (US), January 2021
18. French, M.A., et al.: Precision rehabilitation: optimizing function, adding value to health care. Arch. Phys. Med. Rehabil. **103**, 1233–1239 (2022)
19. Ghorbani, S., et al.: MoVi: a large multi-purpose human motion and video dataset. PLoS ONE **16**(6), e0253157 (2021)
20. Karashchuk, P., et al.: Anipose: a toolkit for robust markerless 3D pose estimation. Cell Rep. **36**, 1–27 (2020)
21. Khosla, P., et al.: Supervised contrastive learning. Adv. Neural Inf. Syst. **33**, 18661–18673 (2020)
22. Kidger, P., Garcia, C.: Equinox: Neural networks in JAX via callable PyTrees and filtered transformations, October 2021
23. Liu, H., et al.: Towards Better Few-Shot and Finetuning Performance with Forgetful Causal Language Models, January 2023
24. Loshchilov, I., Hutter, F.: Decoupled Weight Decay Regularization, January 2019
25. Mahmood, N., Ghorbani, N., Troje, N.F., Pons-Moll, G., Black, M.: AMASS: archive of motion capture as surface shapes. In: 2019 IEEE/CVF International Conference on Computer Vision (ICCV), pp. 5441–5450 (2019)
26. Markus, A.F., Kors, J.A., Rijnbeek, P.R.: The role of explainability in creating trustworthy artificial intelligence for health care: a comprehensive survey of the terminology, design choices, and evaluation strategies. J. Biomed. Inform. **113**, 103655 (2021)
27. McDonough, A.L., Batavia, M., Chen, F.C., Kwon, S., Ziai, J.: The validity and reliability of the GAITRite system's measurements: a preliminary evaluation. Arch. Phys. Med. Rehabil. **82**(3), 419–425 (2001)
28. van den Oord, A., Li, Y., Vinyals, O.: Representation Learning with Contrastive Predictive Coding, July 2018
29. Pearl, J., Mackenzie, D.: The Book of Why: The New Science of Cause and Effect. Basic Books, May 2018
30. Radford, A., Wu, J., Child, R., Luan, D., Amodei, D., Sutskever, I.: Language Models are Unsupervised Multitask Learners (2019)

31. Sárándi, I., Hermans, A., Leibe, B.: Learning 3D Human Pose Estimation from Dozens of Datasets using a Geometry-Aware Autoencoder to Bridge Between Skeleton Formats, December 2022
32. Su, J., Lu, Y., Pan, S., Murtadha, A., Wen, B., Liu, Y.: RoFormer: Enhanced Transformer with Rotary Position Embedding, August 2022
33. Vaswani, A., et al.: Attention is all you need (NIPS) (2017)
34. Werling, K., et al.: Rapid bilevel optimization to concurrently solve musculoskeletal scaling, marker registration, and inverse kinematic problems for human motion reconstruction, August 2022
35. Winner, T.S., Rosenberg, M.C., Kesar, T.M., Ting, L.H., Berman, G.J.: Discovering individual-specific gait signatures from data-driven models of neuromechanical dynamics. Preprint, Neuroscience, December 2022
36. Winters, C., van Wegen, E.E.H., Daffertshofer, A., Kwakkel, G.: Generalizability of the proportional recovery model for the upper extremity after an ischemic stroke. Neurorehabil. Neural Repair **29**(7), 614–622 (2015)
37. Zhang, Y., et al.: MotionGPT: Finetuned LLMs are General-Purpose Motion Generators, June 2023

Author Index

A

Abdou, Kayan 277
Acevedo Trebbau, Gabriela T. 241
Adeli, Vida 265
Aghdam, Ehsan Khodapanah 83
Anarwala, Shawana 277
Aqil, K. H. 58
Arimond, René 83
Azad, Reza 83, 146, 159

B

Bandini, Andrea 241
Bayram, Hizir Can 35
Boité, Hugo Le 1
Bozorgpour, Afshin 146
Brahim, Ikram 1
Broeders, Ivo A. M. J. 218
Butzkueven, Helmut 108

C

Carlini, Lucas Pereira 231
Çelebi, Mehmet Serdar 35
Chae, Allison 46
Chao, Chun-Hung 70
Cho, Yongwon 184
Cimorelli, Anthony 277
Cochener, Béatrice 1
Conze, Pierre-Henri 1
Cotton, R. James 277

D

Daho, Mostafa El Habib 1
Darby, David 108
de Almeida Sá Coutrin, Gabriel 231
de Moraes Barros, Marina Carvalho 231
DeLillo, Allison 277
Duda, Jeffrey 46

F

Fasano, Alfonso 265
Ferreira, Leonardo Antunes 231

G

Gao, Xingyu 25
Ge, Zongyuan 108
Gee, James C. 46
Gerats, Beerend G. A. 218
Gershov, Sapir 253
Gorodetsky, Carolina 265
Gresle, Melissa 108
Guarin, Diego L. 241
Guinsburg, Ruth 231
Gündoğdu, Emircan 14
Guo, Qinghai 134

H

Heideirich, Tatiany Marcondes 231
Hu, Yanan 108
Hwang, Sung Ho 184

I

Iaboni, Andrea 265

J

Jayakumar, Jaikishan 58

K

Kahn Jr., Charles E. 46
Karakostas, Tasos 277
Karimijafarbigloo, Sanaz 159
Kazerouni, Amirhossein 83, 146
Kulkarni, Tanvi 58

L

Lamard, Mathieu 1
Laufer, Shlomi 253
Lee, Seungeun 184

Li, Gang 120
Li, Yihao 1
Lin, Weili 120
Liu, Manhua 25

M

MacLean, Matthew T. 46
Mahameed, Fadi 253
Malin-Mayor, Caroline 265
Massin, Pascal 1
Mehta, Deval 108
Merhof, Dorit 83, 146, 159
Merlo, Daniel 108
Muzammel, Muhammad 206

N

Niethammer, Marc 70
Noritsyn, Sergey 265

O

Oh, Saelin 184
Othmani, Alice 206

P

Park, Beom Jin 184
Peiffer, J. D. 277
Peng, Wei 172
Pistos, Michalis 120
Pohl, Kilian M. 172

Q

Quellec, Gwenolé 1

R

Rader, Daniel 46
Rajadhyaksha, Nishant 96
Ram, Keerthi 58
Raz, Aeyal 253
Rekik, Islem 14, 35, 96, 120, 194

S

Sabo, Andrea 265
Sadegheih, Yousef 146
Sagreiya, Hersh 46
Shah, Kunal 277
Shen, Dinggang 25, 120
Shi, Feng 25
Sivaprakasam, Mohanasankar 58
Sun, Chunli 134

T

Taati, Babak 265
Tadayoni, Ramin 1
Tapert, Susan F. 172
Thomaz, Carlos Eduardo 231
Torigian, Drew A. 46

V

van der Walt, Anneke 108
Verma, Anurag 46

W

Wang, Yixin 172
Witschey, Walter R. 46
Wolterink, Jelmer M. 218

X

Xu, Chun 194

Y

Yang, Gang 134
Yao, Michael S. 46

Z

Zeghlache, Rachid 1
Zhang, Xin 108
Zhao, Feng 134
Zhao, Qingyu 172
Zhu, Chao 108

Printed in the United States
by Baker & Taylor Publisher Services